NCERT EXEMPLAR

Problems - Solutions

Physics 12th

BEST Solution
Guaranteed •••

NCERT EXEMPLAR
Problems - Solutions

Physics 12th

Author
Sushant Batra

arihant
SUCCESS AND NOTHING LESS

arihant
SUCCESS AND NOTHING LESS

ARIHANT PRAKASHAN (Series), MEERUT

卐 **Administrative & Production Offices**

Regd. Office

'Ramchhaya' 4577/15, Agarwal Road, Darya Ganj, New Delhi -110002
Tele: 011- 47630600, 43518550

卐 **Head Office**

Kalindi, TP Nagar, Meerut (UP) - 250002
Tel: 0121-7156203, 7156204

卐 **Sales & Support Offices**

Agra, Ahmedabad, Bengaluru, Bareilly, Chennai, Delhi, Guwahati, Hyderabad, Jaipur, Jhansi, Kolkata, Lucknow, Nagpur & Pune.

卐 **PRICE** ₹225.00

卐 **PO No. :** TXT-59-T071670-6-26

Published by Arihant Publications (India) Ltd.

For further information about the books published by Arihant, log on to www.arihantbooks.com or e-mail at info@arihantbooks.com

Follow us on

PREFACE

NCERT Exemplar Problems, published by the NCERT, are designed to provide students with a diverse range of quality questions in formats such as Multiple Choice Questions, Multiple Choice Questions (More Than One Options), Very Short Answer Type Questions, Short Answer Type Questions and Long Answer Type Questions catering to varying levels of difficulty.

These problems are essential for success in school and board exams, as well as competitive exams like engineering and medical entrances. Regular practice with these problems prepares students to tackle challenging questions effectively.

This book, **NCERT Exemplar Problems-Solutions Physics12th**, offers precise and detailed solutions to all the questions in the NCERT Exemplar Physics textbook. Each solution is complemented by explanatory notes and authentic explanations, enabling students to deepen their conceptual understanding and enhance their analytical skills.

Key features

- **Thinking Process** Provides simple steps to approach and solve the question, clearing up any confusion.
- **Concept Insight** Explains the main ideas and concepts needed to answer the questions correctly.
- **Mistake Alert!** Points out common mistakes students might make and helps them avoid these errors.
- **Notes** Highlights important points and useful tips to make learning easier.

I hope this book proves to be a valuable resource, aiding students in their academic journey and leading them to great success.

Author

CONTENTS

***Note(*)** This Chapter has been deleted from latest NCERT.*

Chapter

01

Electric Charges and Fields

Multiple Choice Questions (MCQs)

Q.1 In figure two positive charges q_2 and q_3 fixed along the y-axis, exert a net electric force in the $+ x$-direction on a charge q_1 fixed along the x-axis. If a positive charge Q is added at $(x, 0)$, the force on q_1

(i) 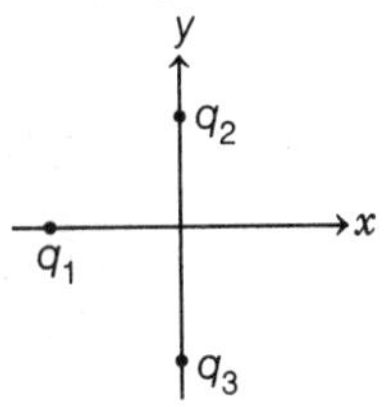

(ii) 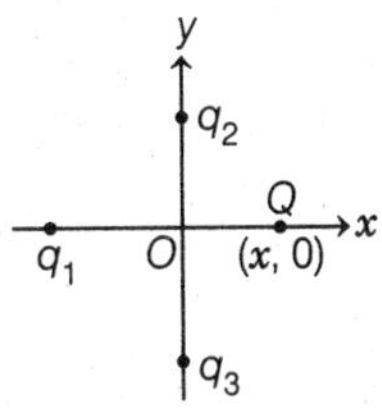

(a) shall increase along the positive x-axis.
(b) shall decrease along the positive x-axis.
(c) shall point along the negative x-axis.
(d) shall increase but the direction changes because of the intersection of Q with q_2 and q_3.

Thinking Process Find out the polarity of the charge q_1 by studying the nature of forces between $q_1 - q_2$ and $q_1 - q_3$. Then, find the nature of force between $q_1 - Q$.

Ans. *(a)* The net force on q_1 by q_2 and q_3 is along the $+ x$-direction, so nature of force between q_1, q_2 and q_1, q_3 is attractive. This can be represented by the figure given below.

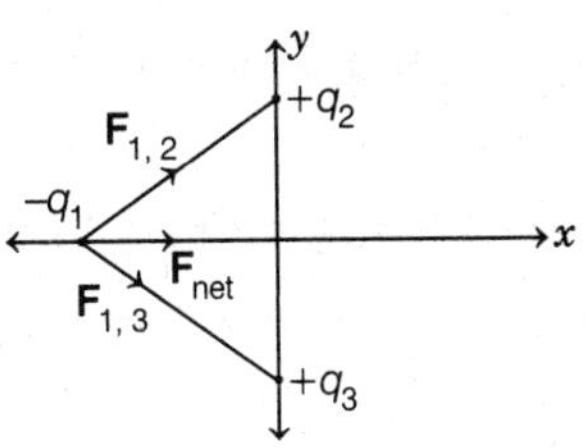

The attractive force between these charges states that q_1 is a negative charge (since, q_2 and q_3 are positive).

Thus, nature of force between q_1 and newly introduced charge Q (positive) is attractive and net force on q_1 by q_2, q_3 and Q are along the same direction as given in the diagram below.

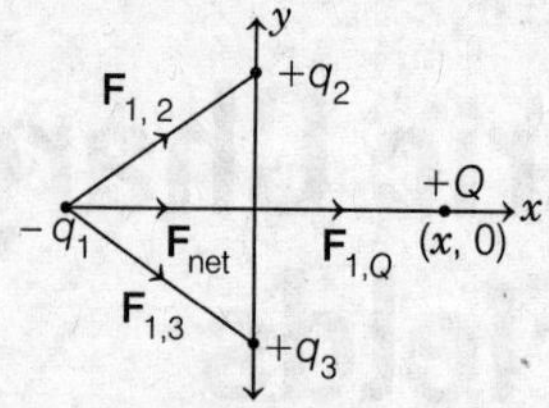

The figure given above clearly shows that the force on q_1 shall increase along the positive x-axis due to the positive charge Q.

Q.2 A point positive charge is brought near an isolated conducting sphere (figure). The electric field is best given by

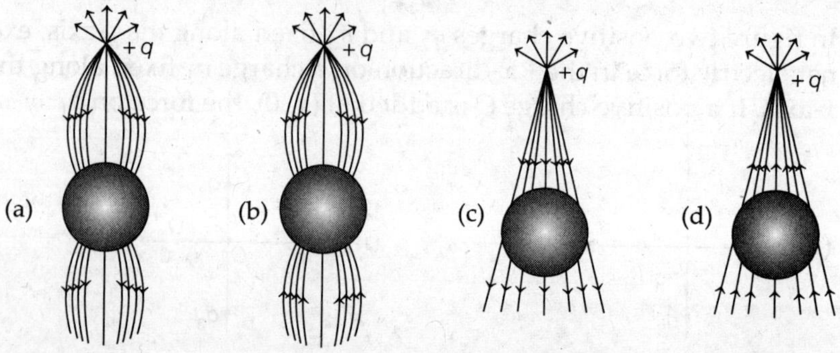

Thinking Process Bringing the point positive charge towards the conducting sphere, charges the sphere by induction process.

Ans. *(a)* When a positive point charge is brought near an isolated conducting sphere without touching the sphere, then the free electrons in the sphere are attracted towards the positive charge. This leaves an excess of positive charge on the rear (right) surface of sphere.

Both kinds of charges are bound in the metal sphere and cannot escape. They, therefore, reside on the surface.

Thus, the left surface of sphere has an excess of negative charge and the right surface of sphere has an excess of positive charge as given in the figure below

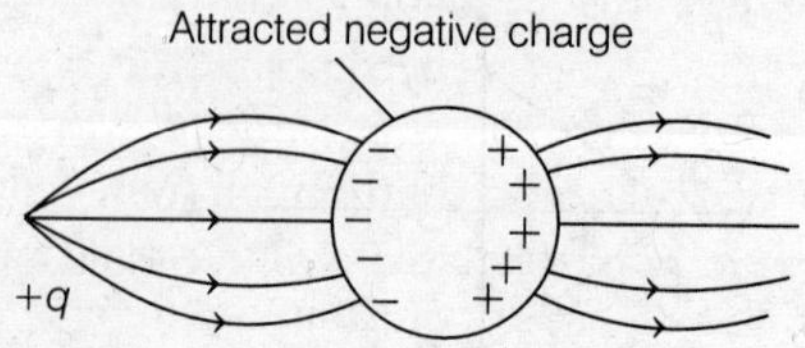

An electric field lines start from positive charge and ends at negative charge (in this case from point positive charge to negative charge created inside the sphere). Also, electric field line emerges from a positive charge, in case of single charge and ends at infinity.

Q.3 The electric flux through the surface

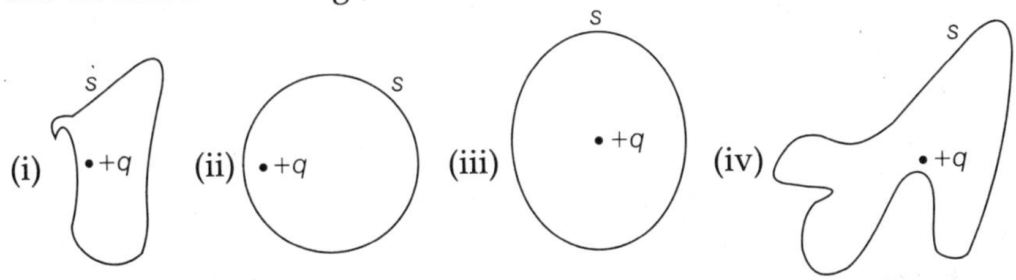

(a) in Fig. (iv) is the largest
(b) in Fig. (iii) is the least
(c) in Fig. (ii) is same as Fig. (iii) but is smaller than Fig. (iv)
(d) is the same for all the figures

- **Concept insight** According to Gauss' law electric flux through a closed surface is $\frac{1}{\varepsilon_0}$ times the charge enclosed by the surface.

Ans. ***(d)*** Gauss' law of electrostatics state that the total of the electric flux out of a closed surface is equal to the charge enclosed divided by the permittivity *i.e.*, $\phi_E = \frac{Q}{\varepsilon_0}$. Thus, electric flux through a surface doesn't depend on the shape, size or area of a surface but it depends on the number of charges enclosed by the surface.

So, here in this question, all the figures have the same electric flux as all of them has single positive charge.

Q.4 Five charges q_1, q_2, q_3, q_4 and q_5 are fixed at their positions as shown in figure, S is a Gaussian surface. The Gauss' law is given by $\oint_s \mathbf{E} \cdot d\mathbf{S} = \frac{q}{\varepsilon_0}$. Which of the following statements is correct?

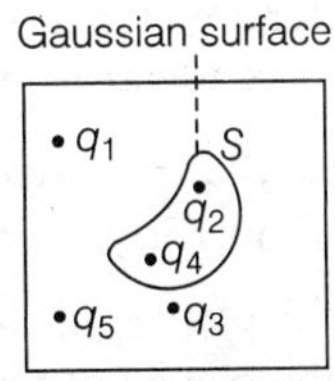

(a) **E** on the LHS of the above equation will have a contribution from q_1, q_5 and q_3 while q on the RHS will have a contribution from q_2 and q_4 only.
(b) **E** on the LHS of the above equation will have a contribution from all charges while q on the RHS will have a contribution from q_2 and q_4 only.
(c) **E** on the LHS of the above equation will have a contribution from all charges while q on the RHS will have a contribution from q_1, q_3 and q_5 only.
(d) Both **E** on the LHS and q on the RHS will have contributions from q_2 and q_4 only.

- **Concept Insight** In Gauss' law, electric field on the LHS is due to all the charges present whereas on the RHS, q is the charge enclosed by the Gaussian surface.

Ans. ***(b)*** According to Gauss' law, the term q on the right side of the equation $\int_s \mathbf{E} \cdot d\mathbf{S} = \frac{q}{\varepsilon_0}$ includes the sum of all charges enclosed by the surface.

The charges may be located anywhere inside the surface. If the surface is so chosen that there are some charges inside and some outside, the electric field on the left side of equation is due to all the charges, both inside and outside S.

So, **E** on LHS of the above equation will have a contribution from all charges while q on the RHS will have a contribution from q_2 and q_4 only.

Mistake Alert ! *Sometimes students thinks that total charge inside and outside of the Gaussian surface contribute to the flux, but only charges inside the surface will contribute to the flux.*

Q.5 Figure shows electric field lines in which an electric dipole p is placed as shown. Which of the following statements is correct?

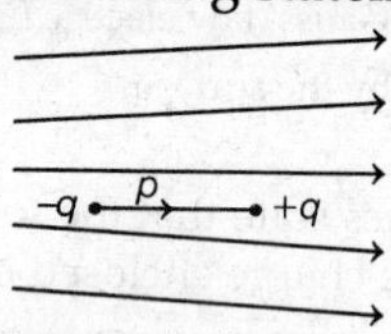

(a) The dipole will not experience any force.
(b) The dipole will experience a force towards right.
(c) The dipole will experience a force towards left.
(d) The dipole will experience a force upwards.

Thinking Process Find the electric field strength on the charges of dipole.
Force varies directly with electric field strength *i.e.,* higher the electric field strength greater the force and *vice-versa.*

Ans. ***(c)*** The space between the electric field lines is increasing from left to right and its properties state that, strength of electric field decreases with the increase in the space between electric field lines. As a result force on charges also decreases from left to right. Thus, the force on charge $-q$ is greater than force on charge $+q$ in turn dipole will experience a force towards left.

Q.6 A point charge $+q$ is placed at a distance d from an isolated conducting plane. The field at a point P on the other side of the plane is

(a) directed perpendicular to the plane and away from the plane
(b) directed perpendicular to the plane but towards the plane
(c) directed radially away from the point charge
(d) directed radially towards the point charge

Ans. ***(a)*** When a point positive charge brought near an isolated conducting plane, some negative charge developes on the surface of the plane towards the charge and an equal positive charge develops on opposite side of the plane. This process is called charging by induction.

Q.7 A hemisphere is uniformly charged positively. The electric field at a point on a diameter away from the centre is directed

(a) perpendicular to the diameter
(b) parallel to the diameter
(c) at an angle tilted towards the diameter
(d) at an angle tilted away from the diameter

Ans. ***(a)*** According to question we wish to find out the electric field at ponit P as shown in the figure.

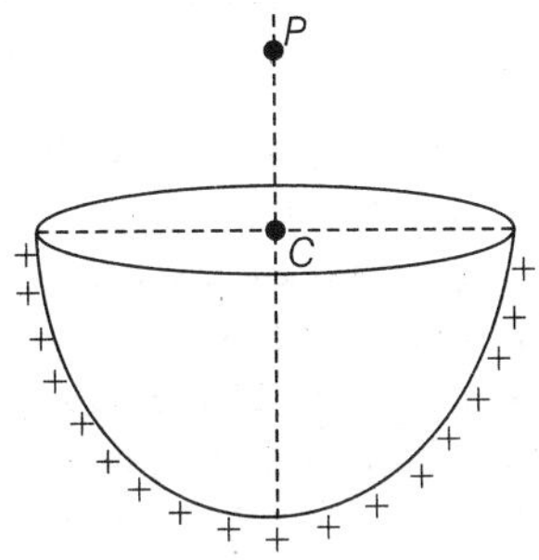

Due to the symmetry of the hemisphere, the components of electric field parallel to the diameter will cancel out and the net electric field at P will be in a direction perpendicular to the diameter.

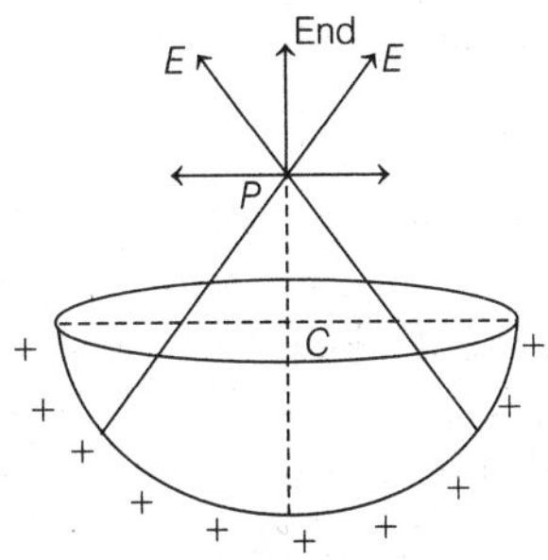

Multiple Choice Questions (More Than One Options)

Q.8 If $\oint_S \mathbf{E} \cdot d\mathbf{S} = 0$ over a surface, then

(a) the electric field inside the surface and on it is zero
(b) the electric field inside the surface is necessarily uniform
(c) the number of flux lines entering the surface must be equal to the number of flux lines leaving it
(d) all charges must necessarily be outside the surface

Thinking Process Go through Gauss' law in detail.

Ans. ***(c, d)*** $\oint_S \mathbf{E} \cdot d\mathbf{S}$ represents electric flux over the closed surface.

In general, $\oint_S \mathbf{E} \cdot d\mathbf{S}$ means the algebraic sum of number of flux lines entering the surface and number of flux lines leaving the surface.

When $\oint_S \mathbf{E} \cdot d\mathbf{S} = 0$, it means that the number of flux lines entering the surface must be equal to the number of flux lines leaving it.

Now, from Gauss' law, we know that $\oint_S \mathbf{E} \cdot d\mathbf{S} = \frac{q}{\varepsilon_0}$ where q is charge enclosed by the surface. When $\oint_S \mathbf{E} \cdot d\mathbf{S} = 0 \Rightarrow q = 0$ *i.e.,* net charge enclosed by the surface must be zero. Therefore, all other charges must necessarily be outside the surface. This is because of the fact that charges outside the surface do not contribute to the electric flux.

Q.9 The electric field at a point is

(a) always continuous
(b) continuous if there is no charge at that point
(c) discontinuous only if there is a negative charge at that point
(d) discontinuous if there is a charge at that point

Thinking Process Use the properties of electric field lines.

Ans. *(b, d)* The electric field due to a charge Q at a point in space may be defined as the force that a unit positive charge would experience if placed at that point. Thus, electric field due to the charge Q will be continuous, if there is no charge at that point. It will be discontinuous if there is a charge at that point.

Q.10 If there were only one type of charge in the universe, then

(a) $\oint_s \mathbf{E} \cdot d\mathbf{S} \neq 0$ on any surface
(b) $\oint_s \mathbf{E} \cdot d\mathbf{S} = 0$ if the charge is outside the surface
(c) $\oint_s \mathbf{E} \cdot d\mathbf{S}$ could not be defined
(d) $\oint_s \mathbf{E} \cdot d\mathbf{S} = \frac{q}{\varepsilon_0}$, if charges of magnitude q were inside the surface

Ans. *(b, d)* Gauss' law states that $\oint_s \mathbf{E} \cdot d\mathbf{S} = \frac{q}{\varepsilon_0}$, where q is the charge enclosed by the surface. If the charge is outside the surface, then charge enclosed by the surface is $q = 0$ and thus, $\oint_s \mathbf{E} \cdot d\mathbf{S} = 0$. Here, electric flux doesn't depend on the type or nature of charge.

Q.11 Consider a region inside which there are various types of charges but the total charge is zero. At points outside the region,

(a) the electric field is necessarily zero
(b) the electric field is due to the dipole moment of the charge distribution only
(c) the dominant electric field is $\propto \frac{1}{r^3}$, for large r, where r is the distance from a origin in this region
(d) the work done to move a charged particle along a closed path, away from the region, will be zero

Ans. *(c, d)* When there are various types of charges in a region, but the total charge is zero, the region can be supposed to contain a number of electric dipoles.

Therefore, at points outside the region (may be anywhere w.r.t. electric dipoles), the dominant electric field $\propto \frac{1}{r^3}$ for large r.

Further, as electric field is conservative, work done to move a charged particle along a closed path, away from the region will be zero.

Q.12 Refer to the arrangement of charges in figure and a Gaussian surface of radius R with Q at the centre. Then,

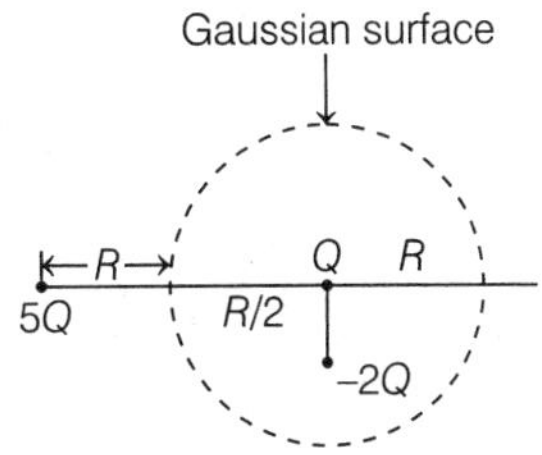

(a) total flux through the surface of the sphere is $\frac{-Q}{\varepsilon_0}$

(b) field on the surface of the sphere is $\frac{-Q}{4\pi\varepsilon_0 R^2}$

(c) flux through the surface of sphere due to $5Q$ is zero

(d) field on the surface of sphere due to $-2Q$ is same everywhere

Ans. ***(a, c)*** Gauss' law states that total electric flux of an enclosed surface is given by $\frac{q}{\varepsilon_0}$.

where q is the charge enclosed by the surface. Thus, from figure,

Total charge inside the surface is $= Q - 2Q = -Q$

$\therefore$ Total flux through the surface of the sphere $= \frac{-Q}{\varepsilon_0}$

Now, considering charge $5Q$. Charge $5Q$ lies outside the surface, thus it makes no contribution to electric flux through the given surface.

Q.13 A positive charge Q is uniformly distributed along a circular ring of radius R. A small test charge q is placed at the centre of the ring as shown in figure. Then,

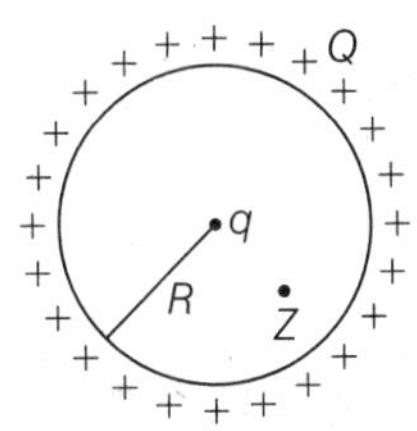

(a) if $q > 0$ and is displaced away from the centre in the plane of the ring, it will be pushed back towards the centre.

(b) if $q < 0$ and is displaced away from the centre in the plane of the ring, it will never return to the centre and will continue moving till it hits the ring.

(c) if $q < 0$, it will perform SHM for small displacement along the axis.

(d) q at the centre of the ring is in an unstable equilibrium within the plane of the ring for $q > 0$.

Ans. ***(a, b, c, d)*** The positive charge Q is uniformly distributed at the outer surface of the enclosed sphere. Thus, electric field at the centre of the sphere is zero.

So, the effect of electric field on charge q at the centre due to the positive charge Q is zero.

Now, the only governing factor is the attractive and repulsive forces between charges (Q and q) there are two cases arise.

Case I When charge $q > 0$ *i.e.*, q is a positive charge, there creates a repulsive force between charge q and Q. The repulsive forces of charge Q from all around the charge q will push it towards the centre, if it is displaced from the centre of the ring.

Case II When charge $q < 0$ *i.e.*, q is a negative charge, then there is an attractive force between charge Q and q. If q is shifted from the centre, then the positive charges nearer to this charge will attract it towards itself and charge q will never return to the centre.

Very Short Answer Type Questions

Q.14 An arbitrary surface encloses a dipole. What is the electric flux through this surface?

Ans. From Gauss' law, the electric flux through an enclosed surface is given by $\oint_s \mathbf{E} \cdot d\mathbf{S} = \frac{q}{\varepsilon_0}$.

Here, q is the net charge inside that enclosed surface.

Now, the net charge on a dipole is given by $-q + q = 0$

$\therefore$ Electric flux through a surface enclosing a dipole $= \frac{-q+q}{\varepsilon_0} = \frac{0}{\varepsilon_0} = 0$

Q.15 A metallic spherical shell has an inner radius R_1 and outer radius R_2. A charge Q is placed at the centre of the spherical cavity. What will be surface charge density on

(i) the inner surface

(ii) the outer surface?

Thinking Process Let us draw the diagram as per the given situation. Using the induction process of charging and distribute the charge on whole spherical shell. Now, find the required surface charge density.

Ans. Here, the charge placed at the centre of the spherical cavity is positively charged. So, the charge created at the inner surface of the sphere, due to induction will be $-Q$ and due to this, charge created at outer surface of the sphere is $+Q$.

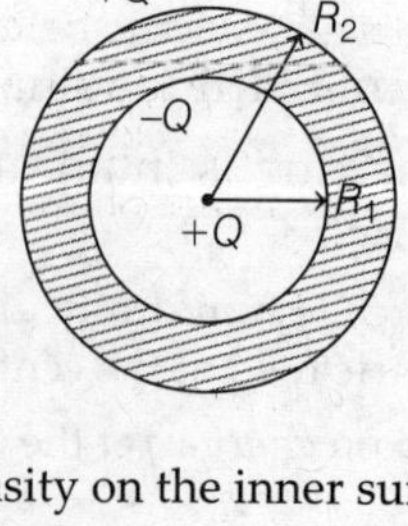

(i) Now, surface charge density on the inner surface $= \frac{-Q}{4\pi R_1^2}$

(ii) Surface charge density on the outer surface $= \frac{+Q}{4\pi R_2^2}$

Q.16 The dimensions of an atom are of the order of an Angstrom. Thus, there must be large electric fields between the protons and electrons. Why, then is the electrostatic field inside a conductor zero?

Ans. Inside an atom, there is a large electric field between an electron and a proton but there are a large number of atoms inside a conductor and their electric fields are aligned in random directions. Thus, the net electric field inside a conductor is zero.

Q.17 If the total charge enclosed by a surface is zero, does it imply that the electric field everywhere on the surface is zero? Conversely, if the electric field everywhere on a surface is zero, does it imply that net charge inside is zero.

Ans. Gauss' law also implies that when the surface is so chosen that there are some charges inside and some outside.

The flux in such situation is given by $\oint \mathbf{E} \cdot d\mathbf{S} = \frac{q}{\varepsilon_0}$.

In such situations, the electric field in the LHS is due to all the charges both inside and outside the surface. The term q on the right side of the equation given by Gauss' law represents only the total charge inside the surface.

Thus, despite being total charge enclosed by a surface zero, it doesn't imply that the electric field everywhere on the surface is zero.

Conversely if the electric field everywhere on a surface is zero, it implies that net charge inside it is zero.

i.e., Putting $E = 0$ in $\oint \mathbf{E} \cdot \mathbf{dS} = \frac{q}{\varepsilon_0}$

we get, $q = 0$

Q. 18 Sketch the electric field lines for a uniformly charged hollow cylinder shown in figure.

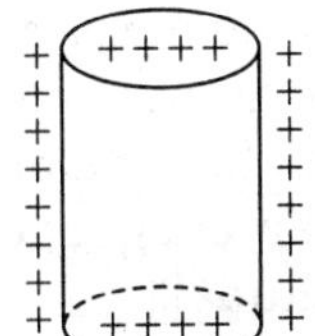

Ans. According to general properties, electric field lines start from positive charges and end at negative charges. If there is a single charge, they may start or end at infinity. Thus, the electric field lines will start from positive charges and move towards infinity as given in the figure below

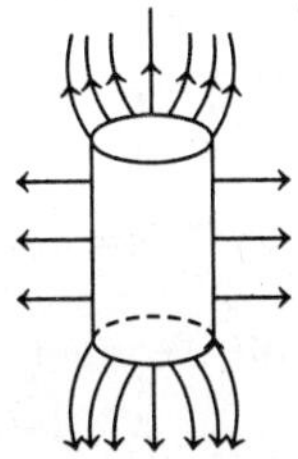
Side view

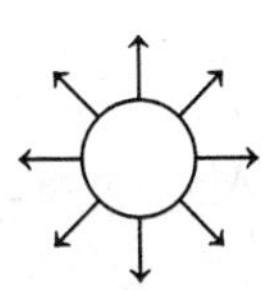
Top view

Q.19 What will be the total flux through the faces of the cube as given in the figure with side of length a if a charge q is placed at?

(a) A a corner of the cube

(b) B mid-point of an edge of the cube

(c) C centre of a face of the cube

(d) D mid-point of B and C

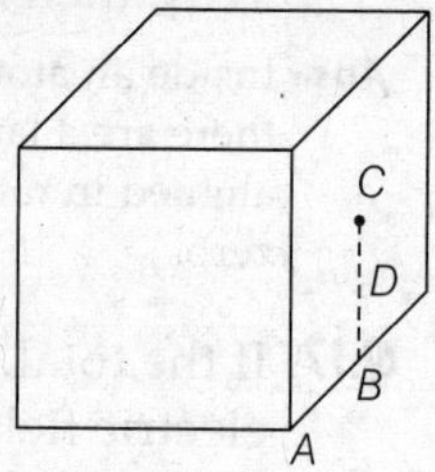

Thinking Process Imagine a symmetric figure in such a way that placed charge arrives at the centre of imaginary figure. Then, apply Gauss' theorem to find flux linked with imaginary figure. Thereafter, find flux linked with the given figure.

Ans. (a) There are eight corners in a cube so, total charge for the cube is $\frac{q}{8}$.

Thus, electric flux at $A = \frac{q}{8\varepsilon_0}$.

(b) When the charge q is place at B, middle point of an edge of the cube, it is being shared equally by 4 cubes. Therefore, total flux through the faces of the given cube $= q / 4\,\varepsilon_0$.

(c) When the charge q is placed at C, the centre of a face of the cube, it is being shared equally by 2 cubes. Therefore, total flux through the faces of the given cube $= q / 2\,\varepsilon_0$.

(d) Similarly, when charge q is placed at D, the mid-point of B and C, it is being shared equally by 2 cubes. Therefore, total flux through the faces of the given cube $= q / 2\varepsilon_0$.

Short Answer Type Questions

Q.20 A paisa coin is made up of Al-Mg alloy and weights 0.75 g. It has a square shape and its diagonal measures 17 mm. It is electrically neutral and contains equal amounts of positive and negative charges. Treating the paisa coins made up of only Al, find the magnitude of equal number of positive and negative charges. What conclusion do you draw from this magnitude?

- **Concept insight** Number of atoms in 1 mol of substance $= N_A = 6.023 \times 10^{23}$.

Ans. Here, given quantities are

Mass of a paisa coin = 0.75 g

Atomic mass of aluminium = 26.9815 g

Avogadro's number $= 6.023 \times 10^{23}$

$\therefore$ Number of aluminium atoms in one paisa coin,

$$N = \frac{6.023 \times 10^{23}}{26.9815} \times 0.75 = 1.6742 \times 10^{22}$$

As charge number of Al is 13, each atom of Al contains 13 protons and 13 electrons.

$\therefore$ Magnitude of positive and negative charges in one paisa coin $= N z e$

$$= 1.6742 \times 10^{22} \times 13 \times 1.60 \times 10^{-19} \text{C}$$

$$= 3.48 \times 10^{4} \text{ C} = 34.8 \text{ kC}$$

This is a very large amount of charge. Thus, we can conclude that ordinary neutral matter contains enormous amount of ± charges.

Q.21 Consider a coin of Question 20. It is electrically neutral and contains equal amounts of positive and negative charge of magnitude 34.8 kC. Suppose that these equal charges were concentrated in two point charges separated by

(i) 1 cm $\left(\sim \frac{1}{2} \times \text{diagonal of the one paisa coin}\right)$

(ii) 100 m (~ length of a long building)

(iii) 10^6 m (radius of the earth). Find the force on each such point charge in each of the three cases. What do you conclude from these results?

- **Concept Insight** Force between two point charges q_1 and q_2 separated by a distance r is $f = \frac{1}{4\pi\varepsilon_0}\frac{|q_1 q_2|}{r^2}$.

Ans. Here, $q = \pm 34.8 \text{ kC} = \pm 3.48 \times 10^4 \text{ C}$

$r_1 = 1 \text{cm} = 10^{-2}$ m, $r_2 = 100$ m, $r_3 = 10^6$ m and $\frac{1}{4\pi\varepsilon_0} = 9 \times 10^9 \frac{\text{Nm}^2}{\text{C}^2}$

(i) $F_1 = \frac{|q|^2}{4\pi\varepsilon_0 r_1^2} = \frac{9 \times 10^9 (3.48 \times 10^4)^2}{(10^{-2})^2} = 1.09 \times 10^{23}$ N

(ii) $F_2 = \frac{|q|^2}{4\pi\varepsilon_0 r_2^2} = \frac{9 \times 10^9 (3.48 \times 10^4)^2}{(100)^2} = 1.09 \times 10^{15}$ N

(iii) $F_3 = \frac{|q|^2}{4\pi\varepsilon_0 r_3^2} = \frac{9 \times 10^9 (3.48 \times 10^4)^2}{(10^6)^2} = 1.09 \times 10^{7}$ N

Conclusion from this result We observe that when ± charges in ordinary neutral matter are separated as point charges, they exert an enormous force. Hence, it is very difficult to disturb electrical neutrality of matter.

Q.22 Figure represents a crystal unit of cesium chloride, CsCl. The cesium atoms, represented by open circles are situated at the corners of a cube of side 0.40nm, whereas a Cl atom is situated at the centre of the cube. The Cs atoms are deficient in one electron while the Cl atom carries an excess electron.

(i) What is the net electric field on the Cl atom due to eight Cs atoms?

(ii) Suppose that the Cs atom at the corner A is missing. What is the net force now on the Cl atom due to seven remaining Cs atoms?

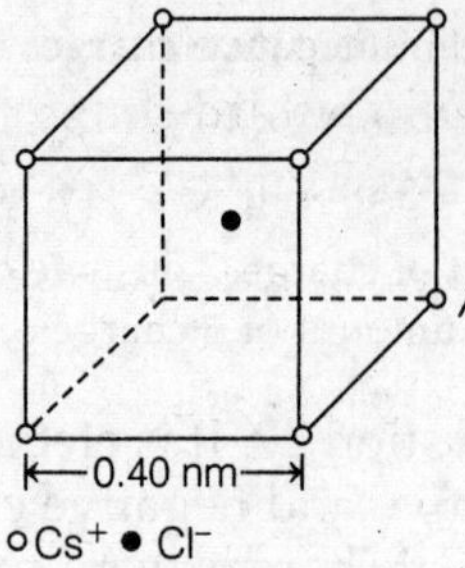

Thinking Process

(i) Net force on a charge due to two equal and opposite charges will be zero. Also electric field on a charge is given by $E = \frac{F}{q}$ where E = electric field, F = force on charge q due to electric field, q = magnitude of charge q.

(ii) If a Cs atom is removed from the corner A. Then the net force will be due to Cs ion located opposite Cl on the body diagonal.

Ans. (i) From the given figure, we can analyse that the chlorine atom is at the centre of the cube *i.e.*, at equal distance from all the eight corners of cube where cesium atoms are placed. Thus, due to symmetry, the forces due to all Cs ions on Cl atom will cancel out.

Hence, $$E = \frac{F}{q} \quad \text{where } F = 0$$

$$\therefore \quad E = 0$$

(ii) Thus, net force on Cl atom at A would be due to B

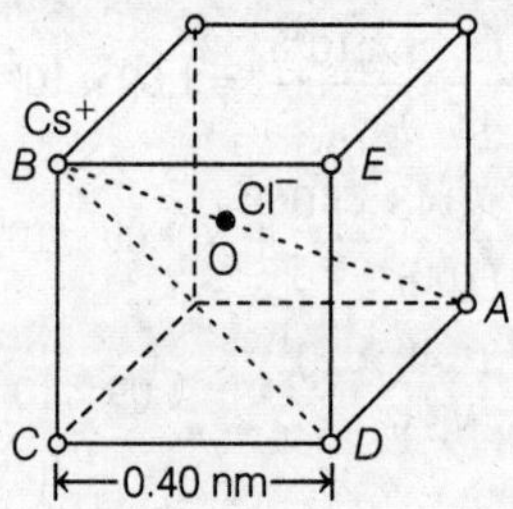

Using pythagoras theorem in ΔBCD,

$$(BD)^2 = (0.40)^2 + (0.40)^2$$

$$(BD)^2 = 0.3200$$

Using pythagoras theorem in ΔABD,

$$(AB)^2 = (BD)^2 + (AD)^2 = 0.32 + 0.16$$

$$= AB = \sqrt{0.48}\text{nm} = 0.69 \text{ nm and } BO = \frac{0.69}{2} = 0.34 \text{ nm}$$

$$f = \frac{1}{4\pi\varepsilon_0} \frac{e^2}{(BO)^2}$$

$$= \frac{9 \times 10^9 \times (1.6 \times 10^{-19})^2}{(0.34 \times 10^{-9})^2} = 1.99 \times 10^{-9} \text{N}$$

Q.23 Two charges q and $-3q$ are placed fixed on X-axis separated by distance d. Where should a third charge $2q$ be placed such that it will not experience any force?

Thinking Process The force on any charge will be zero only if all forces are balanced *i.e.*, force of attraction is balanced by force of repulsion.

Ans. Here, let us keep the charge $2q$ at a distance x from A such that it does not experience any force.

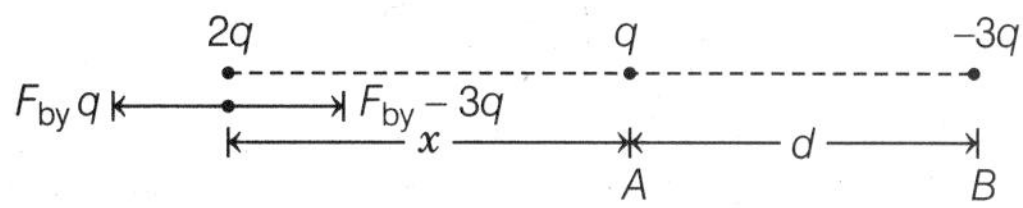

Thus, force of attraction by $-3q$ = Force of repulsion by q

$$\Rightarrow \quad \frac{2q \times q}{4\pi\varepsilon_0 x^2} = \frac{2q \times 3q}{4\pi\varepsilon_0 (x+d)^2}$$

$$\Rightarrow \quad (x+d)^2 = 3x^2$$

$$\Rightarrow \quad x^2 + d^2 + 2xd = 3x^2$$

$$\therefore \quad 2x^2 - 2dx - d^2 = 0$$

$$x = \frac{d}{2} \pm \frac{\sqrt{3}d}{2}$$

(Since, x cannot be negative, therefore $x \neq \frac{d}{2} - \frac{\sqrt{3d}}{2}$)

$$x = \frac{d}{2} + \frac{\sqrt{3}d}{2} = \frac{d}{2}(1+\sqrt{3}) \text{ to the left of } q.$$

Q.24 Figure shows the electric field lines around three point charges A, B and C.

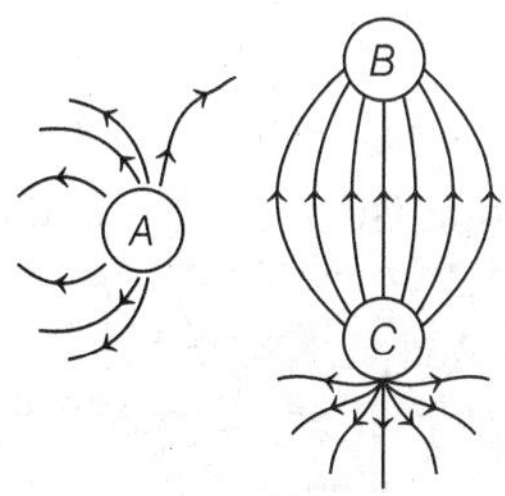

(i) Which charges are positive?

(ii) Which charge has the largest magnitude? Why?

(iii) In which region or regions of the picture could the electric field be zero? Justify your answer.

(a) Near A (b) Near B (c) Near C (d) Nowhere

- **Concept Insight**

(i) Electric lines of forces always starts from a positive charge and ends at a negative charge. In case of a single charge, electric lines of force start from positive charge ends at infinity.

(ii) The magnitude of a charge depends on the number of lines of force enamating from a charge *i.e.*, higher the number of lines of forces, higher the magnitude of charge and *vice-versa*.

Ans. (i) Here, in the figure, the electric lines of force emanate from A and C. Therefore, charges A and C must be positive.

(ii) The number of electric lines of forces enamating is maximum for charge C, so C must have the largest magnitude.

(iii) Point between two like charges where electrostatic force is zero is called netural point. So, the neutral point lies between A and C only.

Now, the position of neutral point depends on the strength of the forces of charges. Here, more number of electric lines of forces shows higher strength of charge C than A. So, neutral point lies near A.

Q.25 Five charges, q each are placed at the corners of a regular pentagon of sides.

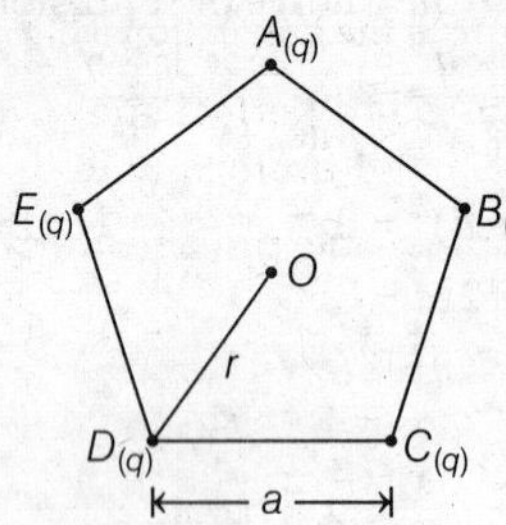

(a) (i) What will be the electric field at O, the centre of the pentagon?

(ii) What will be the electric field at O if the charge from one of the corners (say A) is removed?

(iii) What will be the electric field at O if the charge q at A is replaced by $-q$?

(b) How would your answer to (a) be affected if pentagon is replaced by n-sided regular polygon with charge q at each of its corners?

Thinking Process Due to symmetry, forces by all the charges are cancelled out.

Ans. (a) (i) The point O is equidistant from all the charges at the end point of pentagon. Thus, due to symmetry, the forces due to all the charges are cancelled out. As a result electric field at O is zero.

(ii) When charge q is removed, a negative charge can be assumed at A giving electric field $E = \dfrac{q \times 1}{4\pi\varepsilon_0 r^2}$ along OA.

(iii) If charge q at A is replaced by $-q$, then two negative charges $-2q$ will develop there. Thus, the value of electric field $E = \dfrac{2q}{4\pi\varepsilon_0 r^2}$ along OA.

(b) When pentagon is replaced by n sided regular polygon with charge q at each of its corners, the electric field at O would continue to be zero as symmetricity of the charges is due to the regularity of the polygon. It doesn't depend on the number of sides or the number of charges.

Long Answer Type Questions

Q.26 In 1959 Lyttleton and Bondi suggested that the expansion of the universe could be explained if matter carried a net charge. Suppose that the universe is made up of hydrogen atoms with a number density N, which is maintained a constant. Let the charge on the proton be $e_p = -(1+y)e$, where e is the electronic charge.

(a) Find the critical value of y such that expansion may start.

(b) Show that the velocity of expansion is proportional to the distance from the centre.

Thinking Process Expansion of the universe will start if the coulomb repulsion on a hydrogen atom, at R, is larger than the gravitational attraction.

Ans. (a) Let us suppose that universe is a perfect sphere of radius R and its constituent hydrogen atoms are distributed uniformly in the sphere.

As hydrogen atom contains one proton and one electron, charge on each hydrogen atom.

$$e_H = e_p + e = -(1+y)e + e = -ye = |ye|$$

The total number of Hydrogen atoms in the universe.

$$= \text{density} \times \text{volume} = N \times \frac{4}{3}\pi R^3$$

The total charge in the universe

$$= \text{Number of Hydrogen atoms} \times \text{charge per atom}$$

$$q_{\text{net}} = N \times \frac{4}{3}\pi R^3 \times |y_e|$$

If E is electric field intensity at distance R, on the surface of the sphere, then according to Gauss' theorem,

$$\oint \mathbf{E} \cdot d\mathbf{S} = \frac{q_{\text{net}}}{\varepsilon_0} \quad i.e., \; E(4\pi R^2) = \frac{4}{3}\frac{\pi R^3 N|ye|}{\varepsilon_0}$$

$$E = \frac{1}{3}\frac{N|ye|R}{\varepsilon_0} \qquad \text{...(i)}$$

Now, suppose, mass of each hydrogen atom $\approx m_p$ = Mass of a proton, G_R = gravitational field at distance R on the sphere.

The gravitational force = $F_G = \dfrac{GMm_p}{R^2}$

where, M is the mass of the universe

$$M = \text{Total no. of H-atom} \times \text{Mass of H-atom}$$

$$M = N \times \frac{4}{3}\pi R^3 \times m_p$$

$$\therefore \quad F_G = \frac{4G}{3} N\pi R m_p^2 = \frac{4\pi}{3} GNRm_p^2$$

Coulomb force on hydrogen atom at R is $F_C = |ye|\,E = \dfrac{1}{3}\dfrac{Ny^2e^2R}{\varepsilon_0}$ [from Eq.(i)]

Now, to start expansion $F_C > F_G$ and critical value of y to start expansion would be when

$$F_C = F_G \Rightarrow \frac{1}{3}\frac{Ny^2e^2R}{\varepsilon_0} = \frac{4\pi}{3}Gm_p^2NR$$

$$\Rightarrow \quad y^2 = (4\pi\varepsilon_0)\,G\left(\frac{m_p}{e}\right)^2 = \frac{1}{9\times 10^9}\times(6.67\times 10^{-11})\left(\frac{(1.66\times 10^{-27})^2}{(1.6\times 10^{-19})^2}\right)$$

$$= 79.8\times 10^{-38}$$

$$\Rightarrow \quad y = \sqrt{79.8\times 10^{-38}} = 8.9\times 10^{-19} \approx 10^{-18}$$

Thus, 10^{-18} is the required critical value of y corresponding to which expansion of universe would start.

(b) Net force experienced by the hydrogen atom is given by

$$F = F_C - F_G = \frac{1}{3}\frac{Ny^2e^2R}{\varepsilon_0} - \frac{4\pi}{3}Gm_p^2NR$$

If acceleration of hydrogen atom is represent by d^2R/dt^2, then

$$m_p\frac{d^2R}{dt^2} = F = \frac{1}{3}\frac{Ny^2e^2R}{\varepsilon_0} - \frac{4\pi}{3}Gm_p^2NR = \left(\frac{1}{3}\frac{Ny^2e^2}{\varepsilon_0} - \frac{4\pi}{3}Gm_p^2N\right)R$$

$$\therefore \quad \frac{d^2R}{dt^2} = \frac{1}{m_p}\left[\frac{1}{3}\frac{Ny^2e^2}{\varepsilon_0} - \frac{4\pi}{3}Gm_p^2N\right]R = \alpha^2R \qquad \text{...(iv)}$$

where, $$\alpha^2 = \frac{1}{m_p}\left[\frac{1}{3}\frac{Ny^2e^2}{\varepsilon_0} - \frac{4\pi}{3}Gm_p^2N\right]$$

The general solution of Eq. (iv) is given by $R = Ae^{\alpha t} + Be^{-\alpha t}$. We are looking for expansion, here, so $B = 0$ and $R = Ae^{\alpha t}$.

$\Rightarrow$ Velocity of expansion, $v = \dfrac{dR}{dt} = Ae^{\alpha t}(\alpha) = \alpha Ae^{\alpha t} = \alpha R$

Hence, $v \propto R$ *i.e.*, velocity of expansion is proportional to the distance from the centre.

Q.27 Consider a sphere of radius R with charge density distributed as

$$\rho(r) = kr \text{ for } r \le R$$
$$= 0 \text{ for } r > R$$

(a) Find the electric field at all points r.

(b) Suppose the total charge on the sphere is $2e$, where e is the electronic charge. Where can two protons be embedded such that the force on each of them is zero? Assume that, the introduction of the proton does not alter the negative charge distribution.

Thinking Process According to the given charge density distribution of the sphere of radius R *i.e.*, $\rho(r) = kr$ for $r \le R$; $= 0$ for $r > R$, it is obvious that the electric field is radial.

Ans. (a) Let us consider a sphere S of radius R and two hypothetic sphere of radius $r < R$ and $r > R$.

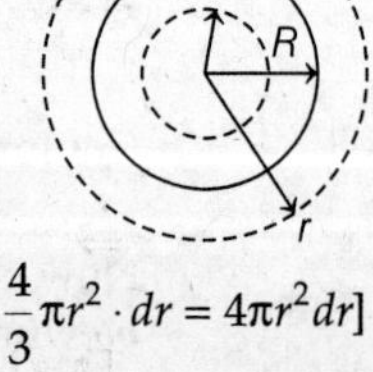

Now, for point $r < R$, electric field intensity will be given by,

$$\oint \mathbf{E}\cdot d\mathbf{S} = \frac{1}{\varepsilon_0}\int \rho\, dV \qquad [\because q = \int \rho\, dV]$$

$$\left[\text{For } dV,\ V = \frac{4}{3}\pi r^3 \Rightarrow dV = 3\times\frac{4}{3}\pi r^2\cdot dr = 4\pi r^2 dr\right]$$

$\Rightarrow \qquad \oint \mathbf{E} \cdot d\mathbf{S} = \frac{1}{\varepsilon_0} 4\pi k \int_0^r r^3 dr \qquad [\because \rho(r) = kr]$

$\Rightarrow \qquad (E)\, 4\pi r^2 = \frac{4\pi k}{\varepsilon_0} \frac{r^4}{4} \Rightarrow E = \frac{1}{4\varepsilon_0} kr^2$

Here, charge density is positive.

So, direction of **E** is radially outwards.

For points $r > R$, electric field intensity will be given by

$$\oint \mathbf{E} \cdot d\mathbf{S} = \frac{1}{\varepsilon_0} \int \rho . dV$$

$\Rightarrow \qquad E(4\pi r^2) = \frac{4\pi k}{\varepsilon_0} \int_0^R r^3 dr = \frac{4\pi k}{\varepsilon_0} \frac{R^4}{4}$

$\Rightarrow \qquad E = \frac{k}{4\varepsilon_0} \frac{R^4}{r^2}$

Charge density is again positive. So, the direction of **E** is radially outward.

(b) The two protons must be on the opposite sides of the centre along a diameter following the rule of symmetry. This can be shown by the figure given below. Charge on the sphere,

$$q = \int_0^R \rho dV = \int_0^R (kr)\, 4\pi r^2 dr$$

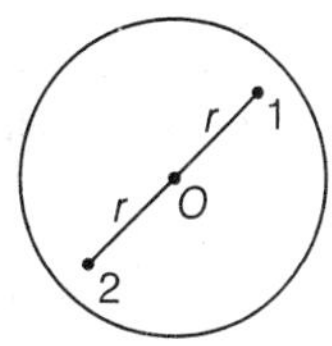

$$q = 4\pi k \frac{R^4}{4} = 2e$$

$\therefore \qquad k = \frac{2e}{\pi R^4}$

If protons 1 and 2 are embedded at distance r from the centre of the sphere as shown, then attractive force on proton 1 due to charge distribution is

$$F_1 = eE = \frac{-ekr^2}{4\varepsilon_0}$$

Repulsive force on proton 1 due to proton 2 is

$$F_2 = \frac{e^2}{4\pi\varepsilon_0 (2r)^2}$$

Net force on proton 1, $F = F_1 + F_2$

$$F = \frac{-ekr^2}{4\varepsilon_0} + \frac{e^2}{16\pi\varepsilon_0 r^2}$$

So, $\qquad F = \left[\frac{-er^2}{4\varepsilon_0} \frac{2e}{\pi R^4} + \frac{e^2}{16\pi\varepsilon_0 r^2}\right]$

Thus, net force on proton 1 will be zero, when

$$\frac{er^2 2e}{4\varepsilon_0 \pi R^4} = \frac{e^2}{16\pi\varepsilon_0 r^2} \Rightarrow r^4 = \frac{R^4}{8}$$

$\Rightarrow \qquad r = \frac{R}{(8)^{1/4}}$

This is the distance of each of the two protons from the centre of the sphere.

Q.28 Two fixed, identical conducting plates (α and β), each of surface area S are charged to $-Q$ and q, respectively, where $Q > q > 0$. A third identical plate (γ), free to move is located on the other side of the plate with charge q at a distance d (figure). The third plate is released and collides with the plate β. Assume the collision is elastic and the time of collision is sufficient to redistribute charge amongst β and γ.

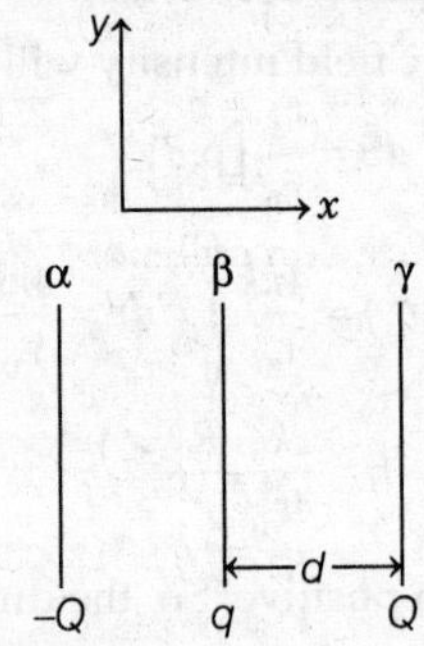

(a) Find the electric field acting on the plate γ before collision.
(b) Find the charges on β and γ after the collision.
(c) Find the velocity of the plate γ after the collision and at a distance d from the plate β.

- **Concept Insight**

(i) Electric field due to an uniformly charged plane sheet of charge is $\frac{\sigma}{2\varepsilon_0} = \frac{Q}{2A\varepsilon_0}$.

(ii) Work energy theorem states that work done by all the forces is equal to change in kinetic energy of the system.

Ans. (a) Net electric field at plate γ before collision is equal to the sum of electric field at plate γ due to plate α and β.

The electric field at plate γ due to plate α is $E_1 = \frac{-Q}{S(2\varepsilon_0)}$, to the left.

The electric field at plate γ due to plate β is $E_2 = \frac{q}{S(2\varepsilon_0)}$, to the right.

Hence, the net electric field at plate γ before collision.

$$E = E_1 + E_2 = \frac{q-Q}{S(2\varepsilon_0)}, \text{ to the left}$$

(b) During collision, plates β and γ are together. Their potentials become same. Suppose charge on plate β is q_1 and charge on plate γ is q_2. At any point O, in between the two plates, the electric field must be zero.

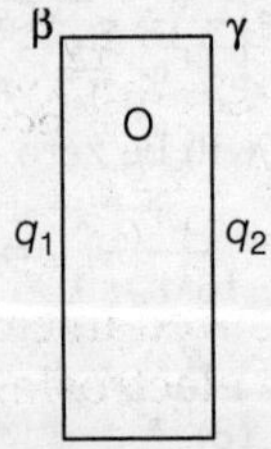

Electric field at O due to plate $\alpha = \frac{-Q}{S(2\varepsilon_0)}$, to the left

Electric field at O due to plate $\beta = \frac{q_1}{S(2\varepsilon_0)}$, to the right

Electric field at O due to plate $\gamma = \frac{-q_2}{S(2\varepsilon_0)}$, to the left

As the electric field at O is zero, therefore

$$\frac{Q+q_2}{S(2\varepsilon_0)} = \frac{q_1}{S(2\varepsilon_0)}$$

$$\therefore \quad Q + q_2 = q_1$$

$$Q = q_1 - q_2 \quad \text{...(i)}$$

As there is no loss of charge on collision,

$$Q + q = q_1 + q_2 \quad \text{...(ii)}$$

On solving Eqs. (i) and (ii), we get

$$q_1 = (Q + q/2) = \text{charge on plate } \beta$$

$$q_2 = (q/2) = \text{charge on plate } \gamma$$

(c) After collision, at a distance d from plate β,

Let the velocity of plate γ be v. After the collision, electric field at plate γ is

$$E_2 = \frac{-Q}{2\varepsilon_0 S} + \frac{(Q+q/2)}{2\varepsilon_0 S} = \frac{q/2}{2\varepsilon_0 S} \text{ to the right.}$$

Just before collision, electric field at plate γ is $E_1 = \frac{Q-q}{2\varepsilon_0 S}$.

If F_1 is force on plate γ before collision, then $F_1 = E_1 Q = \frac{(Q-q)\,Q}{2\varepsilon_0 S}$

If F_2 is force on plate r after collision, then $F_2 = E_2 \frac{q}{2} = \frac{(q/2)^2}{2S}$

Total work done by the electric field is round trip movement of plate γ

$$W = (F_1 + F_2)\,d$$

$$= \frac{[(Q-q)\,Q + (q/2)^2]\,d}{2\varepsilon_0 S} = \frac{(Q-q/2)^2 d}{2\varepsilon_0 S}$$

If m is mass of plate γ, the KE gained by plate $\gamma = \frac{1}{2}mv^2$

According to work-energy principle, $\frac{1}{2}mv^2 = W = \frac{(Q-q/2)^2 d}{2\varepsilon_0 S}$

$$v = (Q - q/2)\left(\frac{d}{m\varepsilon_0 S}\right)^{1/2}$$

Q.29 There is another useful system of units, besides the SI/MKS. A system, called the CGS (Centimeter-Gram-Second) system. In this system, Coulomb's law is given by $\mathbf{F} = \frac{Qq}{r^2}\hat{\mathbf{r}}$.

Where the distance r is measured in cm $(= 10^{-2}\text{m})$, F in dynes $(= 10^{-5}\text{N})$ and the charges in electrostatic units (es units), where 1 es unit of charge $= \frac{1}{[3]} \times 10^{-9}$C.

The number [3] actually arises from the speed of light in vacuum which is now taken to be exactly given by $c = 2.99792458 \times 10^8$ m/s. An approximate value of c, then is $c = 3 \times 10^8$ m/s.

(i) Show that the Coulomb's law in CGS units yields 1 esu of charge $= 1\ (\text{dyne})^{1/2}$ cm. Obtain the dimensions of units of charge in terms of mass M, length L and time T. Show that it is given in terms of fractional powers of M and L.

(ii) Write 1 esu of charge $= xC$, where x is a dimensionless number. Show that this gives $\dfrac{1}{4\pi\varepsilon_0} = \dfrac{10^{-9}}{x^2}\dfrac{\text{Nm}^2}{\text{C}^2}$.

With $x = \dfrac{1}{[3]} \times 10^{-9}$, we have $\dfrac{1}{4\pi\varepsilon_0} = [3]^2 \times 10^9 \dfrac{\text{Nm}^2}{\text{C}^2}$,

$\dfrac{1}{4\pi\varepsilon_0} = (2.99792458)^2 \times 10^9 \dfrac{\text{Nm}^2}{\text{C}^2}$ (exactly).

Ans. (i) From the relation, $F = \dfrac{Qq}{r^2} \Rightarrow 1 \text{ dyne} = \dfrac{[1 \text{ esu of charge}]^2}{[1 \text{ cm}]^2}$

So, 1 esu of charge $= (1 \text{ dyne})^{1/2} \times 1 \text{ cm} = F^{1/2}.L = [\text{MLT}^{-2}]^{1/2}\text{L}$

$\Rightarrow$ 1 esu of charge $= \text{M}^{1/2}\text{L}^{3/2}\text{T}^{-1}$.

Thus, esu of charge is represented in terms of fractional powers $\dfrac{1}{2}$ of M and $\dfrac{3}{2}$ of L.

(ii) Let 1 esu of charge $= xC$, where x is a dimensionless number. Coulomb force on two charges, each of magnitude 1 esu separated by 1 cm is dyne $= 10^{-5}$N. This situation is equivalent to two charges of magnitude xC separated by 10^{-2} m.

$$\therefore \quad F = \frac{1}{4\pi\varepsilon_0}\frac{x^2}{(10^{-2})^2}$$

$$= 1 \text{ dyne} = 10^{-5}\text{N}$$

$$\therefore \quad \frac{1}{4\pi\varepsilon_0} = \frac{10^{-9}}{x^2}\frac{\text{Nm}^2}{\text{C}^2}$$

Taking,
$$x = \frac{1}{|3| \times 10^9}$$

we get,
$$\frac{1}{4\pi\varepsilon_0} = 10^{-9} \times |3|^2 \times 10^{18}\frac{\text{Nm}^2}{\text{C}^2}$$

$$= 9 \times 10^9 \frac{\text{Nm}^2}{\text{C}^2}$$

If $|3| \to 2.99792458$, we get $\dfrac{1}{4\pi\varepsilon_0} = 8.98755 \times 10^9 \text{ Nm}^2\text{C}^{-2}$.

Q.30 Two charges $-q$ each are fixed separated by distance $2d$. A third charge q of mass m placed at the mid-point is displaced slightly by $x (x << d)$ perpendicular to the line joining the two fixed charged as shown in figure. Show that q will perform simple harmonic oscillation of time period.

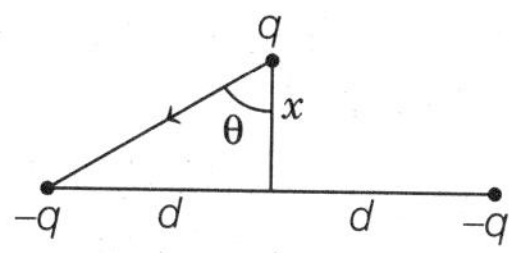

$$T = \left[\frac{8\pi^3 \varepsilon_0 m d^3}{q^2}\right]^{1/2}$$

- **Concept Insight** For motion of charge q to be simple harmonic, force on charge q must be proportional to its distance from the centre O and directed towards $O (f = -kx)$.

Ans. Let us elaborate the figure first.

Given, two charge $-q$ at A and B

$$AB = AO + OB = 2d$$

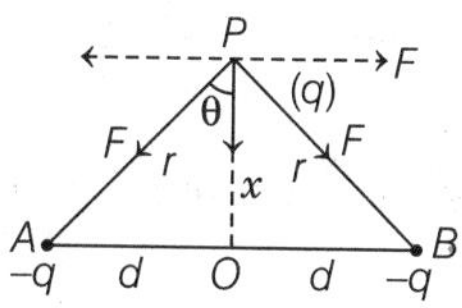

x = small distance perpendicular to O.

i.e., $x < d$ mass of charge q is. So, force of attraction at P towards A and B are each $F = \dfrac{q(q)}{4\pi\varepsilon_0 r^2}$, where $AP = BP = r$

Horizontal components of these forces F_n are cancel out. Vertical components along PO add.

If $\angle APO = \theta$, the net force on q along PO is $F' = 2F\cos\theta$

$$= \frac{2q^2}{4\pi\varepsilon_0 r^2}\left(\frac{x}{r}\right)$$

$$\Rightarrow \qquad \mathbf{F'} = \frac{2q^2 x}{4\pi\varepsilon_0 (d^2 + x^2)^{3/2}}(-\hat{\mathbf{j}})$$

When, $\qquad x << d,\ F' = \dfrac{-2q^2 x}{4\pi\varepsilon_0 d^3} = -kx$

where, $\qquad k = \dfrac{2q^2}{4\pi\varepsilon_0 d^3}$

$$\Rightarrow \qquad F \propto x$$

i.e., force on charge q is proportional to its displacement from the centre O and it is directed towards O.

Hence, motion of charge q would be simple harmonic, where

$$\omega = \sqrt{\frac{k}{m}} \qquad (\because k = m\omega^2)$$

and
$$T = \frac{2\pi}{\omega} = 2\pi\sqrt{\frac{m}{k}}$$

$$= 2\pi\sqrt{\frac{m.4\pi\varepsilon_0 d^3}{2q^2}} = \left[\frac{8\pi^3 \varepsilon_0 m d^3}{q^2}\right]^{1/2}$$

Q.31 Total charge $-Q$ is uniformly spread along length of a ring of radius R. A small test charge $+q$ of mass m is kept at the centre of the ring and is given a gentle push along the axis of the ring.

(a) Show that the particle executes a simple harmonic oscillation.

(b) Obtain its time period.

Thinking Process For simple harmonic oscillation, force on q is proportional to negative of its displacement.

Ans. (a) Let us draw the figure according to question,

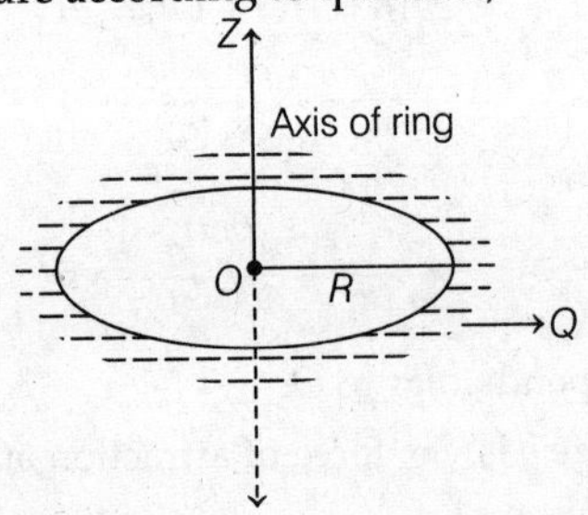

A gentle push on q along the axis of the ring gives rise to the situation shown in the figure below.

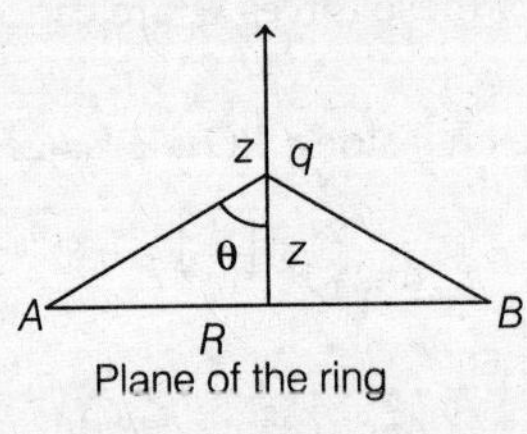

Electric field at the axis of the ring at a distance z from the centre along the axis is

$$\mathbf{E} = \frac{1}{4\pi\varepsilon_0} \frac{Qz}{(R^2 + z^2)^{\frac{3}{2}}}(-\hat{\mathbf{j}})$$

Net force on charge q, $\mathbf{F}_{net} = q\mathbf{E}$

$$\Rightarrow \qquad \mathbf{F}_{net} = \frac{1}{4\pi\varepsilon_o} = \frac{qQz}{(R^2 + z^2)^{\frac{3}{2}}} - \hat{\mathbf{j}}$$

$$= \frac{1}{4\pi\varepsilon_0} \frac{qQz}{R^3\left(1 + \frac{z^2}{R^2}\right)^{\frac{3}{2}}}(-\hat{\mathbf{j}})$$

For $$z << R$$

$$\Rightarrow \quad \frac{z}{R} << 1$$

$$\Rightarrow \quad \left(\frac{z}{R}\right)^2 \approx 0$$

$$\Rightarrow \quad f_{\text{net}} = -\frac{1}{4\pi\varepsilon_o}\frac{qQz}{R^3}$$

Comparing with $$f = -kz$$

$$\Rightarrow \quad k = \frac{qQ}{4\pi\varepsilon_0 R^3}$$

$$\Rightarrow \quad F \propto -z$$

Clearly, force on q is proportional to negative of its displacement. Therefore, motion of q is simple harmonic.

(b) $$\omega = \sqrt{\frac{k}{m}}$$

and $$T = \frac{2\pi}{\omega} = 2\pi\sqrt{\frac{m}{k}}$$

$$T = 2\pi\sqrt{\frac{m\,4\pi\varepsilon_0 R^3}{Qq}}$$

$$\Rightarrow \quad T = 2\pi\sqrt{\frac{4\pi\varepsilon_0\, m\, R^3}{Qq}}$$

Chapter 02

Electrostatic Potential and Capacitance

Multiple Choice Questions (MCQs)

Q.1 A capacitor of 4 μF is connected as shown in the circuit. The internal resistance of the battery is 0.5Ω. The amount of charge on the capacitor plates will be

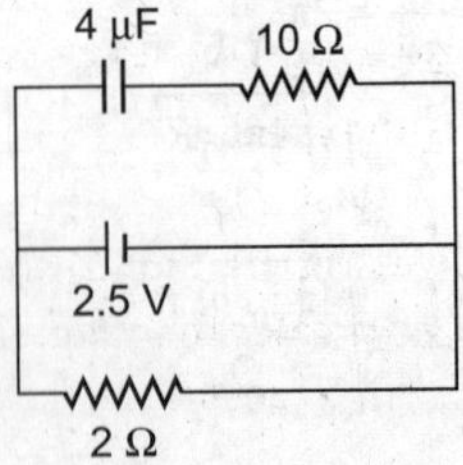

(a) 0 (b) 4 μC (c) 16μC (d) 8 μC

Thinking Process In this problem, the three parallel branches of circuit have the same potential difference. The capacitor offers infinite resistance in DC circuit, therefore no current flows through capacitor and 10Ω resistance, leaving zero potential difference across 10 Ω resistance.

Thus, potential difference across lower and middle branch of circuit is same as that across the capacitor in the upper branch of circuit.

Ans. ***(d)*** Current flows through 2Ω resistance from left to right, is given by

$$I = \frac{V}{R+r} = \frac{2.5\text{V}}{2+0.5} = 1\text{A}$$

The potential difference across 2Ω resistance, $V = IR = 1 \times 2 = 2$ V

Since, capacitor is in parallel with 2Ω resistance, so it also has 2V potential difference across it.

The charge on capacitor

$$q = CV = (4\mu\text{F}) \times 2\text{V} = 8\mu\text{C}$$

Note The potential difference across 2Ω resistance solely occurs across capacitor as no potential drop occurs across 10Ω resistance.

Q.2 A positively charged particle is released from rest in a uniform electric field. The electric potential energy of the charge

(a) remains a constant because the electric field is uniform

(b) increases because the charge moves along the electric field

(c) decreases because the charge moves along the electric field

(d) decreases because the charge moves opposite to the electric field

Thinking Process In this problem, the relationship between E and V is brought into effect.

Ans. *(c)* The direction of electric field is always perpendicular to one equipotential surface maintained at high electrostatic potential to other equipotential surface maintained at low electrostatic potential.

The positively charged particle experiences electrostatic force along the direction of electric field *i.e.*, from high electrostatic potential to low electrostatic potential. Thus, the work is done by the electric field on the positive charge, hence electrostatic potential energy of the positive charge decreases.

Q.3 Figure shows some equipotential lines distributed in space. A charged object is moved from point A to point B.

(a) The work done in Fig. (i) is the greatest

(b) The work done in Fig. (ii) is least

(c) The work done is the same in Fig. (i), Fig.(ii) and Fig. (iii)

(d) The work done in Fig. (iii) is greater than Fig. (ii) but equal to that in Fig. (i).

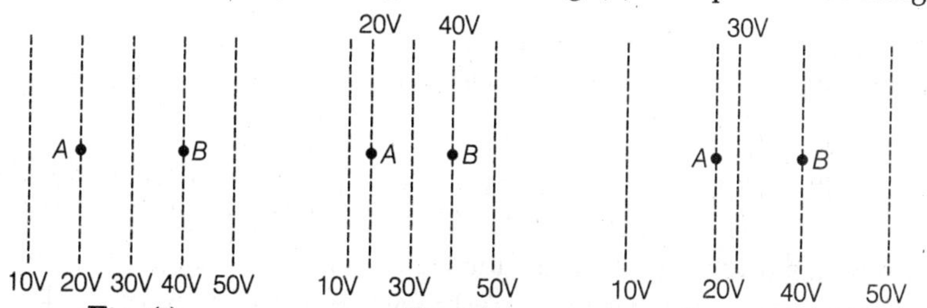

Fig. (i) Fig. (ii) Fig. (iii)

Ans. *(c)* The work done by an electrostatic force is given by $W_{AB} = q(V_B - V_A)$. Here, the potential difference between points A and B remains the same in all three cases and same charge is moved, so work done is same in all three cases.

Q.4 The electrostatic potential on the surface of a charged conducting sphere is 100V. Two statements are made in this regard

S_1 : At any point inside the sphere, electric field intensity is zero.

S_2 : At any point inside the sphere, the electrostatic potential is 100V.

Which of the following is a correct statement?

(a) S_1 is true but S_2 is false.

(b) Both S_1 and S_2 are false.

(c) S_1 is true, S_2 is also true and S_1 is the cause of S_2.

(d) S_1 is true, S_2 is also true but the statements are independent.

Ans. ***(c)*** In this problem, the electric field intensity E and electric potential V are related as

$$E = -\frac{dV}{dr}$$

Electric field intensity $E = 0$ suggests that $\frac{dV}{dr} = 0$

This implies that V = constant.

Thus, $E = 0$ inside the charged conducting sphere causes the same electrostatic potential 100V at any point inside the sphere.

Note V equals zero does not necessary imply that $E = 0$ *e.g.*, the electric potential at any point on the perpendicular bisector due to electric dipole is zero but E not.

$E = 0$ does not necessary imply that $V = 0$ *e.g.*, the electric field intensity at any point inside the charged spherical shell is zero but there may exist non-zero electric potential.

Q.5 Equipotentials at a great distance from a collection of charges whose total sum is not zero are approximately

(a) spheres (b) planes
(c) paraboloids (d) ellipsoids

Ans. ***(a)*** In this problem, the collection of charges whose total sum is not zero, with regard to great distance can be considered as a point charge. The equipotentials due to point charge are spherical in shape as electric potential due to point charge q is given by

$$V = k_e \frac{q}{r}$$

This suggests that electric potential due to point charge is same for all equidistant points. The locus of these equidistant points, which are at same potential, forms spherical surface.

Q.6 A parallel plate capacitor is made of two dielectric blocks in series. One of the blocks has thickness d_1 and dielectric constant K_1 and the other has thickness d_2 and dielectric constant K_2 as shown in figure. This arrangement can be thought as a dielectric slab of thickness $d\,(= d_1 + d_2)$ and effective dielectric constant K. The K is

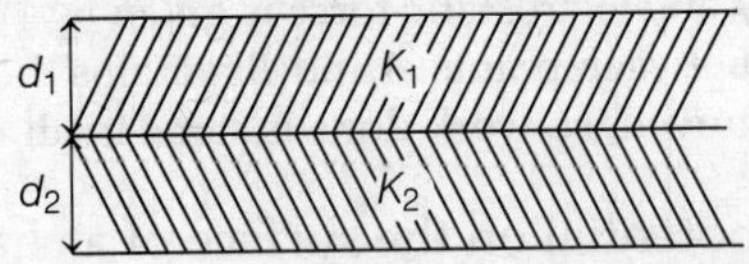

(a) $\dfrac{K_1 d_1 + K_2 d_2}{d_1 + d_2}$ (b) $\dfrac{K_1 d_1 + K_2 d_2}{K_1 + K_2}$

(c) $\dfrac{K_1 K_2 (d_1 + d_2)}{(K_1 d_2 + K_2 d_1)}$ (d) $\dfrac{2 K_1 K_2}{K_1 + K_2}$

Thinking Process In this problem, the system can be considered as the series combination of two capacitors which are of thicknesses d_1 with dielectric constant K_1 and thicknesses d_2 with dielectric constant K_2.

Ans. *(c)* The capacitance of parallel plate capacitor filled with dielectric block having thickness d_1 and dielectric constant K_1 is given by

$$C_1 = \frac{K_1 \varepsilon_0 A}{d_1}$$

Similarly, capacitance of parallel plate capacitor filled with dielectric block having thickness d_2 and dielectric constant K_2 is given by

$$C_2 = \frac{K_2 \varepsilon_0 A}{d_2}$$

Since, the two capacitors are in series combination, the equivalent capacitance is given by

$$\frac{1}{C} = \frac{1}{C_1} + \frac{1}{C_2}$$

or $$C = \frac{C_1 C_2}{C_1 + C_2} = \frac{\frac{K_1\varepsilon_0 A}{d_1} \frac{K_2\varepsilon_0 A}{d_2}}{\frac{K_1\varepsilon_0 A}{d_1} + \frac{K_2\varepsilon_0 A}{d_2}} = \frac{K_1 K_2 \varepsilon_0 A}{K_1 d_2 + K_2 d_1} \quad \text{...(i)}$$

But the equivalent capacitance is given by

$$C = \frac{K\varepsilon_0 A}{d_1 + d_2} \quad \text{...(ii)}$$

On comparing (i) and (ii) we have

$$K = \frac{K_1 K_2 (d_1 + d_2)}{K_1 d_2 + K_2 d_1}$$

Note For the equivalent capacitance of the combination, thickness is equal to the separation between two plates *i.e.*, $d_1 + d_2$ and dielectric constant K.

Multiple Choice Questions (More Than One Options)

Q.7 Consider a uniform electric field in the z-direction. The potential is a constant

(a) in all space
(b) for any x for a given z
(c) for any y for a given z
(d) on the XY-plane for a given z

Ans. *(b, c, d)*

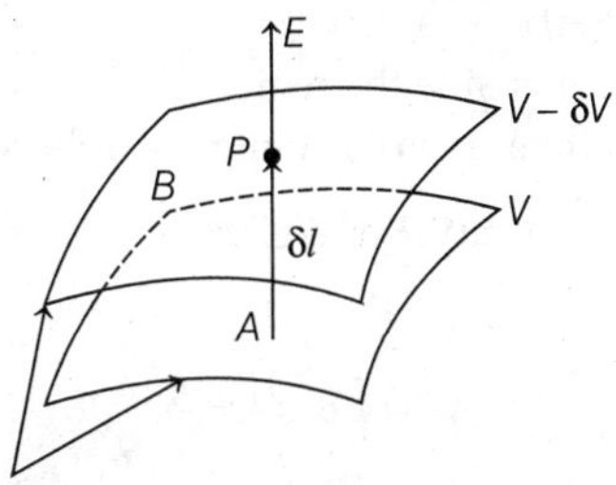

The electric field is always remains in the direction in which the potential decreases steepest. Its magnitude is given by the change in the magnitude of potential per unit displacement normal to the equipotential surface at the point. The electric field in z-direction suggests that equipotential surfaces are in X-Y plane. Therefore, the potential is constant for any x for a given z, for any y for a given z and on the X-Y plane for a given z.

Note The shape of equipotential surfaces depends on the nature and type of distribution of charge *e.g.*, point charge produces spherical surfaces whereas line charge distribution produces cylindrical equipotential surfaces.

Q.8 Equipotential surfaces

(a) are closer in regions of large electric fields compared to regions of lower electric fields
(b) will be more crowded near sharp edges of a conductor
(c) will be more crowded near regions of large charge densities
(d) will always be equally spaced

- **Concept Insight** The relation between the electric field intensity E and electric potential V is given by

$$E = -\frac{dV}{dr}$$

Ans. ***(a,b,c)*** The electric field intensity E is inversely proportional to the separation between equipotential surfaces. So, equipotential surfaces are closer in regions of large electric fields. Since, the electric field intensities are large near sharp edges of charged conductor and near regions of large charge densities. Therefore, equipotential surfaces are closer at such places.

Q.9 The work done to move a charge along an equipotential from A to B

(a) cannot be defined as $-\int_A^B \mathbf{E} \cdot d\mathbf{l}$
(b) must be defined as $-\int_A^B \mathbf{E} \cdot d\mathbf{l}$
(c) is zero
(d) can have a non-zero value

Ans. ***(b, c)*** Work done in displacing a charge particle is given by $W_{AB} = q(V_B - V_A)$ and the line integral of electrical field from point 1 to 2 gives potential difference $V_B - V_A = -\int_A^B \mathbf{E} \cdot d\mathbf{l}$. For equipotential surface, $V_B - V_A = 0$ and $W = 0$.

Q.10 In a region of constant potential,

(a) the electric field is uniform
(b) the electric field is zero
(c) there can be no charge inside the region
(d) the electric field shall necessarily change, if a charge is placed outside the region

Ans. ***(b, c)*** The electric field intensity E and electric potential V are related $E = \frac{-dV}{dr}$. If $V =$ Constant, then $E = 0$.

From Gauss' law
$$\phi_E = \oint \mathbf{E} \cdot d\mathbf{A} = \frac{q_{in}}{\varepsilon_0}$$

Since, $E = 0$, than $\phi_E = 0$

$\therefore$
$$\frac{q_{in}}{\epsilon_0} = 0 \Rightarrow q_{in} = 0$$

Q.11 In the circuit shown in figure, initially key K_1 is closed and key K_2 is open. Then, K_1 is opened and K_2 is closed (order is important).
[Take Q_1' and Q_2' as charges on C_1 and C_2 and V_1 and V_2 as voltage respectively].

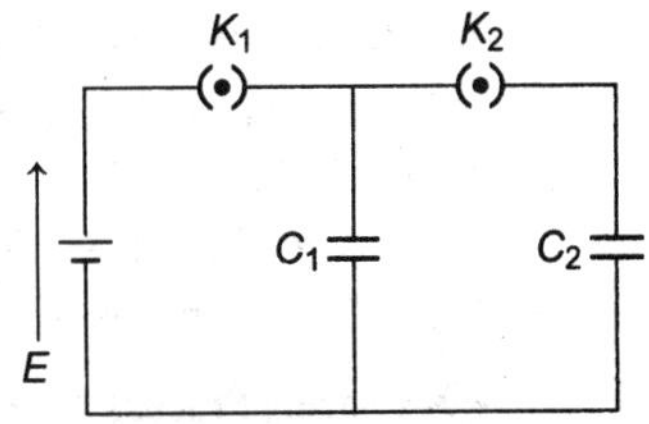

Then,
(a) charge on C_1 gets redistributed such that $V_1 = V_2$
(b) charge on C_1 gets redistributed such that $Q_1' = Q_2'$
(c) charge on C_1 gets redistributed such that $C_1V_1 + C_2V_2 = C_1E$
(d) charge on C_1 gets redistributed such that $Q_1' + Q_2' = Q$

Ans. ***(a, d)*** When key K_1 is closed and key K_2 is open, the capacitor C_1 is charged by cell and when K_1 is opened and K_2 is closed, the charge stored by capacitor C_1 gets redistributed between C_1 and C_2. till their potentials become same i.e., $V_2 = V_1$. By law of conservation of charge, the charge stored in capacitor C_1 when key K_1 is closed and key K_2 is open is equal to sum of charges on capacitors C_1 and C_2 when K_1 is opened and K_2 is closed i.e.,

$$Q_1' + Q_2' = Q$$

Q.12 If a conductor has a potential $V \neq 0$ and there are no charges anywhere else outside, then
(a) there must be charges on the surface or inside itself
(b) there cannot be any charge in the body of the conductor
(c) there must be charges only on the surface
(d) there must be charges inside the surface

- **Concept Insight** The electric field of the conducting body is written as, $E = \dfrac{Q}{4\pi\varepsilon_0 r^2}$.

Ans. ***(a, b)*** The potential of any body or a surface is due to the amount of charge present on it. It may also be due to the amount of charge inside it and outside of it. In order to have non-zero potential these should be some charge either inside or on the surface of the body. For a closed charged conductor, there will be no charge inside of it but it has non-zero potential. The charge resides on the outer surface of a closed charged conductor.

Q.13 A parallel plate capacitor is connected to a battery as shown in figure. Consider two situations.

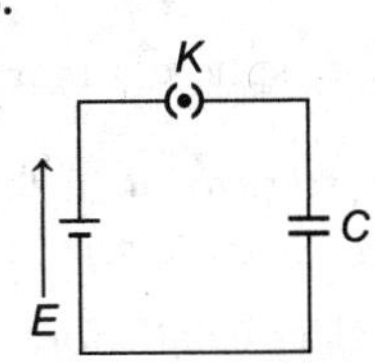

A. Key K is kept closed and plates of capacitors are moved apart using insulating handle.
B. Key K is opened and plates of capacitors are moved apart using insulating handle.

Choose the correct option(s).

(a) In **A**, Q remains same but C changes.

(b) In **B**, V remains same but C changes.

(c) In **A**, V remains same and hence Q changes.

(d) In **B**, Q remains same and hence V changes.

Thinking Process The cell is responsible for maintaining potential difference equal to its emf across connected capacitor in every circumstance. However, charge stored by disconnected charged capacitor remains conserved.

Ans. ***(c, d) Case* A** When key K is kept closed and plates of capacitors are moved apart using insulating handle, the separation between two plates increases which in turn decreases its capacitance $\left(C = \frac{K\varepsilon_0 A}{d}\right)$ and hence the charge stored decreases as $Q = CV$ (potential continues to be the same as capacitor is still connected with cell).

***Case* B** When key K is opened and plates of capacitors are moved apart using insulating handle, charge stored by disconnected charged capacitor remains conserved and with the decrease of capacitance, potential difference V increases as $V = Q/C$.

Very Short Answer Type Questions

Q.14 Consider two conducting spheres of radii R_1 and R_2 with $R_1 > R_2$. If the two are at the same potential, the larger sphere has more charge than the smaller sphere. State whether the charge density of the smaller sphere is more or less than that of the larger one.

Thinking Process The electric potentials on spheres due to their charge need to be written in terms of their charge densities.

Ans. Since, the two spheres are at the same potential, therefore

$$\frac{kq_1}{R_1} = \frac{kq_2}{R_2} \Rightarrow \frac{kq_1 R_1}{4\pi R_1^2} = \frac{kq_2 R_2}{4\pi R_2^2}$$

or
$$\sigma_1 R_1 = \sigma_2 R_2 \Rightarrow \frac{\sigma_1}{\sigma_2} = \frac{R_2}{R_1}$$

$$R_1 > R_2$$

This implies that $\sigma_2 > \sigma_1$.

The charge density of the smaller sphere is more than that of the larger one.

Q.15 Do free electrons travel to region of higher potential or lower potential?

Ans. The free electrons experience electrostatic force in a direction opposite to the direction of electric field being negatively charged. The electric field is always directed from higher potential to lower potential.

Hence, free electrons will move from lower potential to higher potential.

Q.16 Can there be a potential difference between two adjacent conductors carrying the same charge?

Thinking Process The capacity of conductor depends on its geometry *i.e.*, length and breadth . For given charge, potential $V \propto 1/C$, so two adjacent conductors carrying the same charge of different dimensions may have different potentials.

Ans. *Yes*, if the sizes are different.

Q.17 Can the potential function have a maximum or minimum in free space?

Ans. *No*, the absence of atmosphere around conductor prevents the phenomenon of electric discharge or potential leakage and hence potential function does not have a maximum or minimum in free space.

Q.18 A test charge q is made to move in the electric field of a point charge Q along two different closed paths as shown in figure. First path has sections along and perpendicular to lines of electric field. Second path is a rectangular loop of the same area as the first loop. How does the work done compare in the two cases?

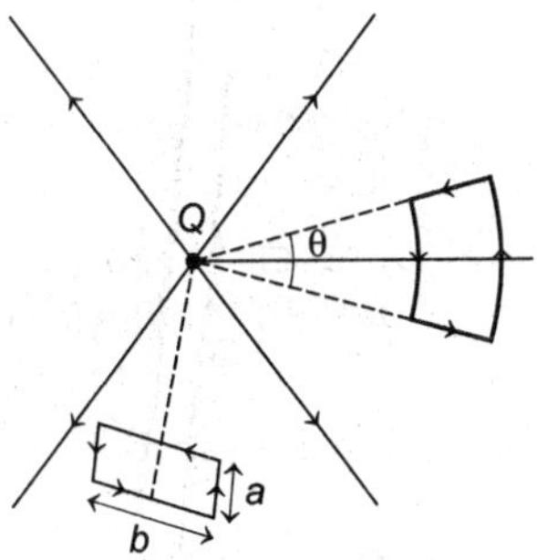

Ans. As electrostatic field is conservative, work done will be zero in both the cases.

Note Conservative forces (like electrostatic force or gravitational force) are those forces, work done by which depends only on initial position and final position of object *viz* charge, but not on the path through which it goes from initial position to final position.

Short Answer Type Questions

Q.19 Prove that a closed equipotential surface with no charge within itself must enclose an equipotential volume.

Thinking Process In this problem, we need to know that the electric field intensity E and electric potential V are related as $E = -\frac{dV}{dr}$ and the field lines are always perpendicular to one equipotential surface maintained at high electrostatic potential to other equipotential surface maintained at low electrostatic potential.

Ans. Let's assume contradicting statement that the potential is not same inside the closed equipotential surface. Let the potential just inside the surface is different from that at the surface causing a potential gradient $\left(\frac{dV}{dr}\right)$.

Consequently, electric field comes into existence, which is given by as $E = -\frac{dV}{dr}$.

Consequently, there will be field lines pointing inwards or outwards from the surface. These lines cannot be again on the surface as the surface is equipotential. It is possible only when the other end of the field lines are originated from the charges inside.

This contradicts the original assumption. Hence, the entire volume inside must be equipotential.

Q.20 A capacitor has some dielectric between its plates and the capacitor is connected to a DC source. The battery is now disconnected and then the dielectric is removed . State whether the capacitance, the energy stored in it, electric field, charge stored and the voltage will increase, decrease or remain constant.

Thinking Process Here, the charge stored by the capacitor remains conserved after its disconnection from battery.

Ans. The capacitance of the parallel plate capacitor, filled with dielectric medium of dielectric constant K is given by

$$C = \frac{K\varepsilon_0 A}{d}$$

The capacitance of the parallel plate capacitor decreases with the removal of dielectric medium as for air or vacuum, $K = 1$.

After disconnection from battery, charge stored will remain the same due to conservation of charge.

The energy stored in an isolated charge capacitor $= \frac{q^2}{2C}$; as q is constant,

energy stored $\propto \frac{1}{C}$ and C decreases with the removal of dielectric medium, therefore energy stored increases. Since, q is constant and $V = q / C$ and C decreases which in turn increases V and therefore E increases as $E = V / d$.

Note One of the very important questions with the competitive point of view.

Q.21 Prove that, if an insulated, uncharged conductor is placed near a charged conductor and no other conductors are present, the uncharged body must be intermediate in potential between that of the charged body and that of infinity.

Thinking Process The electric field $E = -\frac{dV}{dr}$ suggests that electric potential decreases along the direction of electric field.

Ans. Let us take any path from the charged conductor to the uncharged conductor along the direction of electric field. Therefore, the elèctric potential decreases along this path.

Now, another path from the uncharged conductor to infinity will again continually lower the potential further. This ensures that the uncharged body must be intermediate in potential between that of the charged body and that of infinity.

Q.22 Calculate potential energy of a point charge $-q$ placed along the axis due to a charge $+Q$ uniformly distributed along a ring of radius R. Sketch PE as a function of axial distance z from the centre of the ring. Looking at graph, can you see what would happen if $-q$ is displaced slightly from the centre of the ring (along the axis)?

Thinking Process The work done or PE stored in a system of charges can be obtained using $U = W = q \times$ potential difference.

Ans. Let us take point P to be at a distance z from the centre of the ring, as shown in figure. The charge element dq is at a distance r from point P. Therefore, V can be written as

$$V = k_e \int \frac{dq}{r} = k_e \int \frac{dq}{\sqrt{z^2 + R^2}}$$

where, $k_e = \frac{1}{4\pi\varepsilon_0}$, since each element dq is at the same distance from point P, so we have net potential

$$V = \frac{k_e}{\sqrt{z^2 + R^2}} \int dq = \frac{k_e Q}{\sqrt{z^2 + R^2}} \qquad \left[\because \int dq = Q\right]$$

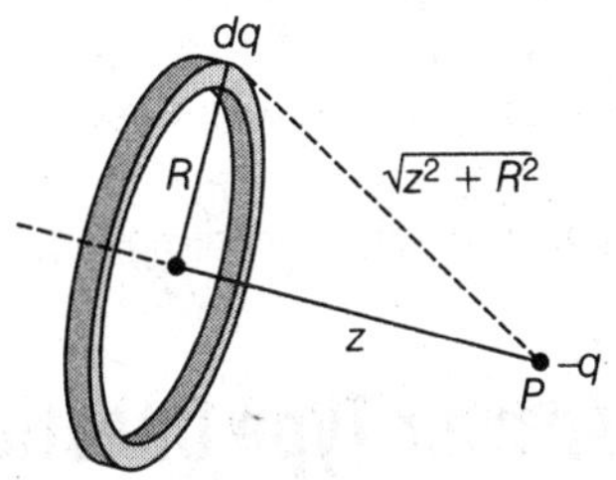

Considering $-q$ charge at P, the potential energy is given by

$$U = W = -q \times \text{potential difference}$$

$$U = \frac{k_e Q(-q)}{\sqrt{z^2 + R^2}}$$

or

$$U = \frac{1}{4\pi\varepsilon_0} \frac{-Qq}{\sqrt{z^2 + R^2}} = \frac{1}{4\pi\varepsilon_0 R} \frac{-Qq}{\sqrt{1 + \left(\frac{z}{R}\right)^2}}$$

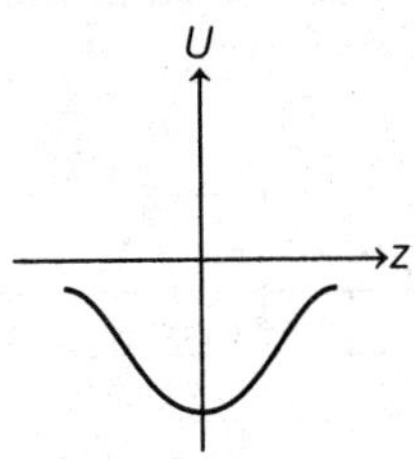

This is the required expression.

The variation of potential energy with z is shown in the figure. The charge $-q$ displaced would perform oscillations.

Nothing can be concluded just by looking at the graph.

Q.23 Calculate potential on the axis of a ring due to charge Q uniformly distributed along the ring of radius R.

Ans. Let us take point P to be at a distance x from the centre of the ring,as shown in figure. The charge element dq is at a distance r from point P. Therefore, V can be written as

$$V = k_e \int \frac{dq}{r} = k_e \int \frac{dq}{\sqrt{x^2 + R^2}}$$

where, $k_e = \frac{1}{4\pi\varepsilon_0}$, since each element dq is at the same distance from point P, so we have net potential,

$$V = \frac{k_e}{\sqrt{x^2 + R^2}} \int dq = \frac{k_e Q}{\sqrt{x^2 + R^2}} \qquad [\because \int dq = Q]$$

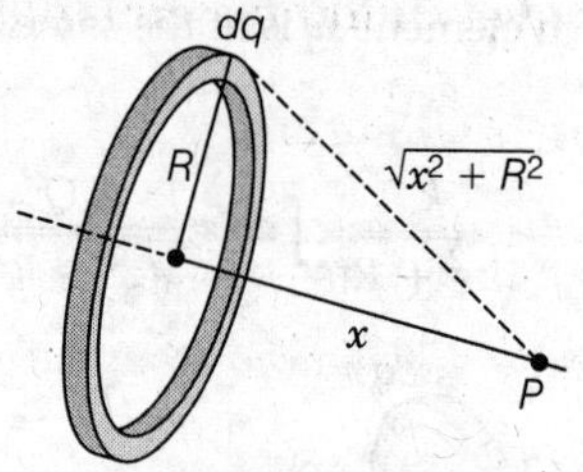

The net electric potential, $V = \frac{1}{4\pi\varepsilon_0} \frac{Q}{\sqrt{x^2 + R^2}}$

Long Answer Type Questions

Q.24 Find the equation of the equipotentials for an infinite cylinder of radius r_0 carrying charge of linear density λ.

Thinking Process The electric field due to line charge needs to be obtained in order to find the potential at distance r from the line charge. As line integral of electric field gives potential difference between two points.

$$V(r) - V(r_0) = -\int_{r_0}^{r} \mathbf{E} \cdot dl$$

Ans. Draw a cylindrical Gaussian surface of radius r and length l. Then, applying Gauss' theorem,

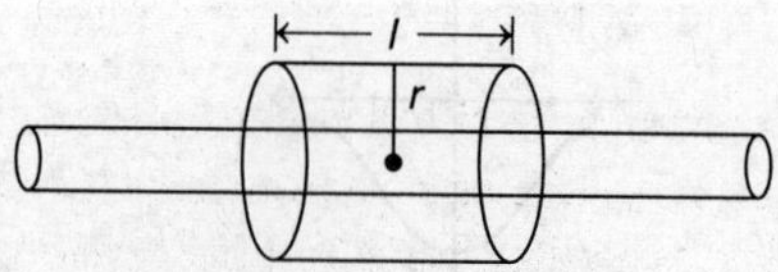

$$\oint \mathbf{E} \cdot d\mathbf{S} = \frac{1}{\varepsilon_0} \lambda l$$

or $$E_r 2\pi rl = \frac{1}{\varepsilon_0} \lambda l \Rightarrow E_r = \frac{\lambda}{2\pi\varepsilon_0 r}$$

Hence, if r_0 is the radius, $V(r) - V(r_0) = -\int_{r_0}^{r} \mathbf{E} \cdot d\mathbf{l} = \frac{\lambda}{2\pi\varepsilon_0} \ln \frac{r_0}{r}$

Since, $$\int_{r_0}^{r} \frac{\lambda}{2\pi\varepsilon_0 r} dr = \frac{\lambda}{2\pi\varepsilon_0} \int_{r_0}^{r} \frac{1}{r} dr = \frac{\lambda}{2\pi\varepsilon_0} \ln \frac{r}{r_0}$$

For a given V,

$$\ln \frac{r}{r_0} = -\frac{2\pi\varepsilon_0}{\lambda}[V(r) - V(r_0)]$$

$$r = r_0 e^{-2\pi\varepsilon_0 [V(r) - V(r)_0]/\lambda}$$

The equipotential surfaces are cylinders of this radius.

Q.25 Two point charges of magnitude $+q$ and $-q$ are placed at $\left(\frac{-d}{2}, 0, 0\right)$ and $\left(\frac{d}{2}, 0, 0\right)$, respectively. Find the equation of the equipotential surface where the potential is zero.

Thinking Process The net electric potential at any point due to system of point charges is equal to the algebraic sum of electric potential due to each individual charges.

Ans. Let the required plane lies at a distance x from the origin as shown in figure.

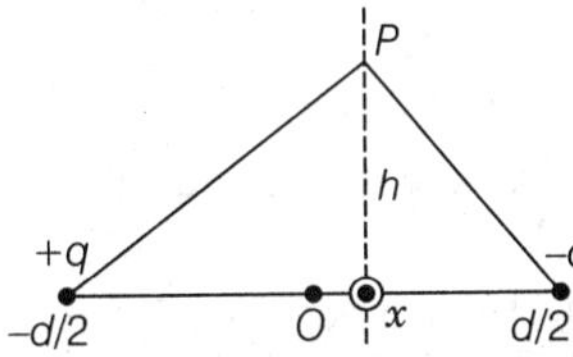

The potential at the point P due to charges is given by

$$\frac{1}{4\pi\varepsilon_0} \frac{q}{[(x + d/2)^2 + h^2]^{1/2}} - \frac{1}{4\pi\varepsilon_0} \frac{q}{[(x - d/2)^2 + h^2]^{1/2}}$$

If net electric potential is zero, then

$$\frac{1}{[(x + d/2)^2 + h^2]^{1/2}} = \frac{1}{[(x - d/2)^2 + h^2]^{1/2}}$$

or $$(x - d/2)^2 + h^2 = (x + d/2)^2 + h^2$$

$\Rightarrow$ $$x^2 - dx + d^2/4 = x^2 + dx + d^2/4$$

or $$2dx = 0 \Rightarrow x = 0$$

The equation of the required plane is $x = 0$ *i.e.*, YZ-plane.

Q. 26 A parallel plate capacitor is filled by a dielectric whose relative permittivity varies with the applied voltage (U) as $\varepsilon = \alpha U$, where $\alpha = 2V^{-1}$. A similar capacitor with no dielectric is charged to $U_0 = 78$ V. It is then connected to the uncharged capacitor with the dielectric. Find the final voltage on the capacitors.

Thinking Process In this problem, the dielectric of variable permittivity is used which gives new insight in the ordinary problem.

Ans. Assuming the required final voltage be U. If C is the capacitance of the capacitor without the dielectric, then the charge on the capacitor is given by $Q_1 = CU$.

Since, the capacitor with the dielectric has a capacitance εC. Hence, the charge on the capacitor is given by

$$Q_2 = \varepsilon CU = (\alpha\ U)\ CU = \alpha\ CU^2$$

The initial charge on the capacitor is given by

$$Q_0 = CU_0$$

From the conservation of charges, $Q_0 = Q_1 + Q_2$

Or $$CU_0 = CU + \alpha\ CU^2 \Rightarrow \alpha\ U^2 + U - U_0 = 0$$

$\therefore$ $$U = \frac{-1 \pm \sqrt{1 + 4\alpha U_0}}{2\alpha}$$

On solving for $U_0 = 78$ V and $\alpha = 2\ V^{-1}$, we get $U = 6$ V

Mistake Alert ! *Be careful while relating charge (Q) with voltage (v), it should be $Q = CU$.*

Q.27 A capacitor is made of two circular plates of radius R each, separated by a distance $d << R$. The capacitor is connected to a constant voltage. A thin conducting disc of radius $r << R$ and thickness $t << r$ is placed at a centre of the bottom plate. Find the minimum voltage required to lift the disc, if the mass of the disc is m.

Thinking Process The disc will be lifted when weight is balanced by electrostatic force.

Ans. Assuming initially the disc is in touch with the bottom plate, so the entire plate is an equipotential.

The electric field on the disc, when potential difference V is applied across it, given by

$$E = \frac{-V}{d}$$

Let charge q' is transferred to the disc during the process, therefore by Gauss' theorem,

$\therefore$ $$q' = -\varepsilon_0 \frac{V}{d} \pi r^2$$

Since, Gauss' theorem states that $\phi = \dfrac{q}{\varepsilon_0}$ or $q = \varepsilon_0 \phi = \varepsilon_0 EA = \dfrac{-\varepsilon_0 V}{d} A$

The force acting on the disc is $-\dfrac{V}{d} \times q' = \varepsilon_0 \dfrac{V^2}{d^2} \pi r^2$

If the disc is to be lifted, then $\varepsilon_0 \dfrac{V^2}{d^2} \pi r^2 = mg \Rightarrow V = \sqrt{\dfrac{mgd^2}{\pi \varepsilon_0 r^2}}$

This is the required expression.

Q.28 (a) In a quark model of elementary particles, a neutron is made of one up quarks [charge (2/3) e] and two down quarks [charges $-(1/3)\ e$]. Assume that they have a triangle configuration with side length of the order of 10^{-15} m. Calculate electrostatic potential energy of neutron and compare it with its mass 939 MeV.

(b) Repeat above exercise for a proton which is made of two up and one down quark.

Ans. (a) (a) This system is made up of three charges. The potential energy of the system is equal to the algebraic sum of PE of each pair. So,

$$U = \frac{1}{4\pi\varepsilon_0}\left\{\frac{q_d q_d}{r} - \frac{q_u q_d}{r} - \frac{q_u q_d}{r}\right\}$$

$$= \frac{9\times 10^9}{10^{-15}}(1.6\times 10^{-19})^2\ [\{(1/3)^2 - (2/3)(1/3) - (2/3)(1/3)\}]$$

$$= 2.304\times 10^{-13}\left\{\frac{1}{9} - \frac{4}{9}\right\} = -7.68\times 10^{-14}\text{J}$$

$$= -4.8\times 10^5\ \text{eV} = -0.48\ \text{MeV} = -5.11\times 10^{-4}(m_n c^2)$$

(b) Since proton consists of 2 up and 1 down quark,

$$q_u = \frac{2e}{3}, q_d = \frac{-e}{3}$$

The potential energy of the system is given by $U = \frac{1}{4\pi\varepsilon_0 r}(q_u q_u + q_d q_u + q_d q_u)$

$$= \frac{9\times 10^9}{10^{-12}}\left[\left(\frac{2e}{3}\right)\left(\frac{2e}{3}\right) + \left(\frac{-e}{3}\right)\left(\frac{2e}{3}\right) + \left(\frac{-e}{3}\right)\left(\frac{2e}{3}\right)\right]$$

$$= \left(\frac{9\times 10^9}{10^{-12}}\right)\left(\frac{4e^2}{9} - \frac{4e^2}{9}\right) = 0$$

Q.29 Two metal spheres, one of radius R and the other of radius $2R$, both have same surface charge density σ. They are brought in contact and separated. What will be new surface charge densities on them?

Ans. The charges on two metal spheres, before coming in contact, are given by

$$Q_1 = \sigma\cdot 4\pi R^2$$
$$Q_2 = \sigma\cdot 4\pi(2R)^2$$
$$= 4(\sigma\cdot 4\pi R^2) = 4Q_1$$

Let the charges on two metal spheres, after coming in contact becomes Q_1' and Q_2'.

Now, applying law of conservation of charges is given by

$$Q_1' + Q_2' = Q_1 + Q_2 = 5Q_1$$
$$= 5(\sigma\cdot 4\pi R^2)$$

After coming in contact, they acquire equal potentials. Therefore, we have

$$\frac{1}{4\pi\varepsilon_0}\frac{Q_1'}{R} = \frac{1}{4\pi\varepsilon_0}\frac{Q_2'}{2R}$$

On solving, we get

$\therefore$ $$Q_1' = \frac{5}{3}(\sigma\cdot 4\pi R^2) \text{ and } Q_2' = \frac{10}{3}(\sigma\cdot 4\pi R^2)$$

$\therefore$ $$\sigma_1 = \frac{5}{3}\sigma \text{ and}$$

$\therefore$ $$\sigma_2 = \frac{5}{6}\sigma$$

Q.30 **In the circuit shown in figure, initially K_1 is closed and K_2 is open. What are the charges on each capacitors?**
Then, K_1 was opened and K_2 was closed (order is important), what will be the charge on each capacitor now? [$C = 1\mu F$]

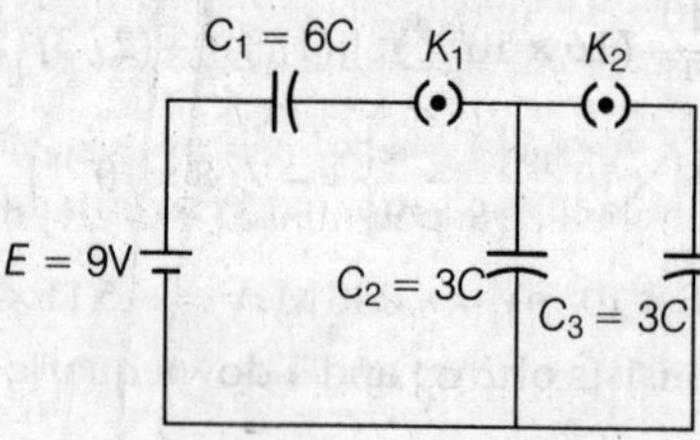

Ans. In the circuit, when initially K_1 is closed and K_2 is open, the capacitors C_1 and C_2 acquire potential difference V_1 and V_2 respectively. So, we have

$$V_1 + V_2 = E$$

and $$V_1 + V_2 = 9V$$

Also, in series combination, $$V \propto 1/C$$

$$V_1 : V_2 = 1/6 : 1/3$$

On solving,

$\Rightarrow$ $$V_1 = 3V \text{ and } V_2 = 6V$$

$\therefore$ $$Q_1 = C_1V_1 = 6C \times 3 = 18\,\mu C$$

$$Q_2 = 9\,\mu C \text{ and } Q_3 = 0$$

Then, K_1 was opened and K_2 was closed, the parallel combination of C_2 and C_3 is in series with C_1.

$$Q_2 = Q_2' + Q_3$$

and considering common potential of parallel combination as V, then we have

$$C_2V + C_3V = Q_2$$

$\Rightarrow$ $$V = \frac{Q_2}{C_2 + C_3} = (3/2)V$$

On solving, $$Q_2' = (9/2)\,\mu C \text{ and } Q_3 = (9/2)\,\mu C$$

Q.31 **Calculate potential on the axis of a disc of radius R due to a charge Q uniformly distributed on its surface.**

Ans. Let the point P lies at a distance x from the centre of the disk and take the plane of the disk to be perpendicular to the X-axis. Let the disc is divided into a number of charged rings as shown in figure.

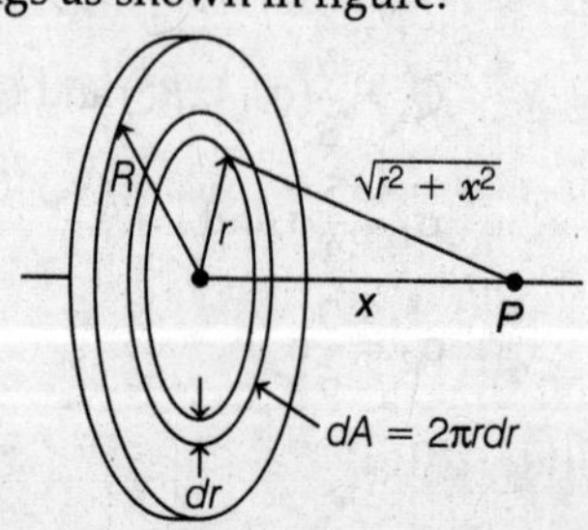

The electric potential of each ring, of radius r and width dr, have charge dq is given by

$$\sigma\, dA = \sigma 2\pi r dr$$

and potential is given by

(Refer the solution of Q. 23)

$$dV = \frac{k_e dq}{\sqrt{r^2 + x^2}} = \frac{k_e \sigma 2\pi r\, dr}{\sqrt{r^2 + x^2}}$$

where, $k_e = \frac{1}{4\pi\varepsilon_0}$, the total electric potential at P is given by

$$V = \pi k_e \sigma \int_0^R \frac{2rdr}{\sqrt{r^2 + x^2}}$$

Substituting $\quad r^2 + x^2 = t$

$\Rightarrow \quad 2rdr = dt$

$\Rightarrow \quad V = \pi k_e \sigma \int_{x^2}^{R^2+x^2} \frac{dt}{\sqrt{t}} \Rightarrow V = \pi k_e \sigma [2t^{\frac{1}{2}}]_{x^2}^{R^2+x^2}$

$\Rightarrow \quad V = 2\pi k_e \sigma [\sqrt{R^2 + x^2} - x^2]$

$\Rightarrow \quad V = \frac{2\pi}{4\pi\varepsilon_0} \frac{Q}{\pi R^2} [\sqrt{R^2 + x^2} - x^2]$

$\Rightarrow \quad V = \frac{2Q}{4\pi\varepsilon_0 R^2} [\sqrt{R^2 + x^2} - (\sqrt{x^2})]$

$$V = \frac{2Q}{4\pi\varepsilon_0 R^2} [\sqrt{R^2 + x^2} - x]$$

Q.32 Two charges q_1 and q_2 are placed at (0, 0, d) and (0, 0, – d) respectively. Find locus of points where the potential is zero.

Thinking Process Here, 3-dimensional imagination is required to actualise the problem. Also, the net electric potential at any point due to system of point charges is equal to the algebraic sum of electric potential due to each individual charges.

Ans. Let any arbitrary point on the required plane is (x, y, z). The two charges lie on Z-axis at a separation of $2d$.

The potential at the point P due to two charges is given by

$$\frac{q_1}{\sqrt{x^2 + y^2 + (z - d)^2}} + \frac{q_2}{\sqrt{x^2 + y^2 + (z + d)^2}} = 0$$

$$\therefore \quad \frac{q_1}{\sqrt{x^2 + y^2 + (z - d)^2}} = \frac{-q_2}{\sqrt{x^2 + y^2 + (z + d)^2}}$$

On squaring and simplifying, we get

$$x^2 + y^2 + z^2 + \left[\frac{(q_1/q_2)^2 + 1}{(q_1/q_2)^2 - 1}\right](2zd) + d^2 = 0$$

This is the equation of a sphere with centre at $\left(0, 0, -2d\left[\frac{q_1^2 + q_2^2}{q_1^2 - q_2^2}\right]\right)$

Note The centre and radius of sphere $(x - a)^2 + (y - b)^2 + (z - c)^2 = r^2$ is (a, b, c) and r, respectively.

Q.33 Two charges $-q$ each are separated by distance $2d$. A third charge $+q$ is kept at mid-point O. Find potential energy of $+q$ as a function of small distance x from O due to $-q$ charges. Sketch PE *versus* x and convince yourself that the charge at O is in an unstable equilibrium.

Ans. Let third charge $+q$ is slightly displaced from mean position towards first charge. So, the total potential energy of the system is given by

$$U = \frac{1}{4\pi\varepsilon_0}\left\{\frac{-q^2}{(d-x)} + \frac{-q^2}{(d+x)}\right\}$$

$$U = \frac{-q^2}{4\pi\varepsilon_0}\frac{2d}{(d^2-x^2)}$$

$$\frac{dU}{dx} = \frac{-q^2.2d}{4\pi\varepsilon_0}\cdot\frac{2x}{(d^2-x^2)^2}$$

The system will be in equilibrium, if

$$F = -\frac{dU}{dx} = 0$$

On solving, $x = 0$. So for $+q$ charge to be in stable/unstable equilibrium, finding second derivative of PE.

$$\frac{d^2U}{dx^2} = \left(\frac{-2dq^2}{4\pi\varepsilon_0}\right)\left[\frac{2}{(d^2-x^2)^2} + \frac{8x^2}{(d^2-x^2)^3}\right]$$

$$= \left(\frac{-2dq^2}{4\pi\varepsilon_0}\right)\frac{1}{(d^2-x^2)^3}[2(d^2-x^2)^2 + 8x^2]$$

At $x = 0$,

$$\frac{d^2U}{dx^2} = \left(\frac{-2dq^2}{4\pi\varepsilon_0}\right)\left(\frac{1}{d^6}\right)(2d^2), \text{ which is} < 0.$$

This shows that system will be in unstable equilibrium.

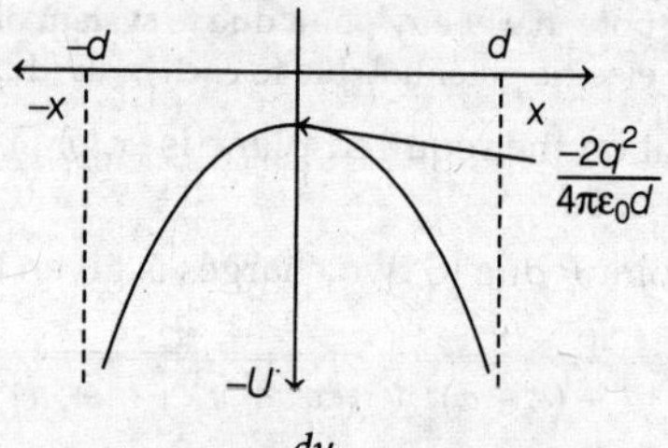

Note For function $y = f(x)$, solving $\frac{dy}{dx} = 0$ gives critical points *i.e.*, points of local maxima or local minima. If $x = x_1$ is a critical point, then $\frac{d^2y}{dx^2} > 0$ implies that y acquires minimum value at $x = x_1$ and $\frac{d^2y}{dx^2} < 0$ implies that y acquires maximum value at $x = x_1$.

Chapter

03 Current Electricity

Multiple Choice Questions (MCQs)

Q.1 Consider a current carrying wire (current I) in the shape of a circle. Note that as the current progresses along the wire, the direction of J (current density) changes in an exact manner, while the current I remain unaffected. The agent that is essentially responsible for is

(a) source of emf
(b) electric field produced by charges accumulated on the surface of wire
(c) the charges just behind a given segment of wire which push them just the right way by repulsion
(d) the charges ahead

Ans. ***(b)*** Current per unit area (taken normal to the current), I/A, is called current density and is denoted by $\hat{J}$. The SI unit of the current density is A/m^2. The current density is also directed along E and is also a vector and the relationship is given by

$$\hat{J} = \sigma \hat{E}$$

The J changes due to electric field produced by charges accumulated on the surface of wire.

Q.2 Two batteries of emf ε_1 and $\varepsilon_2 (\varepsilon_2 > \varepsilon_1)$ and internal resistances r_1 and r_2 respectively are connected in parallel as shown in figure.

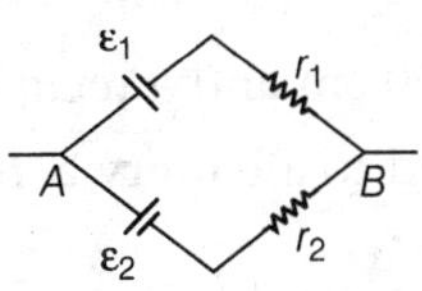

(a) The equivalent emf ε_{eq} of the two cells is between ε_1 and ε_2, *i.e.*, $\varepsilon_1 < \varepsilon_{eq} < \varepsilon_2$.
(b) The equivalent emf ε_{eq} is smaller than ε_1.
(c) The ε_{eq} is given by $\varepsilon_{eq} = \varepsilon_1 + \varepsilon_2$ always.
(d) ε_{eq} is independent of internal resistances r_1 and r_2.

Ans. ***(a)*** The equivalent emf of this combination is given by

$$\varepsilon_{eq} = \frac{\varepsilon_2 r_1 + \varepsilon_1 r_2}{r_1 + r_2}$$

This suggests that the equivalent emf ε_{eq} of the two cells is

$$\varepsilon_1 < \varepsilon_{eq} < \varepsilon_2$$

Q.3 A resistance R is to be measured using a meter bridge. Student chooses the standard resistance S to be 100Ω. He finds the null point at $l_1 = 2.9$ cm. He is told to attempt to improve the accuracy. Which of the following is a useful way?

(a) He should measure l_1 more accurately.
(b) He should change S to 1000Ω and repeat the experiment.
(c) He should change S to 3Ω and repeat the experiment.
(d) He should give up hope of a more accurate measurement with a meter bridge.

Thinking Process Here, the concept of balanced wheatstone bridge is to be used.

Ans. ***(c)*** The percentage error in R can be minimised by adjusting the balance point near the middle of the bridge *i.e.*, when l_1 is close to 50 cm. This requires a suitable choice of S.

Since, $\frac{R}{S} = \frac{l_1}{100 - l_1}$

Since here, $R : S :: 2.9 : 97.1$ imply that the S is nearly 33 times to that of R. In order to make this ratio 1:1, it is necessary to reduce the value of S nearly $\frac{1}{33}$ times *i.e.*, nearly 3Ω.

Q.4 Two cells of emfs approximately 5 V and 10 V are to be accurately compared using a potentiometer of length 400 cm.

(a) The battery that runs the potentiometer should have voltage of 8V.
(b) The battery of potentiometer can have a voltage of 15 V and R adjusted so that the potential drop across the wire slightly exceeds 10 V.
(c) The first portion of 50 cm of wire itself should have a potential drop of 10 V.
(d) Potentiometer is usually used for comparing resistances and not voltages.

Thinking Process The potential drop across wires of potentiometer should be greater than emfs of primary cells.

Ans. ***(b)*** In a potentiometer experiment, the emf of a cell can be measured, if the potential drop along the potentiometer wire is more than the emf of the cell to be determined. Here, values of emfs of two cells are given as 5V and 10V, therefore the potential drop along the potentiometer wire must be more than 10V.

Q.5 A metal rod of length 10 cm and a rectangular cross-section of $1\text{cm} \times \frac{1}{2}$ cm is connected to a battery across opposite faces. The resistance will be

(a) maximum when the battery is connected across $1 \text{ cm} \times \frac{1}{2}$ cm faces.
(b) maximum when the battery is connected across 10 cm x 1 cm faces.
(c) maximum when the battery is connected across $10 \text{ cm} \times \frac{1}{2}$ cm faces.
(d) same irrespective of the three faces.

Thinking Process The resistance of wire depends on its geometry as $R = \rho \frac{l}{A}$.

Ans. ***(a)*** The resistance of wire is given by

$$R = \rho \frac{l}{A}$$

For greater value of R, l must be higher and A should be lower and it is possible only when the battery is connected across 1 cm x $\left(\frac{1}{2}\right)$ cm (area of cross-section A).

Q.6 Which of the following characteristics of electrons determines the current in a conductor?

(a) Drift velocity alone
(b) Thermal velocity alone
(c) Both drift velocity and thermal velocity
(d) Neither drift velocity nor thermal velocity

Ans. ***(a)*** The relationship between current and drift speed is given by

$$I = neAv_d$$

Here, I is the current and v_d is the drift velocity.

So, $$I \propto v_d$$

Thus, only drift velocity determines the current in a conductor.

Multiple Choice Questions (More Than One Options)

Q.7 Kirchhoff's junction rule is a reflection of

(a) conservation of current density vector
(b) conservation of charge
(c) the fact that the momentum with which a charged particle approaches a junction is unchanged (as a vector) as the charged particle leaves the junction
(d) the fact that there is no accumulation of charges at a junction

Ans. ***(b, d)*** Kirchhoff's junction rule is also known as Kirchhoff's current law which states that the algebraic sum of the currents flowing towards any point in an electric network is zero *i.e.*, charges are conserved in an electric network.

So, Kirchhoff's junction rule is the reflection of conservation of charge.

Q.8 Consider a simple circuit shown in figure, where 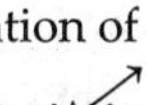 stands for a variable resistance R'. R' can vary from R_0 to infinity. r is internal resistance of the battery ($r << R << R_0$).

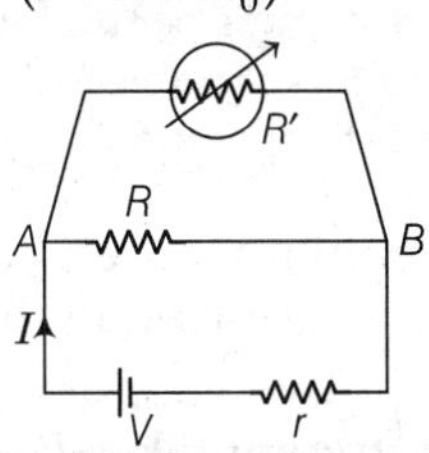

(a) Potential drop across AB is nearly constant as R' is varied
(b) Current through R' is nearly a constant as R' is varied
(c) Current I depends sensitively on R'
(d) $I \geq \frac{V}{r+R}$ always

Ans. ***(a, d)*** Here, the potential drop is taking place across AB and r. Since, the equivalent resistance of parallel combination of r and R is always less than R', therefore $I \geq \frac{V}{r+R}$ always.

Note In parallel combination of resistances, the equivalent resistance is smaller than smallest resistance present in combination.

Alternate Method

Current, $I = \dfrac{V}{r + \dfrac{RR'}{R+R'}}$

As, $R' >> R$, So $R + R' \geq R'$

Hence, $I \geq \dfrac{V}{r + \dfrac{RR'}{R'}} = \dfrac{V}{r+R}$

Thus, option (d) is correct

Potential difference across A and B

$$V_{AB} = I \times \frac{RR'}{R+R'}$$

$$\therefore \quad V_{AB} = \frac{V}{r + \dfrac{RR'}{R+R'}} \times \frac{RR'}{(R+R')} = \frac{V \times RR'}{rR' + RR'} = \frac{VR}{r+R} \quad [\because r << R << R']$$

$\therefore V_{AB}$ is constant if R' is varied. Hence, option (a) is correct.

Current through R', $I' = \dfrac{V_{AB}}{R'} = \dfrac{VR}{(r+R)R'} = \dfrac{VR}{rR' + RR'}$

Thus I' is not constant as R' is varied. The current I does not depend sensitivity on R'.

Q.9 Temperature dependence of resistivity $\rho(T)$ of semiconductors, insulators and metals is significantly based on the following factors

(a) number of charge carriers can change with temperature T

(b) time interval between two successive collisions can depend on T

(c) length of material can be a function of T

(d) mass of carriers is a function of T

Ans. ***(a, b)*** The resistivity of a metallic conductor is given by

$$\rho = \frac{m}{ne^2\tau}$$

where, n is number of charge carriers per unit volume which can change with temperature T and τ is time interval between two successive collisions which decreases with the increase of temperature.

Q.10 The measurement of an unknown resistance R is to be carried out using Wheatstone's bridge as given in the figure below. Two students perform an experiment in two ways. The first student takes $R_2 = 10\Omega$ and $R_1 = 5\Omega$. The other student takes $R_2 = 1000\Omega$ and $R_1 = 500\Omega$. In the standard arm, both take $R_3 = 5\Omega$.

Both find $R = \frac{R_2}{R_1}$, $R_3 = 10\Omega$ within errors.

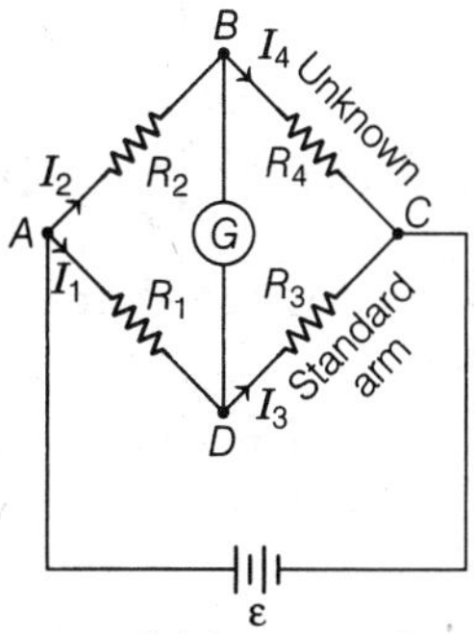

(a) The errors of measurement of the two students are the same.

(b) Errors of measurement do depend on the accuracy with which R_2 and R_1 can be measured.

(c) If the student uses large values of R_2 and R_1, the currents through the arms will be feeble. This will make determination of null point accurately more difficult.

(d) Wheatstone bridge is a very accurate instrument and has no errors of measurement.

Ans. ***(b, c)*** Given, for first student, $R_2 = 10\ \Omega$, $R_1 = 5\ \Omega$, $R_3 = 5\ \Omega$

For second student, $R_2 = 1000\ \Omega$, $R_1 = 500\ \Omega$, $R_3 = 5\ \Omega$

Now, according to Wheatstone bridge rule,

$$\frac{R_2}{R_4} = \frac{R_1}{R_3} \Rightarrow R_4 = R_3 \times \frac{R_2}{R_1} \quad ...(i)$$

Now putting all the values in Eq. (i), we get $R = 10\ \Omega$ for both students. Thus, we can analyse that the Wheatstone bridge is most sensitive and accurate if resistances are of same value. Thus, the errors of measurement of the two students depend on the accuracy and sensitivity of the bridge, which in turn depend on the accuracy with which R_2 and R_1 can be measured. When R_2 and R_1 are large, the currents through the arms of bridge is very weak. This can make the determination of null point accurately more difficult.

Q.11 In a meter bridge, the point D is a neutral point (figure).

(a) The meter bridge can have no other neutral points for this set of resistances

(b) When the jockey contacts a point on meter wire left of D, current flows to B from the wire

(c) When the jockey contacts a point on the meter wire to the right of D, current flows from B to the wire through galvanometer

(d) When R is increased, the neutral point shifts to left

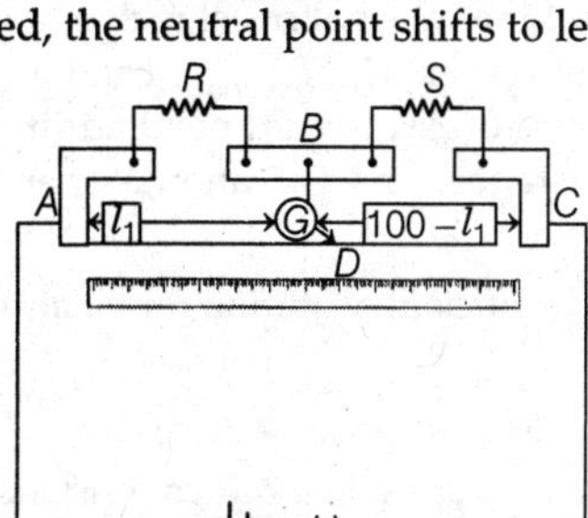

Ans. ***(a, c)*** At neutral point, potential at B and neutral point are same. When jockey is placed to the right of D, the potential drop across AD is more than potential drop across AB, which brings the potential of point D less than that of B, hence current flows from B to D.

Very Short Answer Type Questions

Q.12 Is the momentum conserved when charge crosses a junction in electric circuit ? Why or why not?

Ans. When an electron approaches a junction, in addition to the uniform electric field **E** facing it normally. It keeps the drift velocity fixed as drift velocity depends on E. By the relation drift velocity,

$$v_d = \frac{eE\tau}{m}$$

This results into accumulation of charges on the surface of wires at the junction. These produce additional electric field. These fields change the direction of momentum. Thus, the momentum is not conserved when the charge crosses a junction in an electric circuit.

Q.13 The relaxation time τ is nearly independent of applied electric field E whereas it changes significantly with temperature T. First fact is (in part) responsible for Ohm's law whereas the second fact leads to variation of ρ with temperature. Elaborate why?

Thinking Process The higher drift velocities of electrons make collisions more frequent which in turn decreases the time interval between two successive collision.

Ans. Relaxation time is inversely proportional to the velocities of electrons and ions. The applied electric field produces the insignificant change in velocities of electrons at the order of 1mm/s, whereas the change in temperature (T), affects velocities at the order of 10^2m/s. This decreases the relaxation time considerably in metals and consequently resistivity of metal or conductor increases as

$$\rho = \frac{1}{\sigma} = \frac{m}{ne^2\tau}$$

Q.14 What are the advantages of the null-point method in a Wheatstone bridge? What additional measurements would be required to calculate R_{unknown} by any other method?

Ans. The advantage of null-point method in a Wheatstone bridge is that the resistance of galvanometer does not affect the balance point, there is no need to determine current in resistances and the internal resistance of a galvanometer. It is easy and convenient method for observer. The R_{unknown} can be calculated by applying Kirchhoff's rules to the circuit. We would need additional accurate measurement of all the currents in resistances and galvanometer and internal resistance of the galvanometer.

Note The necessary and sufficient condition for balanced Wheatstone bridge is

$$\frac{P}{Q} = \frac{R}{S}$$

where, P and Q are ratio arms, R is known resistance and S is unknown resistance.

Q.15 What is the advantage of using thick metallic strips to join wires in a potentiometer?

Ans. In potentiometer, the thick metallic strips are used as they have negligible resistance and need not to be counted in the length l_1 of the null point of potentiometer. It is for the convenience of experimenter as he measures only their lengths along the straight wires each of lengths 1 m.

This measurement is done with the help of centimetre scale or metre scale with accuracy.

Q.16 For wiring in the home, one uses Cu wires or Al wires. What considerations are involved in this?

Thinking Process The availability, conductivity and the cost of the metal are main criterion for the selection of metal for wiring in home.

Ans. The Cu wires or Al wires are used for wiring in the home.

The main considerations involved in this process are cost of metal wire and good conductivity of metal wire.

Q.17 Why are alloys used for making standard resistance coils?

Ans. Alloys have small value of temperature coefficient of resistance with less temperature sensitivity.

This keeps the resistance of the wire almost constant even in small temperature change. The alloy also has high resistivity and hence high resistance, because for given length and cross-sectional area of conductor.

$$R \propto \rho$$

Q.18 Power P is to be delivered to a device *via* transmission cables having resistance R_c. If V is the voltage across R and I the current through it, find the power wasted and how can it be reduced.

Ans. The power consumption in transmission lines is given by $P = I^2 R_c$, where R_c is the resistance of transmission lines. The power is given by

$$P = VI$$

The given power can be transmitted in two ways namely (i) at low voltage and high current or (ii) high voltage and low current. In power transmission at low voltage and high current, more power is wasted as $P \propto I^2$ whereas power transmission at high voltage and low current facilitates the power transmission with minimal power wastage.

The power wastage can be reduced by transmitting power at high voltage.

Q.19 AB is a potentiometer wire as shown in figure. If the value of R is increased, in which direction will the balance point J shift?

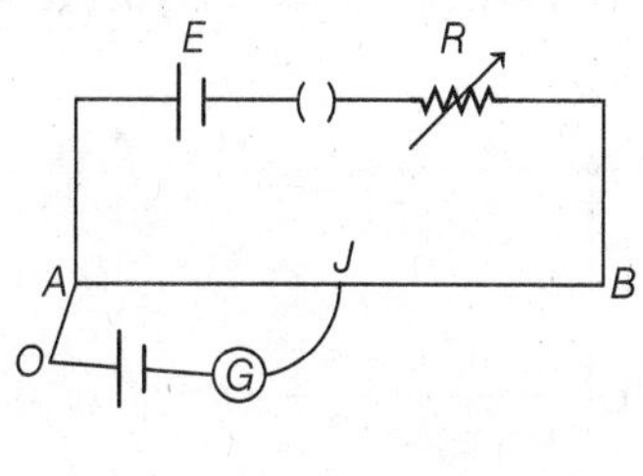

Ans. With the increase of R, the current in main circuit decreases which in turn, decreases the potential difference across AB and hence potential gradient (k) across AB decreases. Since, at neutral point, for given emf of cell, l increases as potential gradient (k) across AB has decreased because

$$E = kl$$

Thus, with the increase of l, the balance point J will shift towards B.

Q.20 While doing an experiment with potentiometer as shown in figure, it was found that the deflection is one sided and (i) the deflection decreased while moving from one end A of the wire to the end B; (ii) the deflection increased while the jockey was moved towards the end B.

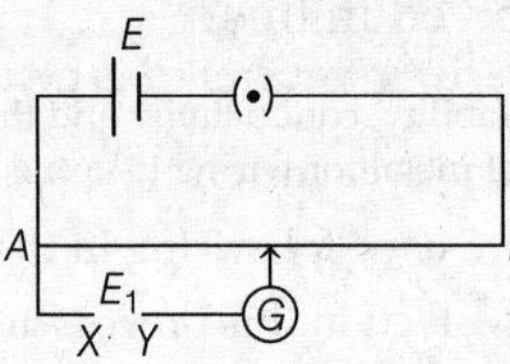

(i) Which terminal positive or negative of the cell E_1 is connected at X in case (i) and how is E_1, related to E?

(ii) Which terminal of the cell E_1 is connected at X in case (ii)?

Ans. (i) The deflection in galvanometer is one sided and the deflection decreased while moving from one end 'A' of the wire to the end 'B'. This implies that current in auxiliary circuit (lower circuit containing primary cell) decreases while potential difference across A and jockey increases. This is possible only when positive terminal of the cell E_1 is connected at X and $E_1 > E$.

(ii) The deflection in galvanometer is one sided and the deflection increased while moving from one end A of the wire to the end B. This implies that current in auxiliary circuit (lower circuit containing primary cell) increases while potential difference across A and jockey increases.

This is possible only when negative terminal of the cell E_1 is connected at X.

Q.21 A cell of emf E and internal resistance r is connected across an external resistance R. Plot a graph showing the variation of potential difference across R, *versus* R.

Thinking Process When the cell of emf E and internal resistance r is connected across an external resistance R, the relationship between the voltage across R is given by

$$V = \frac{E}{1 + \frac{r}{R}}$$

With the increase of R, V approaches closer to E and when R is infinite, V becomes equal to E.

Ans. The graphical relationship between voltage across R and the resistance R is given below.

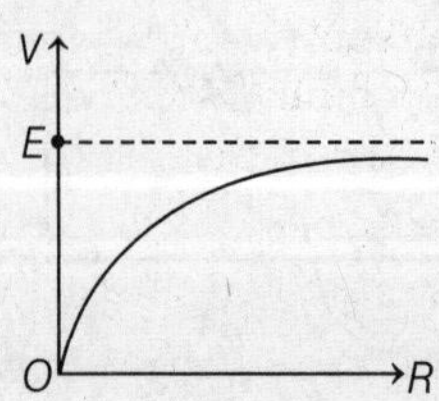

Short Answer Type Questions

Q.22 First a set of n equal resistors of R each are connected in series to a battery of emf E and internal resistance R, a current I is observed to flow. Then, the n resistors are connected in parallel to the same battery. It is observed that the current is increased 10 times. What is 'n'?

- **Concept Insight** Here, in series combination of resistors, the equivalent resistance of series combination is in series with the internal resistance R of battery resistors whereas in parallel combination of resistors , the equivalent resistance of parallel combination is in series with the internal resistance of battery.

Ans. In series combination of resistors, current I is given by $I = \dfrac{E}{R+nR}$

whereas in parallel combination, current 10 I is given by

$$\frac{E}{R+\frac{R}{n}} = 10I$$

Now, according to problem,

$$\frac{1+n}{1+\frac{1}{n}} = 10 \Rightarrow 10 = \left(\frac{1+n}{n+1}\right)n \Rightarrow n = 10$$

Q.23 Let there be n resistors $R_1 .... R_n$ with $R_{max} = \max(R_1 .... R_n)$ and $R_{min} = \min\{R_1 .... R_n\}$. Show that when they are connected in parallel, the resultant resistance $R_p = R_{min}$ and when they are connected in series, the resultant resistance $R_s > R_{max}$. Interpret the result physically.

Ans. When all resistances are connected in parallel, the resultant resistance R_p is given by

$$\frac{1}{R_p} = \frac{1}{R_1} + ... + \frac{1}{R_n}$$

On multiplying both sides by R_{min}, we have

$$\frac{R_{min}}{R_p} = \frac{R_{min}}{R_1} + \frac{R_{min}}{R_2} + ... + \frac{R_{min}}{R_n}$$

Here, in RHS, there exists one term $\dfrac{R_{min}}{R_{min}} = 1$ and other terms are positive, so we have

$$\frac{R_{min}}{R_p} = \frac{R_{min}}{R_1} + \frac{R_{min}}{R_2} + ... + \frac{R_{min}}{R_n} > 1$$

This shows that the resultant resistance $R_p < R_{min}$.

Thus, in parallel combination, the equivalent resistance of resistors is less than the minimum resistance available in combination of resistors . Now, in series combination, the equivalent resistance is given by

$$R_s = R_1 + ... + R_n$$

Here, in RHS, there exist one term having resistance R_{max}.

So, we have

or $$R_s = R_1 + ... + R_{max} + ... + R_n$$

$\Rightarrow$ $$R_s = R_{max} + R_1 + ... R_n$$

$\Rightarrow$ $$R_s \geq R_{max}$$

Thus, in series combination, the equivalent resistance of resistors is greater than the maximum resistance available in combination of resistors.

Physical interpretation

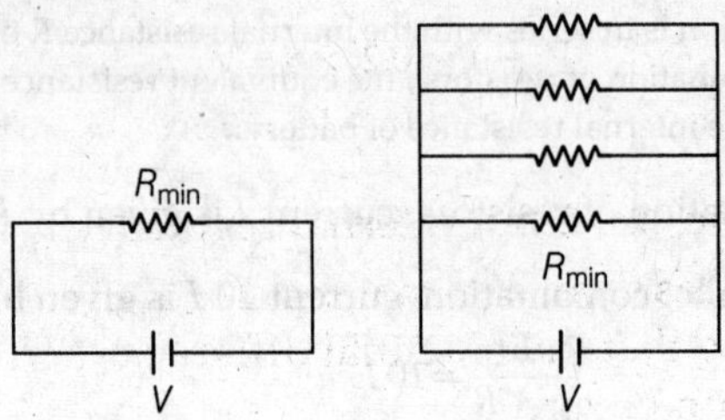

(a) (b)

In Fig. (b), R_{min} provides an equivalent route as in Fig. (a) for current. But in addition, there are $(n-1)$ routes by the remaining $(n-1)$ resistors. Current in Fig. (b) is greater than current in Fig. (a). Effective resistance in Fig. (b) < R_{min}. Second circuit evidently affords a greater resistance.

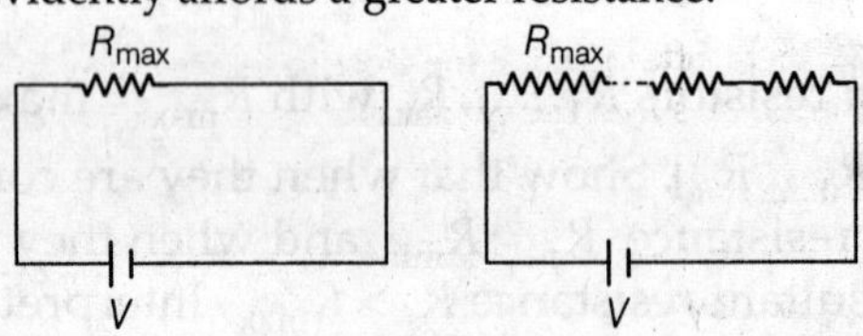

(c) (d)

In Fig. (d), R_{max} provides an equivalent route as in Fig. (c) for current. Current in Fig. (d) < current in Fig. (c). Effective resistance in Fig. (d) > R_{max}. Second circuit evidently affords a greater resistance.

Q.24 The circuit in figure shows two cells connected in opposition to each other. Cell E_1 is of emf 6V and internal resistance 2Ω, the cell E_2 is of emf 4V and internal resistance 8Ω. Find the potential difference between the points A and B.

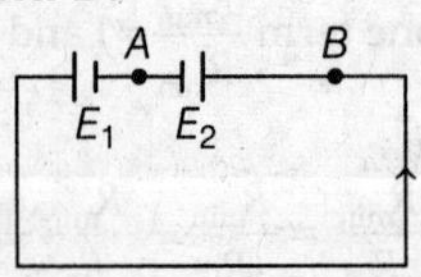

Thinking Process Here, after finding the electric current flow in the circuit by using Kirchhoff's law or Ohm's law, the potential difference across AB can be obtained.

Ans. Applying Ohm's law,

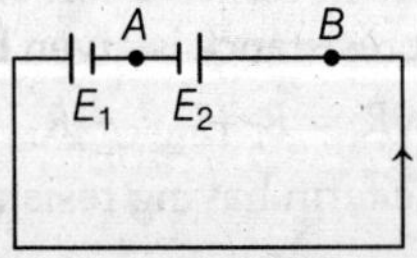

effective resistance = $2\Omega + 8\Omega = 10\Omega$ and effective emf of two cells = $6 - 4 = 2V$, so the electric current is given by

$$I = \frac{6-4}{2+8} = 0.2A$$

along anti-clockwise direction, since $E_1 > E_2$.

The direction of flow of current is always from high potential to low potential. Therefore, $V_B > V_A$.

$\Rightarrow$ $$V_B - 4 - (0.2) \times 8 = V_A$$

Therefore, $$V_B - V_A = 5.6\text{ V}$$

Q.25 Two cells of same emf E but internal resistance r_1 and r_2 are connected in series to an external resistor R (figure). What should be the value of R, so that the potential difference across the terminals of the first cell becomes zero?

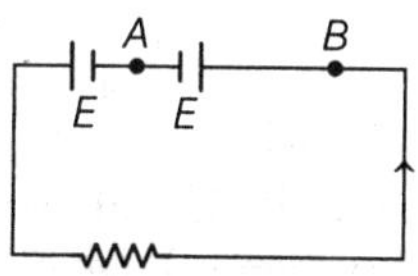

Thinking Process Here, after finding the electric current flow in the circuit by using Kirchhoff 's law or Ohm 's law, the potential difference across first cell can be obtained.

Ans. Applying Ohm's law,

effective resistance = $R + r_1 + r_2$ and effective emf of two cells = $E + E = 2E$, so the electric current is given by

$$I = \frac{E+E}{R + r_1 + r_2}$$

The potential difference across the terminals of the first cell and putting it equal to zero.

$$V_1 = E - Ir_1 = E - \frac{2E}{r_1 + r_2 + R} r_1 = 0$$

or $$E = \frac{2Er_1}{r_1 + r_2 + R} \Rightarrow 1 = \frac{2r_1}{r_1 + r_2 + R}$$

$$r_1 + r_2 + R = 2r_1 \Rightarrow R = r_1 - r_2$$

This is the required relation.

Mistake Alert! *Students sometimes get confused to relate terminal voltage (V) of cell with the cell emf (E). The correct relation would be $V = E - Ir$.*

Q.26 Two conductors are made of the same material and have the same length. Conductor A is a solid wire of diameter 1mm. Conductor B is a hollow tube of outer diameter 2 mm and inner diameter 1mm. Find the ratio of resistance R_A to R_B.

- **Concept Insight** The resistance of wire is given by $R = \rho \frac{l}{A}$ where, A is cross-sectional area of conductor.

Ans. The resistance of first conductor,

$$R_A = \frac{\rho l}{\pi(10^{-3} \times 0.5)^2}$$

The resistance of second conductor,

$$R_B = \frac{\rho l}{\pi[(10^{-3})^2 - (0.5 \times 10^{-3})^2]}$$

Now, the ratio of two resistors is given by

$$\frac{R_A}{R_B} = \frac{(10^{-3})^2 - (0.5 \times 10^{-3})^2}{(0.5 \times 10^{-3})^2} = 3:1$$

Q.27 Suppose there is a circuit consisting of only resistances and batteries. Suppose one is to double (or increase it to n-times) all voltages and all resistances. Show that currents are unaltered. Do this for circuit of Examples 3.7 in the NCERT Text Book for Class XII.

Thinking Process The electric current in two cases is obtained and then shown equal to each other.

Ans. Let the effective internal resistance of the battery is R_{eff}, the effective external resistance R and the effective voltage of the battery is V_{eff}.

Applying Ohm's law,

then current through R is given by

$$I = \frac{V_{eff}}{R_{eff} + R}$$

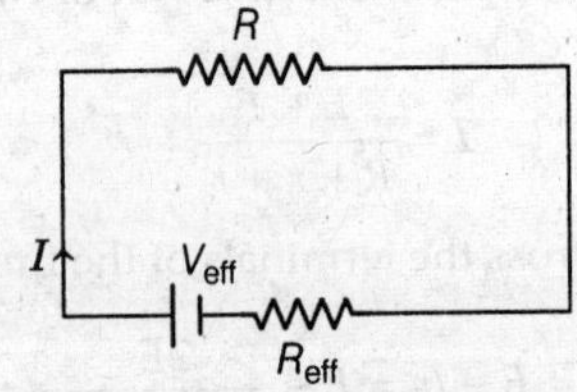

If all the resistances and the effective voltage are increased n-times, then we have

$$V_{eff}^{new} = nV_{eff}, R_{eff}^{new} = nR_{eff}$$

and $$R^{new} = nR$$

Then, the new current is given by

$$I' = \frac{nV_{eff}}{nR_{eff} + nR}$$

$$= \frac{n(V_{eff})}{n(R_{eff} + R)}$$

$$= \frac{(V_{eff})}{(R_{eff} + R)} = I$$

Thus, current remains the same.

Long Answer Type Questions

Q.28 Two cells of voltage 10V and 2V and internal resistances 10Ω and 5Ω respectively, are connected in parallel with the positive end of 10V battery connected to negative end of 2V battery (figure). Find the effective voltage and effective resistance of the combination.

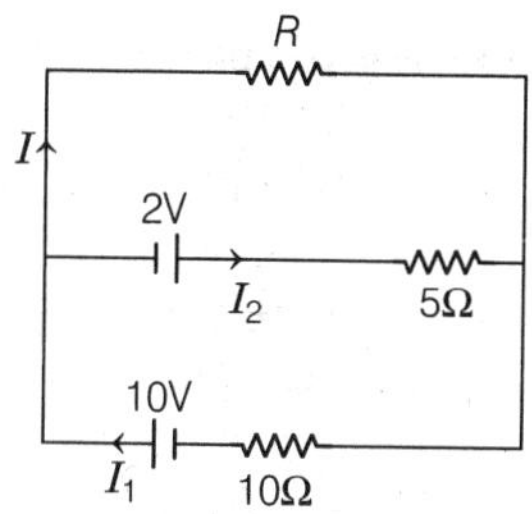

Thinking Process The question can be solved by using Kirchhoff's voltage rule/ loop rule.

Ans. Applying Kirchhoff's junction rule, $I_1 = I + I_2$

Applying Kirchhoff's II law / loop rule in outer loop containing 10V cell and resistance R, we have

$$10 = IR + 10I_1 \quad \ldots(i)$$

Applying Kirchhoff's II law / loop rule in loop containing 2V cell and resistance R, we have

$$2 = 5I_2 - RI = 5(I_1 - I) - RI$$

or
$$4 = 10I_1 - 10I - 2RI \quad \ldots(ii)$$

Solving Eqs. (i) and (ii), we have

$\Rightarrow$
$$6 = 3RI + 10I$$
$$2 = I\left(R + \frac{10}{3}\right)$$

Also, the external resistance is R. The Ohm's law states that

$$V = I(R + R_{eff})$$

On comparing, we have $V = 2V$ and effective internal resistance,

$$R_{eff} = \left(\frac{10}{3}\right)\Omega$$

Since, the effective internal resistance (R_{eff}) of two cells is $\left(\frac{10}{3}\right)\Omega$, being the parallel combination of 5Ω and 10Ω. The equivalent circuit is given below

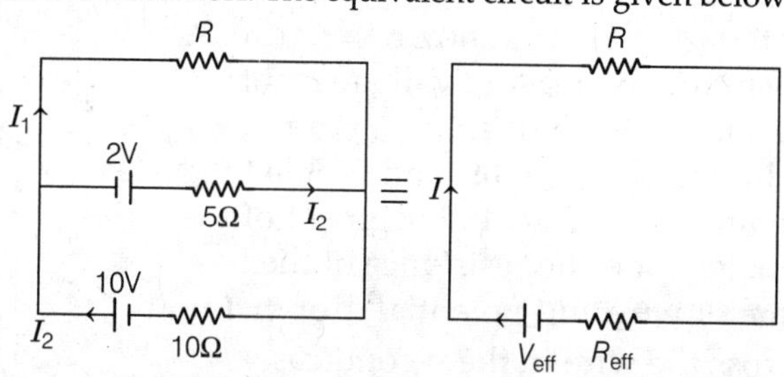

Mistake Alert! *While solving kirchhoff's loop problem, remember the direction of flow of current in the circuit otherwise result will be incorrect.*

Q.29 A room has AC run for 5 hours a day at a voltage of 220V. The wiring of the room consists of Cu of 1 mm radius and a length of 10 m. Power consumption per day is 10 commercial units. What fraction of it goes in the joule heating in wires? What would happen, if the wiring is made of aluminium of the same dimensions?
$[\rho_{Cu} = 1.7 \times 10^{-8}\ \Omega m, \rho_{Al} = 2.7 \times 10^{-8}\ \Omega m]$

Thinking Process The power consumption in a current carrying resistor is given by $P = I^2R$.

Ans. Power consumption in a day *i.e.,* in 5 hours = 10 units

or power consumption per hour = 2 units

or power consumption = 2 units = 2 kW = 2000 J/s

Also, we know that power consumption in resistor,

$$P = V \times I$$

$$\Rightarrow \quad 2000\,W = 220\,V \times I \text{ or } I \approx 9\text{ A}$$

Now, the resistance of wire is given by $R = \rho \frac{l}{A}$

where, A is cross-sectional area of conductor.

Power consumption in first current carrying wire is given by

$$P = I^2 R$$

$$P = \rho \frac{l}{A} I^2 = 1.7 \times 10^{-8} \times \frac{10}{\pi \times 10^{-6}} \times 81\ \text{J/s} \approx 4\ \text{J/s}$$

The fractional loss due to the joule heating in first wire $= \frac{4}{2000} \times 100 = 0.2\%$

Comparing the power loss of aluminium and copper

$$\frac{\rho_{Al}}{\rho_{Cu}} = \frac{I^2 R_{Al}}{I^2 R_{Cu}^2} = \frac{I^2 \rho_{Al}\left(\frac{l}{A}\right)}{I^2 \rho_{Cu}\left(\frac{l}{A}\right)}$$

$$\frac{\rho_{Al}}{\rho_{Cu}} = \frac{\rho_{Al}}{\rho_{Cu}} = \frac{2.7}{1.7}$$

Power loss in Al wire, $\rho_{Al} = 4 \times 1.6 = 6.4\ \text{J/s}$

The fractional loss due to the joule heating in second wire $= \frac{6.4}{2000} \times 100 = 0.32\%$

Q.30 In an experiment with a potentiometer, $V_B = 10$ V. R is adjusted to be 50Ω as shown in figure. A student wanting to measure voltage E_1 of a battery (approx. 8V) finds no null point possible. He then diminishes R to 10Ω and is able to locate the null point on the last (4th) segment of the potentiometer. Find the resistance of the potentiometer wire and potential drop per unit length across the wire in the second case.

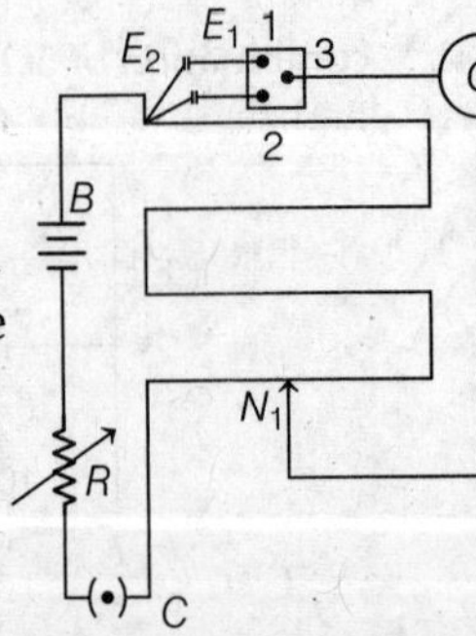

Thinking Process The null point is obtained only when emf of primary cell is less than the potential difference across the wires of potentiometer.

Ans. Let R' be the resistance of the potentiometer wire.

Effective resistance of potentiometer and variable resistor ($R = 50\Omega$) is $50\Omega + R'$.

Effective voltage applied across potentiometer = 10 V.

The current through the main circuit,

$$I = \frac{V}{50\Omega + R'} = \frac{10}{50\Omega + R'}$$

Potential difference across wire of potentiometer,

$$IR' = \frac{10R'}{50\Omega + R'}$$

Since, with 50 Ω resistor, null point is not obtained, it's possible only when

$$\frac{10 \times R'}{50 + R'} < 8$$

$$\Rightarrow \quad 10R' < 400 + 8R'$$

$$2R' < 400 \text{ or } R' < 200\Omega \; .$$

Similarly with 10Ω resistor, null point is obtained, it's possible only when

$$\frac{10 \times R'}{10 + R'} > 8$$

$$\Rightarrow \quad 2R' > 80$$

$$\Rightarrow \quad R' > 40$$

Also,
$$\frac{10 \times \frac{3}{4} R'}{10 + R'} < 8$$

$$\Rightarrow \quad 7.5R' < 80 + 8R'$$

$$R' > 160$$

$$\Rightarrow \quad 160 < R' < 200.$$

Hence, the value of R' could be anywhere between 160 Ω and 200 Ω.

Since, the null point is on the last (4th) segment of the potentiometer, therefore potential drop across 400 cm of wire > 8 V.

This implies that potential gradient,

$$k \times 400 \text{ cm} > 8 \text{ V}$$

or
$$k \times 4 \text{ m} > 8\text{V}$$

$$k > 2\text{V/m}$$

Similarly, potential drop across 300 cm wire < 8V.

$$k \times 300 \text{ cm} < 8 \text{ V}$$

or
$$k \times 3 \text{ m} < 8 \text{ V}$$

$$k < 2\frac{2}{3} \text{V/m}$$

Thus,
$$2\frac{2}{3} \text{ V/m} > k > 2 \text{ V/m}$$

Q.31 (a) Consider circuit in figure. How much energy is absorbed by electrons from the initial state of no current (ignore thermal motion) to the state of drift velocity ?

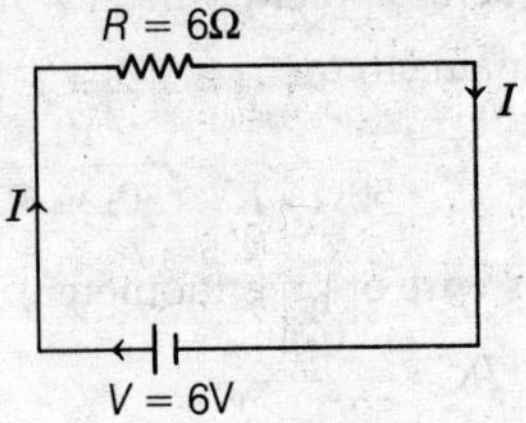

(b) Electrons give up energy at the rate of RI^2 per second to the thermal energy. What time scale would one associate with energy in problem (a) n = number of electron/volume $= 10^{29} / m^3$, length of circuit = 10 cm and cross-section $= A = (1\ mm)^2$.

Thinking Process The current in a conductor and drift velocity of electrons are related as $i = neA\,v_d$, where v_d is drift speed of electrons and n is number density of electrons.

Ans. (a) By Ohm's law, current I is given by

$$I = 6V / 6\Omega = 1A$$

But $$I = neA\,v_d$$

or $$v_d = \frac{I}{neA}$$

On substituting the values for

$$n = \text{number of electron/volume} = 10^{29}/m^3$$

length of circuit = 10 cm and area of cross-section $= A = (1\ mm)^2 = 10^{-6}\ m^2$,

$$v_d = \frac{1}{10^{29} \times 1.6 \times 10^{-19} \times 10^{-6}}$$

$$= \frac{1}{1.6} \times 10^{-4}\ m/s$$

Therefore, the energy absorbed in the form of KE is given by

$$KE = KE \text{ of one electron} \times \text{No. of electrons}$$

$$KE = \frac{1}{2} m_e\, v_d^2 \times nAl \qquad [\because l = 10\ cm = 10^{-1} m]$$

$$= \frac{1}{2} \times 9.1 \times 10^{-31} \times \frac{1}{2.56} \times 10^{-8} \times 10^{29} \times 10^{-6} \times 10^{-1}$$

$$= 2 \times 10^{-17} J$$

(b) Power loss is given by $P = I^2 R = 6 \times 1^2 = 6W = 6J/s$

Since, $$P = \frac{E}{t}$$

Therefore, $$E = P \times t$$

or $$t = \frac{E}{P} = \frac{2 \times 10^{-17}}{6} \approx 10^{-17}\ s$$

Chapter

04

Moving Charges and Magnetism

Multiple Choice Questions (MCQs)

Q.1 Two charged particles traverse identical helical paths in a completely opposite sense in a uniform magnetic field $\mathbf{B} = B_0\hat{\mathbf{k}}$.

(a) They have equal z-components of momenta

(b) They must have equal charges

(c) They necessarily represent a particle, anti-particle pair

(d) The charge to mass ratio satisfy

$$\left(\frac{e}{m}\right)_1 + \left(\frac{e}{m}\right)_2 = 0$$

Thinking Process The uniqueness of helical path is determined by its pitch which is given by

$$\text{Pitch} = \frac{2\pi mv\cos\theta}{qB}$$

Ans. ***(d)*** For given pitch d correspond to charge particle, we have

$$\frac{q}{m} = \frac{2\pi v\cos\theta}{B} = \text{constant}$$

Since, charged particles traverse identical helical paths in a completely opposite sense in a uniform magnetic field **B**, LHS for two particles should be same and of opposite sign. Therefore,

$$\left(\frac{e}{m}\right)_1 + \left(\frac{e}{m}\right)_2 = 0$$

Q.2 Biot-Savart law indicates that the moving electrons (velocity v) produce a magnetic field **B** such that

(a) **B** is perpendicular to v

(b) **B** is parallel to v

(c) it obeys inverse cube law

(d) it is along the line joining the electron and point of.observation

- **Concept Insight** In this problem we use Biot-Savart's law which states that the magnetic field generated by a steady current.

Ans. ***(a)*** In Biot-Savart's law, magnetic field $\mathbf{B} \parallel \hat{\mathbf{i}}\,dl \times \mathbf{r}$ and $\hat{\mathbf{i}}\mathbf{dl}$ due to flow of electron is in opposite direction of **v** and by direction of cross product of two vectors

$$\mathbf{B} \perp \mathbf{v}$$

Q.3 A current carrying circular loop of radius R is placed in the x-y plane with centre at the origin. Half of the loop with $x > 0$ is now bent so that it now lies in the y-z plane.

(a) The magnitude of magnetic moment now diminishes
(b) The magnetic moment does not change
(c) The magnitude of **B** at $(0, 0, z)$, $z > R$ increases
(d) The magnitude of **B** at $(0, 0, z)$, $z >> R$ is unchanged

Thinking Process The magnetic moment of circular loop and the net magnitude of magnetic moment of each semicircular loop of radius R lie in the x-y plane and the y-z plane are compared.

Ans. ***(a)*** The direction of magnetic moment of circular loop of radius R is placed in the x-y plane is along z-direction and given by $M = I(\pi r^2)$, when half of the loop with $x > 0$ is now bent so that it now lies in the y-z plane, the magnitudes of magnetic moment of each semicircular loop of radius R lie in the x-y plane and the y-z plane is $M' = I(\pi r^2)/2$ and the direction of magnetic moments are along z-direction and x-direction respectively.

Their resultant,

$$M_{net} = \sqrt{M'^2 + M'^2} = \sqrt{2}\, M' = \sqrt{2}\, I(\pi r^2)/2$$

So, $M_{net} < M$ or M diminishes.

Q.4 An electron is projected with uniform velocity along the axis of a current carrying long solenoid. Which of the following is true?

(a) The electron will be accelerated along the axis.
(b) The electron path will be circular about the axis.
(c) The electron will experience a force at 45° to the axis and hence execute a helical path.
(d) The electron will continue to move with uniform velocity along the axis of the solenoid.

Thinking Process Here, magnetic lorentz force comes into existence when a charge moves in uniform magnetic field produces by current carrying long solenoid.

Ans. ***(d)*** An electron is projected with uniform velocity along the axis of a current carrying long solenoid $F = -evB\sin 180° = 0$ or $(\theta = 0°)$ as magnetic field and velocity are parallel. The electron will continue to move with uniform velocity along the axis of the solenoid.

***Q.5** In a cyclotron, a charged particle

(a) undergoes acceleration all the time
(b) speeds up between the dees because of the magnetic field
(c) speeds up in a dee
(d) slows down within a dee and speeds up between dees

Thinking Process Here, understanding of working of cyclotron is needed.

Ans. ***(a)*** The charged particle undergoes acceleration as

(i) speeds up between the dees because of the oscillating electric field and
(ii) speed remain the same inside the dees because of the magnetic field but direction undergoes change continuously.

Note (*) Topics related to these question have been removed from latest NCERT.

Q.6 A circular current loop of magnetic moment M is in an arbitrary orientation in an external magnetic field **B**. The work done to rotate the loop by 30° about an axis perpendicular to its plane is

(a) MB (b) $\sqrt{3}\frac{MB}{2}$

(c) $\frac{MB}{2}$ (d) zero

Thinking Process The rotation of the loop by 30° about an axis perpendicular to its plane imply that the axis of the loop still continues to inclined with the same angle with the direction of magnetic field .

Ans. ***(d)*** The rotation of the loop by 30° about an axis perpendicular to its plane make no change in the angle made by axis of the loop with the direction of magnetic field, therefore, the work done to rotate the loop is zero.

Note The work done to rotate the loop in magnetic field, $W = MB(\cos\theta_1 - \cos\theta_2)$. where, signs are as usual.

Multiple Choice Questions (More Than One Options)

Q.7 The gyro-magnetic ratio of an electron in an H-atom, according to Bohr model, is

(a) independent of which orbit it is in
(b) negative
(c) positive
(d) increases with the quantum number n

Thinking Process The gyro-magnetic ratio of an electron in an H-atom is equal to the ratio of the magnetic moment and the angular momentum of the electron.

Ans. ***(a, b)*** If l is the magnitude of the angular momentum of the electron about the central nucleus (orbital angular momentum). Vectorially,

$$\mu_l = -\frac{e}{2m_e} l.$$

The negative sign indicates that the angular momentum of the electron is opposite in direction to the magnetic moment and independent of the orbit of the electron.

Q.8 Consider a wire carrying a steady current, I placed in a uniform magnetic field **B** perpendicular to its length. Consider the charges inside the wire. It is known that magnetic forces do no work. This implies that,

(a) motion of charges inside the conductor is unaffected by **B**, since they do not absorb energy
(b) some charges inside the wire move to the surface as a result of **B**
(c) If the wire moves under the influence of **B**, no work is done by the force
(d) if the wire moves under the influence of **B**, no work is done by the magnetic force on the ions, assumed fixed within the wire.

Ans. ***(b, d)*** Magnetic forces on a wire carrying a steady current, I placed in a uniform magnetic field B, a wire carrying a steady current, I placed in a uniform magnetic field **B** perpendicular to its length is given by

$$F = IlB$$

The direction of force is given by Fleming's left hand rule and F is perpendicular to the direction of magnetic field **B**. Therefore, work done by the magnetic force on the ions is zero.

Q.9 Two identical current carrying coaxial loops, carry current I in an opposite sense. A simple amperian loop passes through both of them once. Calling the loop as C,

(a) $\oint \mathbf{B} \cdot d\mathbf{l} = \mp 2\mu_0 I$

(b) the value of $\oint \mathbf{B} \cdot d\mathbf{l} = \pm 2\mu_0 I$ is independent of sense of C

(c) there may be a point on C where, **B** and $d\mathbf{l}$ are perpendicular

(d) **B** vanishes everywhere on C

- **Concept Insight** In this problem we use the concept of ampere's circuital law which states that the line integral of the magnetic field **B** around any closed loop is equal to μ_0 times the total current enclosed by the loop.

Ans. ***(b, c)*** Applying the Ampere's circuital law, we have

$$\oint_c \mathbf{B} \cdot d\mathbf{l} = \mu_0 (I - I) = 0 \text{(because current is in opposite sense.)}$$

Also, there may be a point on C where **B** and $d\mathbf{l}$ are perpendicular and hence,

$$\oint_c \mathbf{B} \cdot d\mathbf{l} = 0$$

Q.10 A cubical region of space is filled with some uniform electric and magnetic fields. An electron enters the cube across one of its faces with velocity v and a positron enters *via* opposite face with velocity $-v$. At this instant,

(a) the electric forces on both the particles cause identical accelerations

(b) the magnetic forces on both the particles cause equal accelerations

(c) both particles gain or loose energy at the same rate

(d) the motion of the Centre of Mass (CM) is determined by **B** alone

Thinking Process The Lorentz force is experienced by the single moving charge in space is filled with some uniform electric and magnetic fields is given by $\mathbf{F} = q\mathbf{E} + q(\mathbf{v} \times \mathbf{B})$.

Ans. ***(b, c, d)*** The magnetic forces $\mathbf{F} = q(\mathbf{v} \times \mathbf{B})$, on charge particle is either zero or **F** is perpendicular to **v** (or component of **v**) which in turn revolves particles on circular path with uniform speed. In both the cases particles have equal accelerations.

Both the particles gain or loss energy at the same rate as both are subjected to the same electric force ($\mathbf{F} = q\mathbf{E}$) in opposite direction.

Since, there is no change of the Centre of Mass (CM) of the particles , therefore the motion of the Centre of Mass (CM) is determined by **B** alone.

Q.11 A charged particle would continue to move with a constant velocity in a region wherein,

(a) $\mathbf{E} = 0, \mathbf{B} \neq 0$ (b) $\mathbf{E} \neq 0, \mathbf{B} \neq 0$ (c) $\mathbf{E} \neq 0, \mathbf{B} = 0$ (d) $\mathbf{E} = 0, \mathbf{B} = 0$

Thinking Process The Lorentz force is experienced by the single moving charge in space is filled with some uniform electric and magnetic fields is given by $\mathbf{F} = q\mathbf{E} + q(\mathbf{v} \times \mathbf{B})$.

Ans. ***(a, b, d)*** Here, force on charged particle due to electric field $\mathbf{F}_E = q\mathbf{E}$.

Force on charged particle due to magnetic field, $\mathbf{F}_m = q(\mathbf{v} \times \mathbf{B})$

Now, $F_E = 0$ if $E = 0$ and $F_m = 0$ if $\sin\theta = 0$ or $\theta° = 0°$ or $180°$

Hence, $B \neq 0$.

Also, $E = 0$ and $B = 0$ and the resultant force $q\mathbf{E} + q(\mathbf{v} \times \mathbf{B}) = 0$. In this case $E \neq 0$ and $B \neq 0$

Very Short Answer Type Questions

***Q.12** Verify that the cyclotron frequency $\omega = eB/m$ has the correct dimensions of $[T]^{-1}$.

Ans. For a charge particle moving perpendicular to the magnetic field, the magnetic Lorentz force provides necessary centripetal force for revolution.

$$\frac{mv^2}{R} = qvB$$

On simplifying the terms, we have

$$\therefore \qquad \frac{qB}{m} = \frac{v}{R} = \omega$$

Finding the dimensional formula of angular frequency,

$$\therefore \qquad [\omega] = \left[\frac{qB}{m}\right] = \left[\frac{v}{R}\right] = [T]^{-1}$$

Q.13 Show that a force that does no work must be a velocity dependent force.

Ans. Let no work is done by a force , so we have

$$dW = \mathbf{F} \cdot d\mathbf{l} = 0$$

$$\Rightarrow \qquad \mathbf{F} . \mathbf{v}\, dt = 0 \qquad \text{(Since, } d\mathbf{l} = \mathbf{v}\, dt \text{ and } dt \neq 0\text{)}$$

$$\Rightarrow \qquad \mathbf{F} . \mathbf{v} = 0$$

Thus, F must be velocity dependent which implies that angle between F and v is 90°. If v changes (direction), then directions of F should also change so that above condition is satisfied.

Q.14 The magnetic force depends on v which depends on the inertial frame of reference. Does then the magnetic force differ from inertial frame to frame? Is it reasonable that the net acceleration has a different value in different frames of reference?

Note (*) Topics related to these question have been removed from latest NCERT.

Ans. *Yes*, the magnetic force differ from inertial frame to frame. The magnetic force is frame dependent.

The net acceleration which comes into existing out of this is however, frame independent (non-relativistic physics) for inertial frames.

***Q.15** **Describe the motion of a charged particle in a cyclotron if the frequency of the radio frequency (rf) field were doubled.**

Thinking Process The relationship of radio frequency and charge particle frequency must be equal in order to accelerate the charge particle between the dees in cyclotron.

Ans. Here, the condition of magnetic resonance is violated.

When the frequency of the radio frequency (rf) field were doubled, the time period of the radio frequency (rf) field were halved. Therefore, the duration in which particle completes half revolution inside the dees, radio frequency completes the cycle.

Hence, particle will accelerate and decelerate alternatively. So, the radius of path in the dees will remain same.

Q.16 **Two long wires carrying current I_1 and I_2 are arranged as shown in figure. The one carrying current I_1 is along the X-axis. The other carrying current I_2 is along a line parallel to the y-axis given by $x = 0$ and $z = d$. Find the force exerted at O_2 because of the wire along the X-axis.**

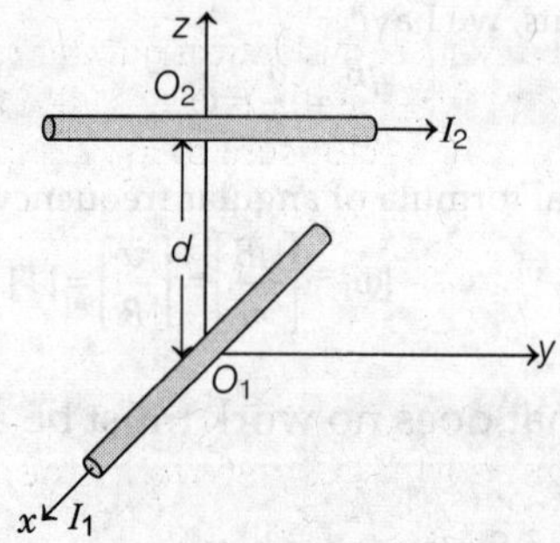

Thinking Process Here, the understanding of application of the rule of finding directions of magnetic field and magnetic force on current carrying wire placed in magnetic field is beautifully tested.

Ans. In Biot- Savart law, magnetic field **B** is parallel to $id\mathbf{l} \times \mathbf{r}$ and $id\mathbf{l}$ have its direction along the direction of flow of current.

The direction of the magnetic field at point O_2 due to the current carrying wire I_1 is

$$\mathbf{B} \parallel id\mathbf{l} \times \mathbf{r} \text{ or } \hat{\mathbf{i}} \times \hat{\mathbf{k}}, \text{ but } \hat{\mathbf{i}} \times \hat{\mathbf{k}} = -\hat{\mathbf{j}}$$

So, the direction at O_2 is along $(-y)$-direction.

The direction of magnetic force exerted at O_2 because of the wire along the, X-axis.

$$\mathbf{F} = I\mathbf{l} \times \mathbf{B} \approx \hat{\mathbf{j}} \times (-\hat{\mathbf{j}}) = 0$$

So, the magnetic field due to I_1 is along the y-axis. The second wire is along the y-axis and hence, the force is zero.

Note (*) Topics related to these question have been removed from latest NCERT.

Short Answer Type Questions

Q.17 A current carrying loop consists of 3 identical quarter circles of radius R, lying in the positive quadrants of the x-y, y-z and z-x planes with their centres at the origin, joined together. Find the direction and magnitude of **B** at the origin.

Thinking Process The magnetic field due to arc of current carrying coil which subtends an angle θ at centre is given by $\mathbf{B} = \frac{\mu_0}{4\pi}\frac{I\,\theta}{R}$.

Ans. For the current carrying loop quarter circles of radius R, lying in the positive quadrants of the x-y plane

$$\mathbf{B}_1 = \frac{\mu_0}{4\pi}\frac{I(\pi/2)}{R}\hat{\mathbf{k}} = \frac{1}{4}\left(\frac{\mu_0 I}{2R}\right)\hat{\mathbf{k}}$$

For the current carrying loop quarter circles of radius R, lying in the positive quadrants of the y-z plane

$$\mathbf{B}_2 = \frac{1}{4}\left(\frac{\mu_0 I}{2R}\right)\hat{\mathbf{i}}$$

For the current carrying loop quarter circles of radius R, lying in the positive quadrants of the z-x plane

$$\mathbf{B}_3 = \frac{1}{4}\left(\frac{\mu_0 I}{2R}\right)\hat{\mathbf{j}}$$

Current carrying loop consists of 3 identical quarter circles of radius R, lying in the positive quadrants of the x-y, y-z and z-x planes with their centres at the origin, joined together is equal to the vector sum of magnetic field due to each quarter and given by

$$\mathbf{B} = \frac{1}{4}(\hat{\mathbf{i}} + \hat{\mathbf{j}} + \hat{\mathbf{k}})\frac{\mu_0 I}{2R}.$$

Q.18 A charged particle of charge e and mass m is moving in an electric field **E** and magnetic field **B**. Construct dimensionless quantities and quantities of dimension $[T]^{-1}$.

Ans. No dimensionless quantity can be constructed using given quantities.
For a charge particle moving perpendicular to the magnetic field, the magnetic Lorentz force provides necessary centripetal force for revolution.

$$\frac{mv^2}{R} = qvB$$

On simplifying the terms, we have

$$\therefore \quad \frac{qB}{m} = \frac{v}{R} = \omega$$

Finding the dimensional formula of angular frequency

$$\therefore \quad [\omega] = \left[\frac{qB}{m}\right] = \left[\frac{v}{R}\right] = [T]^{-1}$$

This is the required expression.

Alternate Method

The necessary centripetal force is provided by the magnetic lorentz force when a charged particle moving perpendicular to the magnetic field.

$$\frac{mv^2}{R} = evB \Rightarrow \frac{eB}{m} = \frac{v}{R} = \omega$$

∴ We know that

$$B = \frac{F}{ev} = \frac{[MLT^{-2}]}{[AT][LT^{-1}]} = [MA^{-1}T^{-2}]$$

$$\therefore \quad [\omega] = \left[\frac{eB}{m}\right] = \left[\frac{v}{R}\right] = \frac{[AT][MA^{-1}T^{-2}]}{[M]} = [T^{-1}]$$

Q.19 An electron enters with a velocity $\mathbf{v} = v_0\hat{\mathbf{i}}$ into a cubical region (faces parallel to coordinate planes) in which there are uniform electric and magnetic fields. The orbit of the electron is found to spiral down inside the cube in plane parallel to the x-y plane. Suggest a configuration of fields **E** and **B** that can lead to it.

Thinking Process The magnetic field revolves the charge particle in uniform circular motion in x-y plane and electric field along negative z-direction.

Ans. Considering magnetic field $\mathbf{B} = B_0\,\hat{\mathbf{k}}$, and an electron enters with a velocity $\mathbf{v} = v_0\,\hat{\mathbf{i}}$ into a cubical region (faces parallel to coordinate planes).

The force on electron, using magnetic Lorentz force, is given by

$$\mathbf{F} = -e\,(v_0\hat{\mathbf{i}} \times B_0\,\hat{\mathbf{k}}) = e\,v_0 B_0\,\hat{\mathbf{j}}$$

which revolves the electron in x-y plane.

The electric force $F = -eE_0\,\hat{\mathbf{k}}$, is acting opposite to the magnetic field. This produces perpendicular component of velocity in the negative z-direction, causing the electron to spiral down with a constant radius.

Q.20 Do magnetic forces obey Newton's third law. Verify for two current elements $d\mathbf{l}_1 = d\mathbf{l}\,\hat{\mathbf{i}}$ located at the origin and $d\mathbf{l}_2 = d\mathbf{l}\,\hat{\mathbf{j}}$ located at (0, R, 0). Both carry current i.

Thinking Process Here, the understanding of application of the rules of finding directions of magnetic field and magnetic force on current carrying wire placed in magnetic field is needed.

Ans. In Biot-Savart's law, magnetic field **B** is parallel (||) to $id\mathbf{l} \times \mathbf{r}$ and $id\mathbf{l}$ have its direction along the direction of flow of current.

Here, for the direction of magnetic field, at $d\mathbf{l}_2$, located at (0, R, 0)due to wire d_1 is given by

$\mathbf{B} \parallel id\mathbf{l} \times \mathbf{r}$ or $\hat{\mathbf{i}} \times \hat{\mathbf{j}}$ (because point (0, R, 0) lies on y-axis), but $\hat{\mathbf{i}} \times \hat{\mathbf{j}} = \hat{\mathbf{k}}$

So, the direction of magnetic field at d_2 is along z-direction.

The direction of magnetic force exerted at d_2 because of the first wire along the X-axis.

$\mathbf{F} = i\,(\mathbf{I} \times \mathbf{B})$ *i.e.*, $\mathbf{F} \parallel (\hat{\mathbf{i}} \times \hat{\mathbf{k}})$ or along $-\hat{\mathbf{j}}$ direction.

Therefore, force due to $d\mathbf{l}_1$ on $d\mathbf{l}_2$ is non-zero.

Now, for the direction of magnetic field, At d_1, located at (0, 0, 0) due to wire d_2 is given by $\hat{B} \parallel i d\mathbf{l} \times \hat{\mathbf{r}}$ or $\hat{\mathbf{j}} \times -\hat{\mathbf{j}}$ (because origin lies on y-direction w.r.t. point (0, R, 0).), but $\hat{\mathbf{j}} \times -\hat{\mathbf{j}} = 0$. So, the magnetic field at d_1 does not exist. Force due to $d\mathbf{l}_2$ on $d\mathbf{l}_1$ is zero. So, magnetic forces do not obey Newton's third law.

Q.21 A multirange voltmeter can be constructed by using a galvanometer circuit as shown in figure. We want to construct a voltmeter that can measure 2V, 20V and 200V using a galvanometer of resistance 10Ω and that produces maximum deflection for current of 1 mA. Find R_1, R_2 and R_3 that have to be used.

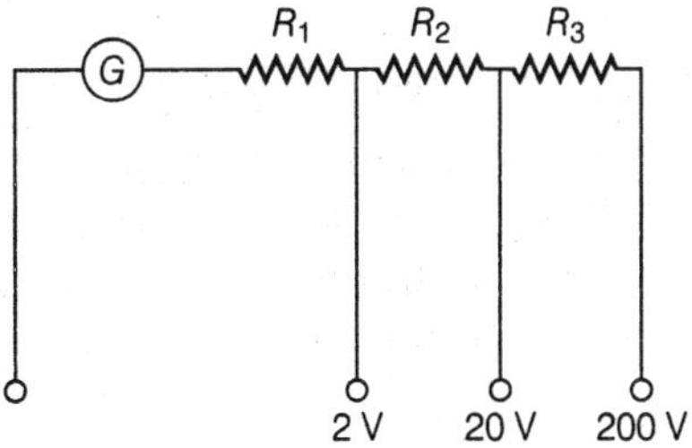

Thinking Process A galvanometer can be converted into voltmeter by connecting a very high resistance wire connected in series with galvanometer. The relationship is given by $I_g(G + R) = V$ where I_g is range of galvanometer, G is resistance of galvanometer and R is resistance of wire connected in series with galvanometer.

Ans.

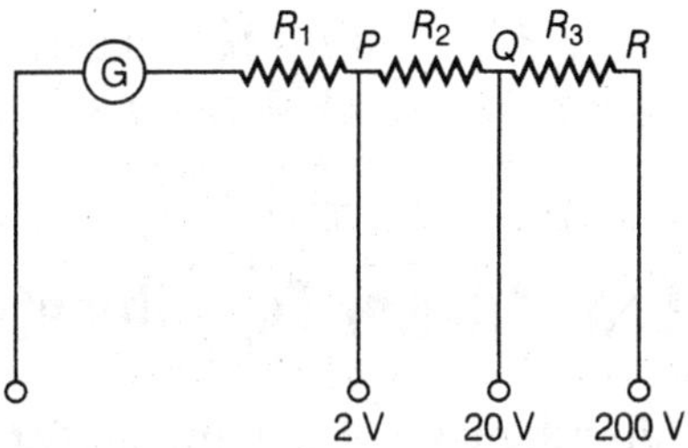

Applying expression in different situations

For $\quad i_G(G + R_1) = 2 \quad$ for 2V range

For $\quad i_G(G + R_1 + R_2) = 20 \quad$ for 20V range

and For $\quad i_G(G + R_1 + R_2 + R_3) = 200 \quad$ for 200V range

On solving, we get

At point P, $R_1 + 10 = \dfrac{2}{10^{-3}} = 2000\Omega \Rightarrow R_1 = 2000 - 10 = 1990\Omega$

At point Q, $R_1 + R_2 + 10 = \dfrac{20}{10^{-3}} = 20000\Omega \Rightarrow R_2 + 2000 = 20000$

$\therefore \quad R_2 = 18000\Omega = 18\text{k}\Omega$

At point R, $R_1 + R_2 + R_3 + 10 = \dfrac{200}{10^{-3}} = 200000\Omega$

$\therefore \quad R_3 = 200000 - 1990 - 18000 - 10 = 180000\Omega = 180\text{k}\Omega$

Q.22 A long straight wire carrying current of 25 A rests on a table as shown in figure. Another wire PQ of length 1m, mass 2.5 g carries the same current but in the opposite direction. The wire PQ is free to slide up and down. To what height will PQ rise?

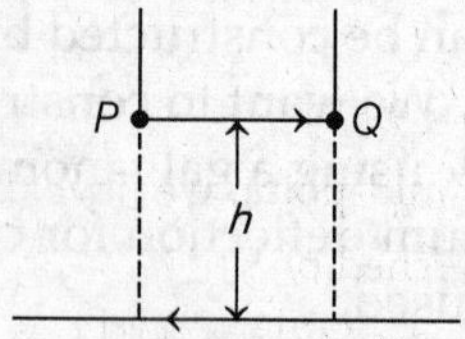

Thinking Process The force applied on PQ by long straight wire carrying current of 25 A rests on a table must balance the weight of small current carrying wire.

Ans. The magnetic field produced by long straight wire carrying current of 25 A rests on a table on small wire

$$B = \frac{\mu_0 I}{2\pi h}$$

The magnetic force on small conductor is

$$F = BIl \sin\theta = BIl$$

Force applied on PQ balance the weight of small current carrying wire.

$$F = mg = \frac{\mu_0 I^2 l}{2\pi h}$$

$$h = \frac{\mu_0 I^2 l}{2\pi\, mg} = \frac{4\pi \times 10^{-7} \times 25 \times 25 \times 1}{2\pi \times 2.5 \times 10^{-3} \times 9.8} = 51 \times 10^{-4}$$

$$h = 0.51 \text{ cm}$$

Long Answer Type Questions

Q.23 A 100 turn rectangular coil $ABCD$ (in x-y plane) is hung from one arm of a balance figure. A mass 500 g is added to the other arm to balance the weight of the coil. A current 4.9 A passes through the coil and a constant magnetic field of 0.2 T acting inward (in x-z plane) is switched on such that only arm CD of length 1 cm lies in the field. How much additional mass m must be added to regain the balance?

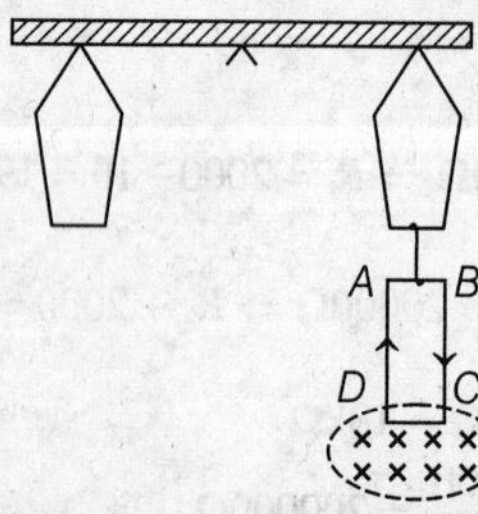

Thinking Process The magnetic force applied on CD by magnetic field must balance the weight.

Ans. For equilibrium/ balance, net torque should also be equal to zero.

When the field is off $\sum t = 0$ considering the separation of each hung from mid-point be l.

$$Mgl = W_{coil}\, l$$
$$500\, g\, l = W_{coil}\, l$$
$$W_{coil} = 500 \times 9.8\, \text{N}$$

Taking moment of force about mid-point, we have the weight of coil

When the magnetic field is switched on

$$Mgl + mgl = W_{coil}\, l + (IBL \sin 90°)\, l$$
$$mgl = BIL\, l$$
$$m = \frac{BIL}{g} = \frac{0.2 \times 4.9 \times 1 \times 10^{-2}}{9.8} = 10^{-3}\ \text{kg} = 1\text{g}$$

Thus, 1g of additional mass must be added to regain the balance.

Mistake Alert! *Ensure that the length L of the arm CD is converted from centimetres to metre, i.e 1 cm = 0.01 m.*
The total force is multiplied by the number of turns N. Missing this step would result in an incorrect force calculation.

Q.24 A rectangular conducting loop consists of two wires on two opposite sides of length l joined together by rods of length d. The wires are each of the same material but with cross-sections differing by a factor of 2. The thicker wire has a resistance R and the rods are of low resistance, which in turn are connected to a constant voltage source V_0. The loop is placed in uniform a magnetic field **B** at 45° to its plane. Find τ, the torque exerted by the magnetic field on the loop about an axis through the centres of rods.

Thinking Process After finding current in both wires, magnetic forces and torques need to be calculated for finding the net torque.

Ans.

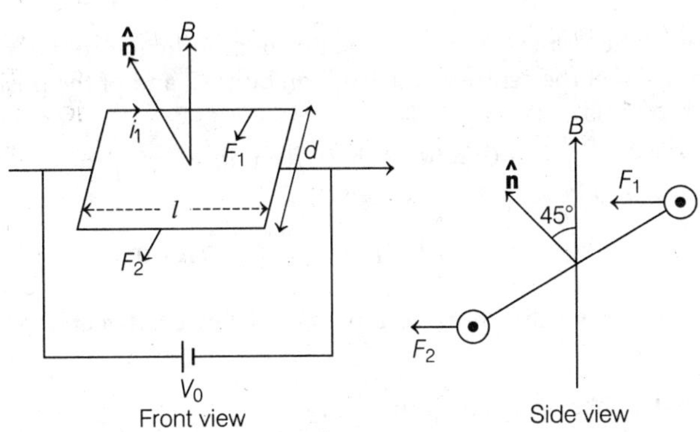

The thicker wire has a resistance R, then the other wire has a resistance $2R$ as the wires are of the same material but with cross-sections differing by a factor 2.

Now, the force and hence, torque on first wire is given by

$$F_1 = i_1\, lB = \frac{V_0}{R}\, lB,\ \tau_1 = \frac{d}{2\sqrt{2}}\, F_1 = \frac{V_0 ldB}{2\sqrt{2}R}$$

Similarly, the force hence torque on other wire is given by

$$F_2 = i_2 lB = \frac{V_0}{2R}\, lB,\ \tau_2 = \frac{d}{2\sqrt{2}}\, F_2 = \frac{V_0 ldB}{4\sqrt{2}\, R}$$

So, net torque, $\tau = \tau_1 - \tau_2$

$$\tau = \frac{1}{4\sqrt{2}} \frac{V_0 ldB}{R}$$

Q.25 An electron and a positron are released from (0, 0, 0) and (0, 0, 1.5*R*) respectively, in a uniform magnetic field $\mathbf{B} = B_0 \hat{\mathbf{i}}$, each with an equal momentum of magnitude $p = eBR$. Under what conditions on the direction of momentum will the orbits be non-intersecting circles?

Thinking Process The circles of the electron and a positron shall not overlap if the distance between the two centers are greater than 2*R*.

Ans. Since, *B* is along the X-axis, for a circular orbit the momentum of the two particles are in the *y-z* plane. Let p_1 and p_2 be the momentum of the electron and positron, respectively. Both traverse a circle of radius *R* of opposite sense. Let p_1 make an angle θ with the *y*-axis p_2 must make the same angle.

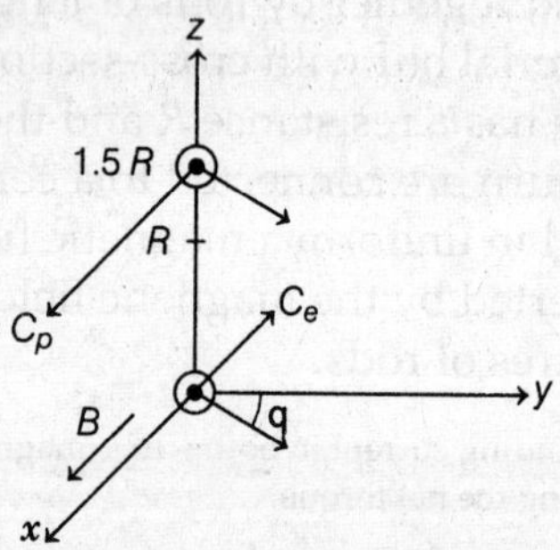

The centres of the respective circles must be perpendicular to the momentum and at a distance *R*. Let the centre of the electron be at C_e and of the positron at C_p. The coordinates of C_e is

$$C_e \equiv (0,\ R\sin\theta,\ R\cos\theta)$$

The coordinates of C_p is

$$C_p \equiv \left(0,\ -R\sin\theta,\ \frac{3}{2}R - R\cos\theta\right)$$

The circles of the two shall not overlap if the distance between the two centres are greater than 2*R*.

Let *d* be the distance between C_p and C_e.

Then, $$d^2 = [R\sin\theta - (-R\sin\theta)]^2 + \left[R\cos\theta - \left(\frac{3}{2}R - R\cos\theta\right)\right]^2$$

$$d^2 = (2R\sin\theta)^2 + \left(2R\cos\theta - \frac{3}{2}R\right)^2$$

$$= 4R^2 \sin^2\theta + \frac{9}{4}R^2 - 6R^2 \cos\theta + 4R^2 \cos^2\theta$$

$$= 4R^2 + \frac{9}{4}R^2 - 6R^2 \cos\theta$$

Since, d has to be greater than $2R$

$$d^2 > 4R^2$$

$$\Rightarrow \quad 4R^2 + \frac{9}{4}R^2 - 6R^2 \cos\theta > 4R^2$$

$$\Rightarrow \quad \frac{9}{4} > 6\cos\theta \quad \text{or} \quad \cos\theta < \frac{3}{8}$$

Mistake Alert ! *Remember that the electron and positron have opposite charges. So, they will rotate in opposite directions.*

Q.26 A uniform conducting wire of length $12a$ and resistance R is wound up as a current carrying coil in the shape of (i) an equilateral triangle of side a, (ii) a square of sides a and, (iii) a regular hexagon of sides a. The coil is connected to a voltage source V_0. Find the magnetic moment of the coils in each case.

Thinking Process The different shapes forms figures of different area and hence, there magnetic moments varies.

Ans. We know that magnetic moment of the coils, $m = nIA$, $n =$ no. of loop

Since, the same wire is used in three cases with same potentials, therefore, same current flows in three cases.

(i) For an equilateral triangle of side a,

$n = 4$ as the total wire of length $= 12a$

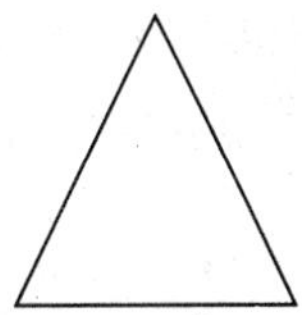

$n = 4$

Magnetic moment of the coils, $m = nIA = 4I\left(\frac{\sqrt{3}}{4}a^2\right)$

From Ohm's Law, $V_0 = IR$

$$\therefore \quad m = \frac{V_0\sqrt{3}a^2}{R}$$

(ii) For a square of sides a,

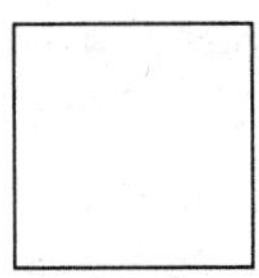

$n = 3$

$A = a^2$

$n = 3$ as the total wire of length $= 12a$

Magnetic moment of the coils, $m = nIA = 3I(a^2) = \frac{3V_0a^2}{R}$ $\quad (\because V_0 = IR)$

(iii) For a regular hexagon of sides a,

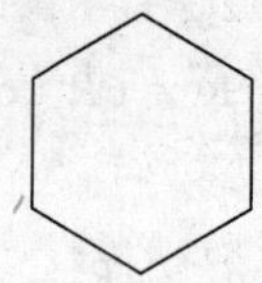

$n = 2$ as the total wire of length $= 12a$

Magnetic moment of the coils, $m = nIA = 2\,I\left(\frac{6\sqrt{3}}{4}a^2\right)$

$$m = \frac{3\sqrt{3}V_0 a^2}{R} \qquad (\because V_0 = IR)$$

m is in a geometric series.

Q.27 Consider a circular current-carrying loop of radius R in the x-yplane with centre at origin. Consider the line integral

$$\Im(\mathbf{L}) = \left|\int_{-L}^{L} \mathbf{B}\cdot d\mathbf{l}\right|$$

taken along Z-axis.

(a) Show that $\Im(L)$ monotonically increases with L

(b) Use an appropriate amperian loop to show that $\Im(\infty) = \mu_0 I$, where I is the current in the wire

(c) Verify directly the above result

(d) Suppose we replace the circular coil by a square coil of sides R carrying the same current I. What can you say about $\Im(L)$ and $\Im(\infty)$?

Thinking Process This question revolves around the application of Ampere circuital law.

Ans. (a) $\mathbf{B}$ (z) points in the same direction on Z-axis and hence, $\Im(L)$ is a monotonically function of L.

Since, B and $d\mathbf{l}$ along the same direction, therefore $\mathbf{B}\cdot d\mathbf{l} = \mathbf{B}\cdot d\mathbf{l}$ as $\cos 0 = 1$

(b) $\Im(L)$ + contribution from large distance on contour $C = \mu_0 I$

$\therefore$ as $L \to \infty$

Contribution from large distance $\to 0$ (as $\mathbf{B} \propto 1/r^3$)

$$\Im(\infty) = \mu_0 I$$

(c) The magnetic field due to circular current-carrying loop of radius R in the x-y plane with centre at origin at any point lying at a distance of from origin.

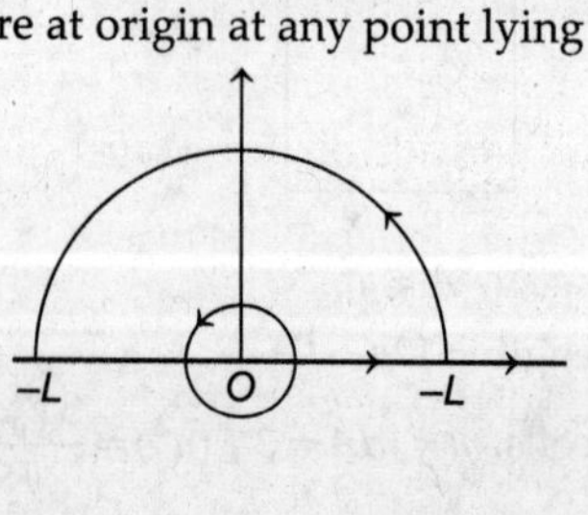

$$B_z = \frac{\mu_0 IR^2}{2(z^2 + R^2)^{3/2}}$$

$$\int_{-\infty}^{\infty} B_z dz = \int_{-\infty}^{\infty} \frac{\mu_0 IR^2}{2(z^2 + R^2)^{3/2}} dz$$

Put $z = R\tan\theta_1$

$\Rightarrow$ $dz = R\sec^2\theta\, d\theta$

$\therefore$ $\int_{-\infty}^{\infty} B_z dz = \frac{\mu_0 I}{2}\int_{-\pi/2}^{\pi/2} \cos\theta\, d\theta = \mu_0 I$

(d) $B(z)_{square} < B(z)_{circular\ coil}$

$\therefore$ $\Im(L)_{square} < \Im(L)_{circular\ coil}$

But by using arguments as in (b)

$$\Im(\infty)_{square} = \Im(\infty)_{circular}$$

Q.28 A multirange current meter can be constructed by using a galvanometer circuit as shown in figure. We want a current meter that can measure 10mA, 100mA and 1mA using a galvanometer of resistance 10Ω and that produces maximum deflection for current of 1mA. Find S_1, S_2 and S_3 that have to be used.

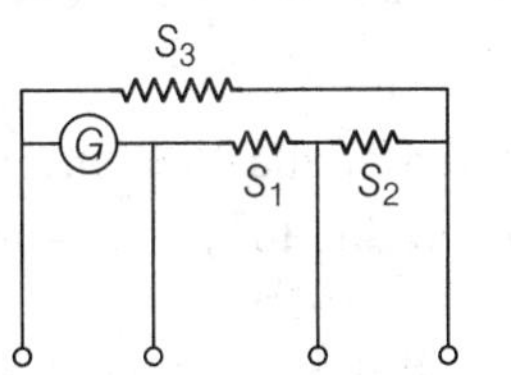

Thinking Process A galvanometer can be converted into ammeter by connecting a very low resistance wire (shunt S) connected in parallel with galvanometer. The relationship is given by $I_g G = (I - I_g) S$, where I_g is range of galvanometer, G is resistance of galvanometer.

Ans. $I_G \cdot G = (I_1 - I_G)(S_1 + S_2 + S_3)$ for $I_1 = 10\text{ mA} = 10^{-2}$

$I_G(G + S_1) = (I_2 - I_G)(S_2 + S_3)$ for $I_2 = 100\text{ mA}$

and $I_G(G + S_1 + S_2) = (I_3 - I_G)(S_3)$ for $I_3 = 1\text{mA}$

gives $S_1 = 1\,\Omega$, $S_2 = 0.1\,\Omega$

and $S_3 = 0.01\,\Omega$

Q.29 Five long wires A, B, C, D and E, each carrying current I are arranged to form edges of a pentagonal prism as shown in figure. Each carries current out of the plane of paper.

(a) What will be magnetic induction at a point on the axis O? Axis is at a distance R from each wire.

(b) What will be the field if current in one of the wires (say A) is switched off?

(c) What if current in one of the wire (say *A*) is reversed?

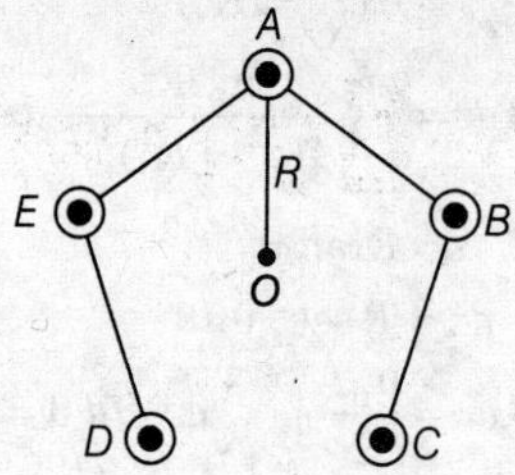

Thinking Process The vector sum of magnetic field produced by each wire at *O* is equal to 0.

Ans. (a) Suppose the five wires *A, B, C, D* and *E* be perpendicular to the plane of paper at locations as shown in above figure.

Thus, magnetic field induction due to five wires will be represented by various sides of a closed pentagon in one order, lying in the plane of paper. So, its value is zero.

(b) Since, the vector sum of magnetic field produced by each wire at *O* is equal to 0. Therefore, magnetic induction produced by one current carrying wire is equal in magnitude of resultant of four wires and opposite in direction.

Therefore, the field if current in one of the wires (say *A*) is switched off is $\frac{\mu_0}{2\pi}\frac{i}{R}$ perpendicular to *AO* towards left.

(c) If current in wire *A* is reversed, then total magnetic field induction at *O*

= Magnetic field induction due to wire *A* + magnetic field induction due to wires *B, C, D* and *E*

$$=\frac{\mu_0}{4\pi R}\frac{2I}{R}$$

(acting perpendicular to *AO* towards left) + $\frac{\mu_0}{\pi}\frac{2I}{R}$ (acting perpendicular *AO* towards left)

$$=\frac{\mu_0 I}{\pi R}$$ acting perpendicular *AO* towards left.

Chapter

05

Magnetism and Matter

Multiple Choice Questions (MCQs)

Q.1 A toroid of n turns, mean radius R and cross-sectional radius a carries current I. It is placed on a horizontal table taken as xy-plane. Its magnetic moment $\mathbf{m}$

(a) is non-zero and points in the z-direction by symmetry

(b) points along the axis of the toroid ($\mathbf{m} = m\,\phi$)

(c) is zero, otherwise there would be a field falling as $\frac{1}{r^3}$ at large distances outside the toroid

(d) is pointing radially outwards

Thinking Process Toroid is a hollow circular ring on which a large number of turns of a wire are closely wound. Thus, in such a case magnetic field is only confined inside the body of toroid.

Ans. ***(c)*** In case of toroid, the magnetic field is only confined inside the body of toroid in the form of concentric magnetic lines of force and there is no magnetic field outside the body of toroid. This is because the loop encloses no current. Thus, the magnetic moment of toroid is zero.

In general, if we take r as a large distance outside the toroid, then $m \propto \frac{1}{r^3}$. But this case is not possible here.

Q.2 The magnetic field of the earth can be modelled by that of a point dipole placed at the centre of the earth. The dipole axis makes an angle of 11.3° with the axis of the earth. At Mumbai, declination is nearly zero. Then,

(a) the declination varies between 11.3° W to 11.3° E

(b) the least declination is 0°

(c) the plane defined by dipole axis and the earth axis passes through Greenwich

(d) declination averaged over the earth must be always negative

Ans. ***(a)*** For the earth's magnetism, the magnetic field lines of the earth resemble that of a hypothetical magnetic dipole located at the centre of the earth.

The axis of the dipole does not coincide with the axis of rotation of the earth but is presently tilted by approxmately 11.3° with respect to the latter. This results into two situations as given in the figure ahead.

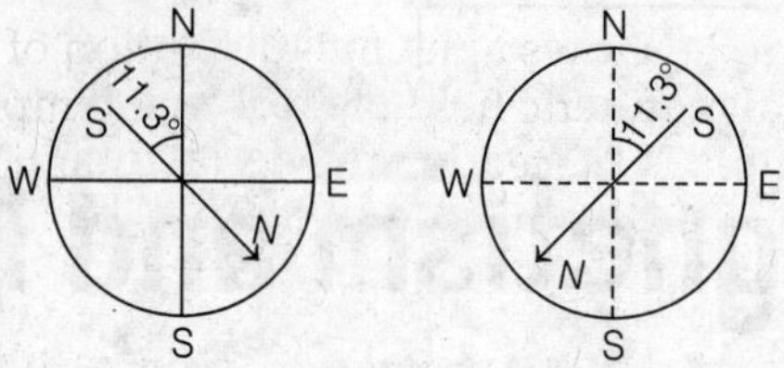

Hence, the declination varies between 11.3° W to 11.3° E.

Q.3 In a permanent magnet at room temperature,

(a) magnetic moment of each molecule is zero
(b) the individual molecules have non-zero magnetic moment which are all perfectly aligned
(c) domains are partially aligned
(d) domains are all perfectly aligned

Thinking Process Permanent magnet at room temperature behaves as a ferromagnetic substance for a long period of time.

Ans. ***(d)*** As we know a permanent magnet is a substance which at room temperature retains ferromagnetic property for a long period of time.

The individual atoms in a ferromagnetic material possess a dipole moment as in a paramagnetic material.

However, they interact with one another in such a way that they spontaneously align themselves in a common direction over a macroscopic volume called domain. Thus, we can say that in a permanent magnet at room temperature, domains are all perfectly aligned.

Q.4 **Consider the two idealised systems (i) a parallel plate capacitor with large plates and small separation and (ii) a long solenoid of length $L \gg R$, radius of cross-section. In (i) E is ideally treated as a constant between plates and zero outside. In (ii) magnetic field is constant inside the solenoid and zero outside. These idealised assumptions, however, contradict fundamental laws as below.**

(a) Case (i) contradicts Gauss' law for electrostatic fields .
(b) Case (ii) contradicts Gauss' law for magnetic fields.
(c) Case (i) agrees with $\oint \mathbf{E} \cdot d\mathbf{l} = 0$.
(d) Case (ii) contradicts $\oint \mathbf{H} \cdot d\mathbf{l} = I_{en}$.

Thinking Process The electric field lines, do not form a continuous closed path while the magnetic field lines form closed loops.

Ans. ***(b)*** As Gauss' law states, $\oint_S \mathbf{E} \cdot d\mathbf{s} = \frac{q}{\varepsilon_0}$ for electrostatic field. It does not contradict for electrostatic fields as the electric field lines do not form continuous closed path.

According to Gauss' law in magnetic field,

$$\oint_S \mathbf{B} \cdot d\mathbf{s} = 0$$

It contradicts for magnetic field, because there is a magnetic field inside the solenoid and no field outside the solenoid carrying current but the magnetic field lines form closed loops.

Q.5 A paramagnetic sample shows a net magnetisation of 8 Am^{-1} when placed in an external magnetic field of 0.6 T at a temperature of 4 K. When the same sample is placed in an external magnetic field of 0.2 T at a temperature of 16 K, the magnetisation will be

(a) $\frac{32}{3}$ Am^{-1} (b) $\frac{2}{3}$ Am^{-1} (c) 6 Am^{-1} (d) 2.4 Am^{-1}

Thinking Process From Curie's law, we know that magnetisation is directly proportional to the magnetic field induction and inversely proportional to the temperature in kelvin.

Ans. ***(b)*** As Curie's law explains, we can deduce a formula for the relation between magnetic field induction, temperature and magnetisation.

i.e., $$I\text{ (magnetisation)} \propto \frac{B\text{ (magnetic field induction)}}{T\text{ (temperature in kelvin)}}$$

$$\Rightarrow \quad \frac{I_2}{I_1} = \frac{B_2}{B_1} \times \frac{T_1}{T_2}$$

Let us suppose, here $I_1 = 8\ Am^{-1}$

$B_1 = 0.6\ T,\ T_1 = 4\ K$

$B_2 = 0.2\ T,\ T_2 = 16\ K$

$I_2 = ?$

$$\Rightarrow \quad \frac{0.2}{0.6} \times \frac{4}{16} = \frac{I_2}{8}$$

$$\Rightarrow \quad I_2 = 8 \times \frac{1}{12} = \frac{2}{3}\ Am^{-1}$$

Multiple Choice Questions (More Than One Options)

Q.6 *S* is the surface of a lump of magnetic material.

(a) Lines of **B** are necessarily continuous across *S*.
(b) Some lines of **B** must be discontinuous across *S*.
(c) Lines of **H** are necessarily continuous across *S*.
(d) Lines of **H** cannot all be continuous across *S*.

Thinking Process According to the properties of magnetic field lines (B), for any magnet, it forms continuous closed loops. This is unlike the electric field lines for electric dipole where the field lines begin from a positive charge and end on the negative charge.
Also, magnetic intensity (*H*) outside any magnet is $H = B / \mu_0$ and for inside the magnet $H = B / \mu_0 \mu_r$, where μ_r is the relative permeability of material (magnetic).

Ans. ***(a, d)*** Magnetic field lines for magnetic induction (**B**) form continuous loops. So, lines of **B** are necessarily continuous across *S*.

Also, magnetic intensity (**H**) varies inside and outside the lump. So, lines of **H** cannot all be continuous across *S*.

Q.7 The primary origin (*s*) of magnetism lies in

(a) atomic currents (b) Pauli exclusion principle
(c) polar nature of molecules (d) intrinsic spin of electron

Ans. *(a, d)* The primary origin of magnetism lies in the fact that the electrons are revolving and spinning about nucleus of an atom, which gives rise to current called atomic current.

This atomic currents give rise to magnetism. The spinning of electron about its axis is called intrinsic spin of electron.

Q.8 A long solenoid has 1000 turns per metre and carries a current of 1 A. It has a soft iron core of $\mu_r = 1000$. The core is heated beyond the Curie temperature, T_c.

(a) The **H** field in the solenoid is (nearly) unchanged but the **B** field decreases drastically.
(b) The **H** and **B** fields in the solenoid are nearly unchanged.
(c) The magnetisation in the core reverses direction.
(d) The magnetisation in the core diminishes by a factor of about 10^8.

Thinking Process The magnetic intensity $\mathbf{H} = nI$, where n is number of turns per unit length of a solenoid and I is current and $B = \mu_0 \mu_r nI$. Also, at normal temperature, a solenoid behaves as a ferromagnetic substance and at the temperature beyond the Curie temperature, it behaves as a paramagnetic substance.

Ans. *(a, d)* Here, for solenoid $\mathbf{H} = nI$.

$$\Rightarrow \quad \mathbf{H} = 1000 \times 1 = 1000 \text{ Am}^{-1}$$

Thus, **H** is a constant ,so it is nearly unchanged.

But $B = \mu_0 \mu_r nI = \mu_0 nI \mu_r = k \text{ (constant) } \mu_r$.

Thus, from above equation, we find that **B** varies with the variation in μ_r.

Now, for magnetisation in the core, when temperature of the iron core of solenoid is raised beyond Curie temperature, then it behaves as paramagnetic material, where

and $$(\chi_m)_{\text{Ferro}} \approx 10^3$$

and $$(\chi_m)_{\text{Para}} \approx 10^{-5}$$

$$\Rightarrow \quad \frac{(\chi_m)_{\text{Ferro}}}{(\chi_m)_{\text{Para}}} = \frac{10^3}{10^{-5}} = 10^8$$

Q.9 Essential difference between electrostatic shielding by a conducting shell and magnetostatic shielding is due to

(a) electrostatic field lines can end on charges and conductors have free charges
(b) lines of **B** can also end but conductors cannot end them
(c) lines of **B** cannot end on any material and perfect shielding is not possible
(d) shells of high permeability materials can be used to divert lines of **B** from the interior region

Ans. *(a, c, d)* Electrostatic shielding is the phenomenon to block the effects of an electric field. The conducting shell can block the effects of an external field on its internal content or the effect of an internal field on the outside environment.

Magnetostatic shielding is done by using an enclosure made of a high permeability magnetic material to prevent a static magnetic field outside the enclosure from reaching objects inside it or to confine a magnetic field within the enclosure.

Q.10 Let the magnetic field on the earth be modelled by that of a point magnetic dipole at the centre of the earth. The angle of dip at a point on the geographical equator

(a) is always zero
(b) can be zero at specific points
(c) can be positive or negative
(d) is bounded

- **Concept Insight** Angle of inclination or dip is the angle that the total magnetic field of the earth makes with the surface of the earth.

Ans. *(b, c, d)* If the total magnetic field of the earth is modelled by a point magnetic dipole at the centre, then it is in the same plane of geographical equator, thus the angle of dip at a point on the geographical equator is bounded in a range from positive to negative value.

Very Short Answer Type Questions

Q.11 A proton has spin and magnetic moment just like an electron. Why then its effect is neglected in magnetism of materials?

Thinking Process Mass of a proton is very larger than the mass of an electron, so its spinning is negligible as compared to that of electron spin.

Ans. The comparison between the spinning of a proton and an electron can be done by comparing their magnetic dipole moment which can be given by

$$M = \frac{eh}{4\pi m} \text{ or } M \propto \frac{1}{m} \qquad \left(\because \frac{eh}{4\pi} = \text{constant}\right)$$

$$\therefore \quad \frac{M_p}{M_e} = \frac{m_e}{m_p}$$

$$= \frac{m_e}{1837 m_e} \qquad (\because m_p = 1837 m_e)$$

$$\Rightarrow \quad \frac{M_p}{M_e} = \frac{1}{1837} << 1$$

$$\Rightarrow \quad M_p << M_e$$

Thus, effect of magnetic moment of proton is neglected as compared to that of electron.

Q.12 A permanent magnet in the shape of a thin cylinder of length 10 cm has $M = 10^6$ A/m. Calculate the magnetisation current I_M.

Ans. Given, M (intensity of magnetisation) = 10^6 A/m.

$$l\,(\text{length}) = 10\text{ cm} = 10 \times 10^{-2}\text{ m} = 0.1\text{ m}$$

and $\quad I_M$ = magnetisation current

We know that $\quad M = \frac{I_M}{l}$

$$\Rightarrow \quad I_M = M \times l = 10^6 \times 0.1 = 10^5\text{ A}$$

Q.13 Explain quantitatively the order of magnitude difference between the diamagnetic susceptibility of $N_2 (\sim 5 \times 10^{-9})$ (at STP) and Cu $(\sim 10^{-5})$.

Thinking Process Magnetic susceptibility is a measure of how a magnetic material responds to an external field.

Ans. We know that

$$\text{density of nitrogen } \rho_{N_2} = \frac{28 \text{ g}}{22.4 \text{ L}} = \frac{28 \text{ g}}{22400 \text{ cc}}$$

Also, density of copper $\rho_{Cu} = 8 \text{ g/cc}$

Now, comparing both densities

$$\frac{\rho_{N_2}}{\rho_{Cu}} = \frac{28}{22400} \times \frac{1}{8} = 1.6 \times 10^{-4}$$

Also given $\dfrac{\chi_{N_2}}{\chi_{Cu}} = \dfrac{5 \times 10^{-9}}{10^{-5}} = 5 \times 10^{-4}$

We know that, $\chi = \dfrac{\text{Magnetisation } (M)}{\text{Magnetic intensity } (H)}$

$$= \frac{\text{Magnetic moment } (M) / \text{Volume } (V)}{H}$$

$$= \frac{M}{HV} = \frac{M}{H\,(\text{mass / density})} = \frac{M\rho}{Hm}$$

$\therefore$ $\chi \propto \rho$ $\qquad \left(\because \dfrac{M}{Hm} = \text{constant}\right)$

Hence, $\dfrac{\chi_{N_2}}{\chi_{Cu}} = \dfrac{\rho_{N_2}}{\rho_{Cu}} = 1.6 \times 10^{-4}$

Thus, we can say that magnitude difference or major difference between the diamagnetic susceptibility of N_2 and Cu is accounted for by density.

Q.14 From molecular view point, discuss the temperature dependence of susceptibility for diamagnetism, paramagnetism and ferromagnetism.

Ans. Susceptibility of magnetic material $\chi = \dfrac{I}{H}$, where I is the intensity of magnetisation induced in the material and H is the magnetic induction.

Diamagnetism is due to orbital motion of electrons in an atom developing magnetic moments opposite to applied field. Thus, the resultant magnetic moment of the diamagnetic material is zero and hence, the susceptibility χ of diamagnetic material is not much affected by temperature.

Paramagnetism and ferromagnetism is due to alignments of atomic magnetic moments in the direction of the applied field. As temperature is raised, the alignment is disturbed, resulting decrease in susceptibility of both with increase in temperature.

Q.15 A ball of superconducting material is dipped in liquid nitrogen and placed near a bar magnet.

(i) In which direction will it move?

(ii) What will be the direction of its magnetic moment?

Thinking Process A superconducting material and nitrogen are diamagnetic in nature.

Ans. When a diamagnetic material is dipped in liquid nitrogen, it again behaves as a diamagnetic material. Thus, superconducting material will again behave as a diamagnetic material. When this diamagnetic material is placed near a bar magnet, it will be feebly magnetised opposite to the direction of magnetising field.

(i) Thus, it will be repelled.

(ii) Also its direction of magnetic moment will be opposite to the direction of magnetic field of magnet.

Short Answer Type Questions

Q.16 Verify the Gauss's law for magnetic field of a point dipole of dipole moment **m** at the origin for the surface which is a sphere of radius R.

Ans. Let us draw the figure for given situation,

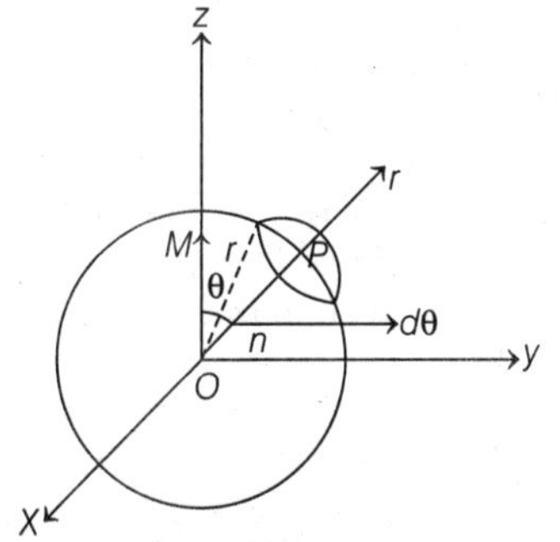

We have to prove that $\oint \mathbf{B} \cdot d\mathbf{S} = 0$. This is called Gauss's law in magnetisation.

According to question,

Magnetic moment of dipole at origin O is

$$\mathbf{M} = M\hat{\mathbf{k}}$$

Let P be a point at distance r from O and OP makes an angle θ with z-axis.

Component of **M** along $OP = M\cos\theta$.

Now, the magnetic field induction at P due to dipole of moment $M\cos\theta$ is

$$\mathbf{B} = \frac{\mu_0}{4\pi}\frac{2M\cos\theta}{r^3}\hat{\mathbf{r}}$$

From the diagram, r is the radius of sphere with centre at O lying in yz-plane. Take an elementary area $d\mathbf{S}$ of the surface at P. Then,

$$d\mathbf{S} = r(r\sin\theta\ d\theta)\hat{\mathbf{r}} = r^2\sin\theta\ d\theta\,\hat{\mathbf{r}}$$

$$\oint \mathbf{B}\cdot d\mathbf{S} = \oint \frac{\mu_0}{4\pi}\frac{2M\cos\theta}{r^3}\hat{\mathbf{r}}\cdot(r^2\sin\theta\ d\theta\,\hat{\mathbf{r}})$$

$$= \frac{\mu_0}{4\pi} \frac{M}{r} \int_0^{2\pi} 2\sin\theta.\cos\theta \, d\theta$$

$$= \frac{\mu_0}{4\pi} \frac{M}{r} \int_0^{2\pi} \sin 2\theta \, d\theta$$

$$= \frac{\mu_0}{4\pi} \frac{M}{r} \left(\frac{-\cos 2\theta}{2} \right)_0^{2\pi}$$

$$= -\frac{\mu_0}{4\pi} \frac{M}{2r} [\cos 4\pi - \cos 0]$$

$$= -\frac{\mu_0}{4\pi} \frac{M}{2r} [1 - 1] = 0$$

Q.17 Three identical bar magnets are rivetted together at centre in the same plane as shown in figure. This system is placed at rest in a slowly varying magnetic field. It is found that the system of magnets does not show any motion. The north-south poles of one magnet is shown in the figure. Determine the poles of the remaining two.

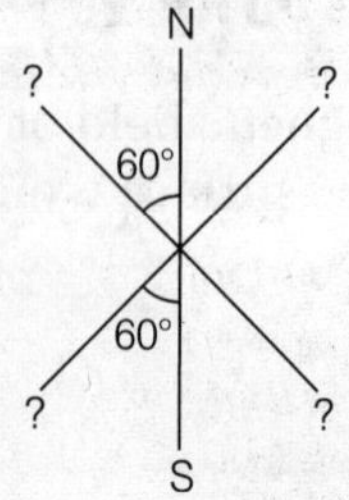

Ans. The system will be in stable equilibrium if the net force on the system is zero and net torque on the system is also zero. This is possible only when the poles of the remaining two magnets are as given in the figure.

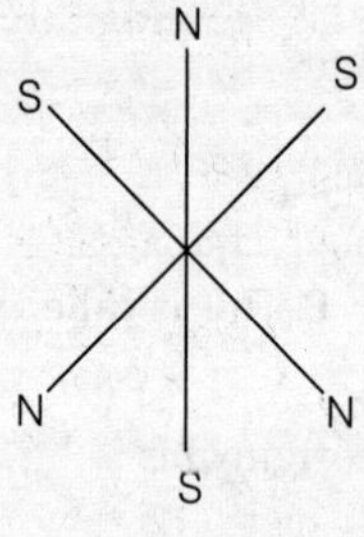

Q.18 Suppose we want to verify the analogy between electrostatic and magnetostatic by an explicit experiment. Consider the motion of (i) electric dipole **p** in an electrostatic field **E** and (ii) magnetic dipole **M** in a magnetic field **B**. Write down a set of conditions on **E, B, p, M** so that the two motions are verified to be identical. (Assume identical initial conditions).

- **Concept Insight** $E(r) = cf(r)$, if the angle between **p** and **E** is θ, torque on electric dipole of moment **p** in electric field **E**, $\tau = pE \sin\theta$.

Ans. Now, suppose that the angle between **M** and **B** is θ.

Torque on magnetic dipole moment **M** in magnetic field **B**,

$$\tau' = MB\sin\theta$$

Two motions will be identical, if

$$pE\sin\theta = MB\sin\theta$$

$$\Rightarrow \qquad pE = MB \qquad \text{...(i)}$$

But, $\quad E = cB$

$\therefore$ Putting this value in Eq. (i),

$$pcB = MB$$

$$\Rightarrow \qquad p = \frac{M}{c}$$

Q.19 A bar magnet of magnetic moment M and moment of inertia I (about centre, perpendicular to length) is cut into two equal pieces, perpendicular to length. Let T be the period of oscillations of the original magnet about an axis through the mid-point, perpendicular to length, in a magnetic field **B**. What would be the similar period T' for each piece?

Thinking Process $\quad T = 2\pi\sqrt{\frac{I}{MB}}$

where, T = time period
I = moment of inertia
m = mass of magnet
B = magnetic field

Ans. Given, I = moment of inertia of the bar magnet

m = mass of bar magnet

l = length of magnet about an any passing through its centre and perpendicular to its length

M = magnetic moment of the magnet

B = uniform magnetic field in which magnet is oscillating, we get time period of oscillation is,

$$T = 2\pi\sqrt{\frac{I}{MB}}$$

Here, $\quad I = \frac{ml^2}{12}.$

When magnet is cut into two equal pieces, perpendicular to length, then moment of inertia of each piece of magnet about an axis perpendicular to length passing through its centre is

$$I' = \frac{m}{2}\frac{(l/2)^2}{12} = \frac{ml^2}{12} \times \frac{1}{8} = \frac{I}{8}$$

Magnetic dipole moment $\quad M' = M/2$

Its time period of oscillation is

$$T' = 2\pi\sqrt{\frac{I'}{M'B}} = 2\pi\sqrt{\frac{I/8}{(M/2)B}} = \frac{2\pi}{2}\sqrt{\frac{I}{MB}}$$

$$T' = \frac{T}{2}.$$

Mistake Alert ! Sometimes students incorrectly assume that the pole strenght will be constant even after cutting a bar magnet. Actually, the pole strength becomes half of its original value when a magnet is cut into two equal pieces along its axis.

Q.20 Use (i) the Ampere's law for **H** and (ii) continuity of lines of **B**, to conclude that inside a bar magnet, (a) lines of **H** run from the *N*-pole to *S*- pole, while (b) lines of **B** must run from the *S*-pole to *N*-pole.

Ans. Consider a magnetic field line of **B** through the bar magnet as given in the figure below.

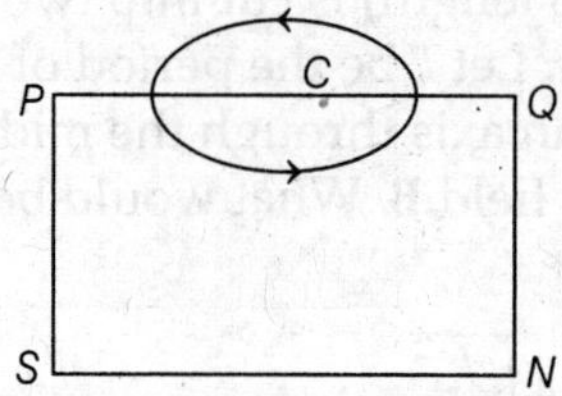

The magnetic field line of *B* through the bar magnet must be a closed loop.

Let *C* be the amperian loop. Then,

$$\int_Q^P \mathbf{H}\cdot dl = \int_Q^P \frac{\mathbf{B}}{\mu_0}\cdot dl$$

We know that the angle between **B** and *dl* is less than 90° inside the bar magnet. So, it is positive.

i.e., $$\int_Q^P \mathbf{H}\cdot dl = \int_Q^P \frac{\mathbf{B}}{\mu_0}\cdot dl > 0$$

Hence, the lines of **B** must run from south pole(*S*) to north pole (*N*) inside the bar magnet.

According to Ampere's law,

$\therefore$ $$\oint_{PQP} \mathbf{H}\cdot dl = 0$$

$\therefore$ $$\oint_{PQP} \mathbf{H}\cdot dl = \int_P^Q \mathbf{H}\cdot dl + \int_Q^P \mathbf{H}\cdot dl = 0$$

As $$\int_Q^P \mathbf{H}\cdot dl > 0, \text{ so, } \int_P^Q \mathbf{H}\cdot dl < 0$$ (*i.e.*, negative)

It will be so if angle between **H** and *dl* is more than 90°, so that $\cos\theta$ is negative.

It means the line of **H** must run from *N*-pole to *S*-pole inside the bar magnet.

Long Answer Type Questions

Q.21 Verify the Ampere's law for magnetic field of a point dipole of dipole moment $\mathbf{M} = M\hat{\mathbf{k}}$. Take C as the closed curve running clockwise along

(i) the z-axis from $z = a > 0$ to $z = R$,

(ii) along the quarter circle of radius R and centre at the origin in the first quadrant of xz-plane,

(iii) along the x-axis from $x = R$ to $x = a$, and

(iv) along the quarter circle of radius a and centre at the origin in the first quadrant of xz-plane

Ans. Let us consider the figure below

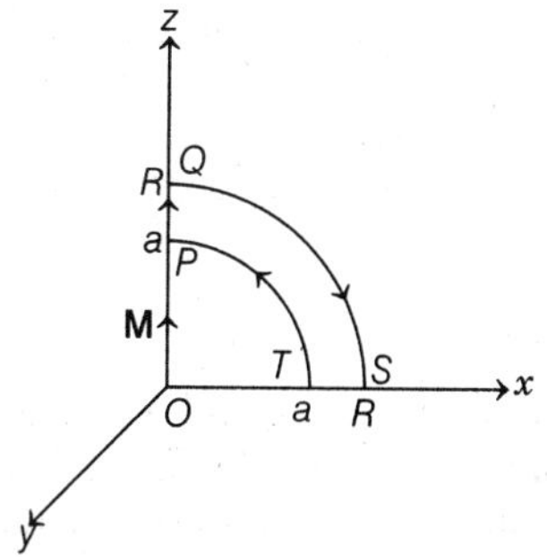

From P to Q, every point on the z-axis lies at the axial line of magnetic dipole of moment M. Magnetic field induction at a point distance z from the magnetic dipole of moment is

$$|\mathbf{B}| = \frac{\mu_0}{4\pi}\frac{2|\mathbf{M}|}{z^3} = \frac{\mu_0 M}{2\pi z^3}$$

(i) Along z-axis from P to Q.

$$\int_P^Q \mathbf{B}\cdot d\mathbf{l} = \int_P^Q \mathbf{B}\cdot d\mathbf{l}\cos 0^\circ = \int_a^R \mathbf{B}\, dz$$

$$= \int_a^R \frac{\mu_0}{2\pi}\frac{M}{z^3}dz = \frac{\mu_0 M}{2\pi}\left(\frac{-1}{2}\right)\left(\frac{1}{R^2} - \frac{1}{a^2}\right)$$

$$= \frac{\mu_0 M}{4\pi}\left(\frac{1}{a^2} - \frac{1}{R^2}\right)$$

(ii) Along the quarter circle QS of radius R as given in the figure below.

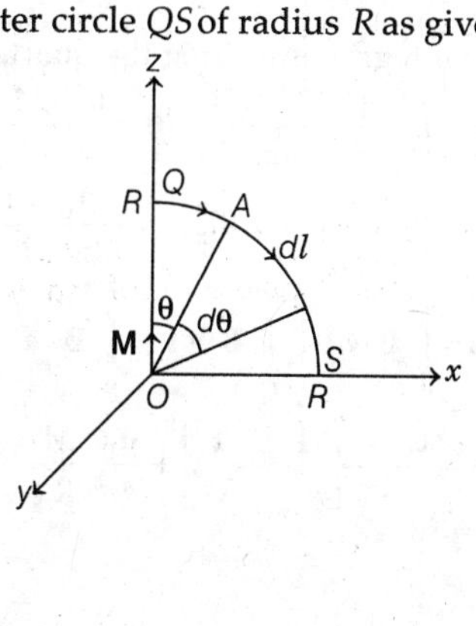

The point A lies on the equatorial line of the magnetic dipole of moment $M\sin\theta$. Magnetic field at point A on the circular arc is

$$B = \frac{\mu_0}{4\pi}\frac{M\sin\theta}{R^3};\ dl = Rd\theta$$

$$\therefore \quad \int \mathbf{B}\cdot d\mathbf{l} = \int \mathbf{B}\cdot d\mathbf{l}\cos\theta = \int_0^{\frac{\pi}{2}} \frac{\mu_0}{4\pi}\frac{M\sin\theta}{R^3} Rd\theta$$

$$\text{Circular arc} = \frac{\mu_0}{4\pi}\frac{M}{R^2}(-\cos\theta)_0^{\pi/2} = \frac{\mu_0}{4\pi}\frac{M}{R^2}$$

(iii) Along x-axis over the path ST, consider the figure given ahead

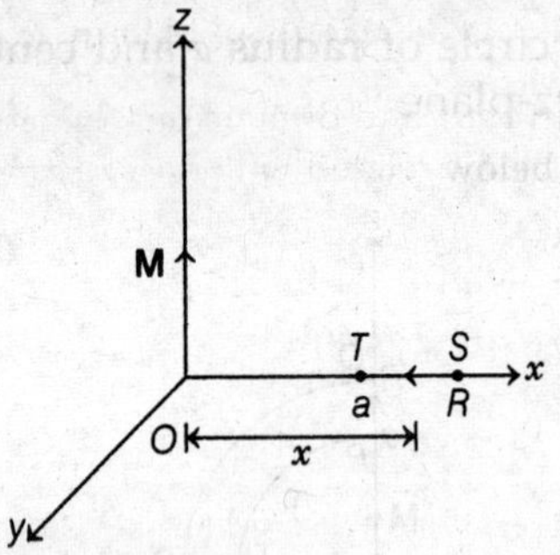

From figure, every point lies on the equatorial line of magnetic dipole. Magnetic field induction at a point distance x from the dipole is

$$B = \frac{\mu_0}{4\pi}\frac{M}{x^3}$$

$$\therefore \quad \int_S^T \mathbf{B}\cdot d\mathbf{l} = \int_R^a -\frac{\mu_0 \mathbf{M}}{4\pi x^3}\cdot d\mathbf{l} = 0 \qquad [\because \text{angle between } (-\mathbf{M}) \text{ and } d\mathbf{l} \text{ is } 90^\circ]$$

(iv) Along the quarter circle TP of radius a. Consider the figure given below

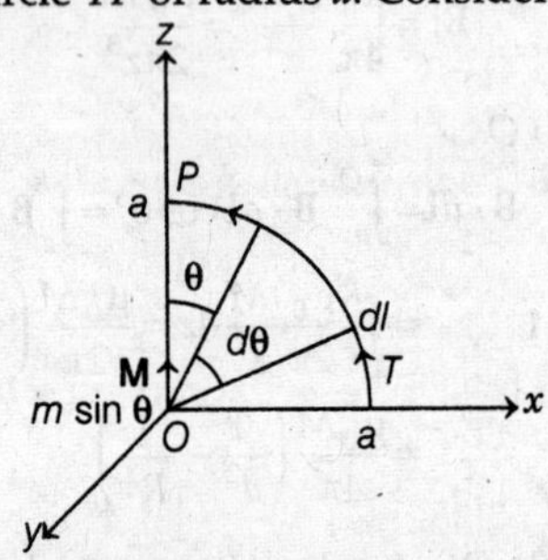

From case (ii), we get line integral of $\mathbf{B}$ along the quarter circle TP of radius a as

$$\int \mathbf{B}.d\mathbf{l} = \int_{\pi/2}^{0} \frac{\mu_0}{4\pi}\frac{\mathbf{M}\sin\theta}{a^3} ad\theta = \frac{\mu_0}{4\pi}\frac{M}{a^2}\int_{\pi/2}^{0} \sin\theta\, d\theta$$

$$= \frac{\mu_0}{4\pi}\frac{M}{a^2}[-\cos\theta]_{\pi/2}^{0} = \frac{-\mu_0}{4\pi}\frac{M}{a^2}$$

$$\therefore \quad \oint_{PQST} \mathbf{B}\cdot d\mathbf{l} = \int_P^Q \mathbf{B}\cdot d\mathbf{l} + \int_Q^S \mathbf{B}\cdot d\mathbf{l} + \int_S^T \mathbf{B}\cdot d\mathbf{l} + \int_T^P \mathbf{B}\cdot d\mathbf{l}$$

$$= \frac{\mu_0 M}{4}\left[\frac{1}{a^2} - \frac{1}{R^2}\right] + \frac{\mu_0}{4\pi}\frac{M}{R^2} + 0 + \left(-\frac{\mu_0}{4\pi}\frac{M}{a^2}\right) = 0$$

Q.22 What are the dimensions of χ, the magnetic susceptibility? Consider an H-atom. Guess an expression for χ, upto a constant by constructing a quantity of dimensions of χ, out of parameters of the atom e, m, v, R and μ_0. Here, m is the electronic mass, v is electronic velocity, R is Bohr radius. Estimate the number so obtained and compare with the value of $|\chi| \sim 10^{-5}$ for many solid materials.

Thinking Process Magnetic susceptibility is a measure of how a magnetic material responds to an external field. *i.e.*, magnetic susceptibility

$$\chi_m = \frac{I}{H} = \frac{\text{(Intensity of magnetisation)}}{\text{(Magnetic Induction)}}$$

Ans. As I and H both have same units and dimensions, hence, χ has no dimensions. Here, in this question, χ is to be related with e, m, v, R and μ_0. We know that dimensions of $\mu_0 = [\text{MLQ}^{-2}]$

From Biot-Savart's law,

$$dB = \frac{\mu_0}{4\pi} \frac{I dl \sin\theta}{r^2}$$

$$\Rightarrow \quad \mu_0 = \frac{4\pi r^2 dB}{I dl \sin\theta} = \frac{4\pi r^2}{I dl \sin\theta} \times \frac{F}{qv \sin\theta} \qquad \left[\because dB = \frac{F}{qv\sin\theta}\right]$$

$$\therefore \quad \text{Dimensions of } \mu_0 = \frac{\text{L}^2 \times (\text{MLT}^{-2})}{(\text{QT}^{-1})(\text{L}) \times 1 \times (\text{Q})(\text{LT}^{-1}) \times (1)} = [\text{MLQ}^{-2}]$$

where Q is the dimension of charge.

As χ is dimensionless, it should have no involvement of charge Q in its dimensional formula. It will be so if μ_0 and e together should have the value $\mu_0 e^2$, as e has the dimensions of charge.

Let $$\chi = \mu_0 e^2 m^a v^b R^c \quad \text{...(i)}$$

where a, b, c are the power of m, v and R respectively, such that relation (i) is satisfied.

Dimensional equation of (i) is

$$[\text{M}^0\text{L}^0\text{T}^0\text{Q}^0] = [\text{MLQ}^{-2}] \times [\text{Q}^2][\text{M}^a] \times (\text{LT}^{-1})^b \times [\text{L}]^c$$
$$= [\text{M}^{1+a} + \text{L}^{1+b+c}\text{T}^{-b}\text{Q}^0]$$

Equating the powers of M, L and T, we get

$$0 = 1 + a \Rightarrow a = -1, \; 0 = 1 + b + c \quad \text{...(ii)}$$
$$0 = -b \Rightarrow b = 0, \; 0 = 1 + 0 + c \text{ or } c = -1$$

Putting values in Eq. (i), we get

$$\chi = \mu_0 e^2 m^{-1} v^2 R^{-1} = \frac{\mu_0 e^2}{mR} \quad \text{...(iii)}$$

Here,
$$\mu_0 = 4\pi \times 10^{-7} \text{Tm A}^{-1}$$
$$e = 1.6 \times 10^{-19} \text{ C}$$
$$m = 9.1 \times 10^{-31} \text{ kg}, \; R = 10^{-10} \text{m}$$
$$\chi = \frac{(4\pi \times 10^{-7}) \times (1.6 \times 10^{-19})^2}{(9.1 \times 10^{-31}) \times 10^{-10}} \approx 10^{-4}$$

$$\therefore \quad \frac{\chi}{\chi_{\text{(given solid)}}} = \frac{10^{-4}}{10^{-5}} = 10$$

Mistake Alert! *When solving dimensional equations, its essential to remember the fundamental dimensions of physical quantities. If the basic dimensions of charge mass, length and speed are not correctly applied the derived dimensional formula may be inconsistent or incorrect.*

Q.23 Assume the dipole model for the earth's magnetic field B which is given by B_V = vertical component of magnetic field $= \frac{\mu_0}{4\pi}\frac{2m\cos\theta}{r^3}$

B_H = horizontal component of magnetic field $= \frac{\mu_0}{4\pi}\frac{m\sin\theta}{r^3}$

$\theta = 90°$ – lattitude as measured from magnetic equator.

Find loci of points for which (a) $|B|$ is minimum (b) dip angle is zero and (c) dip angle is 45°.

Ans. (a)

$$B_V = \frac{\mu_0}{4\pi}\frac{2m\cos\theta}{r^3} \quad \text{...(i)}$$

$$B_H = \frac{\mu_0}{4\pi}\frac{m\sin\theta}{r^3} \quad \text{...(ii)}$$

Squaring both the equations and adding, we get

$$B_V^2 + B_H^2 = \left(\frac{\mu_0}{4\pi}\right)^2 \frac{m^2}{r^6}[4\cos^2\theta + \sin^2\theta]$$

$$B = \sqrt{B_V^2 + B_H^2} = \frac{\mu_0}{4\pi}\frac{m}{r^3}[3\cos^2\theta + 1]^{1/2} \quad \text{...(iii)}$$

From Eq. (iii), the value of B is minimum, if $\theta = \frac{\pi}{2}$

$\theta = \frac{\pi}{2}$. Thus, the magnetic equator is the locus.

(b) Angle of dip,

$$\tan\delta = \frac{B_V}{B_H} = \frac{\frac{\mu_0}{4\pi}\cdot\frac{2m\cos\theta}{r^3}}{\frac{\mu_0}{4\pi}\cdot\frac{\sin\theta\cdot m}{r^3}} = 2\cot\theta \quad \text{...(iv)}$$

$$\tan\delta = 2\cot\theta$$

For dip angle is zero *i.e.*, $\delta = 0$

$$\cot\theta = 0$$

$$\theta = \frac{\pi}{2}$$

It means that locus is again the magnetic equator.

(c) $\tan\delta = \frac{B_V}{B_H}$

Angle of dip *i.e.*, $\delta = \pm 45$

$$\frac{B_V}{B_H} = \tan(\pm 45°)$$

$$\frac{B_V}{B_H} = 1$$

$$2\cot\theta = 1 \quad \text{[From Eq. (iv)]}$$

$$\cot\theta = \frac{1}{2}$$

$$\tan\theta = 2$$

$$\Rightarrow \quad \theta = \tan^{-1}(2)$$

Thus, $\theta = \tan^{-1}(2)$ is the locus.

Q.24 Consider the plane S formed by the dipole axis and the axis of earth. Let P be point on the magnetic equator and in S. Let Q be the point of intersection of the geographical and magnetic equators. Obtain the declination and dip angles at P and Q.

Ans. P is in the plane S, needle is in north, so the declination is zero.

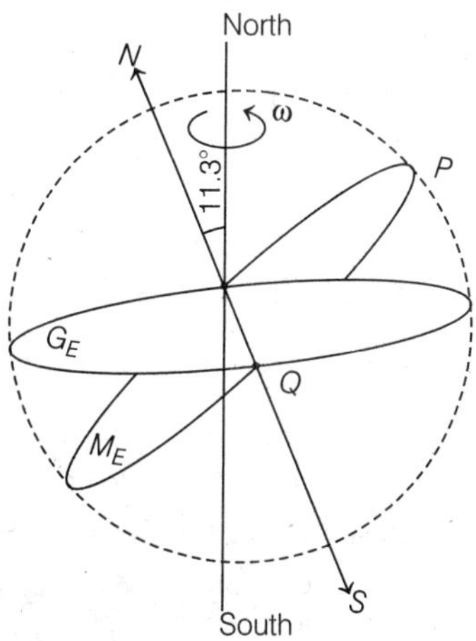

P is also on the magnetic equator, so the angle of dip = 0, because the value of angle of dip at equator is zero. Q is also on the magnetic equator, thus the angle of dip is zero. As earth tilted on its axis by 11.3°, thus the declination at Q is 11.3°.

Q.25 There are two current carrying planar coil made each from identical wires of length L. C_1 is circular (radius R) and C_2 is square (side a). They are so constructed that they have same frequency of oscillation when they are placed in the same uniform **B** and carry the same current. Find a in terms of R.

Ans. C_1 = circular coil of radius R, length L, number of turns per unit length

$$n_1 = \frac{L}{2\pi R}$$

C_2 = square of side a and perimeter L, number of turns per unit length $n_2 = \frac{L}{4a}$

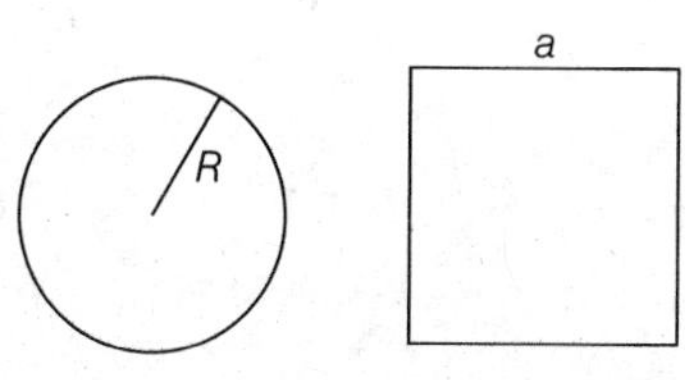

Magnetic moment of C_1

$\Rightarrow \quad m_1 = n_1 I A_1$

Magnetic moment of C_2

$\Rightarrow \quad m_2 = n_2 I A_2$

$$m_1 = \frac{L \cdot I \cdot \pi R^2}{2\pi R}$$

$$m_2 = \frac{L}{4a} \cdot I \cdot a^2$$

$$m_1 = \frac{LIR}{2} \quad \text{...(i)}$$

$$m_2 = \frac{LIa}{4} \quad \text{...(ii)}$$

Moment of inertia of $C_1 \Rightarrow I_1 = \frac{MR^2}{2}$ ...(iii)

Moment of inertia of $C_2 \Rightarrow I_2 = \frac{Ma^2}{12}$ ...(iv)

Frequency of $C_1 \Rightarrow f_1 = \frac{1}{2\pi}\sqrt{\frac{m_1 B}{I_1}}$

Frequency of $C_2 \Rightarrow f_2 = \frac{1}{2\pi}\sqrt{\frac{m_2 B}{I_2}}$

According to question, $f_1 = f_2$

$$\frac{1}{2\pi}\sqrt{\frac{m_1 B}{I_1}} = \frac{1}{2\pi}\sqrt{\frac{m_2 B}{I_2}}$$

$$\frac{m_1}{I_1} = \frac{m_2}{I_2} \text{ or } \frac{m_2}{m_1} = \frac{I_2}{I_1}$$

Plugging the values by Eqs. (i), (ii), (iii) and (iv)

$$\frac{LIa \cdot 2}{4 \times LIR} = \frac{Ma^2 \cdot 2}{12 \cdot MR^2}$$

$$\frac{a}{2R} = \frac{a^2}{6R^2}$$

$$3R = a$$

Thus, the value of a is $3R$.

Chapter

06

Electromagnetic Induction

Multiple Choice Questions (MCQs)

Q.1 A square of side L metres lies in the x-y plane in a region, where the magnetic field is given by $\mathbf{B} = B_0(2\hat{\mathbf{i}} + 3\hat{\mathbf{j}} + 4\hat{\mathbf{k}})$ T, where B_0 is constant. The magnitude of flux passing through the square is

(a) $2B_0L^2$ Wb (b) $3B_0L^2$ Wb (c) $4B_0L^2$ Wb (d) $\sqrt{29}B_0L^2$ Wb

Thinking Process The magnetic flux linked with uniform surface of area A in uniform magnetic field is given by

$$\phi = \mathbf{B}\cdot\mathbf{A}$$

Ans. ***(c)*** Here, $A = L^2\hat{\mathbf{k}}$ and $\mathbf{B} = B_0(2\hat{\mathbf{i}} + 3\hat{\mathbf{j}} + 4\hat{\mathbf{k}})$ T

$$\phi = \mathbf{B}.\mathbf{A} = B_0(2\hat{\mathbf{i}} + 3\hat{\mathbf{j}} + 4\hat{\mathbf{k}}).L^2\hat{\mathbf{k}} = 4B_0L^2 \text{ Wb}$$

Q.2 A loop, made of straight edges has six corners at A (0, 0, 0), B (L, 0, 0), C (L, L, 0), D (0, L, 0), E (0, L, L) and F (0, 0, L). A magnetic field $\mathbf{B} = B_0(\hat{\mathbf{i}} + \hat{\mathbf{k}})$ T is present in the region. The flux passing through the loop $ABCDEFA$ (in that order) is

(a) B_0L^2 Wb (b) $2B_0L^2$ Wb (c) $\sqrt{2}B_0L^2$ Wb (d) $4B_0L^2$ Wb

Thinking Process Here, loop $ABCDA$ lies in x-y plane whose area vector $\mathbf{A}_1 = L^2\hat{\mathbf{k}}$ whereas loop $ADEFA$ lies in y-z plane whose area vector $\mathbf{A}_2 = L^2\hat{\mathbf{i}}$.

Ans. ***(b)*** Also, the magnetic flux linked with uniform surface of area A in uniform magnetic field is given by

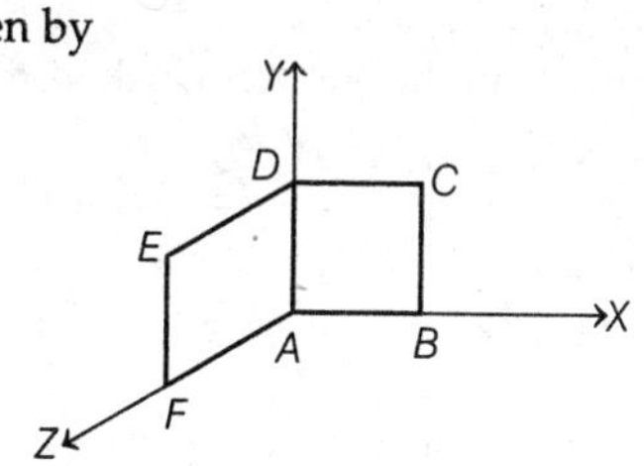

$$\phi = \mathbf{B}\cdot\mathbf{A}$$

$$\mathbf{A} = \mathbf{A}_1 + \mathbf{A}_2 = (L^2\hat{\mathbf{k}} + L^2\hat{\mathbf{i}})$$

and $\mathbf{B} = B_0(\hat{\mathbf{i}} + \hat{\mathbf{k}})T$

Now, $\phi = \mathbf{B}\cdot\mathbf{A} = B_0(\hat{\mathbf{i}} + \hat{\mathbf{k}})\cdot(L^2\hat{\mathbf{k}} + L^2\hat{\mathbf{i}})$

$= 2B_0L^2$ Wb

Q.3 A cylindrical bar magnet is rotated about its axis as shown in figure. A wire is connected from the axis and is made to touch the cylindrical surface through a contact. Then,

(a) a direct current flows in the ammeter A
(b) no current flows through the ammeter A
(c) an alternating sinusoidal current flows through the ammeter A with a time period $T = \frac{2\pi}{\omega}$
(d) a time varying non-sinusoidal current flows through the ammeter A

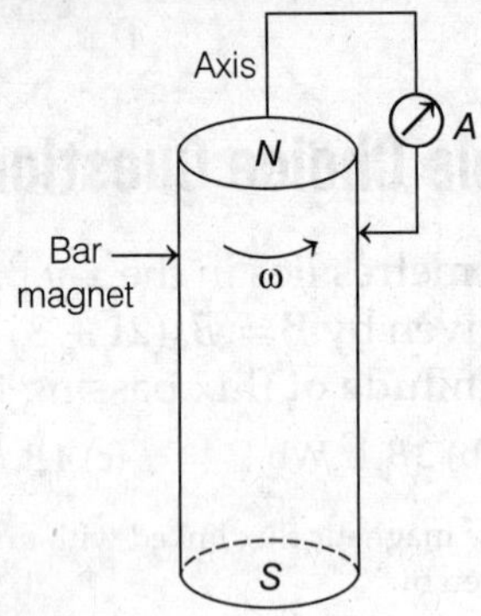

Thinking Process The problem is associated with the phenomenon of electromagnetic induction.

Ans. ***(b)*** When cylindrical bar magnet is rotated about its axis, no change in flux linked with the circuit takes place, consequently no emf is induced and hence, no current flows through the ammeter A.

Q.4 There are two coils A and B as shown in figure. A current starts flowing in B as shown, when A is moved towards B and stops when A stops moving. The current in B is counter clockwise. B is kept stationary when A moves. We can infer that

(a) there is a constant current in the clockwise direction in A.
(b) there is a varying current in A.
(c) there is no current in A.
(d) there is a constant current in the counter clockwise direction in A.

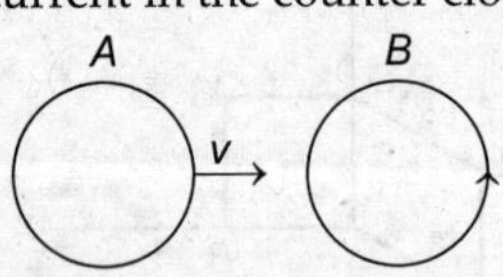

Thinking Process The induced emf in B is due to the variation of magnetic flux in it.

Ans. ***(d)*** When A stops moving, the current in B become zero, it is possible only if the current in A is constant. If the current in A would be variable, there must be an induced emf (current) in B even if the A stops moving.

Q.5 Same as problem 4 except the coil A is made to rotate about a vertical axis (figure). No current flows in B if A is at rest. The current in coil A,when the current in B (at $t = 0$) is counter-clockwise and the coil A is as shown at this instant, $t = 0$, is

(a) constant current clockwise
(b) varying current clockwise
(c) varying current counter clockwise
(d) constant current counter clockwise

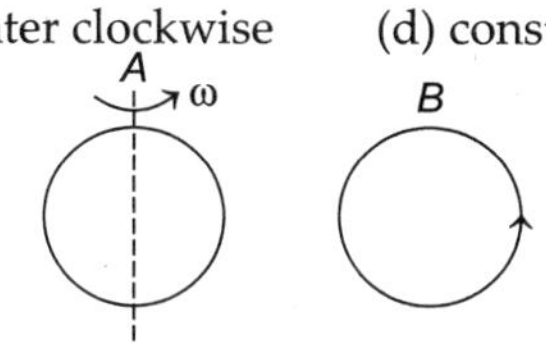

Thinking Process As per Lenz's law, the direction of induced current in the coil is such as to oppose the cause that produces it.

Ans. ***(a)*** The counterclockwise flow of the current in B is equivalent to north pole of magnet and magnetic field lines are emanating upward to coil A. When coil A start rotating at $t = 0$, the current in A is constant along clockwise direction by Lenz's rule.

Q.6 The self inductance L of a solenoid of length l and area of cross-section A, with a fixed number of turns N increases as

(a) l and A increase
(b) l decreases and A increases
(c) l increases and A decreases
(d) both l and A decrease

Thinking Process The self inductance L of a solenoid depends on its geometry (*i.e.*, length, cross-sectional area, number of turns etc.) and on the permeability of the medium.

Ans. ***(b)*** The self-inductance of a long solenoid of cross-sectional area A, length l, and number of turns N, filled with a material of relative permeability (*e.g.*, soft iron, which has a high value of relative permeability) is given by

$$L = \frac{\mu_r \mu_0 N^2 A}{l}$$

So, the self inductance (L) increases as l decreases and A increases.

Note The capacitance, resistance, self and mutual inductance depends on the geometry of the devices as well as permittivity/permeability of the medium.

Multiple Choice Questions (More Than One Options)

Q.7 A metal plate is getting heated. It can be because

(a) a direct current is passing through the plate
(b) it is placed in a time varying magnetic field
(c) it is placed in a space varying magnetic field, but does not vary with time
(d) a current (either direct or alternating) is passing through the plate

Thinking Process This problem is associated with the heating effect of current as well as the phenomenon of electromagnetic induction and eddy currents.

Ans. ***(a, b, d)*** A metal plate gets heated when a DC or AC current is passed through the plate, because of heating effect of current. Also, when metal plate is subjected to time varying magnetic field, the magnetic flux linked with the plate changes and eddy currents comes into existence which make the plate hot.

Q.8 An emf is produced in a coil, which is not connected to an external voltage source. This can be due to

(a) the coil being in a time varying magnetic field
(b) the coil moving in a time varying magnetic field
(c) the coil moving in a constant magnetic field
(d) the coil is stationary in external spatially varying magnetic field, which does not change with time

Thinking Process This problem is associated with the phenomenon of electromagnetic induction.

Ans. *(a, b, c)* Magnetic flux linked with an isolated coil changes when the coil is in a time varying magnetic field, moves through a constant magnetic field or moves through a time varying magnetic field.

Note When magnetic flux linked with the coil change, an emf is induced in the coil. This is known as electromagnetic induction.

Q.9 The mutual inductance M_{12} of coil 1 with respect to coil 2

(a) increases when they are brought nearer
(b) depends on the current passing through the coils
(c) increases when one of them is rotated about an axis
(d) is same as M_{21} of coil 2 with respect to coil 1

Thinking Process Here, it is important to know that the mutual inductance of a pair of coils, solenoids, etc., depends on their separation, their relative orientation as well as the geometry of pair of coils, solenoids, etc.

Ans. *(a, d)* The mutual inductance M_{12} of coil increases when they are brought nearer and is the same as M_{21} of coil 2 with respect to coil 1.

M_{12} *i.e.*, mutual inductance of solenoid S_1 with respect to solenoid S_2 is given by

$$M_{12} = \mu_0 n_1 n_2 \pi r_1^2 l$$

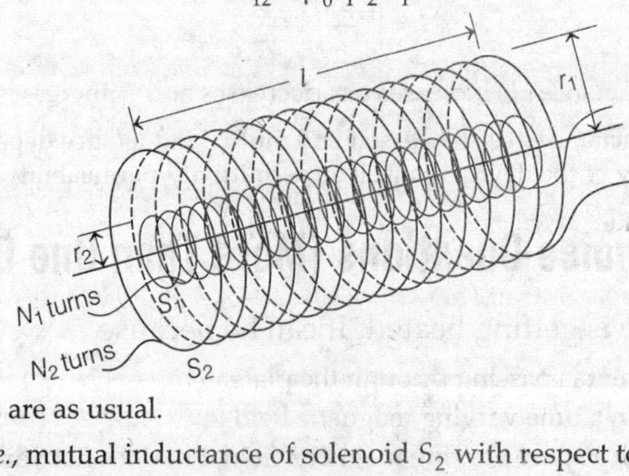

where signs are as usual.

Also, M_{12} *i.e.*, mutual inductance of solenoid S_2 with respect to solenoid S_1 is given by

$$M_{21} = \mu_0 n_1 n_2 \pi r_1^2 l$$

So, we have $\qquad M_{12} = M_{21} = M$

Mistake Alert! *Sometimes students think that mutual inductance depends on the current which is incorrect. The mutual inductance depends on geometrical parameters and not on the current or magnetic field.*

Q.10 A circular coil expands radially in a region of magnetic field and no electromotive force is produced in the coil. This can be because

(a) the magnetic field is constant

(b) the magnetic field is in the same plane as the circular coil and it may or may not vary

(c) the magnetic field has a perpendicular (to the plane of the coil) component whose magnitude is decreasing suitably

(d) there is a constant magnetic field in the perpendicular (to the plane of the coil) direction

Thinking Process The various arrangement are to be thought of in such a way that the magnetic flux linked with the coil do not change even if coil is placed and expanding in magnetic field.

Ans. *(b, c)* When circular coil expands radially in a region of magnetic field such that the magnetic field is in the same plane as the circular coil or the magnetic field has a perpendicular (to the plane of the coil) component whose magnitude is decreasing suitably in such a way that the dot product of magnetic field and surface area of plane of coil remains constant at every instant, then induced emf $= \frac{-d\phi}{dt}$ is zero.

Very Short Answer Type Questions

Q.11 Consider a magnet surrounded by a wire with an on/off switch S (figure). If the switch is thrown from the off position (open circuit) to the on position (closed circuit), will a current flow in the circuit? Explain.

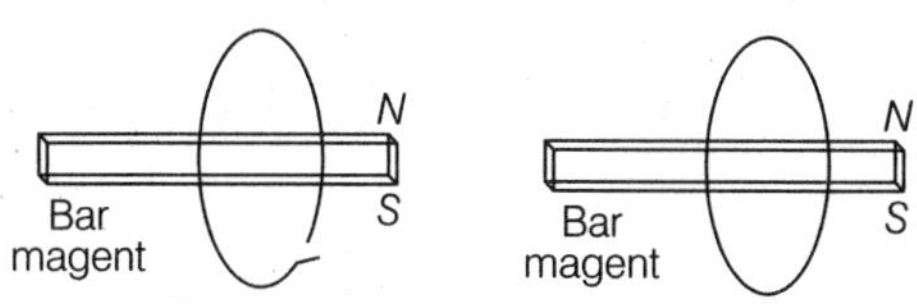

Thinking Process The magnetic flux linked with uniform surface of area A in uniform magnetic field is given by

$$\phi = \mathbf{B} \cdot \mathbf{A} = BA\cos\theta$$

So, flux linked will change only when either B, or A or the angle between $\mathbf{B}$ and $\mathbf{A}$ change.

Ans. When the switch is thrown from the off position (open circuit) to the on position (closed circuit), then neither B, nor A nor the angle between B and A change. Thus, no change in magnetic flux linked with coil occur, hence no electromotive force is produced and consequently no current will flow in the circuit.

Q.12 A wire in the form of a tightly wound solenoid is connected to a DC source, and carries a current. If the coil is stretched so that there are gaps between successive elements of the spiral coil, will the current increase or decrease? Explain.

Thinking Process Here, the application of Lenz's law is tested through this problem.

Ans. When the coil is stretched so that there are gaps between successive elements of the spiral coil *i.e.*, the wires are pulled apart which lead to the flux leak through the gaps. According to Lenz's law, the emf produced must oppose this decrease, which can be done by an increase in current. So, the current will increase.

Mistake Alert! *Students sometimes think that, the flux does not change after stretching the coil which is incorrect. The flux passing through a coil decreases after stretching it.*

Q.13 A solenoid is connected to a battery so that a steady current flows through it. If an iron core is inserted into the solenoid, will the current increase or decrease? Explain.

Ans. When the iron core is inserted in the current carrying solenoid, the magnetic field increase due to the magnetisation of iron core and consequently the flux increases.

According to Lenz's law, the emf produced must oppose this increase in flux, which can be done by decrease in current. So, the current will decrease.

Q.14 Consider a metal ring kept on top of a fixed solenoid (say on a cardboard) (as shown in figure). The centre of the ring coincides with the axis of the solenoid. If the current is suddenly switched on, the metal ring jumps up. Explain.

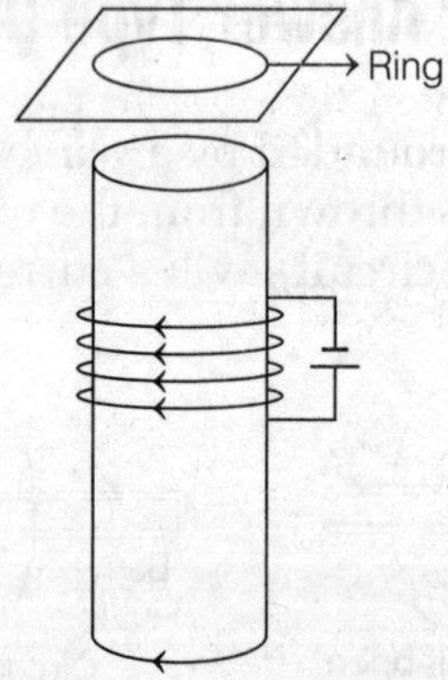

Ans. When the current is switched on, magnetic flux is linked through the ring. Thus, increase in flux takes place. According to Lenz's law, this increase in flux will be opposed and it can happen if the ring moves away from the solenoid.

This happens because the flux increase will cause a counter clockwise current (as seen from the top in the ring in figure.) *i.e.*, opposite direction to that in the solenoid. This makes the same sense of flow of current in the ring (when viewed from the bottom of the ring) and solenoid forming same magnetic pole infront of each other. Hence, they will repel each other and the ring will move upward.

Q.15 Consider a metal ring kept (supported by a cardboard) on top of a fixed solenoid carrying a current I (see figure of Question 14). The centre of the ring coincides with the axis of the solenoid. If the current in the solenoid is switched off, what will happen to the ring?

Ans. *(b)* When the current is switched off, magnetic flux linked through the ring decreases. According to Lenz's law, this decrease in flux will be opposed and the ring experience downward force towards the solenoid.

This happen because the flux decrease will cause a clockwise current (as seen from the top in the ring in figure) *i.e.*, the same direction to that in the solenoid. This makes the opposite sense of flow of current in the ring (when viewed from the bottom of the ring) and solenoid forming opposite magnetic pole infront of each other.

Hence, they will attract each other but as ring is placed at the cardboard it might not be able to move downward.

Q.16 Consider a metallic pipe with an inner radius of 1 cm. If a cylindrical bar magnet of radius 0.8 cm is dropped through the pipe, it takes more time to come down than it takes for a similar unmagnetised cylindrical iron bar dropped through the metallic pipe. Explain.

Thinking Process This problem is based on the concept of eddy current and application of Lenz's law.

Ans. When cylindrical bar magnet of radius 0.8 cm is dropped through the metallic pipe with an inner radius of 1 cm, flux linked with the cylinder changes and consequently eddy currents are produced in the metallic pipe. According to Lenz's law, these currents will oppose the (cause) motion of the magnet.

Therefore, magnet's downward acceleration will be less than the acceleration due to gravity g. On the other hand, an unmagnetised iron bar will not produce eddy currents and will fall with an acceleration due to gravity g.

Thus, the magnet will take more time to come down than it takes for a similar unmagnetised cylindrical iron bar dropped through the metallic pipe.

Short Answer Type Questions

Q.17 A magnetic field in a certain region is given by $\mathbf{B} = B_0 \cos(\omega t)\,\hat{\mathbf{k}}$ and a coil of radius a with resistance R is placed in the x–y plane with its centre at the origin in the magnetic field as shown in figure. Find the magnitude and the direction of the current at $(a, 0, 0)$ at

$$t = \frac{\pi}{2\omega}, \; t = \frac{\pi}{\omega} \text{ and } t = \frac{3\pi}{2\omega}$$

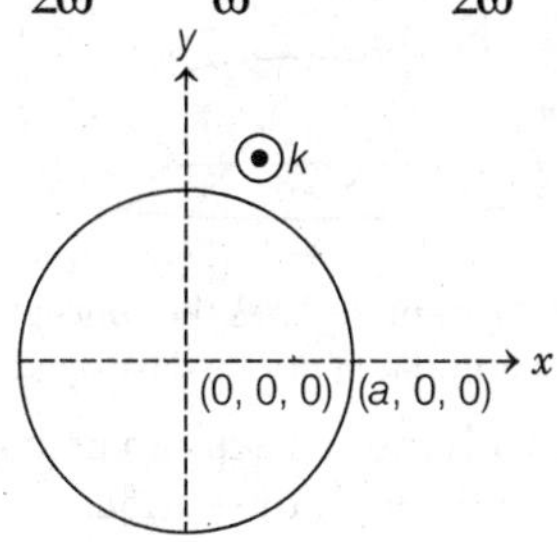

Thinking Process This problem requires application of Faraday's law of EMI and finding mathematical values of emf at different instants.

Ans. At any instant, flux passes through the ring is given by

$$\phi = \mathbf{B} \cdot \mathbf{A} = BA\cos\theta = BA \qquad (\because \theta = 0)$$

or

$$\phi = B_0(\pi a^2)\cos\omega t$$

By Faraday's law of electromagnetic induction,

Magnitude of induced emf is given by

$$\varepsilon = B_0(\pi a^2)\,\omega \sin \omega t$$

This causes flow of induced current, which is given by

$$I = B_0(\pi a^2)\,\omega \sin \omega t / R$$

Now, finding the value of current at different instants, so we have current at

$$t = \frac{\pi}{2\omega}$$

$$I = \frac{B_0(\pi a^2)\omega}{R} \text{ along } \hat{\mathbf{j}}$$

Because, $\sin \omega t = \sin\left(\omega \dfrac{\pi}{2\omega}\right) = \sin \dfrac{\pi}{2} = 1$

At $t = \dfrac{\pi}{\omega}, I = 0$

Because $\sin \omega t = \sin\left(\omega \dfrac{\pi}{\omega}\right) = \sin \pi = 0$

At $t = \dfrac{3\pi}{2\omega}$

$$I = \frac{B(\pi a^2)\omega}{R} \text{ along } -\hat{\mathbf{j}}$$

Because, $\sin \omega t = \sin\left(\omega \dfrac{3\pi}{2\omega}\right) = \sin \dfrac{3\pi}{2} = -1$

Q.18 Consider a closed loop *C* in a magnetic field as shown in figure. The flux passing through the loop is defined by choosing a surface whose edge coincides with the loop and using the formula $\phi = \mathbf{B}_1\, d\mathbf{A}_1$, $\mathbf{B}_2\, d\mathbf{A}_2$ ..... . Now, if we choose two different surfaces S_1 and S_2 having *C* as their edge, would we get the same answer for flux. Justify your answer.

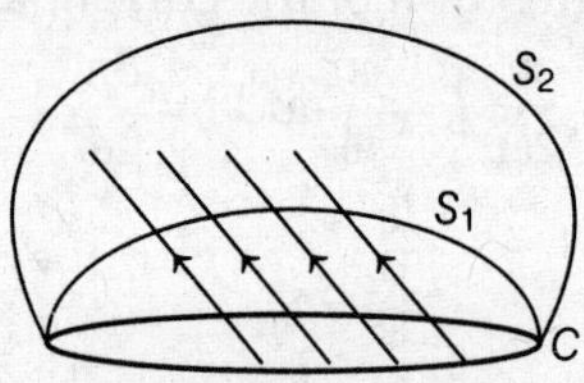

Thinking Process This problem underlines the concept of continuity of magnetic field lines. They can neither be originated nor be destroyed in space.

Ans. The magnetic flux linked with the surface can be considered as the number of magnetic field lines passing through the surface.

By the concept of continuity of lines ***B*** cannot end or start in space, therefore the number of lines passing through surface S_1 must be the same as the number of lines passing through the surface S_2. Therefore, in both the cases we gets the same answer for flux.

Q.19 Find the current in the wire for the configuration shown in figure. Wire PQ has negligible resistance. B, the magnetic field is coming out of the paper. θ is a fixed angle made by PQ travelling smoothly over two conducting parallel wires separated by a distance d.

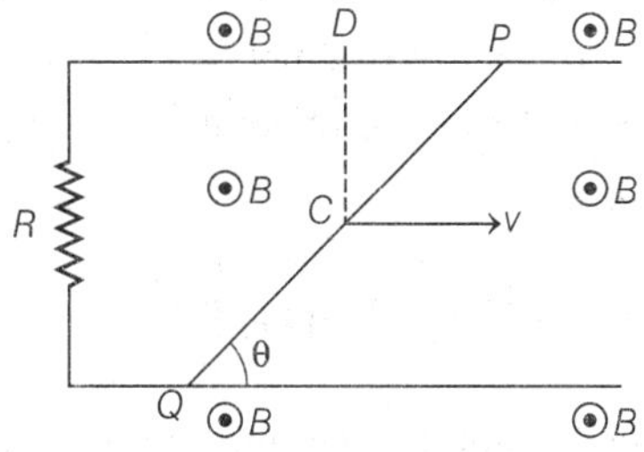

Thinking Process An emf is induced across PQ due to its motion because of change in magnetic flux linked with the loop due to change of enclosed area.

Ans. The motional electric field E along the dotted line CD ($\perp$ to both $\mathbf{v}$ and $\mathbf{B}$ and along $\mathbf{v} \times \mathbf{B}$) $= vB$

Therefore, the motional emf along PQ = (length PQ) $\times$ (field along PQ)

$$= (\text{length } PQ) \times (vB\sin\theta)$$

$$= \left(\frac{d}{\sin\theta}\right) \times (vB\sin\theta) = vBd$$

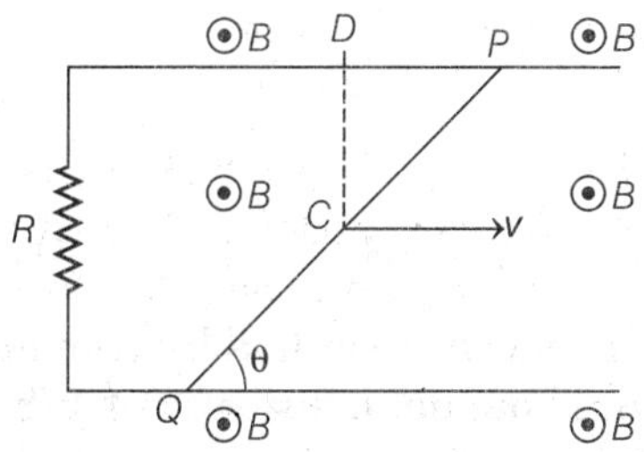

This induced emf make flow of current in closed circuit of resistance R.

$$I = \frac{dvB}{R} \text{ and is independent of } q.$$

Q.20 A (current *versus* time) graph of the current passing through a solenoid is shown in figure. For which time is the back electromotive force (u) a maximum. If the back emf at $t = 3$ s is e, find the back emf at $t = 7$ s, 15s and 40 s. OA, AB and BC are straight line segments.

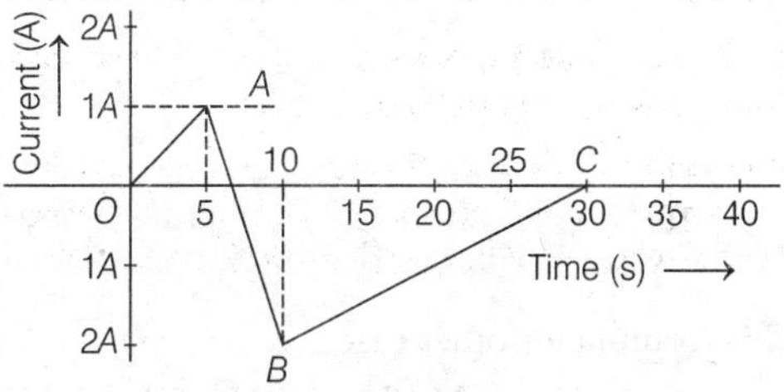

Thinking Process When the current is varied, the flux linked with the coil also changes and an emf is induced in the coil. The induced emf is given by

$$\varepsilon = -\frac{d(N\phi_B)}{dt}$$

$$\varepsilon = -L\frac{dI}{dt}$$

The self-induced emf always opposes any change (increase or decrease) of current in the coil.

Ans. The back electromotive force in solenoid is (u), a maximum when there is maximum rate of change of current. This occurs is in AB part of the graph. So maximum back emf will be obtained between $5\,s < t < 10\,s$.

Since, the back emf at $t = 3\,s$ is e,

Also, the rate of change of current at ($t = 3\,s$) = slope of OA from ($t = 0\,s$) to ($t = 5\,s$) = $1/5$ A/s.

So, we have back emf $\varepsilon = -L\frac{dI}{dt}$

Thus, $e = L1/5 \left(\text{for } t = 3s, \frac{dI}{dt} = 1/5\right)$ (L is a constant). Applying $\varepsilon = -L\frac{dI}{dt}$

Similarly, we have for other values

For $5s < t < 10s$ $\quad u_1 = -L\frac{3}{5} = -\frac{3}{5}L = -3e$

Thus, $\quad$ at $t = 7\,s$, $u_1 = -3\,e$

For $10s < t < 30\,s$

$$u_2 = L\frac{2}{20} = \frac{L}{10} = \frac{1}{2}e$$

For $t > 30\,s$, $u_2 = 0$

Thus, the back emf at $t = 7\,s$, 15 s and 40 s are $-3\,e$, $e/2$ and 0 respectively.

Q.21 There are two coils A and B separated by some distance. If a current of 2A flows through A, a magnetic flux of 10^{-2} Wb passes through B (no current through B). If no current passes through A and a current of 1 A passes through B, what is the flux through A?

Thinking Process A current I_1 is passed through the coil A and the flux linkage with coil B is, $\quad N_2\phi_2 = M_{21}I_1$

where, M_{21} is called the mutual inductance of coil A with respect to coil B and $M_{21} = M_{12}$

And M_{12} is called the mutual inductance of coil B with respect to coil A.

Ans. Applying the mutual inductance of coil A with respect to coil B

$$M_{21} = \frac{N_2\phi_2}{I_1}$$

Therefore, we have

$$\text{Mutual inductance} = \frac{10^{-2}}{2} = 5\,\text{mH}$$

Again applying this formula for other case

$$N_1\phi_1 = M_{12}\,I_2 = 5\,\text{mH} \times 1\,\text{A} = 5\,\text{mWb}.$$

Long Answer Type Questions

Q.22 A magnetic field $\mathbf{B} = B_0 \sin(\omega t)\,\hat{\mathbf{k}}$ covers a large region where a wire AB slides smoothly over two parallel conductors separated by a distance d (figure). The wires are in the x-y plane. The wire AB (of length d) has resistance R and the parallel wires have negligible resistance. If AB is moving with velocity v, what is the current in the circuit. What is the force needed to keep the wire moving at constant velocity?

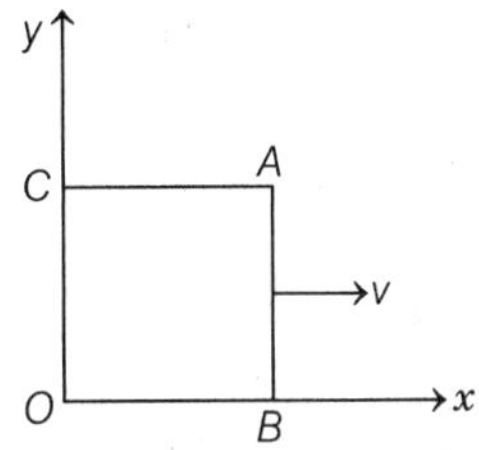

Thinking Process An emf is induced across AB due to its motion because of change in magnetic flux linked with the loop due to change in magnetic field.

Ans. Let us assume that the parallel wires are at $y = 0$ *i.e.*, along x-axis and $y = d$. At $t = 0$, AB has $x = 0$, *i.e.*, along y-axis and moves with a velocity v. Let at time t, wire is at $x(t) = vt$.

Now, the motional emf across AB is

$$= (B_0 \sin \omega t) v d(-\hat{\mathbf{j}})$$

Emf due to change in field (along negative y-axis)

$$= -B_0 \omega \cos \omega t \, x(t)\, d$$

Total emf in the circuit = emf due to change in field (along $OBAC$) + the motional emf across AB

$$= -B_0 d[\omega x \cos(\omega t) + v \sin(\omega t)]$$

Electric current in clockwise direction is given by

$$= \frac{B_0 d}{R}(\omega x \cos \omega t + v \sin \omega t)$$

The force acting on the conductor is given by $F = ilB \sin 90° = ilB$

Substituting the values, we have

$$\text{Force needed along } \hat{\mathbf{i}} = \frac{B_0 d}{R}(\omega x \cos \omega t + v \sin \omega t) \times d \times B_0 \sin \omega t$$

$$= \frac{B_0^2 d^2}{R}(\omega x \cos \omega t + v \sin \omega t) \sin \omega t$$

This is the required expression for force.

Q.23 A conducting wire XY of mass m and negligible resistance slides smoothly on two parallel conducting wires as shown in figure. The closed circuit has a resistance R due to $AC \cdot AB$ and CD are perfect conductors. There is a magnetic field $\mathbf{B} = B(t)\,\hat{\mathbf{k}}$

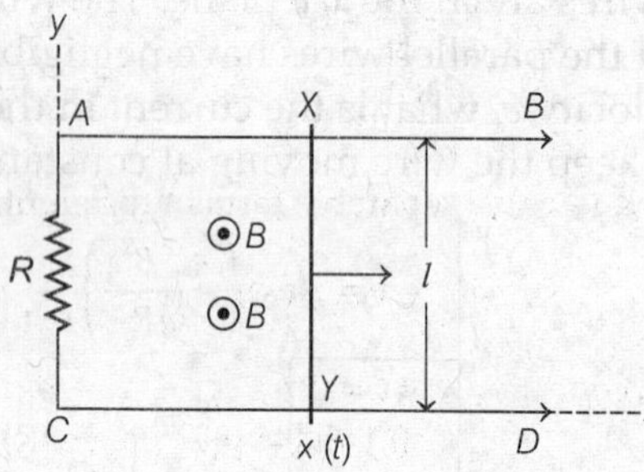

(i) Write down equation for the acceleration of the wire XY.

(ii) If $\mathbf{B}$ is independent of time, obtain $v(t)$, assuming $v(0) = u_0$

(iii) For (ii), show that the decrease in kinetic energy of XY equals the heat lost in R.

Thinking Process This problem relates EMI, magnetic force, power consumption and mechanics.

Ans. Let us assume that the parallel wires are at $y = 0$, *i.e.*, along x-axis and $y = l$. At $t = 0$, XY has $x = 0$ *i.e.*, along y-axis.

(i) Let the wire be at $x = x(t)$ at time t.

The magnetic flux linked with the loop is given by

$$\phi = \mathbf{B} \cdot \mathbf{A} = BA\cos 0 = BA$$

at any instant t Magnetic flux $= B(t)(l \times x(t))$

Total emf in the circuit = emf due to change in field (along $XYAC$) + the motional emf across XY

$$\varepsilon = -\frac{d\phi}{dt} = -\frac{dB(t)}{dt} lx(t) - B(t)\,lv(t)$$

[second term due to motional emf]

Electric current in clockwise direction is given by

$$I = \frac{1}{R}\varepsilon$$

The force acting on the conductor is given by $F = IlB\sin 90° = IlB$

Substituting the values, we have

$$\text{Force} = \frac{lB(t)}{R}\left[-\frac{dB(t)}{dt} l\,x(t) - B(t)lv(t)\right]\hat{\mathbf{i}}$$

Applying Newton's second law of motion,

$$m\frac{d^2x}{dt^2} = -\frac{l^2 B(t)}{R}\frac{dB(t)}{dt}x(t) - \frac{l^2 B^2(t)}{R}\frac{dx(t)}{dt} \quad \text{...(i)}$$

$$a = \frac{1}{m}\left[-\frac{l^2 B(t)}{R}\frac{dB(t)}{dt}x(t) - \frac{l^2 B^2(t)}{R}\frac{dx(t)}{dt}\right] \quad \left[\because \frac{d^2x}{dt^2} = a\right]$$

which is the required equation.

(ii) If **B** is independent of time *i.e.*, $B =$ constant

or $$\frac{dB}{dt} = 0$$

Substituting the above value in Eq (i), we have

$$\frac{d^2x}{dt^2} + \frac{l^2B^2}{mR}\frac{dx}{dt} = 0$$

or $$\frac{dv}{dt} + \frac{l^2B^2}{mR}v = 0$$

Integrating using variable separable form of differential equation, we have

$$v = A\exp\left(\frac{-l^2B^2t}{mR}\right)$$

Applying given conditions, at $t = 0$, $v = u_0$

$$v(t) = u_0\exp(-l^2B^2t/mR)$$

This is the required equation.

(iii) Since the power consumption is given by $P = I^2R$

Here, $$I^2R = \frac{B^2l^2v^2(t)}{R^2} \times R$$

$$= \frac{B^2l^2}{R}u_0^2\exp(-2l^2B^2t/mR)$$

Now, energy consumed in time interval dt is given by energy consumed $= Pdt = I^2Rdt$

Therefore, total energy consumed in time t

$$= \int_0^t I^2Rdt = \frac{B^2l^2}{R}u_0^2\frac{mR}{2l^2B^2}[1 - e^{-(l^2B^2t/mR)}]$$

$$= \frac{m}{2}u_0^2 - \frac{m}{2}v^2(t)$$

$=$ decrease in kinetic energy.

This proves that the decrease in kinetic energy of XY equals the heat lost in R.

Q.24 *ODBAC* is a fixed rectangular conductor of negligible resistance (*CO* is not connected) and *OP* is a conductor which rotates clockwise with an angular velocity ω as shown in figure. The entire system is in a uniform magnetic field **B** whose direction is along the normal to the surface of the rectangular conductor *ABDC*. The conductor *OP* is in electric contact with *ABDC*. The rotating conductor has a resistance of λ per unit length. Find the current in the rotating conductor, as it rotates by 180°.

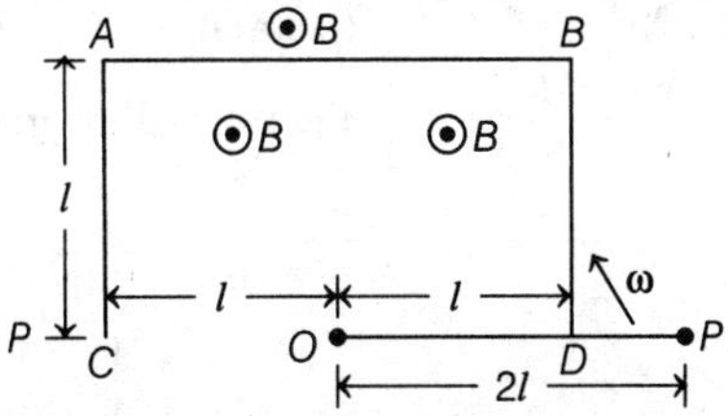

Thinking Process The pattern of rate of change of area (hence flux) can be considered uniform from $0 < \theta < \frac{\pi}{4}; \frac{\pi}{4} < \theta < \frac{3\pi}{4}$ and $\frac{3\pi}{4} < \theta < \frac{\pi}{2}$. Hence, forth finding emf and current.

Ans. Let us consider the position of rotating conductor at time interval

$$t = 0 \text{ to } t = \frac{\pi}{4\omega} \text{ (or } T/8)$$

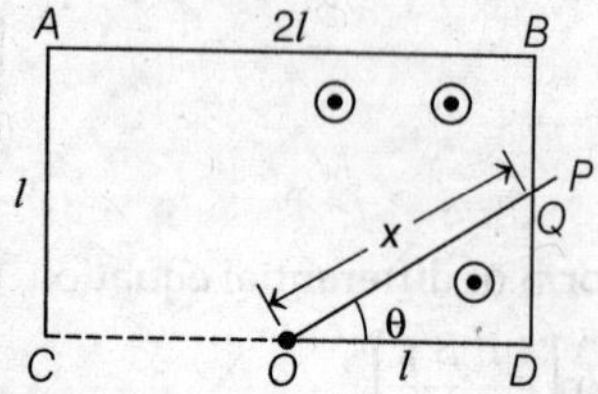

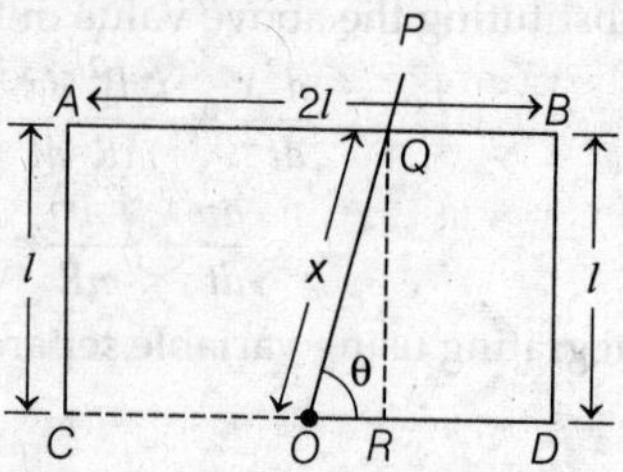

the rod OP will make contact with the side BD. Let the length OQ of the contact at sometime t such that $0 < t < \frac{\pi}{4\omega}$ or $0 < t < \frac{T}{8}$ be x. The flux through the area ODQ is

$$\phi = B\frac{1}{2}QD \times OD = B\frac{1}{2}l\tan\theta \times l$$

$$= \frac{1}{2}Bl^2\tan\theta, \text{ where } \theta = \omega t$$

Applying Faraday's law of EMI,

Thus, the magnitude of the emf generated is $\varepsilon = \frac{d\phi}{dt} = \frac{1}{2}Bl^2\omega\sec^2\omega t$

The current is $I = \frac{\varepsilon}{R}$ where R is the resistance of the rod in contact.

where, $R \propto \lambda$

$$R = \lambda x = \frac{\lambda l}{\cos\omega t}$$

$$\therefore \quad I = \frac{1}{2}\frac{Bl^2\omega}{\lambda l}\sec^2\omega t\cos\omega t = \frac{Bl\omega}{2\lambda\cos\omega t}$$

Let the length OQ of the contact at some time t such that $\frac{\pi}{4\omega} < t < \frac{3\pi}{4\omega}$ or $\frac{T}{8} < t < \frac{3T}{8}$ be x. The rod is in contact with the side AB. The flux through the area $OQBD$ is

$$\phi = \left(2l^2 - \frac{1}{2}\frac{l^2}{\tan\theta}\right)B$$

Where, $\theta = \omega t$

Thus, the magnitude of emf generated in the loop is

$$\varepsilon = \frac{d\phi}{dt} = \frac{1}{2}Bl^2\omega\frac{\sec^2\omega t}{\tan^2\omega t}$$

The current is $I = \frac{\varepsilon}{R} = \frac{\varepsilon}{\lambda x} = \frac{\varepsilon\sin\omega t}{\lambda l} = \frac{1}{2}\frac{Bl\omega}{\lambda\sin\omega t}$

Similarly, for $\frac{3\pi}{4\omega} < t < \frac{\pi}{\omega}$ or $\frac{3T}{8} < t < \frac{T}{2}$, the rod will be in touch with AC.

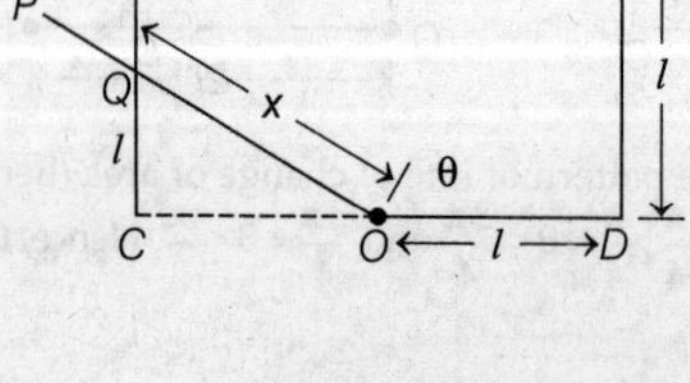

The flux through *OQABD* is given by

$$\phi = \left(2l^2 - \frac{l^2}{2\tan\omega t}\right)B$$

And the magnitude of emf generated in loop is given by

$$\varepsilon = \frac{d\phi}{dt} = \frac{B\omega l^2 \sec^2 \omega t}{2\tan^2 \omega t}$$

$$I = \frac{\varepsilon}{R} = \frac{\varepsilon}{\lambda x} = \frac{1}{2}\frac{Bl\omega}{\lambda \sin \omega t}$$

These are the required expressions.

Q.25 Consider an infinitely long wire carrying a current $I(t)$, with $\frac{dI}{dt} = \lambda =$ constant. Find the current produced in the rectangular loop of wire *ABCD* if its resistance is *R* (figure).

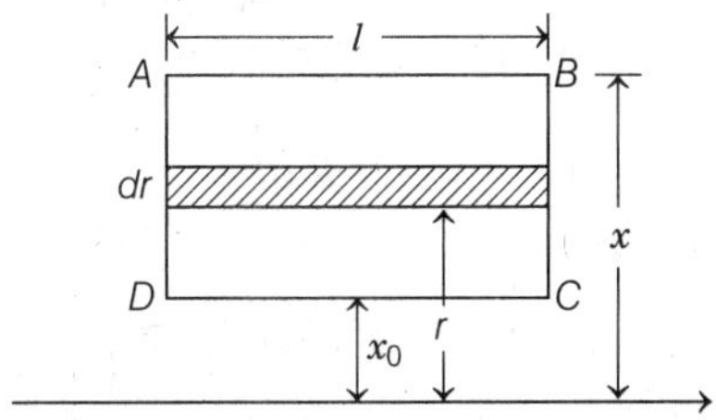

Thinking Process This question needs the use of integration in order to find the total magnetic flux linked with the loop.

Ans. Let us consider a strip of length *l* and width *dr* at a distance *r* from infinite long current carrying wire. The magnetic field at strip due to current carrying wire is given by

$$B(r) = \frac{\mu_0 I}{2\pi r} \text{ (out of paper)}$$

Total flux through the loop is

$$\phi = \frac{\mu_0 I}{2\pi} l \int_{x_0}^{x} \frac{dr}{r} = \frac{\mu_0 Il}{2\pi} \ln \frac{x}{x_0} \qquad \text{...(i)}$$

The emf induced can be obtained by differentiating the Eq. (i) w.r.t. *t* and then applying Ohm's law

$$\frac{\varepsilon}{R} = I$$

We have, $\text{induced current} = \frac{1}{R}\frac{d\phi}{dt} = \frac{\varepsilon}{R} = \frac{\mu_0 l \lambda}{2\pi R} \ln \frac{x}{x_0}$ $\left(\because \frac{dI}{dt} = \lambda\right)$

Q.26 A rectangular loop of wire $ABCD$ is kept close to an infinitely long wire carrying a current $I(t) = I_0(1 - t/T)$ for $0 \le t \le T$ and $I(t) = 0$ for $t > T$ (figure.). Find the total charge passing through a given point in the loop, in time T. The resistance of the loop is R.

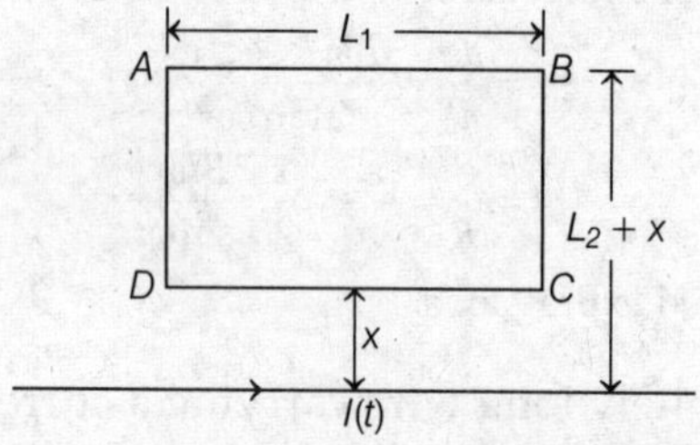

Thinking Process The charge passes through the circuit can be obtained by finding the relation between instantaneous current and instantaneous magnetic flux linked with it.

Ans. The emf induced can be obtained by differentiating the expression of magnetic flux linked w.r.t. t and then applying Ohm's law

$$I = \frac{\varepsilon}{R} = \frac{1}{R}\frac{d\phi}{dt}$$

We know that electric current

$$I(t) = \frac{dQ}{dt} \quad \text{or} \quad \frac{dQ}{dt} = \frac{1}{R}\frac{d\phi}{dt}$$

Integrating the variable separable form of differential equation for finding the charge Q that passed in time t, we have

$$Q(t_1) - Q(t_2) = \frac{1}{R}[\phi(t_1) - \phi(t_2)]$$

$$\phi(t_1) = L_1 \frac{\mu_0}{2\pi}\int_x^{L_2 + x} \frac{dx'}{x'} I(t_1) \quad \text{[Refer to the Eq. (i) of answer no.25]}$$

$$= \frac{\mu_0 L_1}{2\pi} I(t_1) \ln \frac{L_2 + x}{x}$$

The magnitude of charge is given by,

$$= \frac{\mu_0 L_1}{2\pi R} \ln \frac{L_2 + x}{x}[I_0 - 0]$$

$$= \frac{\mu_0 L_1}{2\pi R} I_0 \ln\left(\frac{L_2 + x}{x}\right)$$

This is the required expression.

Q.27 A magnetic field **B** is confined to a region $r \le a$ and points out of the paper (the z-axis), $r = 0$ being the centre of the circular region. A charged ring (charge $= Q$) of radius b, $b > a$ and mass m lies in the x-y plane with its centre at the origin. The ring is free to rotate and is at rest. The magnetic field is brought to zero in time Δt. Find the angular velocity ω of the ring after the field vanishes.

Thinking Process The decrease in magnetic field causes induced emf and hence, electric field around ring. The torque experienced by the ring produces change in angular momentum.

Ans. Since, the magnetic field is brought to zero in time Δt, the magnetic flux linked with the ring also reduces from maximum to zero. This, in turn, induces an emf in ring by the phenomenon of EMI. The induces emf causes the electric field E generation around the ring.

The induced emf = electric field $E \times (2\pi b)$ (Because $V = E \times d$) ...(i)

By Faraday's law of EMI

The induced emf = rate of change of magnetic flux

$$= \text{rate of change of magnetic field} \times \text{area}$$

$$= \frac{B\pi a^2}{\Delta t} \quad \text{...(ii)}$$

From Eqs. (i) and (ii), we have

$$2\pi bE = emf = \frac{B\pi a^2}{\Delta t}$$

Since, the charged ring experiences an electric force = QE

This force tries to rotate the coil, and the torque is given by

$$\text{Torque} = b \times \text{Force}$$

$$= QEb = Q\left[\frac{B\pi a^2}{2\pi b\Delta t}\right]b = Q\frac{Ba^2}{2\Delta t}$$

If ΔL is the change in angular momentum

$$\text{Torque} = \frac{\text{change in angular momentum}}{\text{change in time}}$$

$$\tau = \frac{\Delta L}{\Delta t} = \frac{L_2 - L_1}{\Delta t}$$

$$\therefore \quad L_2 - L_1 = \tau\Delta t$$

$$L_2 - L_1 = \frac{QBa^2\Delta t}{2\Delta t} = \frac{QBa^2}{2}$$

As initial angular momentum, $L_1 = 0$

$$\therefore \quad L_2 = \frac{QBa^2}{2} = I\omega = (mb^2)\omega$$

where, I = moment of inertia of the ring

$$\omega = \frac{QBa^2}{2mb^2}$$

On rearranging the terms, we have the required expression of angular speed.

Q.28 A rod of mass m and resistance R slides smoothly over two parallel perfectly conducting wires kept sloping at an angle θ with respect to the horizontal (figure). The circuit is closed through a perfect conductor at the top. There is a constant magnetic field **B** along the vertical direction. If the rod is initially at rest, find the velocity of the rod as a function of time.

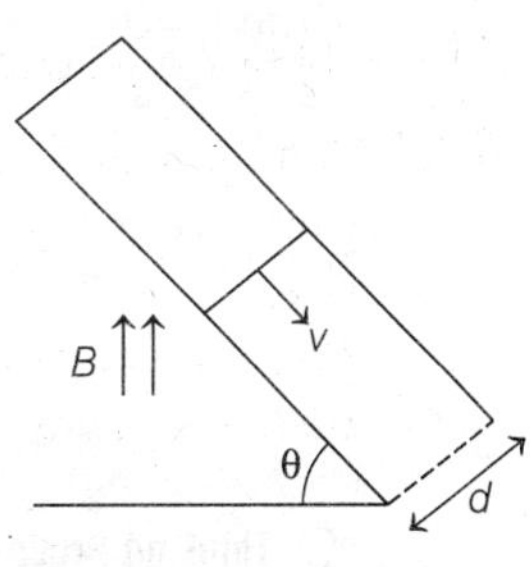

Thinking Process This problem combines mechanics, EMI, magnetic force and linear differential equation.

Ans. Here, the component of magnetic field perpendicular to the plane = $B\cos\theta$

Now, the conductor moves with speed v perpendicular to $B\cos\theta$ component of magnetic field. This causes motional emf across two ends of rod, which is given by $= v(B\cos\theta)d$

This makes flow of induced current $i = \dfrac{v(B\cos\theta)\,d}{R}$ where, R is the resistance of rod. Now, current carrying rod experience force which is given by $F = iBd$ (horizontally in backward direction). Now, the component of magnetic force parallel to incline plane along upward direction =

$F\cos\theta = iBd\cos\theta = \left(\dfrac{v(B\cos\theta)d}{R}\right)Bd\cos\theta$ where, $v = \dfrac{dx}{dt}$

Also, the component of weight (mg) parallel to incline plane along downward direction $= mg\sin\theta$.

Now, by Newton's second law of motion

$$m\frac{d^2x}{dt^2} = mg\sin\theta - \frac{B\cos\theta d}{R}\left(\frac{dx}{dt}\right) \times (Bd)\cos\theta$$

$$\frac{dv}{dt} = g\sin\theta - \frac{B^2d^2}{mR}(\cos\theta)^2 v$$

$$\frac{dv}{dt} + \frac{B^2d^2}{mR}(\cos\theta)^2 v = g\sin\theta$$

But, this is the linear differential equation.

On solving, we get

$$v = \frac{g\sin\theta}{\dfrac{B^2d^2\cos^2\theta}{mR}} + A\exp\left(-\frac{B^2d^2}{mR}(\cos^2\theta)\,t\right)$$

A is a constant to be determine by initial conditions.

The required expression of velocity as a function of time is given by

$$= \frac{mgR\sin\theta}{B^2d^2\cos^2\theta}\left(1 - \exp\left(-\frac{B^2d^2}{mR}(\cos^2\theta)\,t\right)\right)$$

Q.29 Find the current in the sliding rod AB (resistance = R) for the arrangement shown in figure. B is constant and is out of the paper. Parallel wires have no resistance, v is constant. Switch S is closed at time $t = 0$.

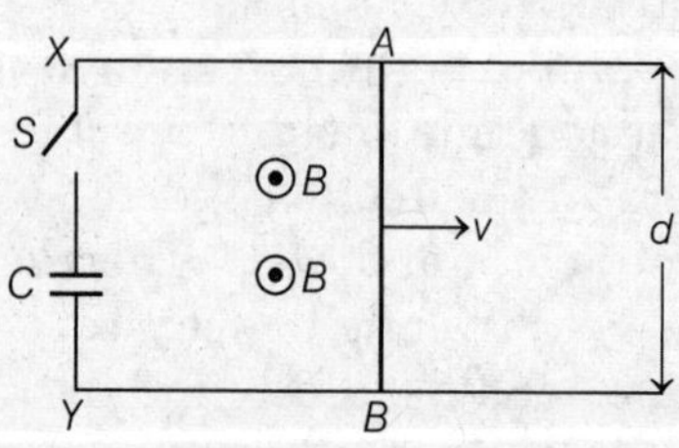

Thinking Process This problem combines the concept of EMI, charging of capacitor and linear differential equation.

Ans. The conductor of length d moves with speed v, perpendicular to magnetic field B as shown in figure. This produces motional emf across two ends of rod, which is given by $= vBd$. Since, switch S is closed at time $t = 0$. capacitor is charged by this potential difference. Let $Q(t)$ is charge on the capacitor and current flows from A to B.

Now, the induced current

$$I = \frac{dQ}{dt} = \frac{vBd}{R} - \frac{Q}{RC}$$

On rearranging the terms, we have

$$\frac{Q}{RC} + \frac{dQ}{dt} = \frac{vBd}{R}$$

This is the linear differential equation. On solving, we get

$$Q = vBdC + Ae^{-t/RC}$$

$\Rightarrow$ $$Q = vBdC[1 - e^{-t/RC}]$$

(At time $t = 0$, $Q = 0 \Rightarrow A = -vBdc$).

Differentiating, we get $I = \frac{vBd}{R} e^{-t/RC}$

This is the required expression of current.

Q.30 Find the current in the sliding rod AB (resistance $= R$) for the arrangement shown in figure. **B** is constant and is out of the paper. Parallel wires have no resistance, **v** is constant. Switch S is closed at time $t = 0$.

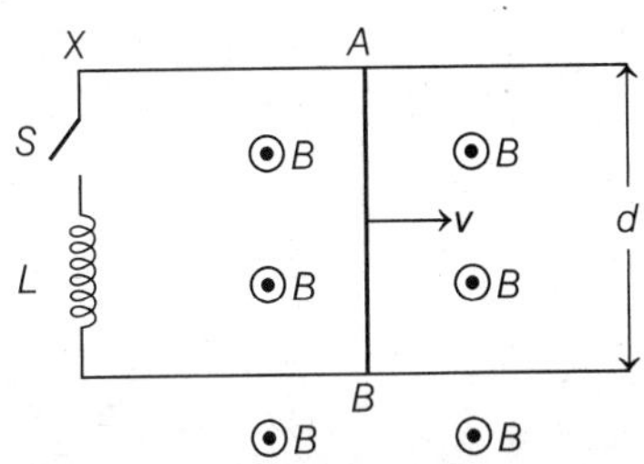

Thinking Process This problem combines the concept of EMI, growth of current in inductor and linear differential equation.

Ans. The conductor of length d moves with speed v, perpendicular to magnetic field **B** as shown in figure. This produces motional emf across two ends of rod, which is given by $= vBd$.

Since, switch S is closed at time $t = 0$, current start growing in inductor by the potential difference due to motional emf.

Applying Kirchhoff's voltage rule, we have

$$-L\frac{dI}{dt} + vBd = IR$$

or $$L\frac{dI}{dt} + IR = vBd$$

This is the linear differential equation. On solving, we get

$$I = \frac{vBd}{R} + Ae^{-Rt/L}$$

$$\text{At } t = 0 \quad I = 0$$

$$\Rightarrow \quad A = -\frac{vBd}{R} \Rightarrow I = \frac{vBd}{R}(1 - e^{-Rt/L}).$$

This is the required expression of current.

Q.31 A metallic ring of mass m and radius l (ring being horizontal) is falling under gravity in a region having a magnetic field. If z is the vertical direction, the z-component of magnetic field is $B_z = B_0(1 + \lambda z)$. If R is the resistance of the ring and if the ring falls with a velocity v, find the energy lost in the resistance. If the ring has reached a constant velocity, use the conservation of energy to determine v in terms of m, B, λ and acceleration due to gravity g.

Thinking Process This problem establishes a relationship between induced current, power lost and velocity acquired by freely falling ring.

Ans. The magnetic flux linked with the metallic ring of mass m and radius l falling under gravity in a region having a magnetic field whose z-component of magnetic field is $B_z = B_0(1 + \lambda z)$ is

$$\phi = B_z(\pi l^2) = B_0(1 + \lambda z)(\pi l^2)$$

Applying Faraday's law of EMI, we have emf induced given by $\frac{d\phi}{dt}$ = rate of change of flux

Also, by Ohm's law

$$B_0(\pi l^2)\lambda \frac{dz}{dt} = IR$$

On rearranging the terms, we have $I = \frac{\pi l^2 B_0 \lambda}{R} v$ $\quad \left(\because V = \frac{dz}{dt}\right)$

$$\text{Energy lost/second} = I^2 R = \frac{(\pi l^2 \lambda)^2 B_0^2 v^2}{R}$$

This must come from rate of change in PE $= mg\frac{dz}{dt} = mgv$

[as kinetic energy is constant for v = constant]

Thus, $$mgv = \frac{(\pi l^2 \lambda B_0)^2 v^2}{R} \quad \text{or} \quad v = \frac{mgR}{(\pi l^2 \lambda B_0)^2}$$

This is the required expression of velocity.

Q.32 A long solenoid S has n turns per meter, with diameter a. At the centre of this coil, we place a smaller coil of N turns and diameter b (where $b < a$). If the current in the solenoid increases linearly, with time, what is the induced emf appearing in the smaller coil. Plot graph showing nature of variation in emf, if current varies as a function of $mt^2 + C$.

Thinking Process This problem requires an insight into magnetic field due to a current carrying solenoid having varying current which induces emf in coil of some radius.

Ans. Magnetic field due to a solenoid S, $B = \mu_0 nI$

Magnetic flux in smaller coil $\phi = NBA$, where

$$A = \pi b^2$$

Applying Faraday's law of EMI, we have

So, $$e = \frac{-d\phi}{dt} = \frac{-d}{dt}(NBA)$$

$$= -N\pi b^2 \frac{d(B)}{dt}$$

where, $$B = \mu_0 nI$$

$\Rightarrow$ $$e = -N\pi b^2 \mu_0 n \frac{dI}{dt}$$

$$= -Nn\pi\mu_0 b^2 \frac{d}{dt}(mt^2 + C) = -\mu_0 Nn\pi b^2 2mt$$

Since, current varies as a function of $mt^2 + C$.

$$e = -\mu_0 Nn\pi b^2 2mt$$

Negative sign signifies opposite nature of induced emf. The magnitude of emf. The magnitude of emf varies with time as shown in the figure.

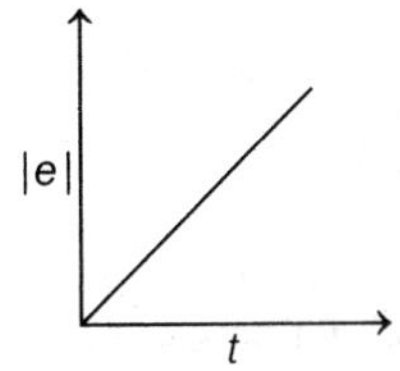

Chapter 07

Alternating Current

Multiple Choice Questions (MCQs)

Q.1 If the rms current in a 50 Hz AC circuit is 5 A, the value of the current 1/300 s after its value becomes zero is

(a) $5\sqrt{2}$ A
(b) $5\sqrt{3/2}$ A
(c) $5/6$ A
(d) $5/\sqrt{2}$ A

Ans. ***(b)*** Given, $\nu = 50\text{ Hz},\ I_{\text{rms}} = 5\text{A}$

$$t = \frac{1}{300}\text{ s}$$

We have to find $I(t)$

$$I_0 = \text{Peak value} = \sqrt{2}\ I_{\text{rms}} = \sqrt{2} \times 5$$
$$= 5\sqrt{2}\ \text{A}$$
$$I = I_0 \sin \omega t = 5\sqrt{2} \sin 2\pi\ \nu t = 5\sqrt{2} \sin\left(2\pi \times 50 \times \frac{1}{300}\right)$$
$$= 5\sqrt{2} \sin \frac{\pi}{3} = 5\sqrt{2} \times \frac{\sqrt{3}}{2} = 5\sqrt{3/2}\ \text{A}$$

Q.2 An alternating current generator has an internal resistance R_g and an internal reactance X_g. It is used to supply power to a passive load consisting of a resistance R_g and a reactance X_L. For maximum power to be delivered from the generator to the load, the value of X_L is equal to

(a) zero
(b) X_g
(c) $-X_g$
(d) R_g

Ans. ***(c)*** For delivering maximum power from the generator to the load, total internal reactance must be equal to conjugate of total external reactance.

Hence, $X_{\text{int}} = (X_{\text{ext}})^*$

$\Rightarrow$ $X_g = (X_L)^* = -X_L$

$\Rightarrow$ $X_L = -X_g$

Q.3 When a voltage measuring device is connected to AC mains, the meter shows the steady input voltage of 220 V. This means

(a) input voltage cannot be AC voltage, but a DC voltage

(b) maximum input voltage is 220 V

(c) the meter reads not v but $< v^2 >$ and is calibrated to read $\sqrt{< v^2 >}$

(d) the pointer of the meter is stuck by some mechanical defect

Ans. *(c)* The voltmeter connected to AC mains reads mean value ($<v^2>$) and is calibrated in such a way that it gives value of $<v^2>$, which is multiplied by form factor to give rms value i.e., $\sqrt{< v^2 >}$.

Q.4 To reduce the resonant frequency in an *L-C-R* series circuit with a generator

(a) the generator frequency should be reduced

(b) another capacitor should be added in parallel to the first

(c) the iron core of the inductor should be removed

(d) dielectric in the capacitor should be removed

Ans. *(b)* We know that resonant frequency in an *L-C-R* circuit is given by

$$\nu_0 = \frac{1}{2\pi\sqrt{LC}}$$

Now to reduce ν_0 either we can increase L or we can increase C.

To increase capacitance, we must connect another capacitor parallel to the first.

Q.5 Which of the following combinations should be selected for better tuning of an *L-C-R* circuit used for communication?

(a) $R = 20\,\Omega$, $L = 1.5\,\text{H}$, $C = 35\,\mu\text{F}$

(b) $R = 25\,\Omega$, $L = 2.5\,\text{H}$, $C = 45\,\mu\text{F}$

(c) $R = 15\,\Omega$, $L = 3.5\,\text{H}$, $C = 30\,\mu\text{F}$

(d) $R = 25\,\Omega$, $L = 1.5\,\text{H}$, $C = 45\,\mu\text{F}$

Thinking Process For better tuning of an L-C-R circuit used for communication, quality factor of the circuit must be as high as possible.

Ans. *(c)* Quality factor (Q) of an *L-C-R* circuit is given by,

$$Q = \frac{1}{R}\sqrt{\frac{L}{C}}$$

where R is resistance, L is inductance and C is capacitance of the circuit. To make Q high, R should be low, L should be high and C should be low.

These conditions are best satisfied by the values given in option (c).

Note We should be careful while writing formula for quality factor, because we are considering series *L-C-R* circuit.

Q.6 An inductor of reactance 1Ω and a resistor of 2Ω are connected in series to the terminals of a 6V (rms) AC source. The power dissipated in the circuit is

(a) 8 W (b) 12 W
(c) 14.4 W (d) 18 W

Ans. ***(c)*** Given, $X_L = 1\Omega$, $R = 2\Omega$

$$E_{rms} = 6\text{ V}, P_{av} = ?$$

Average power dissipated in the circuit,

$$P_{av} = E_{rms} I_{rms} \cos\phi \quad \text{...(i)}$$

$$Z = \sqrt{R^2 + X_L^2}$$

$$= \sqrt{4+1} = \sqrt{5}$$

$$I_{rms} = \frac{V_{rms}}{Z} = \frac{6}{\sqrt{5}}\text{ A}$$

$$\cos\phi = \frac{R}{Z} = \frac{2}{\sqrt{5}}$$

$$P_{av} = 6 \times \frac{6}{\sqrt{5}} \times \frac{2}{\sqrt{5}} \quad \text{[from Eq. (i)]}$$

$$= \frac{72}{\sqrt{5}\sqrt{5}} = \frac{72}{5} = 14.4\text{ W}$$

Q.7 The output of a step-down transformer is measured to be 24 V when connected to a 12 W light bulb. The value of the peak current is

(a) $1/\sqrt{2}$ A (b) $\sqrt{2}$ A
(c) 2 A (d) $2\sqrt{2}$ A

Ans. ***(a)*** Secondary voltage $V_S = 24$ V

Power associated with secondary $P_S = 12$ W

$$I_S = \frac{P_S}{V_S} = \frac{12}{24}$$

$$= \frac{1}{2}\text{ A} = 0.5\text{ A}$$

Peak value of the current in the secondary

$$I_0 = I_S\sqrt{2}$$

$$= (0.5)(1.414) = 0.707 = \frac{1}{\sqrt{2}}\text{ A}$$

Multiple Choice Questions (More Than One Options)

Q.8 As the frequency of an AC circuit increases, the current first increases and then decreases. What combination of circuit elements is most likely to comprise the circuit?

(a) Inductor and capacitor
(b) Resistor and inductor
(c) Resistor and capacitor
(d) Resistor, inductor and capacitor

Thinking Process We can decide the elements, comprising the given circuit by predicting the variation in their reactances with frequency.

Ans. ***(a,d)*** Reactance of an inductor of inductance L is,

$X_L = 2\pi\nu L$

where ν is frequency of the AC circuit.

$$X_c = \text{Reactance of the capacitive circuit}$$
$$= \frac{1}{2\pi\nu C}$$

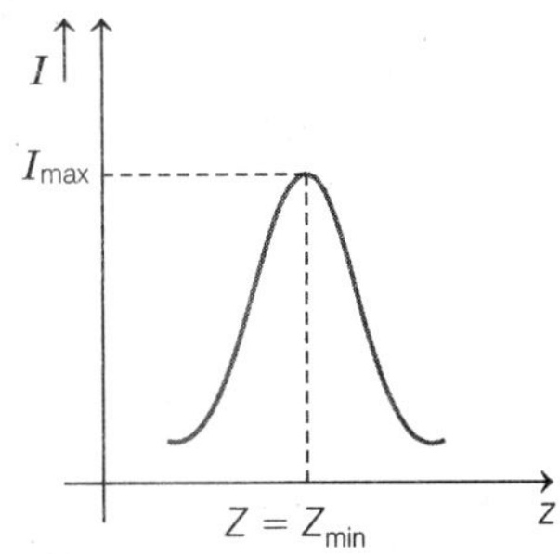

On increasing frequency ν, clearly X_L increases and X_C decreases.

For a *L-C-R* circuit,

$$Z = \text{Impedance of the circuit}$$
$$= \sqrt{R^2 + (X_L - X_C)^2}$$
$$= \sqrt{R^2 + \left(2\pi\nu L - \frac{1}{2\pi\nu C}\right)^2}$$

As frequency (ν) increases, Z decreases and at certain value of frequency know as resonant frequency (ν_0), impedance Z is minimum that is $Z_{min} = R$, current varies inversely with impedance and at Z_{min} current is maximum.

Q.9 In an alternating current circuit consisting of elements in series, the current increases on increasing the frequency of supply. Which of the following elements are likely to constitute the circuit?

(a) Only resistor
(b) Resistor and an inductor
(c) Resistor and a capacitor
(d) Only a capacitor

Ans. ***(c, d)*** According to the question, the current increases on increasing the frequency of supply. Hence, the reactance of the circuit must be decreases as increasing frequency.

For a capacitive circuit,

$$X_C = \frac{1}{\omega C} = \frac{1}{2\pi f C}$$

Clearly when frequency increases, X_C decreases.

For *R-C* circuit, $$X = \sqrt{R^2 + \left(\frac{1}{\omega C}\right)^2}$$

when the frequency increases, X decreases.

Q.10 Electrical energy is transmitted over large distances at high alternating voltages. Which of the following statements is (are) correct?

(a) For a given power level, there is a lower current
(b) Lower current implies less power loss
(c) Transmission lines can be made thinner
(d) It is easy to reduce the voltage at the receiving end using step-down transformers

Thinking Process Power loss due to transmission lines having resistance (R) and rms current flowing I_{rms} is $I^2_{rms} R$.

Ans. ***(a, b, d)*** We have to transmit energy (power) over large distances at high alternating voltages, so current flowing through the wires will be low because for a given power (P).

$$P = E_{rms} I_{rms}, \; I_{rms} \text{ is low when } E_{rms} \text{ is high.}$$

$$\text{Power loss} = I^2_{rms} R = \text{low} \qquad (\because I_{rms} \text{ is low})$$

Now at the receiving end high voltage is reduced by using step-down transformers.

Q.11 For a L-C-R circuit, the power transferred from the driving source to the driven oscillator is $P = I^2 Z \cos\phi$.

(a) Here, the power factor $\cos\phi \geq 0, P \geq 0$.
(b) The driving force can give no energy to the oscillator ($P = 0$) in some cases.
(c) The driving force cannot syphon out ($P < 0$) the energy out of oscillator.
(d) The driving force can take away energy out of the oscillator.

Ans. ***(a, b, c)*** According to question power transferred,

$$P = I^2 Z \cos\phi$$

where I is the current, $Z =$ Impedance and $\cos\phi$ is power factor

As power factor, $\cos\phi = \dfrac{R}{Z}$

where $R > 0$ and $Z > 0$

$\Rightarrow$ $\cos\phi \geq 0 \Rightarrow P \geq 0$

$P = 0$, when $\phi = \dfrac{\pi}{2}$ for L and C and $P < 0$ is not possible.

Q.12 When an AC voltage of 220 V is applied to the capacitor C

(a) the maximum voltage between plates is 220 V.
(b) the current is in phase with the applied voltage.
(c) the charge on the plates is in phase with the applied voltage.
(d) power delivered to the capacitor is zero.

Ans. ***(c, d)*** When the AC voltage is applied to the capacitor, the plate connected to the positive terminal will be at higher potential and the plate connected to the negative terminal will be at lower potential.

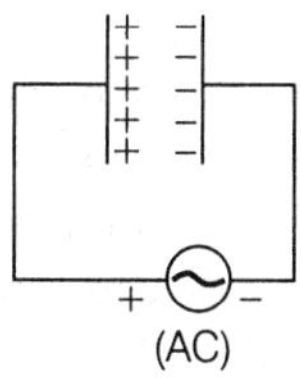

The plate with positive charge will be at higher potential and the plate with negative charge will be at lower potential. So, we can say that the charge is in phase with the applied voltage.

Power applied to a circuit is $P_{av} = V_{rms} I_{rms} \cos \phi$

For capacitive circuit, $\phi = 90°$

$\Rightarrow \quad \cos \phi = 0$

$\Rightarrow \quad P_{av} = \text{Power delivered} = 0$

Q.13 The line that draws power supply to your house from street has

(a) zero average current

(b) 220 V average voltage

(c) voltage and current out of phase by 90°

(d) voltage and current possibly differing in phase ϕ such that $|\phi| < \frac{\pi}{2}$

Ans. ***(a, d)*** For house hold supplies, AC currents are used which are having zero average value over a cycle.

The line is having some resistance so power factor $\cos \phi = \frac{R}{Z} \neq 0$

so, $\phi \neq \pi/2$

$\Rightarrow \quad \phi < \pi/2$

i.e., phase lies between 0 and $\pi/2$.

Very Short Answer Type Questions

Q.14 If a *L-C* circuit is considered analogous to a harmonically oscillating spring block system, which energy of the *L-C* circuit would be analogous to potential energy and which one analogous to kinetic energy?

Ans. If we consider a *L-C* circuit analogous to a harmonically oscillating spring block system.

The electrostatic energy $\frac{1}{2} CV^2$ is analogous to potential energy and energy associated with moving charges (current) that is magnetic energy $\left(\frac{1}{2} LI^2\right)$ is analogous to kinetic energy.

Q.15 Draw the effective equivalent circuit of the circuit shown in figure, at very high frequencies and find the effective impedance.

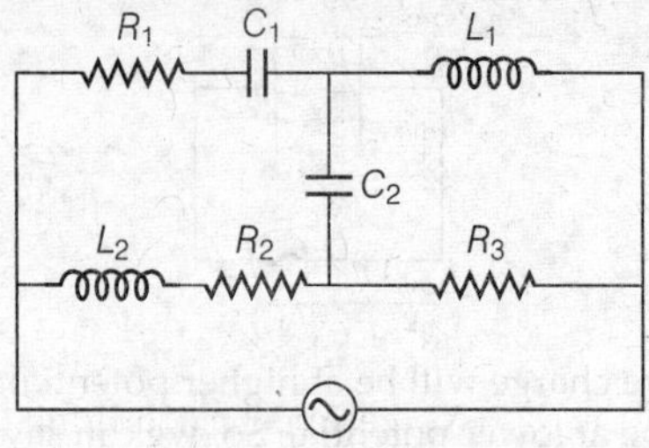

Thinking Process The component with infinite resistance will be considered as open circuit and the component with zero resistance will be considered as short circuited.

Ans. We know that inductive reactance $X_L = 2\pi fL$

and capacitive reactance $X_C = \dfrac{1}{2\pi fC}$

For very high frequencies ($f \to \infty$), $X_L \to \infty$ and $X_C \to 0$

When reactance of a circuit is infinite it will be considered as open circuit. When reactance of a circuit is zero it will be considered as short circuited.

So, $C_1, C_2 \to$ shorted and $L_1, L_2 \to$ opened.

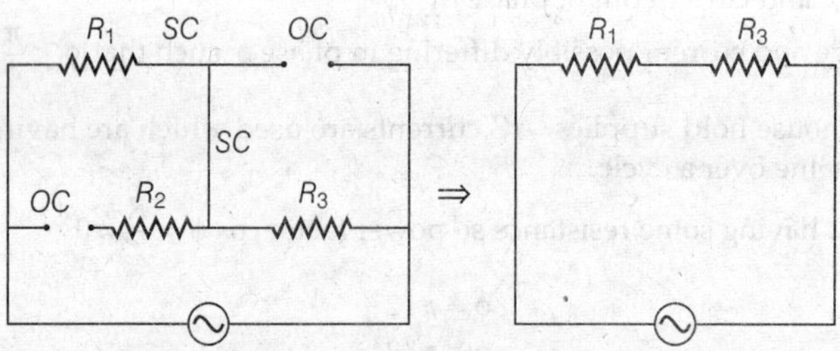

So, effective impedance $= R_{eq} = R_1 + R_3$

Q.16 Study the circuits (a) and (b) shown in figure and answer the following questions.

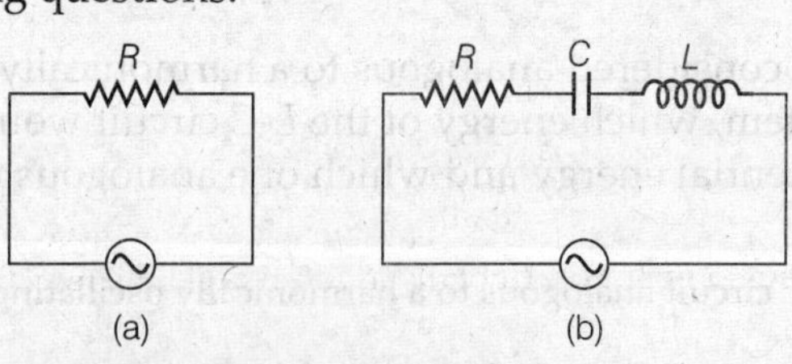

(a) Under which conditions would the rms currents in the two circuits be the same?

(b) Can the rms current in circuit (b) be larger than that in (a)?

Ans. Let,

$$(I_{rms})\,a = \text{rms current in circuit (a)}$$
$$(I_{rms})\,b = \text{rms current in circuit (b)}$$
$$(I_{rms})\,a = \frac{V_{rms}}{R} = \frac{V}{R}$$
$$(I_{rms})\,b = \frac{V_{rms}}{Z} = \frac{V}{\sqrt{R^2 + (X_L - X_C)^2}}$$

(a) When $(I_{rms})\,a = (I_{rms})\,b$

$$R = \sqrt{R^2 + (X_L - X_C)^2}$$

$\Rightarrow$ $X_L = X_C$, resonance condition

(b) As $Z \geq R$

$$\Rightarrow \quad \frac{(I_{rms})a}{(I_{rms})b} = \frac{\sqrt{R^2 + (X_L - X_C)^2}}{R} = \frac{Z}{R} \geq 1$$

$$\Rightarrow \quad (I_{rms})\,a \geq (I_{rms})b$$

No, the rms current in circuit (b), cannot be larger than that in (a).

Q.17 Can the instantaneous power output of an AC source ever be negative? Can the average power output be negative?

Ans. Let the applied emf

$$E = E_0 \sin(\omega t)$$

and current developed is

$$I = I_0 \sin(\omega t \pm \phi)$$

Instantaneous power output of the AC source

$$P = EI = (E_0 \sin \omega t)\, I \qquad [I = I_0 \sin(\omega t \pm \phi)]$$
$$= E_0 I_0 \sin \omega t \cdot \sin(\omega t + \phi)$$
$$= \frac{E_0 I_0}{2}[\cos \phi - \cos(2\omega t + \phi)] \qquad \text{...(i)}$$

Average power

$$P_{av} = \frac{V_0}{\sqrt{2}} \frac{I_0}{\sqrt{2}} \cos \phi$$
$$= V_{rms}\, I_{rms} \cos \phi \qquad \text{...(ii)}$$

where ϕ is the phase difference.

Clearly, from Eq. (i)

when $\cos \phi < \cos(2\,\omega t + \phi)$

$$P < 0$$

Yes, the instantaneous power output of an AC source can be negative.

From Eq. (ii) $P_{av} > 0$

Because $\cos \phi = \dfrac{R}{Z} > 0$

No, the average power output of an AC source cannot be negative.

Q.18 In series *LCR* circuit, the plot of I_{max} *versus* ω is shown in figure. Find the bandwidth and mark in the figure.

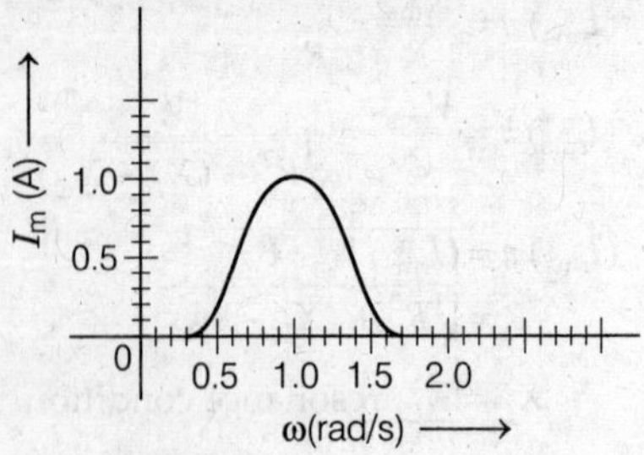

Ans. Consider the diagram .

Bandwidth = $\omega_2 - \omega_1$

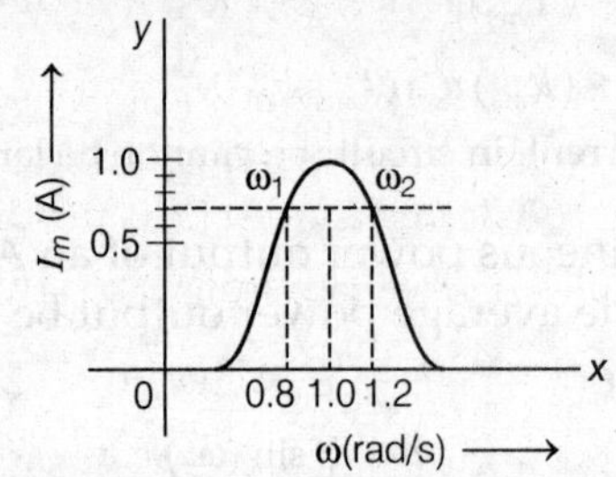

where ω_1 and ω_2 corresponds to frequencies at which magnitude of current is $\frac{1}{\sqrt{2}}$ times of maximum value.

$$I_{rms} = \frac{I_{max}}{\sqrt{2}} = \frac{1}{\sqrt{2}} \approx 0.7 \text{ A}$$

Clearly from the diagram, the corresponding frequencies are 0.8 rad/s and 1.2 rad/s.

$$\Delta\omega = \text{Bandwidth} = 1 \cdot 2 - 0.8 = 0.4 \text{ rad/s}$$

Q.19 The alternating current in a circuit is described by the graph shown in figure. Show rms current in this graph.

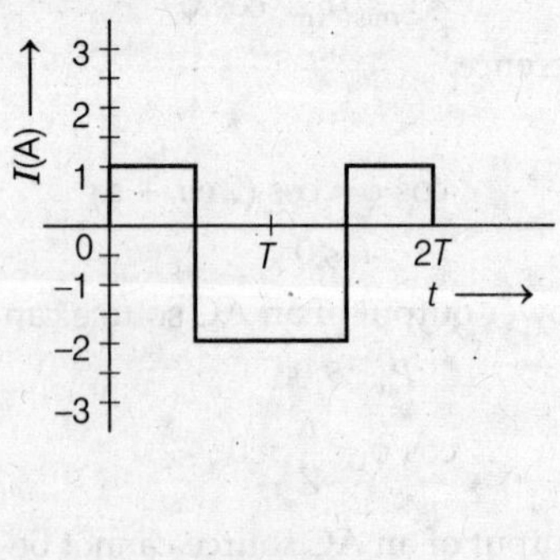

Ans. I_{rms} = rms current

$$= \sqrt{\frac{1^2 + 2^2}{2}} = \sqrt{\frac{5}{2}} = 1.58\text{A} \approx 1.6\text{ A}$$

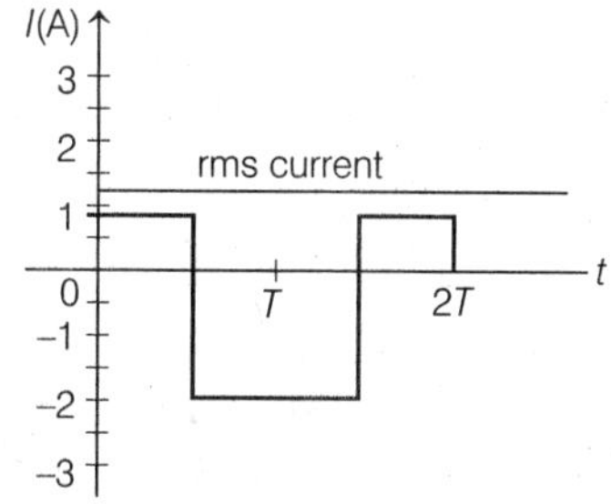

The rms value of the current (I_{rms}) = 1.6 A is indicated in the graph.

Q.20 How does the sign of the phase angle ϕ, by which the supply voltage leads the current in an L-C-R series circuit, change as the supply frequency is gradually increased from very low to very high values.

Ans. The phase angle (ϕ) by which voltage leads the current in L-C-R series circuit is given by

$$\tan\phi = \frac{X_L - X_C}{R} = \frac{2\pi\nu L - \frac{1}{2\pi\nu C}}{R}$$

$$\tan\phi < 0 \text{ (for } \nu < \nu_0)$$

$$\tan\phi > 0 \text{ (for } \nu > \nu_0)$$

$$\tan\phi = 0 \qquad \left(\text{for } \nu = \nu_0 = \frac{1}{2\pi\sqrt{LC}}\right)$$

Short Answer Type Questions

Q.21 A device 'X' is connected to an AC source. The variation of voltage, current and power in one complete cycle is shown in figure.

(a) Which curve shows power consumption over a full cycle?

(b) What is the average power consumption over a cycle?

(c) Identify the device X.

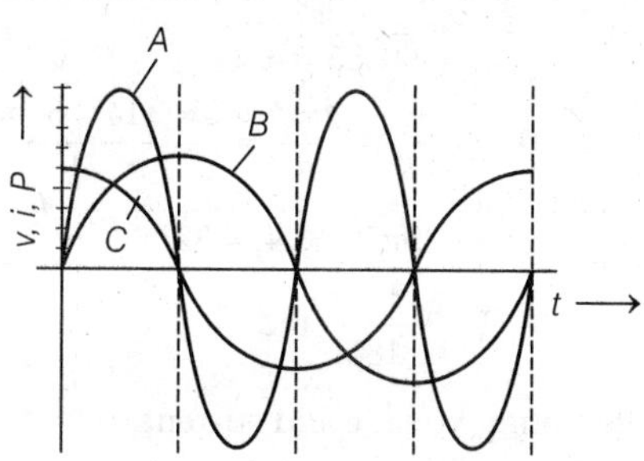

Ans. (a) We know that Power = $P = VI$

that is curve of power will be having maximum amplitude, equals to multiplication of amplitudes of voltage (V) and current (I) curve. So, the curve will be represented by A.

(b) As shown by shaded area in the diagram, the full cycle of the graph consists of one positive and one negative symmetrical area.

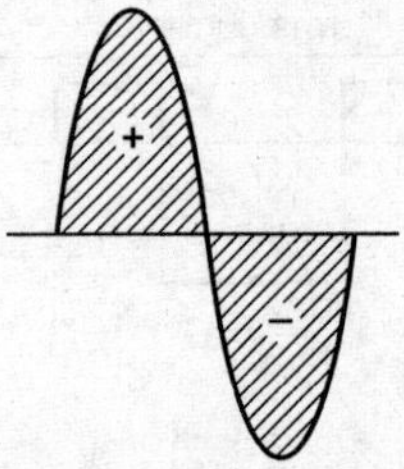

Hence, average power over a cycle is zero.

(c) As the average power is zero, hence the device may be inductor (L) or capacitor (C) or the series combination of L and C.

Q.22 **Both alternating current and direct current are measured in amperes. But how is the ampere defined for an alternating current?**

Ans. For a Direct Current (DC),

$$1 \text{ ampere} = 1 \text{ coulomb/sec}$$

An AC current changes direction with the source frequency and the attractive force would average to zero. Thus, the AC ampere must be defined in terms of some property that is independent of the direction of current.

Joule's heating effect is such property and hence it is used to define rms value of AC.

Q.23 **A coil of 0.01H inductance and 1Ω resistance is connected to 200 V, 50Hz AC supply. Find the impedance of the circuit and time lag between maximum alternating voltage and current.**

Ans. Given, inductance $L = 0.01\,\text{H}$

resistance $R = 1\Omega$, voltage $(V) = 200\,\text{V}$

and frequency $(f) = 50$ Hz.

Impedance of the circuit $Z = \sqrt{R^2 + X_L^2} = \sqrt{R^2 + (2\pi f L)^2}$

$$= \sqrt{1^2 + (2 \times 3.14 \times 50 \times 0.01)^2}$$

or $Z = \sqrt{10.86} = 3.3\Omega$

$$\tan\phi = \frac{\omega L}{R} = \frac{2\pi f L}{R} = \frac{2 \times 3.14 \times 50 \times 0.01}{1} = 3.14$$

$$\phi = \tan^{-1}(3.14) \approx 72°$$

Phase difference $\phi = \frac{72 \times \pi}{180}$ rad.

Time lag between alternating voltage and current

$$\Delta t = \frac{\phi}{\omega} = \frac{72\pi}{180 \times 2\pi \times 50} = \frac{1}{250}\text{ s} = 0.004\text{ s}$$

Q.24 A 60 W load is connected to the secondary of a transformer whose primary draws line voltage. If a current of 0.54 A flows in the load, what is the current in the primary coil? Comment on the type of tansformer being used.

Ans. Given, $P_s = 60\text{ W}, I_s = 0.54\text{ A}$

Current in the primary $I_p = ?$

Taking line or primary voltage as 220 V.

We can write,

$$\Rightarrow \quad P_s = 60\text{W}, I_s = 0.54\text{A}$$

$$\Rightarrow \quad V_s = \frac{60}{0.54} = 110\text{V}. \quad \text{...(i)}$$

Voltage in the secondary (V_S) is less than voltage in the primary (V_P).

Hence, the transformer is step down transformer.

Since, the transformation ratio

$$r = \frac{V_s}{V_p} = \frac{I_p}{I_s}$$

Substituting the values, $\frac{110\text{V}}{220\text{V}} = \frac{I_p}{0.54\text{A}}$

On solving $\quad I_p = 0.27\text{A}$

Q.25 Explain why the reactance provided by a capacitor to an alternating current decreases with increasing frequency.

Ans. A capacitor does not allow flow of direct current through it as the resistance across the gap is infinite. When an alternating voltage is applied across the capacitor plates, the plates are alternately charged and discharged. The current through the capacitor is a result of this changing voltage (or charge).

Thus, a capacitor will pass more current through it if the voltage is changing at a faster rate, *i.e.* the frequency of supply is higher. This implies that the reactance offered by a capacitor is less with increasing frequency.

Mathematically, the reactance can be written as $X_C = \frac{1}{\omega C}$.

Q.26 Explain why the reactance offered by an inductor increases with increasing frequency of an alternating voltage.

Ans. An inductor opposes flow of current through it by developing a back emf according to Lenz's law. The induced voltage has a polarity so as to maintain the current at its present value. If the current is decreasing, the polarity of the induced emf will be so as to increase the current and *vice -versa.*

Since, the induced emf is proportional to the rate of change of current, it will provide greater reactance to the flow of current if the rate of change is faster, *i.e.*, if the frequency is higher. The reactance of an inductor, therefore, is proportional to the frequency. Mathematically, the reactance offered by the inductor is given by $X_L = \omega L$.

Long Answer Type Questions

Q.27 An electrical device draws 2 kW power from AC mains (voltage 223 V (rms) $= \sqrt{50000}$ V). The current differs (lags) in phase by $\phi \left(\tan \phi = \frac{-3}{4} \right)$ as compared to voltage. Find (a) R, (b) $X_C - X_L$ and (c) I_M. Another device has twice the values for R, X_C and X_L. How are the answers affected?

Thinking Process We have to apply the formula for phase relation, net reactance as well as instantaneous power associate with the circuit in terms of voltage and current.

Ans. Given, power drawn $= P = 2\text{kW} = 2000$ W

$$\tan \phi = -\frac{3}{4}, I_M = I_0 = ?, R = ?, X_C - X_L = ?$$

$$V_{\text{rms}} = V = 223 \text{ V}$$

$$\text{Power } P = \frac{V^2}{Z}$$

$$\Rightarrow \quad Z = \frac{V^2}{P} = \frac{223 \times 223}{2 \times 10^3} = 25\ \Omega$$

$$\text{Impedance } Z = 25\ \Omega$$

$$\text{Impedance } Z = \sqrt{R^2 + (X_L - X_C)^2}$$

$$\Rightarrow \quad 25 = \sqrt{R^2 + (X_L - X_C)^2}$$

or $$625 = R^2 + (X_L - X_C)^2 \quad \ldots\text{(i)}$$

Again, $$\tan \phi = \frac{X_L - X_C}{R} = \frac{-3}{4}$$

or $$X_L - X_C = \frac{-3R}{4} \quad \ldots\text{(ii)}$$

From Eq. (ii), we put $X_L - X_C = \frac{-3R}{4}$ in Eq. (i), we get

$$625 = R^2 + \left(\frac{-3R}{4} \right)^2 = R^2 + \frac{9R^2}{16}$$

or $$625 = \frac{25R^2}{16}$$

(a) Resistance $R = \sqrt{25 \times 16} = \sqrt{400} = 20\Omega$

(b) $X_L - X_C = \frac{-3R}{4} = \frac{-3}{4} \times 20 = -15\Omega$

(c) Main current $I_M = \sqrt{2} I = \sqrt{2} \frac{V}{Z} = \frac{223}{25} \times \sqrt{2} = 12.6$ A

As R, X_C, X_L are all doubled, $\tan \phi$ does not change. Z is doubled, current is halved. So, power is also halved.

Q.28 1 MW power is to be delivered from a power station to a town 10 km away. One uses a pair of Cu wires of radius 0.5 cm for this purpose. Calculate the fraction of ohmic losses to power transmitted if

(i) power is transmitted at 220V. Comment on the feasibility of doing this.

(ii) a step-up transformer is used to boost the voltage to 11000V, power transmitted, then a step-down transformer is used to bring voltage to 220 V. ($\rho_{cu} = 1.7 \times 10^{-8}$ SI unit)

Ans. (i) The town is 10 km away, length of pair of Cu wires used, $L = 20$ km $= 20000$ m.

Resistance of Cu wires, $R = \dfrac{\rho_{cu}\, l}{A} = \dfrac{\rho_{cu}\, l}{\pi (r)^2}$

$$= \frac{1.7 \times 10^{-8} \times 20000}{3.14\,(0.5 \times 10^{-2})^2} = 4.3\Omega$$

I at 220 V $\quad VI = 10^6$ W; $I = \dfrac{10^6}{220} = 0.45 \times 10^4$ A

Power loss $= RI^2$

$$= 4.3 \times (0.45)^2 \times 10^8 \text{ W} > 10^6 \text{ W}$$

Therefore, this method cannot be used for transmission.

(ii) When power $P = 10^6$ W is transmitted at 11000 V.

$$V'I' = 10^6 \text{ W} = 11000\, I'$$

Current drawn, $I' = \dfrac{1}{1.1} \times 10^2$

Power loss $= RI^2 = \dfrac{1}{121} \times 4 \times 10^4 = 3.3 \times 10^4$ W

Fraction of power loss $= \dfrac{3.3 \times 10^4}{10^6} = 3.3\%$

Q.29 Consider the L-C-R circuit shown in figure. Find the net current i and the phase of i. Show that $i = \dfrac{V}{Z}$. Find the impedance Z for this circuit.

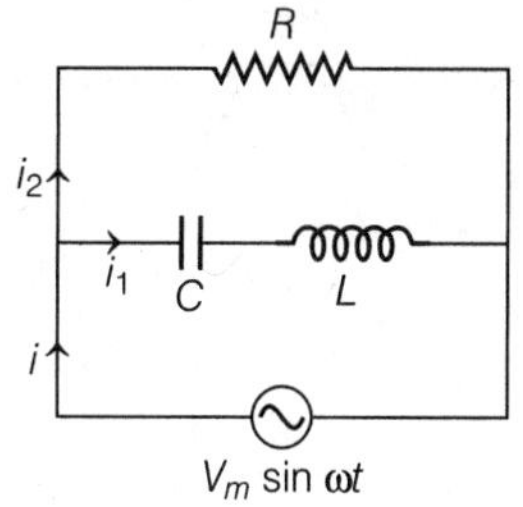

Thinking Process The circuit consists of inductor (L) and capacitor (C) connected in series and the combination is connected parallel with a resistance R. Due to this combination there is oscillation of electromagnetic energy.

Ans. In the given figure i is the total current from the source. It is divided into two parts i_1 through R and i_2 through series combination of C and L.

So, we can write $i = i_1 + i_2$

As, $V_m \sin \omega t = R i_1$ [from the circuit diagram]

$$\Rightarrow \quad i_1 = \frac{V_m \sin \omega t}{R} \quad \text{...(i)}$$

If q_2 is charge on the capacitor at any time t, then for series combination of C and L.

Applying KVL in the Lower circuit as shown,

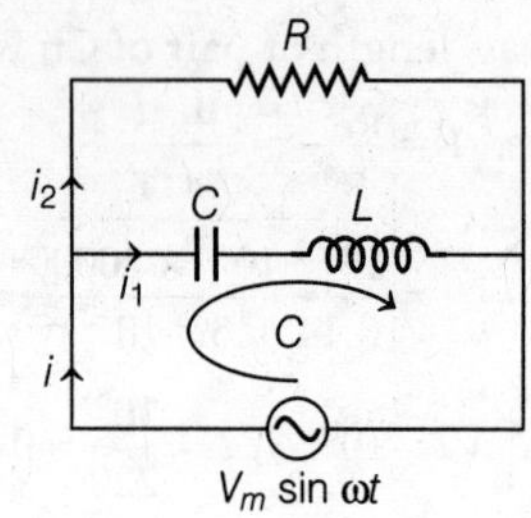

$$\frac{q_2}{C} + \frac{L\,di_2}{dt} - V_m \sin \omega t = 0$$

$$\Rightarrow \quad \frac{q_2}{C} + \frac{L\,d^2 q_2}{dt^2} = V_m \sin \omega t \quad \left[\because i_2 = \frac{dq_2}{dt}\right] \text{... (ii)}$$

Let $$q_2 = q_m \sin (\omega t + \phi) \quad \text{... (iii)}$$

$$\therefore \quad \frac{dq_2}{dt} = q_m \omega \cos (\omega t + \phi)$$

$$\Rightarrow \quad \frac{d^2 q_2}{dt^2} = -q_m \omega^2 \sin (\omega t + \phi)$$

Now putting these values in Eq. (ii), we get

$$q_m \left[\frac{1}{C} + L(-\omega^2)\right] \sin (\omega t + \phi) = V_m \sin \omega t$$

If $\phi = 0$ and $\left(\frac{1}{C} - L\omega^2\right) > 0$,

then $$q_m = \frac{V_m}{\left(\frac{1}{C} - L\omega^2\right)} \quad \text{...(iv)}$$

From Eq. (iii), $$i_2 = \frac{dq_2}{dt} = \omega q_m \cos (\omega t + \phi)$$

using Eq. (iv), $$i_2 = \frac{\omega V_m \cos (\omega t + \phi)}{\frac{1}{C} - L\omega^2}$$

$$\text{Taking } \phi = 0; \; i_2 = \frac{V_m \cos (\omega t)}{\left(\frac{1}{\omega C} - L\omega\right)} \quad \text{...(v)}$$

From Eqs. (i) and (v), we find that i_1 and i_2 are out of phase by $\frac{\pi}{2}$.

Now, $$i_1 + i_2 = \frac{V_m \sin \omega t}{R} + \frac{V_m \cos \omega t}{\left(\frac{1}{\omega C} - L\omega\right)}$$

Put $$\frac{V_m}{R} = A = C\cos\phi \text{ and } \frac{V_m}{\left(\frac{1}{\omega C} - L\omega\right)} = B = C\sin\phi$$

$\therefore$ $$i_1 + i_2 = C\cos\phi\sin\omega t + C\sin\phi\cos\omega t$$
$$= C\sin(\omega t + \phi)$$

where $$C = \sqrt{A^2 + B^2}$$

$$C = \left[\frac{V_m^2}{R^2} + \frac{V_m^2}{\left(\frac{1}{\omega C} - L\omega\right)}\right]^{1/2}$$

and $$\phi = \tan^{-1}\frac{B}{A}$$

and $$\phi = \tan^{-1}\frac{R}{\left(\frac{1}{\omega C} - L\omega\right)}$$

Hence, $$i = i_1 + i_2 = \left[\frac{V_m^2}{R^2} + \frac{V_m^2}{\left(\frac{1}{\omega C} - L\omega\right)^2}\right]^{1/2} \sin(\omega t + \phi)$$

For AC, $i = V / Z\ (\because V = V_m \sin(\omega t + \phi))$

or $$\frac{i}{V} = \frac{1}{Z} = \left[\frac{1}{R^2} + \frac{1}{\left(\frac{1}{\omega C} - L\omega\right)^2}\right]^{1/2}$$

This is the expression for impedance Z of the circuit.

Mistake Alert! *In this problem, we should not apply the formulae of L-C-R series circuit directly.*

Q.30 For a L-C-R circuit driven at frequency ω, the equation reads

$$L\frac{di}{dt} + Ri + \frac{q}{C} = V_i = V_m \sin\omega t$$

(a) Multiply the equation by i and simplify where possible.

(b) Interpret each term physically.

(c) Cast the equation in the form of a conservation of energy statement.

(d) Intergrate the equation over one cycle to find that the phase difference between V and i must be acute.

- **Concept Insight** Apply *KVL* for the given *L-C-R* series circuit and find the required relations. Also find energy loss through the resistors to know net loss of energy through the circuit.

Ans. Consider the *L-C-R* circuit. Applying KVL for the loop, we can write

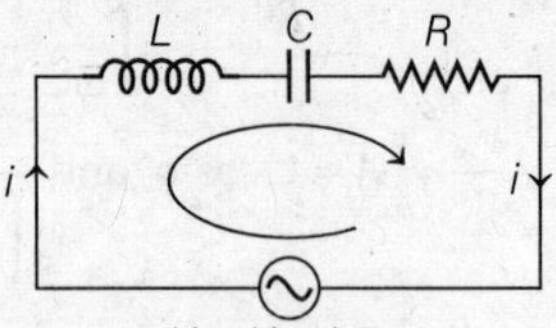

$$\Rightarrow \qquad L\frac{di}{dt} + \frac{q}{C} + iR = V_m \sin \omega t \qquad \text{.... (i)}$$

(a) Multiplying both sides by *i*, we get

$$Li\frac{di}{dt} + \frac{q}{C}i + i^2R = (V_m i)\sin \omega t = Vi \qquad \text{..... (ii)}$$

(b) $Li\frac{di}{dt} = \frac{d}{dt}\left(\frac{1}{2}Li^2\right)$ = rate of change of energy stored in an inductor.

Ri^2 = joule heating loss and $\frac{q}{C}i = \frac{d}{dt}\left(\frac{q^2}{2C}\right)$ = rate of change of energy stored in the capacitor.

Vi = rate at which driving force pours in energy. It goes into (i) ohmic loss and (ii) increase of stored energy.

(c) Hence Eq. (ii) is in the form of conservation of energy statement.

(d) Integrating both sides of Eq. (ii) with respect to time over one full cycle ($0 \to T$) we may write

$$\int_0^T \frac{d}{dt}\left(\frac{1}{2}Li^2 + \frac{q^2}{2C}\right)dt + \int_0^T Ri^2 dt = \int_0^T Vi\,dt \Rightarrow 0 + (+ve) = \int_0^T Vi\,dt$$

$\Rightarrow \int_0^T Vi\,dt > 0$, if phase difference between *V* and *i* is a constant and acute angle.

Mistake Alert! *When integrating over one cycle, it is essential to understand that quantities like current return to their starting values. Forgetting this leads to incorrect simplifications.*

Q.31 In the *L-C-R* circuit, shown in figure the AC driving voltage is $V = V_m \sin \omega t$.

(a) Write down the equation of motion for $q(t)$.

(b) At $t = t_0$, the voltage source stops and *R* is short circuited. Now write down how much energy is stored in each of *L* and *C*.

(c) Describe subsequent motion of charges.

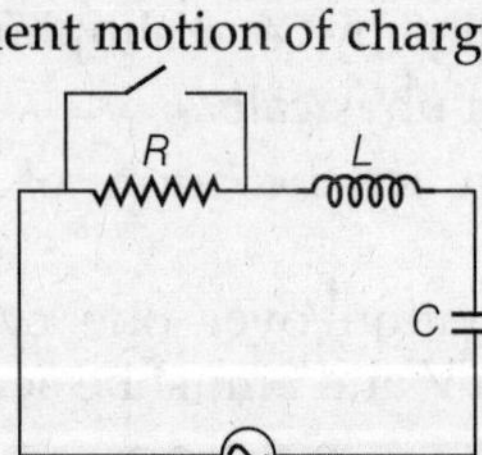

Thinking Process We have to apply KVL write the equations in the form of current and charge double differentiate the equation with respect to time and find the required relations.

Ans. (a) Consider the *R-L-C* circuit shown in the adjacent diagram.

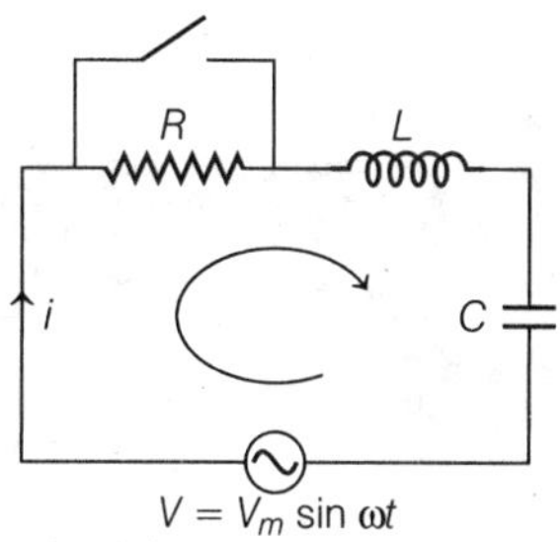

Given $V = V_m \sin \omega t$

Let current at any instant be i

Applying KVL in the given circuit

$$iR + L\frac{di}{dt} + \frac{q}{C} - V_m \sin \omega t = 0 \quad \text{...(i)}$$

Now, we can write $i = \frac{dq}{dt} \Rightarrow \frac{di}{dt} = \frac{d^2q}{dt^2}$

From Eq. (i) $\frac{dq}{dt} R + L\frac{d^2q}{dt^2} + \frac{q}{C} = V_m \sin \omega t$

$\Rightarrow$ $$L\frac{d^2q}{dt^2} + R\frac{dq}{dt} + \frac{q}{C} = V_m \sin \omega t$$

This is the required equation of variation (motion) of charge.

(b) Let $q = q_m \sin (\omega t + \phi) = - q_m \cos (\omega t + \phi)$

$$i = i_m \sin(\omega t + \phi) = q_m \omega \sin (\omega t + \phi)$$

$$i_m = \frac{V_m}{Z} = \frac{V_m}{\sqrt{R^2 + (X_C - X_L)^2}} \Rightarrow \phi = \tan^{-1}\left(\frac{X_C - X_L}{R}\right)$$

When R is short circuited at $t = t_0$, energy is stored in L and C.

$$U_L = \frac{1}{2} Li^2 = \frac{1}{2} L\left[\frac{V_m}{\sqrt{(R^2 + X_C - X_L)^2}}\right]^2 \sin^2 (\omega t_0 + \phi)$$

and $$U_C = \frac{1}{2} \times \frac{q^2}{C} = \frac{1}{2C} [q_m^2 \cos^2 (\omega t_0 + \phi)] = \frac{1}{2C}\left[\frac{V_m}{\sqrt{R^2 + (X_C - X_L)^2}}\right]^2$$

$$= \frac{1}{2C} \times \left(\frac{i_m}{\omega}\right)^2 \cos^2 (\omega t_0 + \phi) = \frac{i_m^2}{2C\omega^2} \cos^2(\omega t_0 + \phi) \quad [\because i_m = q_m\omega]$$

$$= \frac{1}{2C}\left[\frac{V_m}{\sqrt{R^2 + (X_C - X_L)^2}}\right]^2 \frac{\cos^2 (\omega t_0 + \phi)}{\omega^2}$$

$$= \frac{1}{2C\omega^2}\left[\frac{V_m}{\sqrt{R^2 + (X_C - X_L)^2}}\right]^2 \cos^2 (\omega t_0 + \phi)$$

(c) When R is short circuited, the circuit becomes an *L-C* oscillator. The capacitor will go on discharging and all energy will go to L and back and forth. Hence, there is oscillation of energy from electrostatic to magnetic and magnetic to electrostatic.

Chapter

08 Electromagnetic Waves

Multiple Choice Questions (MCQs)

Q.1 One requires 11 eV of energy to dissociate a carbon monoxide molecule into carbon and oxygen atoms. The minimum frequency of the appropriate electromagnetic radiation to achieve the dissociation lies in

(a) visible region
(b) infrared region
(c) ultraviolet region
(d) microwave region

Ans. *(c)* Given, energy required to dissociate a carbon monoxide molecule into carbon and oxygen atoms $E = 11\,\text{eV}$

We know that, $E = h\nu$, where $h = 6.62 \times 10^{-34}$ J-s and ν is frequency of the EM radiation

$$\Rightarrow \quad 11\text{eV} = h\nu$$

$$\Rightarrow \quad \nu = \frac{11 \times 1.6 \times 10^{-19}\,\text{J}}{h}$$

$$= \frac{11 \times 1.6 \times 10^{-19}}{6.62 \times 10^{-34}}\,\text{Hz}$$

$$= 2.65 \times 10^{15}\ \text{Hz}$$

This frequency radiation belongs to ultraviolet region.

Q.2 A linearly polarised electromagnetic wave given as $\mathbf{E} = \text{E}_0 \hat{\mathbf{i}} \cos\,(kz - \omega t)$ is incident normally on a perfectly reflecting infinite wall at $z = a$. Assuming that the material of the wall is optically inactive, the reflected wave will be given as

(a) $\mathbf{E}_r = E_0 \hat{\mathbf{i}}(kz - \omega t)$
(b) $\mathbf{E}_r = E_0 \hat{\mathbf{i}} \cos(kz + \omega t)$
(c) $\mathbf{E}_r = -E_0 \hat{\mathbf{i}} \cos(kz + \omega t)$
(d) $\mathbf{E}_r = E_0 \hat{\mathbf{i}} \sin(kz - \omega t)$

Thinking Process When a wave is reflected from a denser medium, then its phase changes by 180° or π.

Ans. *(b)* When a wave is reflected from denser medium, then the type of wave doesn't change but only its phase changes by 180° or π radian.

Thus, for the reflected wave $z = -z$, $\hat{\mathbf{i}} = -\hat{\mathbf{i}}$ and additional phase of π in the incident wave.

Given, here the incident electromagnetic wave is,

$$\mathbf{E} = E_0 \hat{\mathbf{i}} \cos(kz - \omega t)$$

The reflected electromagnetic wave is given by

$$\mathbf{E}_r = E_0(-\hat{\mathbf{i}}) \cos[k(-z) - \omega t + \pi]$$
$$= -E_0 \hat{\mathbf{i}} \cos[-(kz + \omega t) + \pi]$$
$$= E_0 \hat{\mathbf{i}} \cos(kz + \omega t) \qquad \{\because \cos(\pi - \theta) = -\cos\theta\}$$

Q.3 Light with an energy flux of 20 W/cm^2 falls on a non-reflecting surface at normal incidence. If the surface has an area of 30 cm^2, the total momentum delivered (for complete absorption) during 30 min is

(a) 36×10^{-5} kg-m/s
(b) 36×10^{-4} kg-m/s
(c) 108×10^{4} kg-m/s
(d) 1.08×10^{7} kg-m/s

Ans. ***(b)*** Given, energy flux $\phi = 20 \text{ W} / \text{cm}^2$

Area, $A = 30 \text{ cm}^2$

Time, $t = 30 \text{ min} = 30 \times 60 \text{ s}$

Now, total energy falling on the surface in time t is, $U = \phi A t = 20 \times 30 \times (30 \times 60) \text{ J}$

Momentum of the incident light $= \dfrac{U}{c}$

$$= \frac{20 \times 30 \times (30 \times 60)}{3 \times 10^8}$$
$$= 36 \times 10^{-4} \text{ kg-ms}^{-1}$$

Momentum of the reflected light = 0

$\therefore$ Momentum delivered to the surface $= 36 \times 10^{-4} - 0 = 36 \times 10^{-4} \text{ kg-ms}^{-1}$

Q.4 The electric field intensity produced by the radiations coming from 100 W bulb at a 3 m distance is E. The electric field intensity produced by the radiations coming from 50 W bulb at the same distance is

(a) $\dfrac{E}{2}$
(b) $2E$
(c) $\dfrac{E}{\sqrt{2}}$
(d) $\sqrt{2}E$

Thinking Process Electric field intensity on a surface due to incident radiation is,

$$I_{av} \propto E_0^2$$
$$\frac{P_{av.}}{A} \propto E_0^2$$

Here, $$P_{av} \propto E_0^2 \qquad [\because A \text{ is same in both cases}]$$

Ans. ***(c)*** We know that, $E_0 \propto \sqrt{P_{av}}$

$$\therefore \quad \frac{(E_0)_1}{(E_0)_2} = \sqrt{\frac{(P_{av})_1}{(P_{av})_2}} \Rightarrow \frac{(E_0)_1}{(E_0)_2} = \sqrt{\frac{100}{50}}$$

$$\Rightarrow \quad (E_0)_2 = \frac{(E_0)_1}{\sqrt{2}}$$

$$\Rightarrow \quad (E_0)_2 = \frac{E}{\sqrt{2}}$$

Q.5 If **E** and **B** represent electric and magnetic field vectors of the electromagnetic wave, the direction of propagation of electromagnetic wave is along

(a) **E** (b) **B** (c) $\mathbf{B} \times \mathbf{E}$ (d) $\mathbf{E} \times \mathbf{B}$

Ans. *(d)* The direction of propagation of electromagnetic wave is perpendicular to both electric field vector **E** and magnetic field vector **B**, *i.e.*, in the direction of $\mathbf{E} \times \mathbf{B}$.

This can be seen by the diagram given below.

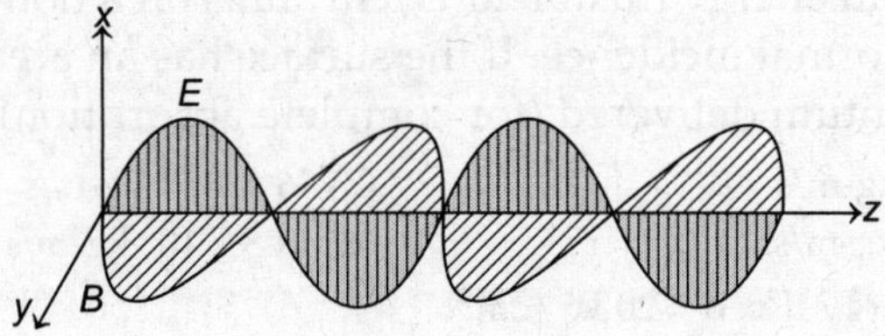

Here, electromagnetic wave is along the z-direction which is given by the cross product of **E** and **B**.

Mistake Alert ! *Students sometimes assume that the direction of* $\mathbf{B} \times \mathbf{E}$ *and* $\mathbf{E} \times \mathbf{B}$ *is same, but both directions are opposite to each other.*

Q.6 The ratio of contributions made by the electric field and magnetic field components to the intensity of an EM wave is

(a) $c : 1$ (b) $c^2 : 1$ (c) $1 : 1$ (d) $\sqrt{c} : 1$

● **Concept Insight** Intensity of electromagnetic wave, $I = U_{av} c$

where, U_{av} = average energy
and c = speed of light

Ans. *(c)* Average energy stored in electric field, $U_{av} = \frac{1}{2} \varepsilon_0 E_0^2$

Average energy stored in magnetic field, $U_{av} = \frac{1}{2} \frac{B_0^2}{\mu_0}$

Now,

$$(U_{av})_E = \frac{1}{2} \varepsilon_0 E_0^2$$

$$\Rightarrow \quad = \frac{1}{2} \varepsilon_0 (cB_0)^2 \qquad (\because E_0 = cB_0)$$

$$= \frac{1}{2} \varepsilon_0 \times c^2 B_0^2$$

But,

$$c = \frac{1}{\sqrt{\mu_0 \varepsilon_0}}$$

$$\therefore \quad (U_{av})_E = \frac{1}{2} \varepsilon_0 \times \frac{1}{\mu_0 \varepsilon_0} B_0^2 = \frac{1}{2} \frac{B_0^2}{\mu_0} = (U_{av})_B$$

Thus, the energy in electromagnetic wave is divided equally between electric field vector and magnetic field vector.

Therefore, the ratio of contributions by the electric field and magnetic field components to the intensity of an electromagnetic wave is 1 : 1.

Q.7 An EM wave radiates outwards from a dipole antenna, with E_0 as the amplitude of its electric field vector. The electric field E_0 which transports significant energy from the source falls off as

(a) $\frac{1}{r^3}$ (b) $\frac{1}{r^2}$

(c) $\frac{1}{r}$ (d) remains constant

Ans. *(c)* From a diode antenna, the electromagnetic waves are radiated outwards. The amplitude of electric field vector (E_0) which transports significant energy from the source falls off inversely with the distance (r) from the antenna, *i.e.*, $E_0 \propto \frac{1}{r}$.

Multiple Choice Questions (More Than One Options)

Q.8 An electromagnetic wave travels in vacuum along z-direction $\mathbf{E} = (E_1\hat{\mathbf{i}} + E_2\hat{\mathbf{j}})\cos(kz - \omega t)$. Choose the correct options from the following

(a) The associated magnetic field is given as

$$\mathbf{B} = \frac{1}{c}(E_1\hat{\mathbf{j}} - E_2\hat{\mathbf{i}})\cos(kz - \omega t)$$

(b) The associated magnetic field is given as

$$\mathbf{B} = \frac{1}{c}(E_1\hat{\mathbf{i}} - E_2\hat{\mathbf{j}})\cos(kz - \omega t)$$

(c) The given electromagnetic field is circularly polarised

(d) The given electromagnetic wave is plane polarised

- **Concept Insight** From Maxwell's equations, it is seen that the electric and the magnetic field vectors in an electromagnetic wave are related as

$$\mathbf{B} = \frac{\hat{\mathbf{k}} \times \mathbf{E}}{c}$$

Ans. *(a, d)* Here, in electromagnetic wave, the electric field vector is given as,

$$\mathbf{E} = (E_1\hat{\mathbf{i}} + E_2\hat{\mathbf{j}})\cos(kz - \omega t)$$

Since this wave is propagating in + z direction *i.e.*, $\hat{\mathbf{k}}$ direction

$$\therefore \quad \mathbf{B} = \frac{\mathbf{E}}{c} = \frac{\hat{\mathbf{k}} \times \mathbf{E}}{c} = \frac{1}{c}[\hat{\mathbf{k}} \times (E_1\hat{\mathbf{i}} + E_2\hat{\mathbf{j}})\cos(kz - \omega t)]$$

$$\Rightarrow \quad \mathbf{B} = \frac{1}{c}[(E_1\hat{\mathbf{j}} - E_2\hat{\mathbf{i}})\cos(kz - \omega t)]$$

Also, **E** and **B** are perpendicular to each other and the propagation of electromagnetic wave is perpendicular to **E** as well as **B**, so the given electromagnetic wave is plane polarised.

Q.9 An electromagnetic wave travelling along z-axis is given as $\mathbf{E} = \mathbf{E}_0 \cos(kz - \omega t)$. Choose the correct options from the following

(a) The associated magnetic field is given as $\mathbf{B} = \frac{1}{c}\hat{\mathbf{k}} \times \mathbf{E} = \frac{1}{\omega}(\hat{\mathbf{k}} \times \mathbf{E})$

(b) The electromagnetic field can be written in terms of the associated magnetic field as $\mathbf{E} = c(\mathbf{B} \times \hat{\mathbf{k}})$

(c) $\hat{\mathbf{k}} \cdot \mathbf{E} = 0$, $\hat{\mathbf{k}} \cdot \mathbf{B} = 0$

(d) $\hat{\mathbf{k}} \times \mathbf{E} = 0$, $\hat{\mathbf{k}} \times \mathbf{B} = 0$

Ans. ***(a, b, c)*** Suppose an electromagnetic wave is travelling along positive z-direction. Its electric field is given by

$$\mathbf{E} = \mathbf{E}_o \cos(kz - \omega t)$$

which is perpendicular to z-axis.

The associated magnetic field **B** in electromagnetic wave is along $\hat{\mathbf{k}} \times \mathbf{E}$

$$\therefore \quad \mathbf{B} = \frac{1}{c}(\hat{\mathbf{k}} \times \mathbf{E}) = \frac{1}{\omega}(\hat{\mathbf{k}} \times \mathbf{E}) \qquad \left(\because c = \frac{\omega}{k}\right)$$

The associated electric field can be written in terms of magnetic field as

$$\mathbf{E} = c(\mathbf{B} \times \hat{\mathbf{k}}).$$

Angle between $\hat{\mathbf{k}}$ and **E** and between $\hat{\mathbf{k}}$ and **B** are 90°.

Therefore, $\hat{\mathbf{k}} \cdot \mathbf{E} = 1E\cos 90° = 0$ and $\hat{\mathbf{k}} \cdot \mathbf{B} = 1\, E\cos 90° = 0$.

Q.10 A plane electromagnetic wave propagating along *x*-direction can have the following pairs of **E** and **B**.

(a) E_x, B_y (b) E_y, B_z (c) B_x, E_y (d) E_z, B_y

Ans. ***(b, d)*** Electric and magnetic field vectors **E** and **B** are perpendicular to each other as well as perpendicular to the direction of propagation of electromagnetic wave.

Here in the question electromagnetic wave is propagating along *x*-direction. So, electric and magnetic field vectors should have either *y*-direction or *z*-direction.

Q.11 A charged particle oscillates about its mean equilibrium position with a frequency of 10^9 Hz. The electromagnetic waves produced

(a) will have frequency of 10^9 Hz

(b) will have frequency of 2×10^9 Hz

(c) will have wavelength of 0.3 m

(d) fall in the region of radiowaves

Thinking Process The frequency of electromagnetic waves produced by a charged particle is equal to the frequency with which it oscillates about its mean equilibrium position.

Ans. ***(a, c, d)*** Given, frequency with which the charged particles oscillates about its mean equilibrium position = 10^9Hz.

So, frequency of electromagnetic waves produced by the charged particle is $\nu = 10^9$ Hz.

$$\text{Wavelength } \lambda = \frac{c}{\nu} = \frac{3 \times 10^8}{10^9} = 0.3 \text{ m}$$

Also, frequency of 10^9 Hz falls in the region of radiowaves.

Q.12 The source of electromagnetic waves can be a charge

(a) moving with a constant velocity
(b) moving in a circular orbit
(c) at rest
(d) falling in an electric field

Thinking Process An electromagnetic wave can be produced by accelerated or oscillating charge.

Ans. ***(b, d)*** In circular motion, the direction of the motion of charge is changing continuously, thus it is an accelerated motion and accelerated charges can be considered as source of electromagnetic wave.

Also, we know that a charge starts accelerating when it falls in an electric field.

Q.13 An EM wave of intensity I falls on a surface kept in vacuum and exerts radiation pressure p on it. Which of the following are true?

(a) Radiation pressure is $\frac{I}{c}$ if the wave is totally absorbed

(b) Radiation pressure is $\frac{I}{c}$ if the wave is totally reflected

(c) Radiation pressure is $\frac{2I}{c}$ if the wave is totally reflected

(d) Radiation pressure is in the range $\frac{I}{c} < p < \frac{2I}{c}$ for real surfaces

Ans. ***(a, c, d)*** Radiation pressure (p) is the force exerted by electromagnetic wave on unit area of the surface, *i.e.*, rate of change of momentum per unit area of the surface.

Momentum per unit time per unit area $= \frac{\text{Intensity}}{\text{Speed of wave}} = \frac{I}{c}$

Change in momentum per unit time per unit area $= \frac{\Delta I}{c} =$ radiation pressure (p)

i.e., $$p = \frac{\Delta I}{c}$$

Momentum of incident wave per unit time per unit area $= \frac{I}{c}$

When wave is fully absorbed by the surface, the momentum of the reflected wave per unit time per unit area = 0.

Radiation pressure (p) = change in momentum per unit time per unit area

$$= \frac{\Delta I}{c} = \frac{I}{c} - 0 = \frac{I}{c}.$$

When wave is totally reflected, then momentum of the reflected wave per unit time per unit area $= -\frac{I}{c}$, Radiation pressure $p = \frac{I}{c} - \left(-\frac{I}{c}\right) = \frac{2I}{c}$.

Here, p lies between $\frac{I}{c}$ and $\frac{2I}{c}$.

Very Short Answer Type Questions

Q.14 Why is the orientation of the portable radio with respect to broadcasting station important?

Ans. The orientation of the portable radio with respect to broadcasting station is important because the electromagnetic waves are plane polarised, so the receiving antenna should be parallel to the vibration of the electric or magnetic field of the wave.

Q.15 Why does microwave oven heats up a food item containing water molecules most efficiently?

Ans. Microwave oven heats up the food items containing water molecules most efficiently because the frequency of microwaves matches the resonant frequency of water molecules.

Q.16 The charge on a parallel plate capacitor varies as $q = q_0 \cos 2\pi\nu t$. The plates are very large and close together (area = A, separation = d). Neglecting the edge effects, find the displacement current through the capacitor.

Ans. The displacement current through the capacitor is,

$$I_d = I_c = \frac{dq}{dt} \quad \text{...(i)}$$

Here, $q = q_0 \cos 2\pi\nu t$ (given)

Putting this value in Eq (i), we get

$$I_d = I_c = -q_0 \sin 2\pi\nu t \times 2\pi\nu$$

$$I_d = I_c = -2\pi\nu q_0 \sin 2\pi\nu t$$

Q.17 A variable frequency AC source is connected to a capacitor. How will the displacement current change with decrease in frequency?

- **Concept Insight** Capacitive reactance X_c is inversely proportional to the displacement current *i.e.*, $X_c \propto \frac{1}{I}$

Ans. Capacitive reactance $X_c = \frac{1}{2\pi fC}$

$$\therefore \quad X_c \propto \frac{1}{f}$$

As frequency decreases, X_c increases and the conduction current is inversely proportional to $X_c \left(\because I \propto \frac{1}{X_c} \right)$.

So, displacement current decreases as the conduction current is equal to the displacement current.

Q.18 The magnetic field of a beam emerging from a filter facing a floodlight is given by $B_0 = 12 \times 10^{-8} \sin(1.20 \times 10^7 z - 3.60 \times 10^{15} t)$ T. What is the average intensity of the beam?

Ans. Magnetic field $B = B_0 \sin \omega t$

Given, equation $B = 12 \times 10^{-8} \sin(1.20 \times 10^7 z - 3.60 \times 10^{15} t)$ T.

On comparing this equation with standard equation, we get

$$B_0 = 12 \times 10^{-8}$$

The average intensity of the beam $I_{av} = \frac{1}{2}\frac{B_0^2}{\mu_0} \cdot c = \frac{1}{2} \times \frac{(12 \times 10^{-8})^2 \times 3 \times 10^8}{4\pi \times 10^{-7}}$

$$= 1.71 \text{ W/m}^2$$

Q.19 Poynting vectors **S** is defined as a vector whose magnitude is equal to the wave intensity and whose direction is along the direction of wave propogation. Mathematically, it is given by $\mathbf{S} = \frac{1}{\mu_o} \mathbf{E} \times \mathbf{B}$. Show the nature of **S** *versus* t graph.

Ans. Consider an electromagnetic wave, let **E** be varying along y-axis, **B** is along z-axis and propagation of wave be along x-axis. Then $\mathbf{E} \times \mathbf{B}$ will tell the direction of propagation of energy flow in electromagnetic wave, along x-axis.

Let
$$\mathbf{E} = E_o \sin(\omega t - kx)\hat{\mathbf{j}}$$
$$\mathbf{B} = B_o \sin(\omega t - kx)\hat{\mathbf{k}}$$
$$\mathbf{S} = \frac{1}{\mu_o}(\mathbf{E} \times \mathbf{B}) = \frac{1}{\mu_o} E_o B_o \sin^2(\omega t - kx)[\hat{\mathbf{j}} \times \hat{\mathbf{k}}]$$
$$= \frac{E_o B_o}{\mu_o} \sin^2(\omega t - kx)\,\hat{\mathbf{i}}$$

The variation of $|\mathbf{S}|$ with time t will be as given in the figure below.

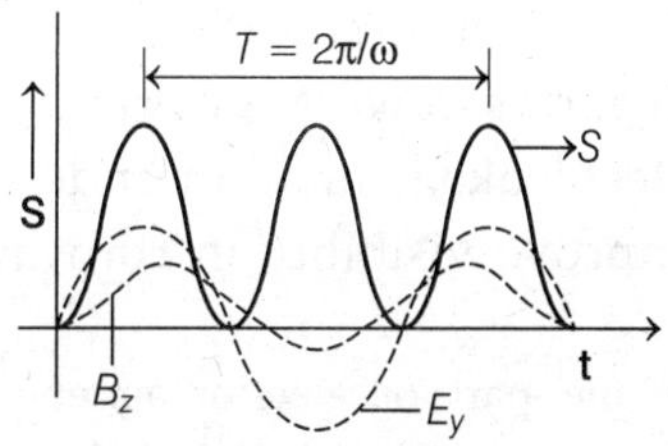

Q.20 Professor CV Raman surprised his students by suspending freely a tiny light ball in a transparent vacuum chamber by shining a laser beam on it. Which property of EM waves was he exhibiting? Give one more example of this property.

Ans. An electromagnetic wave carries energy and momentum like other waves. Since, it carries momentum, an electromagnetic wave also exerts pressure called radiation pressure. This property of electromagnetic waves helped professor CV Raman surprise his students by suspending freely a tiny light ball in a transparent vacuum chamber by shining a laser beam on it. The tails of the comets are also due to radiation pressure.

Short Answer Type Questions

Q.21 Show that the magnetic field B at a point in between the plates of a parallel plate capacitor during charging is $\frac{\mu_o \varepsilon_o r}{2}\frac{dE}{dt}$ (symbols having usual meaning).

Ans. Consider the figure given below to prove that the magnetic field B at a point in between the plates of a parallel plate capacitor during charging is $\frac{\varepsilon_0 \mu_0 r}{2}\frac{dE}{dt}$.

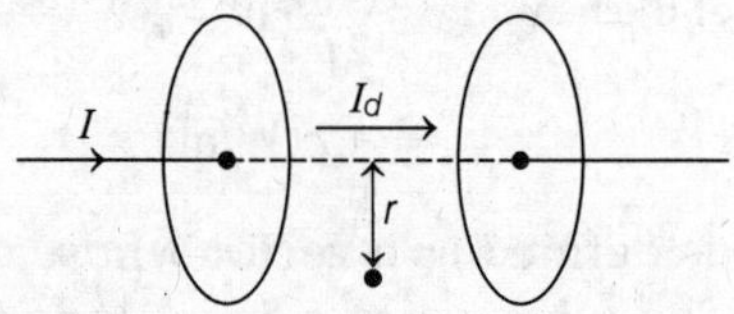

Let I_d be the displacement current in the region between two plates of parallel plate capacitor, in the figure.

The magnetic field induction at a point in a region between two plates of capacitor at a perpendicular distance r from the axis of plates is

$$B = \frac{\mu_0 2I_d}{4\pi r} = \frac{\mu_0}{2\pi r} I_d = \frac{\mu_0}{2\pi r} \times \varepsilon_0 \frac{d\phi_E}{dt} \qquad \left[\because I_d = \frac{\varepsilon_0 d\phi_E}{dt}\right]$$

$$= \frac{\mu_0 \varepsilon_0}{2\pi r}\frac{d}{dt}(E\pi r^2) = \frac{\mu_0 \varepsilon_0}{2\pi r}\pi r^2 \frac{dE}{dt} \qquad [\because \phi_E = E\pi r^2]$$

$$B = \frac{\mu_0 \varepsilon_0 r}{2}\frac{dE}{dt}$$

Mistake Alert! *Students sometimes think that the displacement current and conventional current both have same nature but displacement current is modification of Ampere's circuital law without using negative sign.*

Q.22 Electromagnetic waves with wavelength

(i) λ_1 is used in satellite communication.

(ii) λ_2 is used to kill germs in water purifies.

(iii) λ_3 is used to detect leakage of oil in underground pipelines.

(iv) λ_4 is used to improve visibility in runways during fog and mist conditions.

(a) Identify and name the part of electromagnetic spectrum to which these radiations belong.

(b) Arrange these wavelengths in ascending order of their magnitude.

(c) Write one more application of each.

Ans. (a) (i) Microwave is used in satellite communications.
So, λ_1 is the wavelength of microwave.

(ii) Ultraviolet rays are used to kill germs in water purifier. So, λ_2 is the wavelength of UV rays.

(iii) X-rays are used to detect leakage of oil in underground pipelines. So, λ_3 is the wavelength of X-rays.

(iv) Infrared is used to improve visibility on runways during fog and mist conditions. So, λ_4 is the wavelength of infrared waves.

(b) Wavelength of X-rays < wavelength of UV < wavelength of infrared < wavelength of microwave.

$$\Rightarrow \qquad \lambda_3 < \lambda_2 < \lambda_4 < \lambda_1$$

(c) (i) Microwave is used in radar.

(ii) UV is used in LASIK eye surgery.

(iii) X-ray is used to detect a fracture in bones.

(iv) Infrared is used in optical communication.

Q.23 Show that average value of radiant flux density S over a single period T is given by $S = \frac{1}{2c\mu_0} E_0^2$.

Ans. Radiant flux density $S = \frac{1}{\mu_0}(\mathbf{E} \times \mathbf{B}) = c^2 \varepsilon_o (\mathbf{E} \times \mathbf{B})$ $\left[\because c = \frac{1}{\sqrt{\mu_0 \varepsilon_0}}\right]$

Suppose electromagnetic wave is propagating along x-axis. The electric field vector of electromagnetic wave is along y-axis and magnetic field vector is along z-axis. Therefore,

$$\mathbf{E} = \mathbf{E}_0 \cos(kx - \omega t)$$

and

$$\mathbf{B} = \mathbf{B}_0 \cos(kx - \omega t)$$

$$\mathbf{E} \times \mathbf{B} = (\mathbf{E}_0 \times \mathbf{B}_0)\cos^2(kx - \omega t)$$

$$\mathbf{S} = c^2 \varepsilon_o (\mathbf{E} \times \mathbf{B})$$

$$= c^2 \varepsilon_0 (\mathbf{E}_0 \times \mathbf{B}_0)\cos^2(kx - \omega t)$$

Average value of the magnitude of radiant flux density over complete cycle is

$$S_{av} = c^2 \varepsilon_0 |\mathbf{E}_0 \times \mathbf{B}_0| \frac{1}{T}\int_o^T \cos^2(kx - \omega t)dt$$

$$= c^2 \varepsilon_0 E_0 B_0 \times \frac{1}{T} \times \frac{T}{2} \qquad \left[\because \int_o^T \cos^2(kx - \omega t)dt = \frac{T}{2}\right]$$

$$\Rightarrow \qquad S_{av} = \frac{c^2}{2} \varepsilon_0 E_0 \left(\frac{E_0}{c}\right) \qquad \left[\text{As, } c = \frac{E_0}{B_0}\right]$$

$$= \frac{c}{2} \varepsilon_0 E_0^2 = \frac{c}{2} \times \frac{1}{c^2 \mu_0} E_0^2 \qquad \left[c = \frac{1}{\sqrt{\mu_0 \varepsilon_0}} \text{ or } \varepsilon_0 = \frac{1}{c^2 \mu_0}\right]$$

Hence it is proved that $S_{av} = \frac{E_0^2}{2\mu_0 c}$

Q.24 You are given a 2μF parallel plate capacitor. How would you establish an instantaneous displacement current of 1 mA in the space between its plates?

Ans. Given, capacitance of capacitor $C = 2\mu F$,

Displacement current $I_d = 1\,mA$

Charge $\qquad q = CV$

$$I_d dt = C dV \qquad [\because q = it]$$

or

$$I_d = C\frac{dV}{dt}$$

$$1\times 10^{-3} = 2\times 10^{-6}\times \frac{dV}{dt}$$

or $$\frac{dV}{dt} = \frac{1}{2}\times 10^{+3} = 500 \text{ V/s}$$

So, by applying a varying potential difference of 500 V/s, we would produce a displacement current of desired value.

Q.25 Show that the radiation pressure exerted by an EM wave of intensity I on a surface kept in vacuum is $\frac{I}{c}$.

Ans. Pressure $= \frac{\text{Force}}{\text{Area}} = \frac{F}{A}$

Force is the rate of change of momentum

i.e., $$F = \frac{\Delta p}{\Delta t}$$

$\therefore$ $$P = \frac{1}{A}\frac{\Delta p}{\Delta t}$$

$$P = \frac{1}{A}\cdot\frac{\Delta u}{\Delta tc} \qquad (\Delta pc = \Delta u = \text{energy imparted by wave in time } \Delta t)$$

$$P = \frac{I}{c} \qquad \left[\because \text{Intensity, } I = \frac{\Delta u}{A\cdot\Delta t}\right]$$

Q.26 What happens to the intensity of light from a bulb if the distance from the bulb is doubled? As a laser beam travels across the length of room, its intensity essentially remain constant.

What geometrical characteristic of LASER beam is responsible for the constant intensity which is missing in the case of light from the bulb?

Ans. As the distance is doubled, the area of spherical region ($4\pi r^2$) will become four times, so the intensity becomes one fourth the initial value $\left(\because I \propto \frac{1}{r^2}\right)$ but in case of laser it does not spread, so its intensity remain same.

Geometrical characteristic of LASER beam which is responsible for the constant intensity are as following

(i) Unidirection (ii) Monochromatic

(iii) Coherent light (iv) Highly collimated

These characteristic are missing in the case of light from the bulb.

Q.27 Even though an electric field **E** exerts a force $q\mathbf{E}$ on a charged particle yet electric field of an EM wave does not contribute to the radiation pressure (but transfers energy). Explain.

Ans. Since, electric field of an EM wave is an oscillating field and so is the electric force caused by it on a charged particle. This electric force averaged over an integral number of cycles is zero, since its direction changes every half cycle. Hence, electric field is not responsible for radiation pressure.

Long Answer Type Questions

Q.28 An infinitely long thin wire carrying a uniform linear static charge density λ is placed along the *z*-axis as shown in given figure. The wire is set into motion along its length with a uniform velocity $\mathbf{v} = v\hat{\mathbf{k}}_z$. Calculate the pointing vector $\mathbf{S} = \frac{1}{\mu_0}(\mathbf{E} \times \mathbf{B})$.

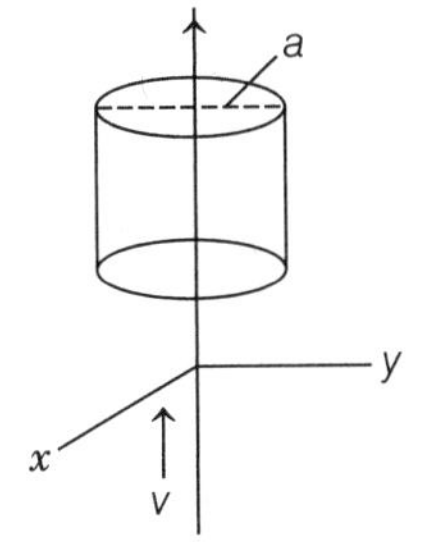

Ans. We know that,

$$\mathbf{E} = \frac{\lambda}{2\pi\varepsilon_0 a}\hat{\mathbf{j}}$$

$$\mathbf{B} = \frac{\mu_0 i}{2\pi a}\hat{\mathbf{i}} = \frac{\mu_0 \lambda v}{2\pi a}\hat{\mathbf{i}} \qquad [\because I = \lambda v]$$

$\therefore$

$$\mathbf{S} = \frac{1}{\mu_0}[\mathbf{E} \times \mathbf{B}] = \frac{1}{\mu_0}\left[\frac{\lambda\hat{\mathbf{j}}}{2\pi\varepsilon_0 a} \times \frac{\mu_0}{2\pi a}\lambda v\hat{\mathbf{i}}\right]$$

$$= \frac{\lambda^2 v}{4\pi^2\varepsilon_0 a^2}(\hat{\mathbf{j}} \times \hat{\mathbf{i}}) = -\frac{\lambda^2 v}{4\pi^2\varepsilon_0 a^2}\hat{\mathbf{k}}$$

Q.29 Sea water at frequency $\nu = 4 \times 10^8$ Hz has permittivity $\varepsilon \approx 80\varepsilon_0$, permeability $\mu \approx \mu_0$ and resistivity $\rho = 0.25\ \Omega$-m. Imagine a parallel plate capacitor immersed in sea water and driven by an alternating voltage source $V(t) = V_0 \sin(2\pi\nu t)$. What fraction of the conduction current density is the displacement current density?

Thinking Process The conduction current density is given by the Ohm's law = Conductivity × Electric field between the plates.

Ans. Suppose distance between the parallel plates is *d* and applied voltage $V(t) = V_0 \sin(2\pi\nu t)$.

Thus, electric field

$$E = \frac{V_0}{d}\sin(2\pi\nu t)$$

Now using Ohm's law,

$$J_c = \frac{1}{\rho}E = \frac{1}{\rho}\frac{V_0}{d}\sin(2\pi\nu t)$$

$\Rightarrow$

$$= \frac{V_0}{\rho d}\sin(2\pi\nu t) = J_0^c \sin 2\pi\nu t$$

Here,

$$J_0^c = \frac{V_0}{\rho d}$$

Now the displacement current density is given as

$$J_d = \varepsilon \frac{dE}{dt}$$

$$= \frac{\varepsilon 2\pi \nu V_0}{d} \cos(2\pi\nu t) \quad \left[\because E = \frac{V_0}{d}\sin(2\pi\nu t)\right]$$

$$= J_0^d \cos(2\pi\nu t)$$

where, $$J_0^d = \frac{2\pi\nu\varepsilon V_0}{d}$$

$$\Rightarrow \quad \frac{J_0^d}{J_0^c} = \frac{2\pi\nu\varepsilon V_0}{d} \cdot \frac{\rho d}{V_0} = 2\pi\nu\varepsilon\rho$$

$$= 2\pi \times 80\varepsilon_0 \nu \times 0.25 = 4\pi\varepsilon_0 \nu \times 10$$

$$= \frac{10\nu}{9 \times 10^9} = \frac{10 \times 4 \times 10^8}{9 \times 10^9} = \frac{4}{9}$$

Q.30 A long straight cable of length l is placed symmetrically along z-axis and has radius $a(<< l)$. The cable consists of a thin wire and a co-axial conducting tube. An alternating current $I(t) = I_0 \sin(2\pi\nu t)$ flows down the central thin wire and returns along the co-axial conducting tube. The induced electric field at a distance s from the wire inside the cable is $\mathbf{E}(s, t) = \mu_0 I_0 \nu \cos(2\pi\nu t) \ln\left(\frac{s}{a}\right)\hat{\mathbf{k}}$.

(i) Calculate the displacement current density inside the cable.

(ii) Integrate the displacement current density across the cross-section of the cable to find the total displacement current I_d.

(iii) Compare the conduction current I_0 with the displacement current I_{0d}.

- **Concept Insight** Displacement current density

$$\mathbf{J}_d = \varepsilon_0 \frac{d\mathbf{E}}{dt}$$

Ans. (i) Given, the induced electric field at a distance r from the wire inside the cable is

$$\mathbf{E}(s,t) = \mu_0 I_0 \nu \cos(2\pi\nu t) \ln\left(\frac{s}{a}\right)\hat{\mathbf{k}}$$

Now, displacement current density,

$$\mathbf{J}_d = \varepsilon_0 \frac{d\mathbf{E}}{dt} = \varepsilon_0 \frac{d}{dt}\left[\mu_0 I_0 \nu \cos(2\pi\nu t) \ln\left(\frac{s}{a}\right)\hat{\mathbf{k}}\right]$$

$$= \varepsilon_0 \mu_0 I_0 \nu \frac{d}{dt}[\cos 2\pi\nu t] \ln\left(\frac{s}{a}\right)\hat{\mathbf{k}}$$

$$= \frac{1}{c^2} I_0 \nu^2 2\pi[-\sin 2\pi\nu t] \ln\left(\frac{s}{a}\right)\hat{\mathbf{k}}$$

$$= \frac{\nu^2}{c^2} 2\pi I_0 \sin 2\pi\nu t \ln\left(\frac{a}{s}\right)\hat{\mathbf{k}} \quad \left[\because \ln\left(\frac{s}{a}\right) = -\ln\left(\frac{a}{s}\right)\right]$$

$$= \frac{1}{\lambda^2} 2\pi I_0 \ln\left(\frac{a}{s}\right) \sin 2\pi\nu t\, \hat{\mathbf{k}} = \frac{2\pi I_0}{\lambda^2} \ln\frac{a}{s} \sin 2\pi\nu t\, \hat{\mathbf{k}}$$

(ii)
$$I_d = \int J_d s ds\, d\theta = \int_{s=0}^{a} J_d s ds \int_0^{2\pi} d\theta = \int_{s=0}^{a} J_d s ds \times 2\pi$$

$$= \int_{s=0}^{a} \left[\frac{2\pi}{\lambda^2} I_0 \ln\left(\frac{a}{s}\right) s ds \sin 2\pi\nu t \right] \times 2\pi$$

$$= \left(\frac{2\pi}{\lambda}\right)^2 I_0 \int_{s=0}^{a} \ln\left(\frac{a}{s}\right) s ds \sin 2\pi\nu t$$

$\Rightarrow$
$$= \left(\frac{2\pi}{\lambda}\right)^2 I_0 \int_{s=0}^{a} \ln\left(\frac{a}{s}\right) \frac{1}{2} d(s^2) . \sin 2\pi\nu t$$

$$= \frac{a^2}{2}\left(\frac{2\pi}{\lambda}\right)^2 I_0 \sin 2\pi\nu t \int_{s=0}^{a} \ln\left(\frac{a}{s}\right) \cdot d\left(\frac{s}{a}\right)^2$$

$$= \frac{a^2}{4}\left(\frac{2\pi}{\lambda}\right)^2 I_0 \sin 2\pi\nu t \int_{s=0}^{a} \ln\left(\frac{a}{s}\right)^2 \cdot d\left(\frac{s}{a}\right)^2$$

$$= -\frac{a^2}{4}\left(\frac{2\pi}{\lambda}\right)^2 I_0 \sin 2\pi\nu t \int_{s=0}^{a} \ln\left(\frac{s}{a}\right)^2 \cdot d\left(\frac{s}{a}\right)^2$$

$$= -\frac{a^2}{4}\left(\frac{2\pi}{\lambda}\right)^2 I_0 \sin 2\pi\nu t \times (-1) \qquad \left[\because \int_{s=0}^{a} \ln\left(\frac{s}{a}\right)^2 d\left(\frac{s}{a}\right)^2 = -1\right]$$

$\therefore$
$$I_d = \frac{a^2}{4}\left(\frac{2\pi}{\lambda}\right)^2 I_0 \sin 2\pi\nu t$$

$$= \left(\frac{2\pi a}{2\lambda}\right)^2 I_0 \sin 2\pi\nu t$$

(iii) The displacement current,

$$I_d = \left(\frac{2\pi a}{2\lambda}\right)^2 I_0 \sin 2\pi\nu t$$

$$= I_{0d} \sin 2\pi\nu t$$

Here, $I_{0d} = \left(\dfrac{2\pi a}{2\lambda}\right)^2 I_0 = \left(\dfrac{a\pi}{\lambda}\right)^2 I_0$

$\therefore$
$$\frac{I_{0d}}{I_0} = \left(\frac{a\pi}{\lambda}\right)^2$$

Q.31 A plane EM wave travelling in vacuum along z-direction is given by $\mathbf{E} = E_0 \sin(kz - \omega t)\,\hat{\mathbf{i}}$ and $\mathbf{B} = B_0 \sin(kz - \omega t)\,\hat{\mathbf{j}}$.

(i) Evaluate $\int \mathbf{E} \cdot dl$ over the rectangular loop 1234 shown in figure.

(ii) Evaluate $\int \mathbf{B} \cdot ds$ over the surface bounded by loop 1234.

(iii) Use equation $\int \mathbf{E} \cdot dl = \dfrac{-d\phi_B}{dt}$ to prove $\dfrac{E_0}{B_0} = c$.

(iv) By using similar process and the equation

$$\int \mathbf{B}\cdot dl = \mu_0 I + \varepsilon_0 \frac{d\phi_E}{dt}, \text{ prove that } c = \frac{1}{\sqrt{\mu_0 \varepsilon_0}}$$

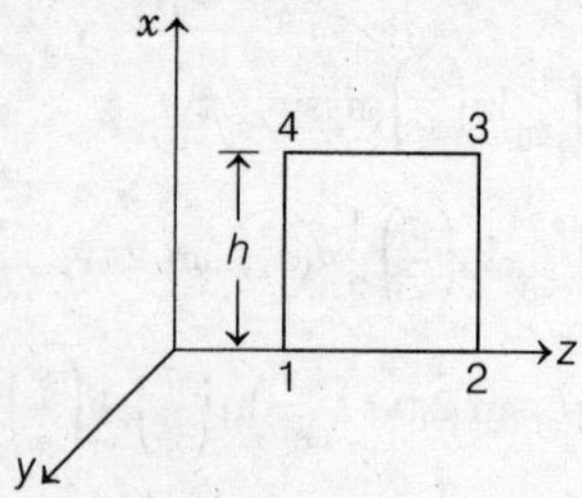

Ans. (i) Consider the figure given below

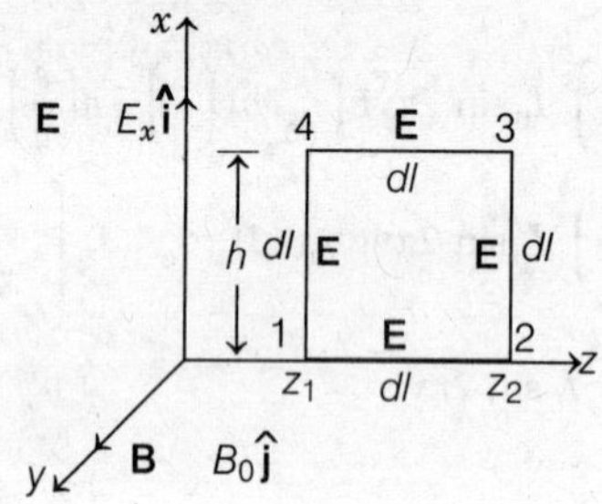

During the propagation of electromagnetic wave along z-axis, let electric field vector (**E**) be along x-axis and magnetic field vector **B** along y-axis, *i.e.*, $\mathbf{E} = E_0 \sin(kz - \omega t)\,\hat{\mathbf{i}}$ and $\mathbf{B} = B_0 \sin(kz - \omega t)\,\hat{\mathbf{j}}$.

Line integral of E over the closed rectangular path 1234 in x-z plane of the figure

$$\oint \mathbf{E}\cdot dl = \int_1^2 \mathbf{E}\cdot dl + \int_2^3 \mathbf{E}\cdot dl + \int_3^4 \mathbf{E}\cdot dl + \int_4^1 \mathbf{E}\cdot dl$$

$$= \int_1^2 \mathbf{E}\cdot dl \cos 90^\circ + \int_2^3 \mathbf{E}\cdot dl \cos 0^\circ + \int_3^4 \mathbf{E}\cdot dl \cos 90^\circ + \int_4^1 \mathbf{E}\cdot dl \cos 180^\circ$$

$$= \int_2^3 E\cdot dl - \int_4^1 E\cdot dl = E_{z_2} h - E_{z_1} h$$

$$= E_0 h[\sin(kz_2 - \omega t) - \sin(kz_1 - \omega t)] \quad \text{...(i)}$$

(ii) For evaluating $\int \mathbf{B}\cdot ds$, let us consider the rectangle 1234 to be made of strips of area $ds = hdz$ each.

$$\int \mathbf{B}\cdot ds = \int \mathbf{B}\cdot ds \cos 0^\circ = \int \mathbf{B}\cdot ds = \int_{Z_1}^{Z_2} B_0 \sin(kz - \omega t) h dz$$

$$= \frac{-B_0 h}{k}[\cos(kz_2 - \omega t) - \cos(kz_1 - \omega t)] \quad \text{...(ii)}$$

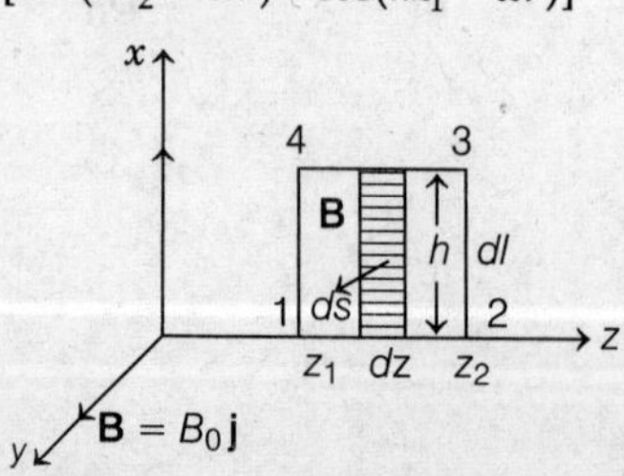

(iii) Given, $\oint \mathbf{E}\cdot dl = \frac{-d\phi_B}{dt} = -\frac{d}{dt}\oint \mathbf{B}\cdot ds$

Putting the values from Eqs. (i) and (ii), we get

$$E_0h[\sin(kz_2 - \omega t) - \sin(kz_1 - \omega t)]$$
$$= \frac{-d}{dt}\left[\frac{B_0h}{k}\{\cos(kz_2 - \omega t) - \cos(kz_1 - \omega t)\}\right]$$
$$= \frac{B_0h}{k}\omega[\sin(kz_2 - \omega t) - \sin(kz_1 - \omega t)]$$

$$\Rightarrow \quad E_0 = \frac{B_0\omega}{k} = B_0c \qquad \left(\because \frac{\omega}{k} = c\right)$$

$$\Rightarrow \quad \frac{E_0}{B_0} = c$$

(iv) For evaluating $\oint \mathbf{B}\cdot dl$, let us consider a loop 1234 in y-z plane as shown in figure given below

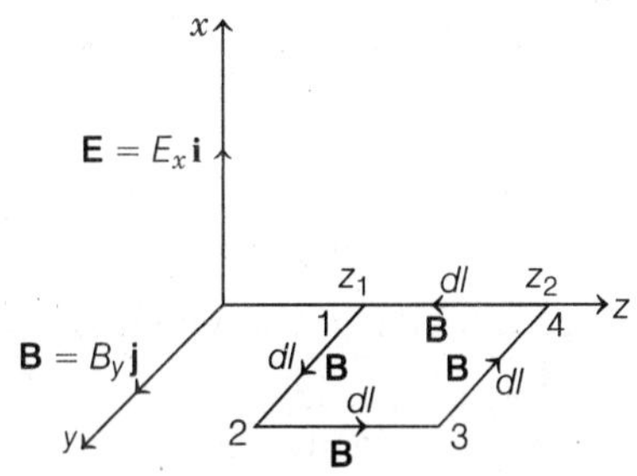

$$\oint \mathbf{B}\cdot dl = \int_1^2 \mathbf{B}\cdot dl + \int_2^3 \mathbf{B}\cdot dl + \int_3^4 \mathbf{B}\cdot dl + \int_4^1 \mathbf{B}\cdot dl$$
$$= \int_1^2 \mathbf{B}\cdot dl\cos 0 + \int_2^3 \mathbf{B}\cdot dl\cos 90° + \int_3^4 \mathbf{B}\cdot dl\cos 180° + \int_4^1 \mathbf{B}\cdot dl\cos 90°$$
$$= \int_1^2 B\cdot dl - \int_3^4 B\cdot dl = B_{z_1}h - B_{z_2}h$$
$$= B_0h[\sin(kz_1 - \omega t) - \sin(kz_2 - \omega t)] \qquad \text{...(iii)}$$

Now to evaluate $\phi_E = \int \mathbf{E}\cdot ds$, let us consider the rectangle 1234 to be made of strips of area hd_2 each.

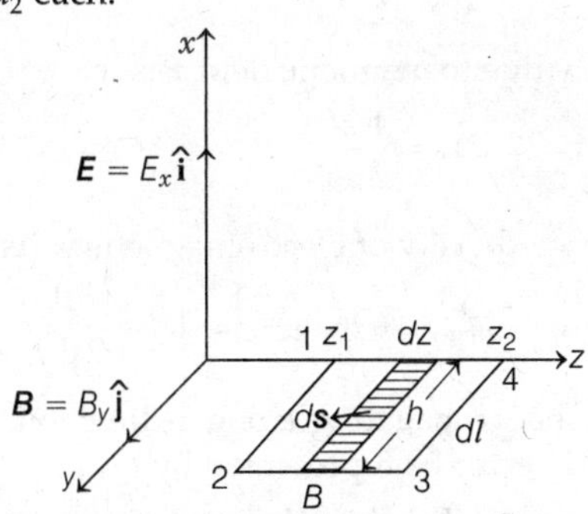

$$\phi_E = \int \mathbf{E}\cdot ds = \int Eds\cos 0° = \int Eds = \int_{z_1}^{z_2} E_0\sin(kz_1 - \omega t)hdz$$
$$= -\frac{E_0h}{k}[\cos(kz_2 - \omega t) - \cos(kz_1 - \omega t)]$$

$\therefore$ $$\frac{d\phi_E}{dt}=\frac{E_0 h\omega}{k}[\sin(kz_1-\omega t)-\sin(kz_2-\omega t)] \quad \text{...(iv)}$$

In $$\oint \mathbf{B}\cdot dl=\mu_0\left(I+\frac{\varepsilon_o d\phi_E}{dt}\right), I = \text{conduction current}$$

$I = 0$ in vacuum

$\therefore$ $$\oint \mathbf{B}\cdot dl=\mu_0\varepsilon_0\frac{d\phi_E}{dt}$$

Using relations obtained in Eqs. (iii) and (iv) and simplifying, we get

$$B_0 = E_0\frac{\omega\mu_0\varepsilon_0}{k}$$

$\Rightarrow$ $$\frac{E_0}{B_0}\frac{\omega}{k}=\frac{1}{\mu_0\varepsilon_0}$$

But $$\frac{E_0}{B_0}=c \text{ and } \omega = ck$$

$\Rightarrow$ $$c\cdot c=\frac{1}{\mu_0\varepsilon_0}, \text{ therefore } c=\frac{1}{\sqrt{\mu_0\varepsilon_0}}$$

Q.32 A plane EM wave travelling along z-direction is described by $\mathbf{E}=E_0\sin(kz-\omega t)\,\hat{\mathbf{i}}$ and $\mathbf{B}=B_0\sin(kz-\omega t)\,\hat{\mathbf{j}}$. Show that

(i) the average energy density of the wave is given by

$$u_{\text{av}}=\frac{1}{4}\varepsilon_0E_0^2+\frac{1}{4}\frac{B_0^2}{\mu_0}$$

(ii) the time averaged intensity of the wave is given by

$$I_{\text{av}}=\frac{1}{2}c\varepsilon_o E_0^2.$$

Ans. (i) The electromagnetic wave carry energy which is due to electric field vector and magnetic field vector. In electromagnetic wave, E and B vary from point to point and from moment to moment. Let E and B be their time averages.

The energy density due to electric field E is

$$u_E=\frac{1}{2}\varepsilon_0E^2$$

The energy density due to magnetic field B is

$$u_B=\frac{1}{2}\frac{B^2}{\mu_0}$$

Total average energy density of electromagnetic wave

$$u_{av}=u_E+u_B=\frac{1}{2}\varepsilon_0E^2+\frac{1}{2}\frac{B^2}{\mu_0}$$

Let the EM wave be propagating along z-direction. The electric field vector and magnetic field vector be represented by

$$E=E_0\sin(kz-\omega t)$$
$$B=B_0\sin(kz-\omega t)$$

The time average value of E^2 over complete cycle $= \frac{E_0^2}{2}$

and time average value of B^2 over complete cycle $= \frac{B_0^2}{2}$

$$u_{av} = \frac{1}{2}\frac{\varepsilon_o E_0^2}{2} + \frac{1}{2\mu_0}\left(\frac{B_0^2}{2}\right)$$

$$= \frac{1}{4}\varepsilon_o E_0^2 + \frac{B_0^2}{4\mu_0}$$

(ii) We know that $E_0 = cB_0$ and $c = \frac{1}{\sqrt{\mu_0 \varepsilon_0}}$

$\therefore$

$$\frac{1}{4}\frac{B_0^2}{\mu_0} = \frac{1}{4}\frac{E_0^2 / c^2}{\mu_0} = \frac{E_0^2}{4\mu_0} \times \mu_0 \varepsilon_0 = \frac{1}{4}\varepsilon_0 E_0^2$$

$\therefore$

$$u_B = u_E$$

Hence,

$$u_{av} = \frac{1}{4}\varepsilon_0 E_0^2 + \frac{1}{4}\frac{B_0^2}{\mu_0}$$

$$= \frac{1}{4}\varepsilon_0 E_0^2 + \frac{1}{4}\varepsilon_0 E_0^2$$

$$= \frac{1}{2}\varepsilon_0 E_0^2 = \frac{1}{2}\frac{B_0^2}{\mu_0}$$

Time average intensity of the wave

$$I_{av} = u_{av} c = \frac{1}{2}\varepsilon_0 E_0^2 c$$

Chapter 09

Ray Optics and Optical Instruments

Multiple Choice Questions (MCQs)

Q.1 A ray of light incident at an angle θ on a refracting face of a prism emerges from the other face normally. If the angle of the prism is 5° and the prism is made of a material of refractive index 1.5, the angle of incidence is

(a) 7.5° (b) 5° (c) 15° (d) 2.5°

Thinking Process The ray refracted by first surface must fall normally on second surface in order to emerge from the other face normally.

Ans. ***(a)*** Since, deviation $\delta = (\mu - 1) A = (1.5 - 1) \times 5° = 2.5°$

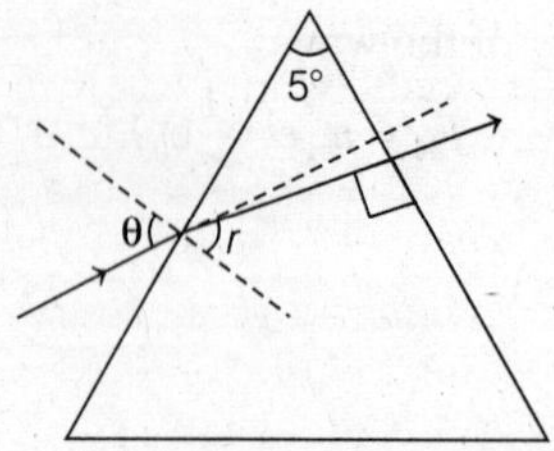

Angle of refraction by first surface is $r = A - r' = 5° - 0 = 5°$

But $\delta = \theta - r$, so, we have, $2.5° = \theta - 5°$ on solving $\theta = 7.5°$.

Q.2 A short pulse of white light is incident from air to a glass slab at normal incidence. After travelling through the slab, the first colour to emerge is

(a) blue (b) green (c) violet (d) red

Thinking Process When light ray goes from one medium to other medium, the frequency of light remains unchanged.

Ans. ***(d)*** Since $v \propto \lambda$, the light of red colour is of highest wavelength and therefore of highest speed. Therefore, after travelling through the slab, the red colour emerge first.

Q.3 An object approaches a convergent lens from the left of the lens with a uniform speed 5 m/s and stops at the focus. The image

(a) moves away from the lens with an uniform speed 5 m/s
(b) moves away from the lens with an uniform acceleration
(c) moves away from the lens with a non-uniform acceleration
(d) moves towards the lens with a non-uniform acceleration

Thinking Process This problem has link with the formation of image when object is at different positions.

Ans. ***(c)*** When an object approaches a convergent lens from the left of the lens with a uniform speed of 5 m/s, the image away from the lens with a non-uniform acceleration.

Q.4 A passenger in an aeroplane shall

(a) never see a rainbow.
(b) may see a primary and a secondary rainbow as concentric circles.
(c) may see a primary and a secondary rainbow as concentric arcs.
(d) shall never see a secondary rainbow.

Ans. ***(b)*** A passenger in an aeroplane may see a primary and a secondary rainbow like concentric circles because there is no ground ahead him.

Q.5 You are given four sources of light each one providing a light of a single colour - red, blue, green and yellow. Suppose the angle of refraction for a beam of yellow light corresponding to a particular angle of incidence at the interface of two media is 90°. Which of the following statements is correct if the source of yellow light is replaced with that of other lights without changing the angle of incidence?

(a) The beam of red light would undergo total internal reflection.
(b) The beam of red light would bend towards normal while it gets refracted through the second medium.
(c) The beam of blue light would undergo total internal reflection.
(d) The beam of green light would bend away from the normal as it gets refracted through the second medium.

Thinking Process This problem is based on the critical angle of total internal reflection.

Ans. ***(c)*** According to VIBGYOR, among all given sources of light, the blue light have smallest wavelength. According to Cauchy relationship, smaller the wavelength higher the refractive index and consequently smaller the critical angle.

So, corresponding to blue colour, the critical angle is least which facilitates total internal reflection for the beam of blue light. The beam of green light would also undergo total internal reflection.

Q.6 The radius of curvature of the curved surface of a plano-convex lens is 20 cm. If the refractive index of the material of the lens be 1.5, it will

(a) act as a convex lens only for the objects that lie on its curved side.
(b) act as a concave lens for the objects that lie on its curved side.
(c) act as a convex lens irrespective of the side on which the object lies.
(d) act as a concave lens irrespective of side on which the object lies.

- **Concept Insight** By lens maker's formula for plano-convex lens, focal length is given by $f = \frac{R}{\mu - 1}$. This is always positive for $\mu > 1$ or optically denser medium of material of lens placed in air.

Ans. ***(c)*** Here, $R = 20$ cm, $\mu = 1.5$, on substituting the values in $f = \frac{R}{\mu - 1} = \frac{20}{1.5 - 1} = 40$ cm

of converging nature as $f > 0$. Therefore, lens act as a convex lens irrespective of the side on which the object lies.

Q.7 The phenomena involved in the reflection of radiowaves by ionosphere is similar to

(a) reflection of light by a plane mirror
(b) total internal reflection of light in air during a mirage
(c) dispersion of light by water molecules during the formation of a rainbow
(d) scattering of light by the particles of air

Ans. ***(b)*** The phenomenon involved in the reflection of radiowaves by ionosphere is similar to total internal reflection of light in air during a mirage *i.e.*, angle of incidence is greater than critical angle.

Q.8 The direction of ray of light incident on a concave mirror is shown by *PQ* while directions in which the ray would travel after reflection is shown by four rays marked 1, 2, 3 and 4 as shown in figure. Which of the four rays correctly shows the direction of reflected ray?

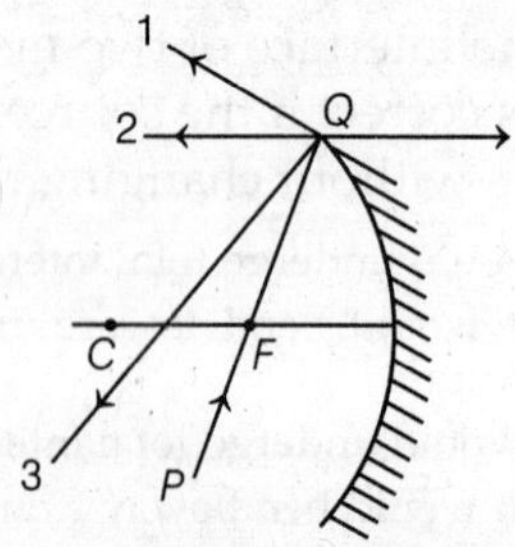

(a) 1 (b) 2 (c) 3 (d) 4

Ans. ***(b)*** The *PQ* ray of light passes through focus *F* and incident on the concave mirror, after reflection, should become parallel to the principal axis shown by ray-2 in the figure.

Q.9 The optical density of turpentine is higher than that of water while its mass density is lower. Figure shows a layer of turpentine floating over water in a container. For which one of the four rays incident on turpentine in figure, the path shown is correct?

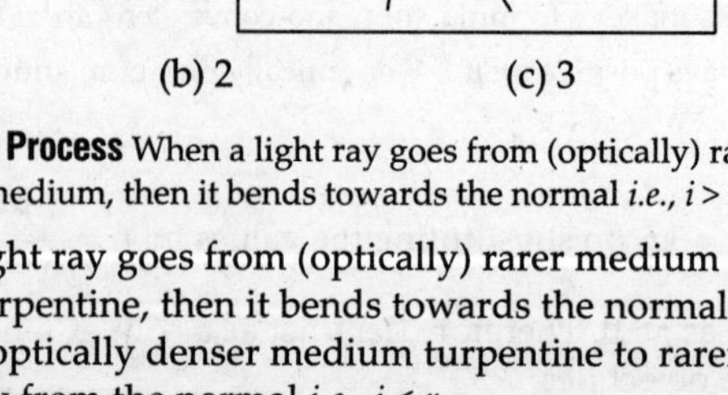

(a) 1 (b) 2 (c) 3 (d) 4

Thinking Process When a light ray goes from (optically) rarer medium to (optically) denser medium, then it bends towards the normal *i.e.*, $i > r$ and *vice-versa.*

Ans. ***(b)*** Here, light ray goes from (optically) rarer medium air to optically denser medium turpentine, then it bends towards the normal *i.e.*, $i > r$ whereas when it goes from optically denser medium turpentine to rarer medium water, then it bends away from the normal *i.e.*, $i < r$.

Q.10 A car is moving with at a constant speed of 60 km h^{-1} on a straight road. Looking at the rear view mirror, the driver finds that the car following him is at a distance of 100 m and is approaching with a speed of 5 km h^{-1}.

In order to keep track of the car in the rear, the driver begins to glance alternatively at the rear and side mirror of his car after every 2 s till the other car overtakes. If the two cars were maintaining their speeds, which of the following statement (s) is/are correct?

(a) The speed of the car in the rear is 65 km h^{-1}.

(b) In the side mirror, the car in the rear would appear to approach with a speed of 5 km h^{-1} to the driver of the leading car.

(c) In the rear view mirror, the speed of the approaching car would appear to decrease as the distance between the cars decreases.

(d) In the side mirror, the speed of the approaching car would appear to increase as the distance between the cars decreases.

Thinking Process The image formed by convex mirror does not depend on the relative position of object w.r.t. mirror.

Ans. ***(d)*** The speed of the image of the car would appear to increase as the distance between the cars decreases.

Q.11 There are certain materials developed in laboratories which have a negative refractive index figure. A ray incident from air (Medium 1) into such a medium (Medium 2) shall follow a path given by

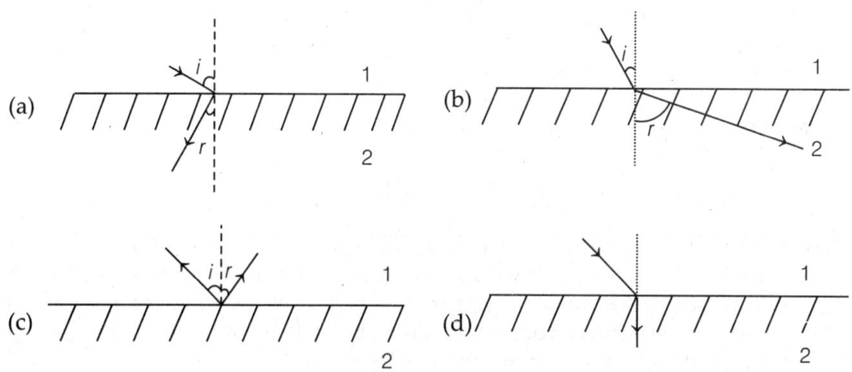

Ans. ***(a)*** The negative refractive index metamaterials are those in which incident ray from air (Medium 1) to them refract or bend differently to that of positive refractive index medium.

Multiple Choice Questions (More Than One Options)

Q.12 Consider an extended object immersed in water contained in a plane trough. When seen from close to the edge of the trough the object looks distorted because

(a) the apparent depth of the points close to the edge are nearer the surface of the water compared to the points away from the edge

(b) the angle subtended by the image of the object at the eye is smaller than the actual angle subtended by the object in air

(c) some of the points of the object far away from the edge may not be visible because of total internal reflection

(d) water in a trough acts as a lens and magnifies the object

Thinking Process This problem is based on the phenomenon of reflection of light when it goes from denser to rarer medium.

Ans. *(a, b, c)* When immersed object is seen from close to the edge of the trough the object looks distorted because the apparent depth of the points close to the edge are nearer the surface of the water compared to the points away from the edge.

The angle subtended by the image of the object at the eye is smaller than the actual angle subtended by the object in air and some of the points of the object far away from the edge may not be visible because of total internal reflection.

Q.13 A rectangular block of glass *ABCD* has a refractive index 1.6. A pin is placed midway on the face *AB* as shown in figure. When observed from the face *AD*, the pin shall

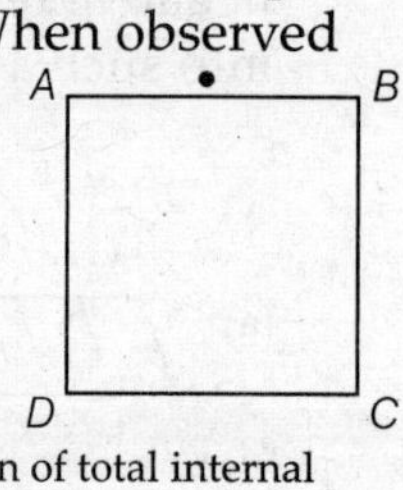

(a) appear to be near *A*

(b) appear to be near *D*

(c) appear to be at the centre of *AD*

(d) not be seen at all

Thinking Process This problem is associated with the phenomenon of total internal reflection.

Ans. *(a, d)* For $\mu = 1.6$, the critical angle, $\mu = 1/\sin C$, we have $C = 38.7°$. As long as the angle of incidence on *AD* of the ray emanating from the pin is less than the critical angle, the pin shall appear to be near *A*. When angle of incidence on *AD* of the ray emanating from pins is greater than the critical angle the light suffers from total internal reflection and cannot be seen through *AD*.

Mistake Alert! *Students sometimes get confused that the TIR occurs when critical angle is less than angle of incident.*

***Q.14** Between the primary and secondary rainbows, there is a dark band known as Alexander's dark band. This is because

(a) light scattered into this region interfere destructively

(b) there is no light scattered into this region

(c) light is absorbed in this region

(d) angle made at the eye by the scattered rays with respect to the incident light of the sun lies between approximately 42° and 50°

Note (✱) Topics related to these question have been removed from latest NCERT.

Ans. ***(a, d)*** Alexandar's dark band lies between the primary and secondary rainbows, forms as the light scattered into this region interfere destructively.

Since, primary rainbows subtends an angle nearly 41° to 42° at observer's eye, whereas, secondary rainbows subtends an angle nearly 51° to 54° at observer's eye w.r.t. incident light ray.

So, the scattered rays with respect to the incident light of the sun lies between approximately 42° and 50°.

Q.15 A magnifying glass is used, as the object to be viewed can be brought closer to the eye than the normal near point. This results in

(a) a larger angle to be subtended by the object at the eye and hence, viewed in greater detail

(b) the formation of a virtual erect image

(c) increase in the field of view

(d) infinite magnification at the near point

Thinking Process The problem is about the case when an object is placed between optical centre and focus of the convergent (magnifying) lens.

Ans. ***(a, b)*** A magnifying glass is used, as the object to be viewed can be brought closer to the eye than the normal near point. This results in a larger angle to be subtended by the object at the eye and hence, viewed in greater detail. Morever, the formation of a virtual erect and enlarged image, takes place.

Q.16 An astronomical refractive telescope has an objective of focal length 20m and an eyepiece of focal length 2 cm.

(a) The length of the telescope tube is 20.02 m.

(b) The magnification is 1000.

(c) The image formed is inverted.

(d) An objective of a larger aperture will increase the brightness and reduce chromatic aberration of the image.

- **Concept Insight** The magnifying power m is the ratio of the angle β subtended at the eye by the final image to the angle α which the object subtends at the lens or the eye. Hence, in normal adjustment

$$m \approx \frac{\beta}{\alpha} \approx \frac{h}{f_e}\frac{f_o}{h} = \frac{f_o}{f_e}$$

In this case, the length of the telescope tube is $f_o + f_e$.

Ans. ***(a, b, c)*** The length of the telescope tube is $f_o + f_e = 20 + (0.02) = 20.02$ m

And magnification, $m = 20 / 0.02 = 1000$

Also, the image formed is inverted .

Very Short Answer Type Questions

Q.17 Will the focal length of a lens for red light be more, same or less than that for blue light?

Ans. As the refractive index for red is less than that for blue, parallel beams of light incident on a lens will be bent more towards the axis for blue light compared to red.

In other words, $\mu_b > \mu_r$

By lens maker's formula, $\frac{1}{f} = (\mu_{21} - 1)\left(\frac{1}{R_1} - \frac{1}{R_2}\right)$

Therefore, $f_b < f_r$.

Thus, the focal length for blue light will be smaller than that for red.

Mistake Alert! *Students sometimes incorrectly assume that the focal length of a lens is always constant irrespective of its surrounding mediums. While the focal length depends on the surrounding medium of the lens.*

Q.18 The near vision of an average person is 25 cm. To view an object with an angular magnification of 10, what should be the power of the microscope?

Ans. Here, $v = D = 25$ cm and $u = f$

But the magnification $m = v/u = D/f$

$$m = \frac{D}{f} \Rightarrow f = \frac{D}{m} = \frac{25}{10} = 2.5 \text{ cm} = 0.025 \text{ m}$$

$$P = \frac{1}{0.025} = 40 \text{ D}$$

This is the required power of lens .

Q.19 An unsymmetrical double convex thin lens forms the image of a point object on its axis. Will the position of the image change if the lens is reversed?

Thinking Process A lens has a unique focal length irrespective of its face or geometry taken for use.

Ans. We know $\frac{1}{f} = (\mu - 1)\left(\frac{1}{R_1} - \frac{1}{R_2}\right)$. In the first case, R_1 is positive and R_2 is negative.

Therefore, $\frac{1}{f} = (\mu - 1)\left(\frac{1}{R_1} + \frac{1}{R_2}\right)$. In the second case, the lens is reversed *i.e* R_1 becomes R_2 and R_2 becomes R_1: Also, this time R_1 is negative and R_2 is positive, so we have

$$\frac{1}{f} = (\mu - 1)\left(\frac{1}{R_2} - \frac{1}{(-R_1)}\right) = (\mu - 1)\left(\frac{1}{R_1} + \frac{1}{R_2}\right)$$

Thus, focal length remains unaffected on reversing the lens.

Q.20 Three immiscible liquids of densities $d_1 > d_2 > d_3$ and refractive indices $\mu_1 > \mu_2 > \mu_3$ are put in a beaker. The height of each liquid column is $\frac{h}{3}$. A dot is made at the bottom of the beaker. For near normal vision, find the apparent depth of the dot.

Thinking Process The image formed by first medium act as an object for second medium.

Ans. Let the apparent depth be O_1 for the object seen from medium 2, then

$$O_1 = \frac{\mu_2}{\mu_1} \frac{h}{3}$$

Since, apparent depth = real depth /refractive index μ.

Also, the image formed by medium 1, O_1 act as an object for medium 2.

If seen from medium 3, the apparent depth is O_2 .

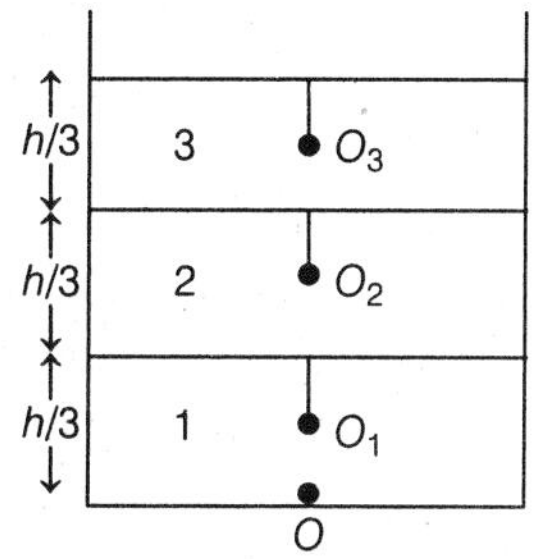

Similarly, the image formed by medium 2 , O_2 act as an object for medium 3

$$O_2 = \frac{\mu_3}{\mu_2}\left(\frac{h}{3} + O_1\right) = \frac{\mu_3}{\mu_2}\left(\frac{h}{3} + \frac{\mu_2}{\mu_1}\frac{h}{3}\right) = \frac{h}{3}\left(\frac{\mu_3}{\mu_2} + \frac{\mu_3}{\mu_1}\right)$$

Seen from outside, the apparent height is

$$O_3 = \frac{1}{\mu_3}\left(\frac{h}{3} + O_2\right) = \frac{1}{\mu_3}\left[\frac{h}{3} + \frac{h}{3}\left(\frac{\mu_3}{\mu_2} + \frac{\mu_3}{\mu_1}\right)\right] = \frac{h}{3}\left(\frac{1}{\mu_1} + \frac{1}{\mu_2} + \frac{1}{\mu_3}\right)$$

This is the required expression of apparent depth.

Q.21 For a glass prism ($\mu = \sqrt{3}$), the angle of minimum deviation is equal to the angle of the prism. Find the angle of the prism.

Ans. The relationship between refractive index, prism angle A and angle of minimum deviation is given by

$$\mu = \frac{\sin\left[\frac{(A + \delta_m)}{2}\right]}{\sin\left(\frac{A}{2}\right)}$$

Here,

∴ Given, $\delta_m = A$

Substituting the value, we have

$$\therefore \quad \mu = \frac{\sin A}{\sin \frac{A}{2}}$$

On solving, we have

$$= \frac{2\sin\frac{A}{2}\cos\frac{A}{2}}{\sin\frac{A}{2}} = 2\cos\frac{A}{2}$$

For the given value of refractive index,

we have

$$\therefore \quad \cos\frac{A}{2} = \frac{\sqrt{3}}{2} \text{ or } \frac{A}{2} = 30°$$

$$\therefore \quad A = 60°$$

This is the required value of prism angle.

Q.22 A short object of length L is placed along the principal axis of a concave mirror away from focus. The object distance is u. If the mirror has a focal length f, what will be the length of the image? You may take $L << |v - f|$.

Thinking Process The length of image is the separation between the images formed by mirror of the extremities of object.

Ans. Since, the object distance is u. Let us consider the two ends of the object be at distance $u_1 = u - L/2$ and $u_2 = u + L/2$, respectively so that $|u_1 - u_2| = l$. Let the image of the two ends be formed at v_1 and v_2, respectively so that the image length would be

$$L' = |v_1 - v_2| \quad \text{... (i)}$$

Applying mirror formula, we have

$$\frac{1}{u} + \frac{1}{v} = \frac{1}{f} \text{ or } v = \frac{fu}{u - f}$$

On solving, the positions of two images are given by

$$v_1 = \frac{f(u - L/2)}{u - f - L/2}, \quad v_2 = \frac{f(u + L/2)}{u - f + L/2}$$

For length, substituting the value in (i), we have

$$L' = |v_1 - v_2| = \frac{f^2 L}{(u - f)^2 \times L^2/4}$$

Since, the object is short and kept away from focus, we have

$$L^2/4 << (u - f)^2$$

Hence, finally $$L' = \frac{f^2}{(u - f)^2} L$$

This is the required expression of length of image.

Mistake Alert ! *Students generally make mistake in the sign convention while solving question using mirror formula. To avoid mistake, distance should be always be measured from the centre of the mirror.*

Q.23 A circular disc of radius R is placed co-axially and horizontally inside an opaque hemispherical bowl of radius 'a' as shown in given figure. The far edge of the disc is just visible when viewed from the edge of the bowl. The bowl is filled with transparent liquid of refractive index μ and the near edge of the disc becomes just visible. How far below the top of the bowl is the disc placed?

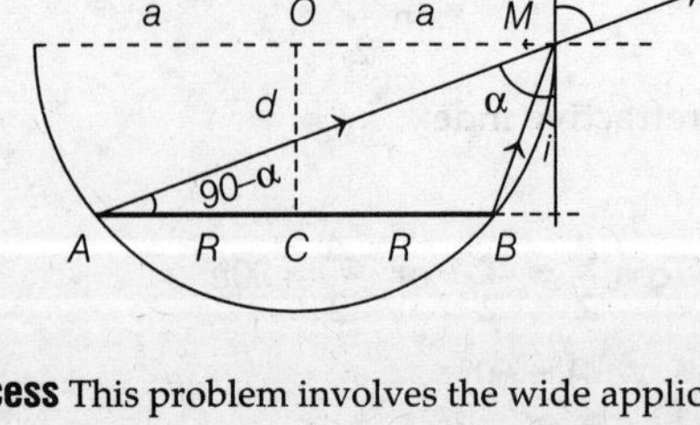

Thinking Process This problem involves the wide application of geometry and Snell's law.

Ans. Refering to the figure, AM is the direction of incidence ray before liquid is filled. After liquid is filled in , BM is the direction of the incident ray. Refracted ray in both cases is same as that along AM. Let the disc is separated by O at a distance d as shown in figure. Also, considering angle

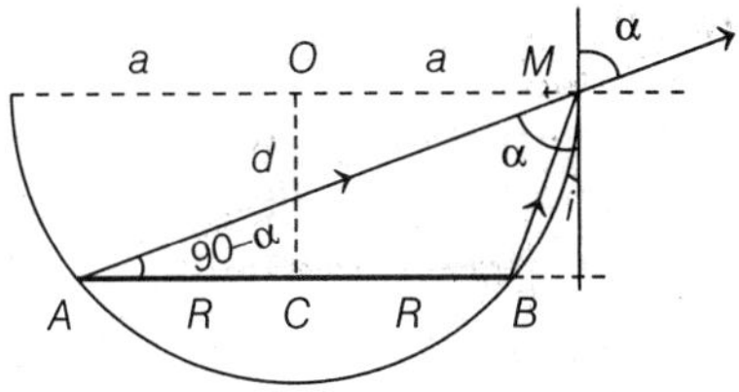

$$N = 90°, OM = a, NB = a - R, AN = a + R$$

Here, in figure $\sin i = \dfrac{a - R}{\sqrt{d^2 + (a - R)^2}}$

and $$\sin \alpha = \cos(90° - \alpha) = \frac{a + R}{\sqrt{d^2 + (a + R)^2}}$$

But on applying Snell's law,

$$\frac{1}{\mu} = \frac{\sin i}{\sin r} = \frac{\sin i}{\sin \alpha}$$

On substituting the values, we have the separation

$$d = \frac{\mu(a^2 - b^2)}{\sqrt{(a + r)^2 - \mu(a - r)^2}}$$

This is the required expression.

Q.24 A thin convex lens of focal length 25 cm is cut into two pieces 0.5cm above the principal axis. The top part is placed at (0,0) and an object placed at (– 50 cm, 0). Find the coordinates of the image.

Thinking Process There is no effect on the focal length of the lens if it is cut as given in the question.

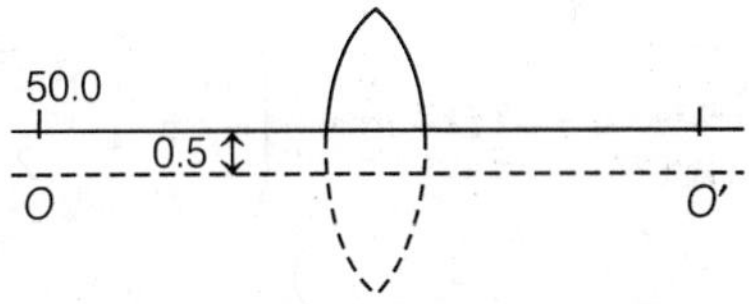

Ans. If there was no cut, then the object would have been at a height of 0.5 cm from the principal axis OO'.

Applying lens formula , we have

$$\frac{1}{v} - \frac{1}{u} = \frac{1}{f}$$

$$\therefore \quad \frac{1}{v} = \frac{1}{u} + \frac{1}{f} = \frac{1}{-50} + \frac{1}{25} = \frac{1}{50}$$

$$\therefore \quad v = 50 \text{ cm}$$

$$\text{Mangnification } m = \frac{v}{u} = -\frac{50}{50} = -1$$

Thus, the image would have been formed at 50 cm from the pole and 0.5 cm below the principal axis. Hence, with respect to the X-axis passing through the edge of the cut lens, the coordinates of the image are (50 cm, –1 cm).

Mistake Alert ! *Sometimes students do not put the values of u, v and f with proper sign.*

Q.25 In many experimental set-ups, the source and screen are fixed at a distance say D and the lens is movable. Show that there are two positions for the lens for which an image is formed on the screen. Find the distance between these points and the ratio of the image sizes for these two points.

Thinking Process This is also one of the methods for finding the focal length of the lens in laboratory and known as displacement method.

Ans. According to displacement method, if the distance between object and screen (D) is greater than $4f$, then there are two positions of lens for which the image of object on the screen is distinct and clear.

On the screen, let the first position be when the lens is at O. Finding u and v and substituting in lens formula.

Given, $$-u + v = D$$

$$\Rightarrow \quad u = -(D - v)$$

Placing it in the lens formula

$$\frac{1}{D-v} + \frac{1}{v} = \frac{1}{f}$$

On solving, we have

$$\Rightarrow \quad \frac{v + D - v}{(D-v)v} = \frac{1}{f}$$

$$\Rightarrow \quad v^2 - Dv + Df = 0$$

$$\Rightarrow \quad v = \frac{D}{2} \pm \frac{\sqrt{D^2 - 4Df}}{2}$$

Hence, finding u

$$u = -(D - v) = -\left(\frac{D}{2} \pm \frac{\sqrt{D^2 - 4Df}}{2}\right)$$

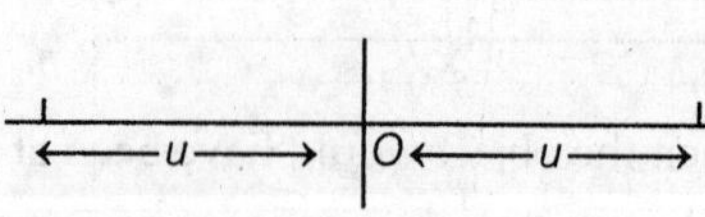

When, the object distance is $\dfrac{D}{2} + \dfrac{\sqrt{D^2 - 4Df}}{2}$

the image forms at $\dfrac{D}{2} - \dfrac{\sqrt{D^2 - 4Df}}{2}$

Similarly, when the object distance is

$$\frac{D}{2} - \frac{\sqrt{D^2 - 4Df}}{2}$$

The image forms at $\dfrac{D}{2} + \dfrac{\sqrt{D^2 - 4Df}}{2}$

The distance between the poles for these two object distance is

$$\frac{D}{2} + \frac{\sqrt{D^2 - 4Df}}{2} - \left(\frac{D}{2} - \frac{\sqrt{D^2 - 4Df}}{2}\right) = \sqrt{D^2 - 4Df}$$

Let $d = \sqrt{D^2 - 4Df}$

If $u = \dfrac{D}{2} + \dfrac{d}{2}$, then the image is at $v = \dfrac{D}{2} - \dfrac{d}{2}$.

$\therefore$ The magnification $m_1 = \dfrac{D-d}{D+d}$

If $u = \dfrac{D-d}{2}$, then $v = \dfrac{D+d}{2}$

$\therefore$ The magnification $m_2 = \dfrac{D+d}{D-d}$

Thus, $\dfrac{m_2}{m_1} = \left(\dfrac{D+d}{D-d}\right)^2$.

This is the required expression of magnification.

Q.26 A jar of height h is filled with a transparent liquid of refractive index μ as shown in figure. At the centre of the jar on the bottom surface is a dot. Find the minimum diameter of a disc, such that when placed on the top surface symmetrically about the centre, the dot is invisible.

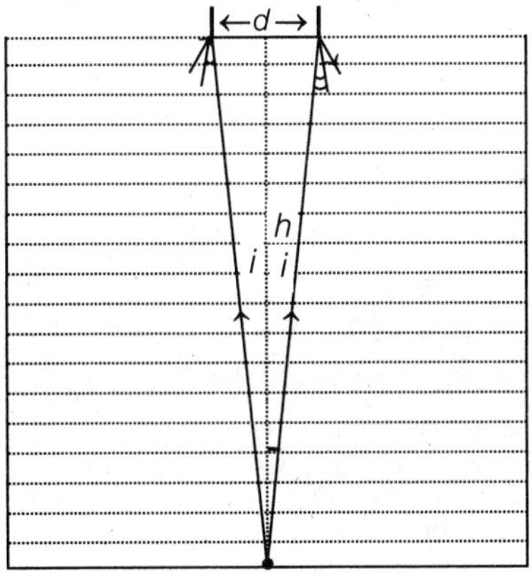

Thinking Process The problem is based on the principle of total internal reflection and area of visibility.

Ans. Let d be the diameter of the disc. The spot shall be invisible if the incident rays from the dot to the surface at $d/2$ exceeds the critical angle.

Let i be the angle of incidence.

Using relationship between refractive index and critical angle,

then, $\sin i = \dfrac{1}{\mu}$

Using geometry and trigonometry.

Now, $$\frac{d/2}{h} = \tan i$$

$\Rightarrow$ $$\frac{d}{2} = h \tan i = h[\sqrt{\mu^2 - 1}]^{-1}$$

$\therefore$ $$d = \frac{2h}{\sqrt{\mu^2 - 1}}$$

This is the required expression of d.

Q.27 A myopic adult has a far point at 0.1 m. His power of accomodation is 4 D.

(i) What power lenses are required to see distant objects?

(ii) What is his near point without glasses?

(iii) What is his near point with glasses? (Take the image distance from the lens of the eye to the retina to be 2 cm.)

- **Concept Insight** If two thin lenses of focal length f_1 and f_2 are in contact, the effective focal length of the combination is given by, $\frac{1}{f} = \frac{1}{f_1} + \frac{1}{f_2}$

Power of combination $P = P_1 + P_2$

Ans. (i) Let the power at the far point be P_f for the normal relaxed eye of an average person. The required power

$$P_f = \frac{1}{f} = \frac{1}{0.1} + \frac{1}{0.02} = 60 \text{ D}$$

By the corrective lens the object distance at the far point is ∞.

The power required is

$$P_f' = \frac{1}{f'} = \frac{1}{\infty} + \frac{1}{0.02} = 50 \text{ D}$$

So for eye + lens system,

we have the sum of the eye and that of the glasses P_g

$\therefore$ $$P_f' = P_f + P_g$$

$\therefore$ $$P_g = -10 \text{ D}$$

(ii) His power of accomodatlon is 4 D for the normal eye. Let the power of the normal eye for near vision be P_n.

Then, $$4 = P_n - P_f \text{ or } P_n = 64 \text{ D}$$

Let his near point be x_n, then

$$\frac{1}{x_n} + \frac{1}{0.02} = 64 \text{ or } \frac{1}{x_n} + 50 = 64$$

$$\frac{1}{x_n} = 14,$$

$\therefore$ $$x_n = \frac{1}{14} = 0.07 \text{ m}$$

(iii) With glasses $P_n' = P_f' + 4 = 54$

$$54 = \frac{1}{x_n'} + \frac{1}{0.02} = \frac{1}{x_n'} + 50$$

$$\frac{1}{x_n'} = 4$$

$\therefore$ $$x_n' = \frac{1}{4} = 0.25 \text{ m}$$

Long Answer Type Questions

Q.28 Show that for a material with refractive index $\mu \geq \sqrt{2}$, light incident at any angle shall be guided along a length perpendicular to the incident face.

Ans. Any ray entering at an angle i shall be guided along AC if the angle ray makes with the face AC (ϕ) is greater than the critical angle as per the principle of total internal reflection $\phi + r = 90°$, therefore $\sin \phi = \cos r$

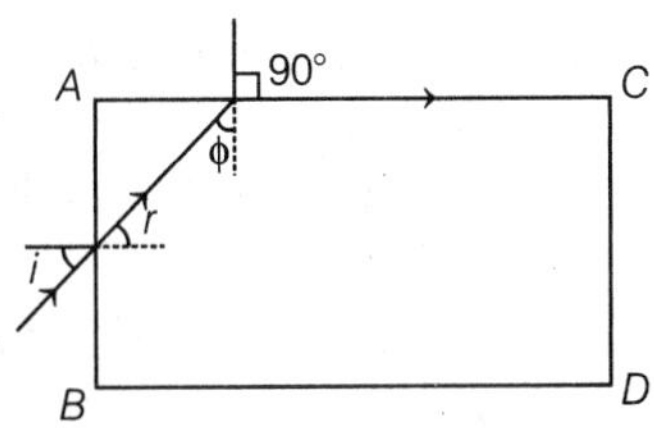

$\Rightarrow$ $$\sin \phi \geq \frac{1}{\mu}$$

$\Rightarrow$ $$\cos r \geq \frac{1}{\mu}$$

or $$1 - \cos^2 r \leq 1 - \frac{1}{\mu^2}$$

i.e., $$\sin^2 r \leq 1 - \frac{1}{\mu^2}$$

since, $$\sin i = \mu \sin r$$

$$\frac{1}{\mu^2} \sin^2 i \leq 1 - \frac{1}{\mu^2}$$

or $$\sin^2 i \leq \mu^2 - 1$$

when $$i = \frac{\pi}{2}$$

Then, we have smallest angle ϕ.

If that is greater than the critical angle, then all other angles of incidence shall be more than the critical angle.

Thus, $$1 \leq \mu^2 - 1 \text{ or } \mu^2 \geq 2$$

$\Rightarrow$ $$\mu \geq \sqrt{2}$$

This is the required result.

Q.29 The mixture of pure liquid and a solution in a long vertical column (*i.e.,* horizontal dimensions << vertical dimensions) produces diffusion of solute particles and hence a refractive index gradient along the vertical dimension. A ray of light entering the column at right angles to the vertical is deviated from its original path. Find the deviation in travelling a horizontal distance $d << h$, the height of the column.

Ans. Let us consider a portion of a ray between x and $x + dx$ inside the liquid. Let the angle of incidence at x be θ and let it enter the thin column at height y. Because of the bending it shall emerge at $x + dx$ with an angle $\theta + d\theta$ and at a height $y + dy$. From Snell's law,

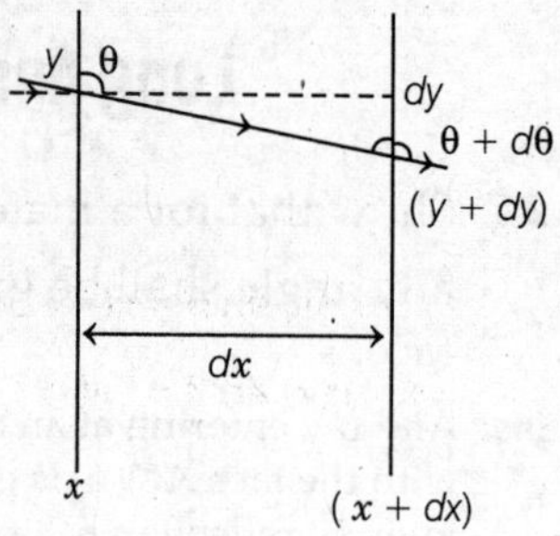

$$\mu(y) \sin \theta = \mu(y + dy) \sin (\theta + d\theta)$$

or $$\mu(y) \sin \theta = \left(\mu(y) + \frac{d\mu}{dy} dy\right) (\sin\theta \cos d\theta + \cos\theta \sin d\theta)$$

or $$\mu(y)\sin\theta = \mu(y) \sin \theta + \mu(y) \cos \theta d\theta + \frac{d\mu}{dy} dy \sin\theta$$

$\{\because \cos d\theta = 1, \sin d\theta \approx d\theta$ as $d\theta$ is small$\}$

or $$\mu(y)\cos\theta d\theta = \frac{-d\mu}{dy} dy\sin \theta$$

$$d\theta = \frac{-d\mu}{\mu\, dy} dy \tan \theta$$

But $$\tan\theta = \frac{dx}{dy}$$ (from the figure)

On solving, we have

$\therefore$ $$d\theta = \frac{-1\, d\mu}{\mu\, dy} dx$$

Solving this variable separable form of differential equation.

$\therefore$ $$\theta = \frac{-1\, d\mu}{\mu\, dy} \int_0^d dx = \frac{-1\, d\mu}{\mu\, dy} d$$

Q.30 If light passes near a massive object, the gravitational interaction causes a bending of the ray. This can be thought of as happening due to a change in the effective refractive index of the medium given by

$$n(r) = 1 + 2GM / rc^2$$

where r is the distance of the point of consideration from the centre of the mass of the massive body, G is the universal gravitational constant, M the mass of the body and c the speed of light in vacuum. Considering a spherical object find the deviation of the ray from the original path as it grazes the object.

Ans. Let us consider two planes at r and $r + dr$. Let the light be incident at an angle θ at the plane at r and leave $r + dr$ at an angle $\theta + d\theta$. Then from Snell's law,

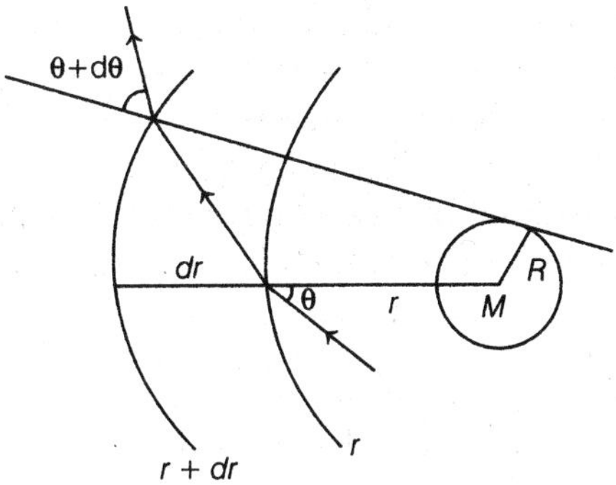

$$n(r)\sin\theta = n(r+dr)\sin(\theta+d\theta)$$

$$\Rightarrow \quad n(r)\sin\theta = \left(n(r)+\frac{dn}{dr}dr\right)(\sin\theta\cos d\theta+\cos\theta\sin d\theta)$$

$$= \left(n(r)+\frac{dn}{dr}dr\right)(\sin\theta+\cos\theta\, d\theta)$$

Ignoring the product of differentials

$$n(r)\sin\theta = n(r)\sin\theta + \frac{dn}{dr}dr\sin\theta + n(r)\cos\theta d\theta$$

or

$$-\frac{dn}{dr}\tan\theta = n(r)\frac{d\theta}{dr}$$

$$\frac{2GM}{r^2c^2}\tan\theta = \left(1+\frac{2GM}{rc^2}\right)\frac{d\theta}{dr} \approx \frac{d\theta}{dr}$$

$$\int_0^{\theta_0} d\theta = \frac{2GM}{c^2}\int_{-\infty}^{\infty}\frac{\tan\theta dr}{r^2}$$

Now substitution for integrals, we have

Now, $$r^2 = x^2 + R^2 \text{ and } \tan\theta = \frac{R}{x}$$

$$2rdr = 2xdx$$

$$\int_0^{\theta_0} d\theta = \frac{2GM}{c^2}\int_{-\infty}^{\infty}\frac{R}{x}\frac{xdx}{(x^2+R^2)^{\frac{3}{2}}}$$

Put $$x = R\tan\phi$$

$$dx = R\sec^2\phi\, d\phi$$

$$\therefore \quad \theta_0 = \frac{2GMR}{c^2}\int_{-\pi/2}^{\pi/2}\frac{R\sec^2\phi d\phi}{R^3\sec^3\phi}$$

$$= \frac{2GM}{Rc^2}\int_{-\pi/2}^{\pi/2}\cos\phi\, d\phi = \frac{4\,GM}{Rc^2}$$

This is the required relation.

Q.31 An infinitely long cylinder of radius R is made of an unusual exotic material with refractive index-1 (figure). The cylinder is placed between two planes whose normals are along the y-direction. The centre of the cylinder O lies along the y-axis. A narrow laser beam is directed along the y-direction from the lower plate. The laser source is at a horizontal distance x from the diameter in the y direction. Find the range of x such that light emitted from the lower plane does not reach the upper plane.

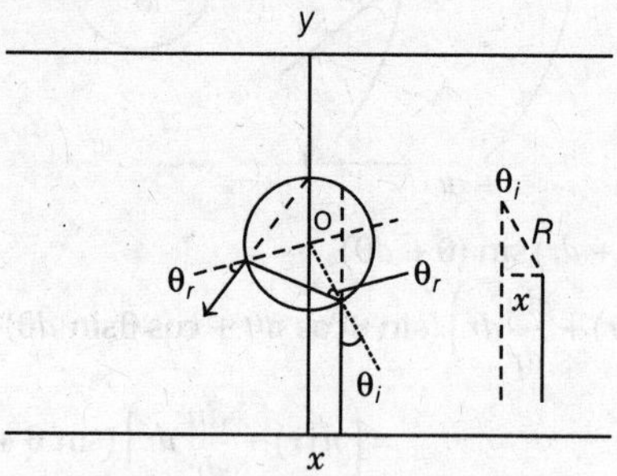

Ans. Since, the material is of refractive index – 1, θ_r, is negative and θ'_r positive.

Now, $$|\theta_i| = |\theta_r| = |\theta'_r|$$

The total deviation of the outcoming ray from the incoming ray is $4\theta_i$. Rays shall not reach the recieving plate if

$$\frac{\pi}{2} \leq 4\theta_i \leq \frac{3\pi}{2} \quad \text{[angles measured clockwise from the } y\text{-axis]}$$

On solving, $$\frac{\pi}{8} \leq \theta_i \leq \frac{3\pi}{8}$$

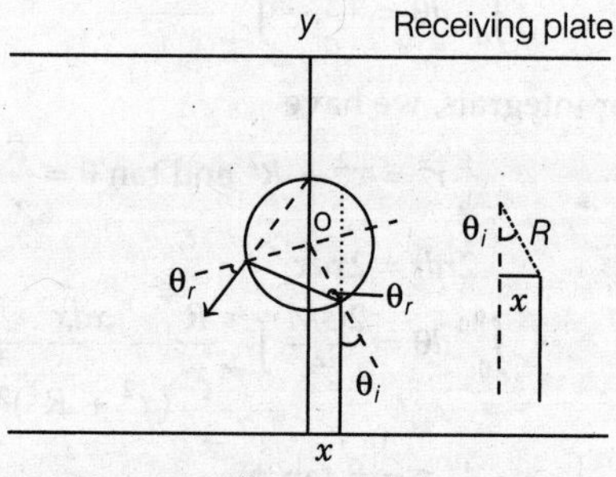

Now, $$\sin\theta_i = \frac{x}{R}$$

$$\frac{\pi}{8} \leq \sin^{-1}\frac{x}{R} \leq \frac{3\pi}{8}$$

or $$\frac{\pi}{8} \leq \frac{x}{R} \leq \frac{3\pi}{8}$$

Thus, for light emitted from the source shall not reach the receiving plate.

If $\frac{R\pi}{8} \leq x \leq \frac{R3\pi}{8}$.

***Q.32** (i) Consider a thin lens placed between a source (S) and an observer (O) (Figure). Let the thickness of the lens vary as $w(b) = w_0 - \frac{b^2}{\alpha}$, where b is the vertical distance from the pole, w_0 is a constant. Using Fermat's principle *i.e.*, the time of transit for a ray between the source and observer is an extremum, find the condition that all paraxial rays starting from the source will converge at a point O on the axis. Find the focal length.

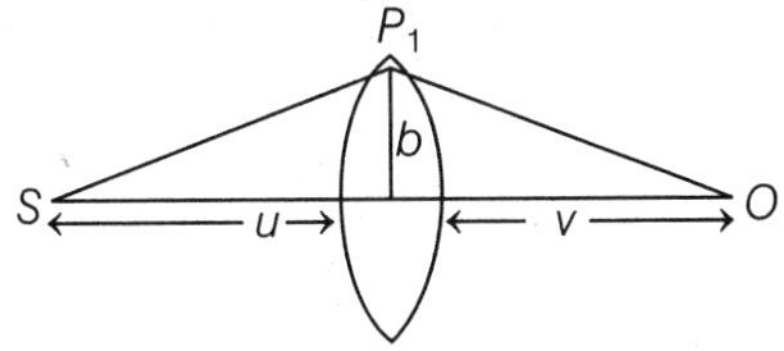

(ii) A gravitational lens may be assumed to have a varying width of the form

$$w(b) = k_1 \ln\left(\frac{k_2}{b}\right); b_{min} < b < b_{max}$$

$$= k_1 \ln\left(\frac{k_2}{b_{min}}\right); b < b_{min}$$

Show that an observer will see an image of a point object as a ring about the centre of the lens with an angular radius

$$\beta = \sqrt{\frac{(n-1)\, k_1 \frac{u}{v}}{u+v}}$$

Ans. (i) The time elapsed to travel from S to P_1 is

$$t_1 = \frac{SP_1}{c} = \frac{\sqrt{u^2 + b^2}}{c}$$

or $\frac{u}{c}\left(1 + \frac{1}{2}\frac{b^2}{u^2}\right)$ assuming $b << u$.

The time required to travel from P_1 to O is

$$t_2 = \frac{P_1O}{c} = \frac{\sqrt{v^2 + b^2}}{c} = \frac{v}{c}\left(1 + \frac{1}{2}\frac{b^2}{v^2}\right)$$

The time required to travel through the lens is

$$3 = \frac{(n-1)\, w(b)}{c}$$

where n is the refractive index.

Thus, the total time is

$$t = \frac{1}{c}\left[u + v + \frac{1}{2} b^2 \left(\frac{1}{u} + \frac{1}{v}\right) + (n-1) w(b)\right]$$

Put $$\frac{1}{D} = \frac{1}{u} + \frac{1}{v}$$

Note (✱) Topics related to these question have been removed from latest NCERT.

Then, $$t = \frac{1}{c}\left(u + v + \frac{1}{2}\frac{b^2}{D} + (n-1)\left(w_0 + \frac{b^2}{\alpha}\right)\right)$$

Fermat's principle states that the time taken should be minimum.

For that first derivative should be zero.

$$\frac{dt}{db} = 0 = \frac{b}{CD} - \frac{2(n-1)b}{c\alpha}$$

$$\alpha = 2(n-1)\, D$$

Thus, a convergent lens is formed if $\alpha = 2(n-1)D$. This is independent of b and hence, all paraxial rays from S will converge at O *i.e.*, for rays

and $(b << v.)$

Since, $\frac{1}{D} = \frac{1}{u} + \frac{1}{v}$, the focal length is D.

(ii) In this case, differentiating expression of time taken t w.r.t. b

$$t = \frac{1}{c}\left(u + v + \frac{1}{2}\frac{b^2}{D} + (n-1)\, k_1 \ln\left(\frac{k_2}{b}\right)\right)$$

$$\frac{dt}{db} = 0 = \frac{b}{D} - (n-1)\frac{k_1}{b}$$

$\Rightarrow$ $$b^2 = (n-1)\, k_1 D$$

$\therefore$ $$b = \sqrt{(n-1)k_1 D}$$

Thus, all rays passing at a height b shall contribute to the image. The ray paths make an angle.

$$\beta = \frac{b}{v} = \frac{\sqrt{(n-1)k_1 D}}{v} = \sqrt{\frac{(n-1)k_1 uv}{v^2(u+v)}} = \sqrt{\frac{(n-1)k_1 u}{(u+v)v}}$$

This is the required expression.

Chapter 10

Wave Optics

Multiple Choice Questions (MCQs)

Q.1 Consider a light beam incident from air to a glass slab at Brewster's angle as shown in figure.

A polaroid is placed in the path of the emergent ray at point P and rotated about an axis passing through the centre and perpendicular to the plane of the polaroid.

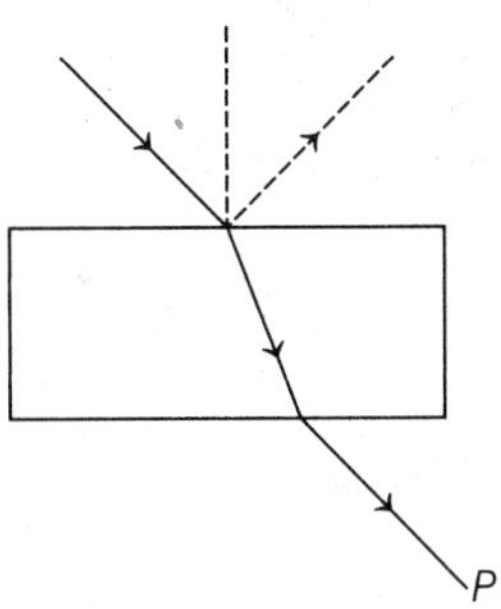

(a) For a particular orientation, there shall be darkness as observed through the polaroid

(b) The intensity of light as seen through the polaroid shall be independent of the rotation

(c) The intensity of light as seen through the polaroid shall go through a minimum but not zero for two orientations of the polaroid

(d) The intensity of light as seen through the polaroid shall go through a minimum for four orientations of the polaroid

Thinking Process When the light beam incident at Brewster's angle, the transmitted beam is unpolarised and reflected beam is polarised.

Ans. *(c)* Consider the diagram, the light beam is incident from air to the glass slab at Brewster's angle (i_B). The incident ray is unpolarised and is represented by dot (.).

The reflected light is plane polarised represented by arrows.

As the emergent ray is unpolarised, hence intensity cannot be zero when passes through polaroid.

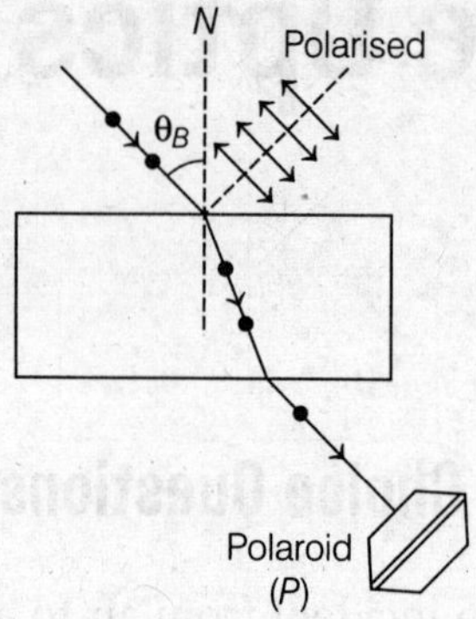

Q.2 Consider sunlight incident on a slit of width 10^4 Å. The image seen through the slit shall

(a) be a fine sharp slit white in colour at the centre

(b) a bright slit white at the centre diffusing to zero intensities at the edges

(c) a bright slit white at the centre diffusing to regions of different colours

(d) only be a diffused slit white in colour

Ans. ***(a)*** Given, width of the slit = 10^4 Å

$$= 10^4 \times 10^{-10} \text{ m} = 10^{-6} \text{ m} = 1 \mu\text{m}$$

Wavelength of (visible) sunlight varies from 4000 Å to 8000 Å.

As the width of slit is comparable to that of wavelength, hence diffraction occurs with maxima at centre. So, at the centre all colours appear *i.e.,* mixing of colours form white patch at the centre.

Q.3 Consider a ray of light incident from air onto a slab of glass (refractive index n) of width d, at an angle θ. The phase difference between the ray reflected by the top surface of the glass and the bottom surface is

(a) $\frac{4\pi d}{\lambda}\left(1-\frac{1}{n^2}\sin^2\theta\right)^{1/2}+\pi$ (b) $\frac{4\pi d}{\lambda}\left(1-\frac{1}{n^2}\sin^2\theta\right)^{1/2}$

(c) $\frac{4\pi d}{\lambda}\left(1-\frac{1}{n^2}\sin^2\theta\right)^{1/2}+\frac{\pi}{2}$ (d) $\frac{4\pi d}{\lambda}\left(1-\frac{1}{n^2}\sin^2\theta\right)^{1/2}+2\pi$

Ans. ***(a)*** Consider the diagram, the ray (P) is incident at an angle θ and gets reflected in the direction P' and refracted in the direction P''. Due to reflection from the glass medium, there is a phase change of π.

Time taken to travel along OP''

$$\Delta t = \frac{OP''}{v} = \frac{d/\cos r}{c/n} = \frac{nd}{c\cos r}$$

From Snell's law, $$n = \frac{\sin\theta}{\sin r}$$

$$\Rightarrow \qquad \sin r = \frac{\sin\theta}{n}$$

$$\cos r = \sqrt{1-\sin^2 r} = \sqrt{1-\frac{\sin^2\theta}{n^2}}$$

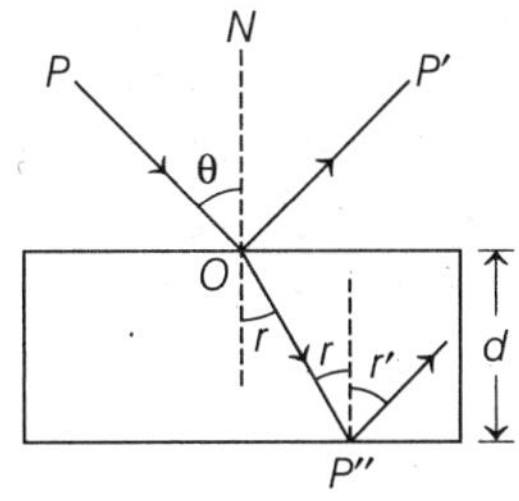

$$\therefore \qquad \Delta t = \frac{nd}{c\left(1-\frac{\sin^2\theta}{n^2}\right)^{1/2}} = \frac{n^2 d}{c}\left(1-\frac{\sin^2\theta}{n^2}\right)^{-1/2}$$

$$\text{Phase difference} = \Delta\phi = \frac{2\pi}{T}\times\Delta t = \frac{2\pi\, nd}{\lambda}\left(1-\frac{\sin^2\theta}{n^2}\right)^{-1/2}$$

$$\text{So, net phase difference} = \Delta\phi + \pi = \frac{4\pi d}{\lambda}\left(1-\frac{1}{n^2}\sin^2\theta\right)^{-1/2} + \pi$$

Q.4 In a Young's double-slit experiment, the source is white light. One of the holes is covered by a red filter and another by a blue filter. In this case,

(a) there shall be alternate interference patterns of red and blue
(b) there shall be an interference pattern for red distinct from that for blue
(c) there shall be no interference fringes
(d) there shall be an interference pattern for red mixing with one for blue

Ans. ***(c)*** For the interference pattern to be formed on the screen, the sources should be coherent and emit light of the same frequency and wavelength.

In a Young's double-slit experiment, when one of the holes is covered by a red filter and another by a blue filter, only red and blue lights are present due to filtration. In YDSE monochromatic light is used for the formation of fringes on the screen. Hence, in this case there shall be no interference fringes.

Q.5 Figure shows a standard two slit arrangement with slits S_1, S_2, P_1, P_2 are the two minima points on either side of P as shown is figure.

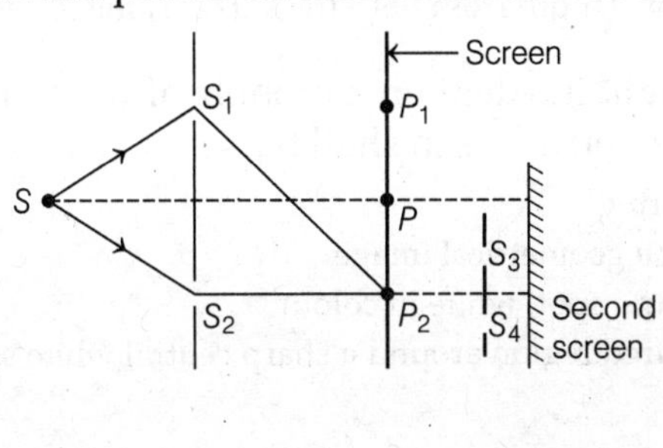

At P_2 on the screen, there is a hole and behind P_2 is a second 2-slit arrangement with slits S_3, S_4 and a second screen behind them.

(a) There would be no interference pattern on the second screen but it would be lighted
(b) The second screen would be totally dark
(c) There would be a single bright point on the second screen
(d) There would be a regular two slit pattern on the second screen

Ans. ***(d)*** According to question, there is a hole at point P_2. From Huygen's principle, wave will propagates from the sources S_1 and S_2. Each point on the screen will acts as secondary sources of wavelets.

Now, there is a hole at point P_2 (minima). The hole will act as a source of fresh light for the slits S_3 and S_4.

Therefore, there will be a regular two slit pattern on the second screen.

Multiple Choice Questions (More Than One Options)

Q.6 Two sources S_1 and S_2 of intensity I_1 and I_2 are placed in front of a screen [Fig. (a)]. The pattern of intensity distribution seen in the central portion is given by Fig. (b).

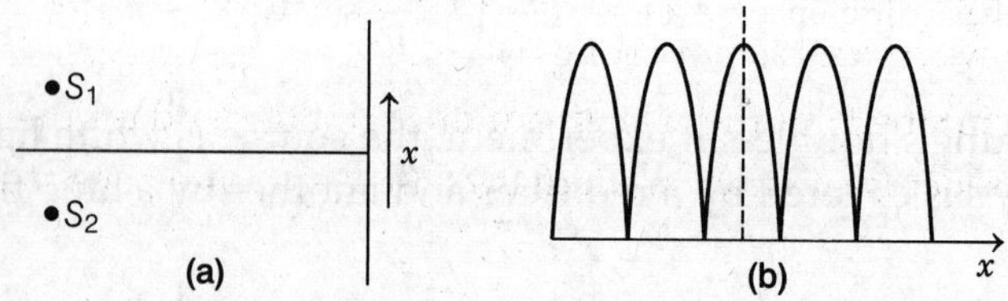

In this case, which of the following statements are true?

(a) S_1 and S_2 have the same intensities
(b) S_1 and S_2 have a constant phase difference
(c) S_1 and S_2 have the same phase
(d) S_1 and S_2 have the same wavelength

Ans. ***(a, b, d)*** Consider the pattern of the intensity shown in the given figure

(a) As intensities of all successive minima is zero, hence we can say that two sources S_1 and S_2 have same intensities.
(b) The intensity is a function of phase difference and is not changing with time as shown in figure (b). Thus the phase difference does not change with time.
(d) The intensity curve obtained is for monochromatic and coherent light source. Hence the wavelength from both the slits is same.

Q.7 Consider sunlight incident on a pinhole of width 10^3 Å. The image of the pinhole seen on a screen shall be

(a) a sharp white ring
(b) different from a geometrical image
(c) a diffused central spot, white in colour
(d) diffused coloured region around a sharp central white spot

Ans. ***(b, d)*** Given, width of pinhole $= 10^3$ Å $= 1000$ Å

We know that wavelength of sunlight ranges from 4000 Å to 8000 Å.

Clearly, wavelength $\lambda <$ width of the slit.

Hence, light is diffracted from the hole. Due to diffraction from the slit, the image formed on the screen will be different from the geometrical image.

Q.8 Consider the diffraction pattern for a small pinhole. As the size of the hole is increased

(a) the size decreases
(b) the intensity increases
(c) the size increases
(d) the intensity decreases

Ans. ***(a, b)***

(a) On increasing width of hole of pinhole, 'd' increases. Hence the size of central maxima decreases.

(b) As the energy passing through hole increased on increasing the size of hole. So the intensity of pattern will increase.

Q.9 For light diverging from a point source,

(a) the wavefront is spherical
(b) the intensity decreases in proportion to the distance squared
(c) the wavefront is parabolic
(d) the intensity at the wavefront does not depend on the distance

Ans. ***(a, b)*** Consider the diagram in which light diverges from a point source (O).

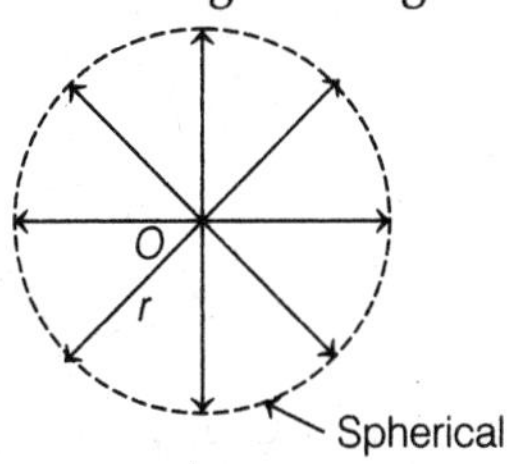

Due to the point source light propagates in all directions symmetrically and hence, wavefront will be spherical as shown in the diagram.

If power of the source is P, then intensity of the source will be

$$I = \frac{P}{4\pi r^2}$$

where, r is radius of the wavefront at any time.

Very Short Answer Type Questions

Q.10 Is Huygen's principle valid for longitudinal sound waves?

Ans. When we are considering a point source of sound wave. The disturbance due to the source propagates in spherical symmetry that is in all directions. The formation of wavefront is in accordance with Huygen's principle.

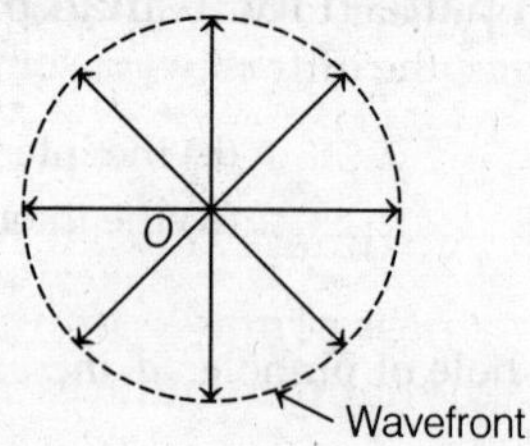

So, Huygen's principle is valid for longitudinal sound waves also.

Q.11 Consider a point at the focal point of a convergent lens. Another convergent lens of short focal length is placed on the other side. What is the nature of the wavefronts emerging from the final image?

Ans. Consider the ray diagram shown below

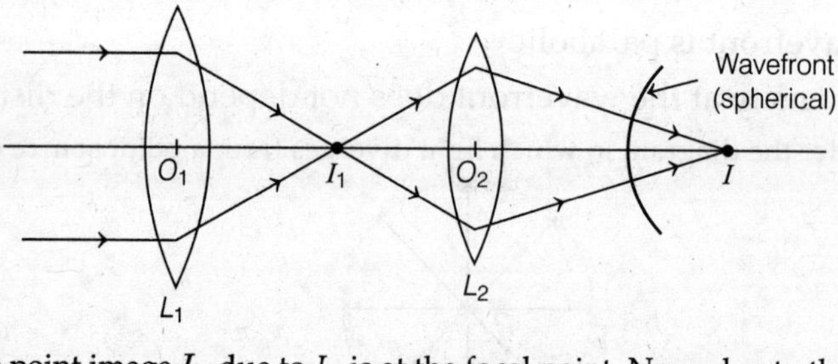

The point image I_1, due to L_1 is at the focal point. Now, due to the converging lense L_2, let final image formed is I which is point image, hence the wavefront for this image will be of spherical symmetry.

Q.12 What is the shape of the wavefront on earth for sunlight?

Ans. We know that the sun is at very large distance from the earth. Assuming sun as spherical, it can be considered as point source situated at infinity.

Due to the large distance the radius of wavefront can be considered as large (infinity) and hence, wavefront is almost plane.

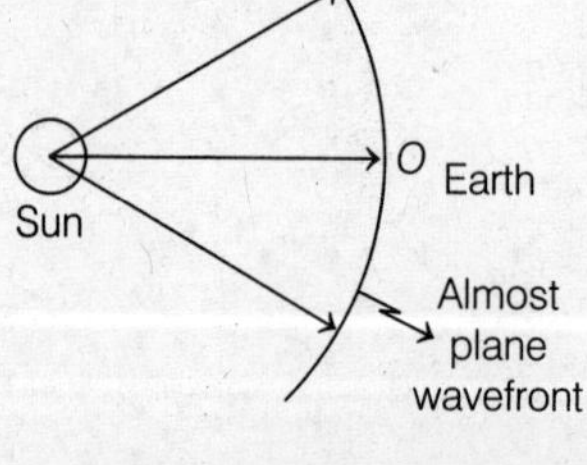

Q.13 Why is the diffraction of sound waves more evident in daily experience than that of light wave?

Ans. As we know that the frequencies of sound waves lie between 20 Hz to 20 kHz so their wavelength ranges between 15 m to 15 mm. The diffraction occurs if the wavelength of waves is nearly equal to slit width or size of obstacle.

As the wavelength of light waves is 7000×10^{-10} m to 4000×10^{-10} m. The slit width or size of obstacle is very near to the wavelength of sound waves as compared to light waves. Thus, the diffraction of sound waves is more evident in daily life than that of light waves.

***Q.14** The human eye has an approximate angular resolution of $\phi = 5.8 \times 10^{-4}$ rad and a typical photoprinter prints a minimum of 300 dpi (dots per inch, 1 inch = 2.54 cm). At what minimal distancez should a printed page be held so that one does not see the individual dots.

Ans. Given, angular resolution of human eye, $\phi = 5.8 \times 10^{-4}$ rad.

and printer prints 300 dots per inch.

The linear distance between two dots is $l = \frac{2.54}{300}$ cm $= 0.84 \times 10^{-2}$ cm.

At a distance of z cm, this subtends an angle, $\phi = \frac{l}{z}$

$$\therefore \quad z = \frac{l}{\phi} = \frac{0.84 \times 10^{-2} \text{ cm}}{5.8 \times 10^{-4}} = 14.5 \text{ cm.}$$

Q.15 A polaroid (I) is placed infront of a monochromatic source. Another polariod (II) is placed in front of this polaroid (I) and rotated till no light passes. A third polaroid (III) is now placed in between (I) and (II). In this case, will light emerge from (II). Explain.

Thinking Process Natural light from the sun is unpolarised. This means the electric vector oscillates in all possible directions in the transverse plane.

Ans. In the diagram shown, a monochromatic light is placed infront of polaroid (I) as shown below.

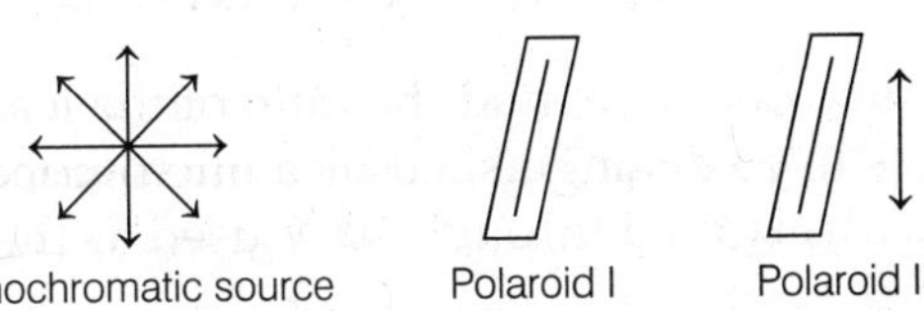

As per the given question, monochromatic light emerging from polaroid (I) is plane polarised. When polaroid (II) is placed infront of this polaroid (I), and rotated till no light passes through polaroid (II), then (I) and (II) are set in crossed positions, *i.e.*, pass axes of I and II are at 90°.

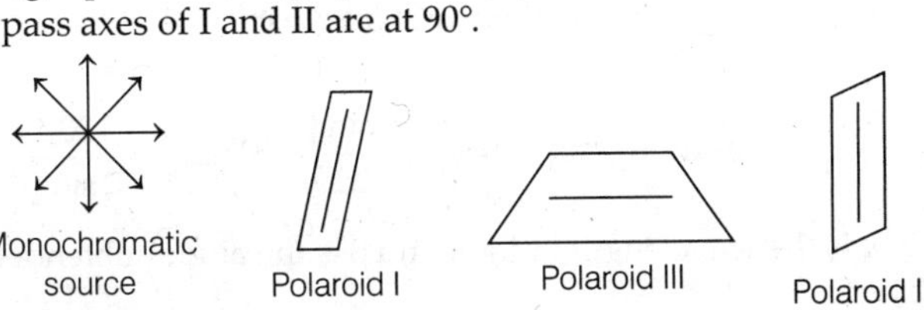

Note (✱) Topics related to these question have been removed from latest NCERT.

Consider the above diagram where a third polaroid (III) is placed between polaroid (I) and polaroid II.

When a third polaroid (III) is placed in between (I) and (II), no light will emerge from (II), if pass axis of (III) is perpendicular to pass axis of (I) or (II). In all other cases, light will emerge from (II), as pass axis of (II) will no longer be at 90° to the pass axis of (III).

Short Answer Type Questions

***Q.16** Can reflection result in plane polarised light if the light is incident on the interface from the side with higher refractive index?

Ans. When angle of incidence is equal to Brewster's angle, the transmitted light is unpolarised and reflected light is plane polarised.

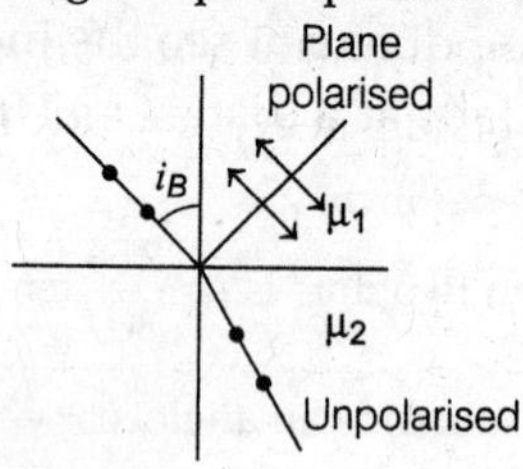

Consider the diagram in which unpolarised light is represented by dot and plane polarised light is represented by arrows. Polarisation by reflection occurs when the angle of incidence is the Brewster's angle

i.e., $$\tan i_B = {}^1\mu_2 = \frac{\mu_2}{\mu_1} \text{ where } \mu_2 < \mu_1$$

when the light rays travels in such a medium, the critical angle is

$$\sin i_c = \frac{\mu_2}{\mu_1}$$

where, $\mu_2 < \mu_1$

As $|\tan i_B| > |\sin i_C|$ for large angles $i_B < i_C$.

Thus, the polarisation by reflection occurs definitely.

Q.17 For the same objective, find the ratio of the least separation between two points to be distinguished by a microscope for light of 5000 Å and electrons accelerated through 100V used as the illuminating substance.

Thinking Process Resolving power of a microscope is calculated by $\frac{2 \sin \beta}{1.22 \lambda}$, where β is the angle subtented by the objective at the object.

Ans. We know that

$$\text{Resolving power} = \frac{1}{d} = \frac{2\sin \beta}{1.22 \lambda} \Rightarrow d_{\min} = \frac{1.22 \lambda}{2 \sin \beta}$$

where, λ is the wavelength of light and β is the angle subtended by the objective at the object.

Note (✱) Topics related to these question have been removed from latest NCERT.

For the light of wavelength 5500 Å,

$$d_{min} = \frac{1.22 \times 5500 \times 10^{-10}}{2 \sin \beta} \quad \text{... (i)}$$

For electrons accelerated through 100 V, the de-Broglie wavelength

$$\lambda = \frac{12.27}{\sqrt{V}} = \frac{12.27}{\sqrt{100}} = 0.12 \times 10^{-9} \text{ m} \Rightarrow d_{min} = \frac{1.22 \times 0.12 \times 10^{-9}}{2 \sin \beta}$$

Ratio of the least separation

$$\therefore \quad \frac{d'_{min}}{d_{min}} = \frac{0.12 \times 10^{-9}}{5500 \times 10^{-10}} = 0.2 \times 10^{-3}$$

Q.18 Consider a two slit interference arrangements as shown in figure such that the distance of the screen from the slits is half the distance between the slits. Obtain the value of D in terms of λ such that the first minima on the screen falls at a distance D from the centre O.

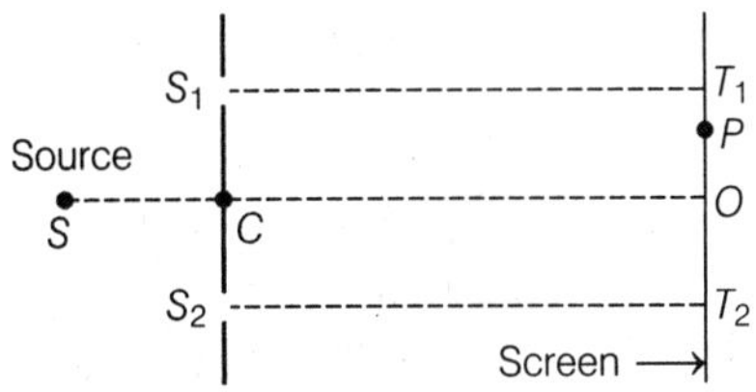

Thinking Process For n^{th} minima to be formed on the screen path difference between the rays coming from S_1 and S_2 must be $(2n-1)\frac{\lambda}{2}$.

Ans. From the given figure of two slit interference arrangements, we can write

$$T_2P = T_2O + OP = D + x$$

and

$$T_1P = T_1O - OP = D - x$$

$$S_1P = \sqrt{(S_1T_1)^2 + (PT_1)^2} = \sqrt{D^2 + (D-x)^2}$$

and

$$S_2P = \sqrt{(S_2T_2)^2 + (T_2P)^2} = \sqrt{D^2 + (D+x)^2}$$

The minima will occur when $S_2P - S_1P = (2n-1)\frac{\lambda}{2}$

i.e., $[D^2 + (D+x)^2]^{1/2} - [D^2 + (D-x)^2]^{1/2} = \frac{\lambda}{2}$ [for first minima $n = 1$]

If $x = D$

we can write $[D^2 + 4D^2]^{1/2} - [D^2 + 0]^{1/2} = \frac{\lambda}{2}$

$$\Rightarrow \quad [5D^2]^{1/2} - [D^2]^{1/2} = \frac{\lambda}{2} \Rightarrow \sqrt{5}D - D = \frac{\lambda}{2}$$

$$\Rightarrow \quad D(\sqrt{5} - 1) = \lambda/2 \text{ or } D = \frac{\lambda}{2(\sqrt{5}-1)}$$

Putting $\sqrt{5} = 2.236 \Rightarrow \sqrt{5} - 1 = 2.236 - 1 = 1.236$

$$D = \frac{\lambda}{2(1.236)} = 0.404\lambda$$

Long Answer Type Questions

Q.19 Figure shown a two slit arrangement with a source which emits unpolarised light. P is a polariser with axis whose direction is not given. If I_0 is the intensity of the principal maxima when no polariser is present, calculate in the present case, the intensity of the principal maxima as well as of the first minima.

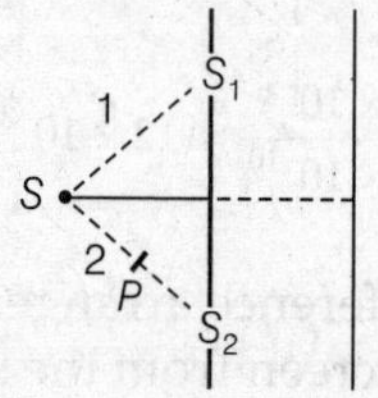

Thinking Process The resultant amplitude will be the sum of amplitude of either beam in perpendicular and parallel polarisation.

Ans. A = Resultant amplitude

$= A$ parallel $(A_{\parallel}) + A$ perpendicular $(A_{\perp})$

$\Rightarrow \quad A = A_{\perp} + A_{\parallel}$

Without P,

$$A = A_{\perp} + A_{\parallel}$$

$$A_{\perp} = A^1{}_{\perp} + A_{\perp}^2 = A_{\perp}^0 \sin(kx - \omega t) + A_{\perp}^0 \sin(kx - \omega t + \phi)$$

$$A_{\parallel} = A_{\parallel}^{(1)} + A_{\parallel}^{(2)}$$

$$A_{\parallel} = A_{\parallel}^0 [\sin(kx - \omega t) + \sin(kx - \omega t + \phi)]$$

where $A_{\perp}^0, A_{\parallel}^0$ are the amplitudes of either of the beam in perpendicular and parallel polarisations.

$\therefore$ Intensity $= \{|A_{\perp}^0|^2 + |A_{\parallel}{}^0|^2\}$

$[\sin^2(kx - \omega t)(1 + \cos^2\phi + 2\sin\phi) + \sin^2(kx - \omega t)\sin^2\phi]$

$$= \{|A_{\perp}^0|^2 + |A_{\parallel}^0|^2\}\left(\frac{1}{2}\right).2(1 + \cos\phi)$$

$$= 2|A_{\perp}^0|^2(1 + \cos\phi), \text{ since, } |A_{\perp}^0|_{av} = |A_{\parallel}{}^0|_{av}$$

With P,

Assume $A_{\perp}^2$ is blocked.

$$\text{Intensity} = (A_{\parallel}^1 + A_{\parallel}^2)^2 + (A_{\perp}^1)^2$$

$$= |A_{\perp}^0|^2(1 + \cos\phi) + |A_{\perp}^0|^2 \cdot \frac{1}{2}$$

Given, $I_0 = 4|A_{\perp}^0|^2$ = Intensity without polariser at principal maxima.

Intensity at principal maxima with polariser

$$= |A_{\perp}^0|^2\left(2 + \frac{1}{2}\right) = \frac{5}{8}I_0$$

Intensity at first minima with polariser

$$= |A_{\perp}^0|^2(1 - 1) + \frac{|A_{\perp}^0|^2}{2} = \frac{I_0}{8}.$$

Q.20 A small transparent slab containing material of $\mu = 1.5$ is placed along AS_2 as shown in figure.

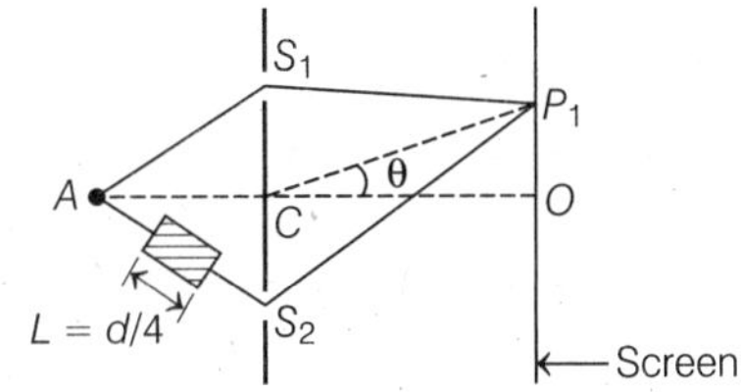

$$AC = CO = D, S_1C = S_2C = d << D$$

What will be the distance from O of the principal maxima and of the first minima on either side of the principal maxima obtained in the absence of the glass slab?

- **Concept Insight** Whenever a transparent slab of refractive index μ and thickness t is inserted in the path of the ray, the fringes on the screen shift by $(\mu - 1)\, t$ towards the slab.

Ans. In case of transparent glass slab of refractive index μ, the path difference will be calculated as $\Delta x = 2d \sin\theta + (\mu - 1) L$.

For the principal maxima, (path difference is zero)

i.e., $$2d \sin\theta_0 + (\mu - 1) L = 0$$

or $$\sin\theta_0 = -\frac{L(\mu - 1)}{2d} = \frac{-L(0.5)}{2d} \qquad [\because L = d/4]$$

or $$\sin\theta_0 = \frac{-1}{16}$$

$\therefore$ $$OP = D\tan\theta_0 \approx D\sin\theta_0 = \frac{-D}{16}$$

For the first minima, the path difference is $\pm \dfrac{\lambda}{2}$

$\therefore$ $$2d \sin\theta_1 + 0.5L = \pm\frac{\lambda}{2}$$

or $$\sin\theta_1 = \frac{\pm\lambda/2 - 0.5L}{2d} = \frac{\pm\lambda/2 - d/8}{2d} = \frac{\pm\lambda/2 - \lambda/8}{2\lambda} = \pm\frac{1}{4} - \frac{1}{16}$$

[$\because$ The diffraction occurs if the wavelength of waves is nearly equal to the side width (d)]

On the positive side $\sin\theta_1^+ = +\dfrac{1}{4} - \dfrac{1}{16} = \dfrac{3}{16}$

On the negative side $\sin\theta_1^- = -\dfrac{1}{4} - \dfrac{1}{16} = -\dfrac{5}{16}$

The first principal maxima on the positive side is at distance

$$D\tan\theta_1'^{+} = D\frac{\sin\theta_1'^{+}}{\sqrt{1 - \sin^2\theta_1'}} = D\frac{3}{\sqrt{16^2 - 3^2}} = \frac{3D}{\sqrt{247}} \text{ above point } O$$

The first principal minima on the negative side is at distance

$$D\tan\theta_1^- = \frac{-5D}{\sqrt{16^2 - 5^2}} = \frac{-5D}{\sqrt{231}} \text{ below point } O.$$

Q.21 Four identical monochromatic sources A, B, C, D as shown in the figure produce waves of the same wavelength λ and are coherent. Two receiver R_1 and R_2 are at great but equal distances from B.

(i) Which of the two receivers picks up the larger signal?

(ii) Which of the two receivers picks up the larger signal when B is turned off?

(iii) Which of the two receivers picks up the larger signal when D is turned off?

(iv) Which of the two receivers can distinguish which of the sources B or D has been turned off?

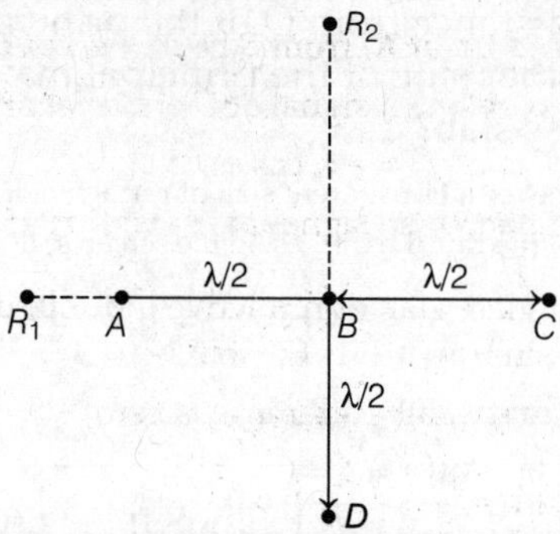

$$R_1B = d = R_2 B$$
$$AB = BC = BD = \lambda/2$$

Thinking Process The resultant disturbance at a point will be calculated by sum of disturbances due to individual sources.

Ans. Consider the disturbances at the receiver R_1 which is at a distance d from B.

Let the wave at R_1 because of A be $y_A = a\cos\omega t$. The path difference of the signal from A with that from B is $\lambda/2$ and hence, the phase difference is π.

Thus, the wave at R_1 because of B is

$$y_B = a\cos(\omega t - \pi) = -a\cos\omega t.$$

The path difference of the signal from C with that from A is λ and hence the phase difference is 2π.

Thus, the wave at R_1 because of C is $y_c = a\cos(\omega t - 2\pi) = a\cos\omega t$

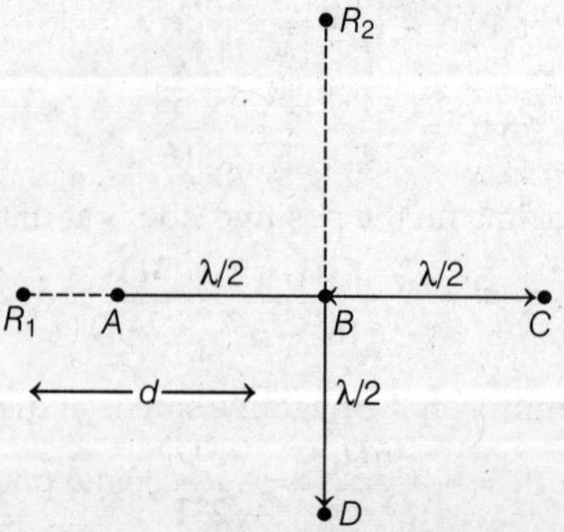

The path difference between the signal from D with that of A is

$$\sqrt{d^2+\left(\frac{\lambda}{2}\right)^2}-(d-\lambda/2)=d\left(1+\frac{\lambda}{4d^2}\right)^{1/2}-d+\frac{\lambda}{2}$$

$$=d\left(1+\frac{\lambda^2}{8d^2}\right)^{1/2}-d+\frac{\lambda}{2}\approx\frac{\lambda}{2} \qquad (\because d>>\lambda)$$

Therefore, phase difference is π.

$\therefore \qquad y_D = a\cos(\omega t-\pi) = -a\cos\omega t$

Thus, the signal picked up at R_1 from all the four sources is $y_{R_1} = y_A + y_B + y_C + y_D$

$$= a\cos\omega t - a\cos\omega t + a\cos\omega t - a\cos\omega t = 0$$

(i) Let the signal picked up at R_2 from B be $y_B = a_1\cos\omega t$.

The path difference between signal at D and that at B is $\lambda/2$.

$\therefore \qquad y_D = -a_1\cos\omega t$

The path difference between signal at A and that at B is

$$\sqrt{(d)^2+\left(\frac{\lambda}{2}\right)^2}-d=d\left(1+\frac{\lambda^2}{4d^2}\right)^{1/2}-d\approx\frac{1\,\lambda^2}{8\,d^2}$$

As $d>>\lambda$, therefore this path difference $\to 0$

and phase difference $=\frac{2\pi}{\lambda}\left(\frac{1}{8}\frac{\lambda^2}{d^2}\right)\to 0$

Hence, $\qquad y_A = a_1\cos(\omega t-\phi)$

Similarly, $\qquad y_C = a_1\cos(\omega t-\phi)$

$\therefore$ Signal picked up by R_2 is

$$y_A+y_B+y_C+y_D = y_{R_2} = 2a_1\cos(\omega t-\phi)$$

$$\therefore \qquad |y_{R_2}|^2 = 4a_1^2\cos^2(\omega t-\phi)$$

$$\therefore \qquad \langle I\rangle = 2a_1^2$$

Thus, R_2 picks up the larger signal.

(ii) If B is switched off,

R_1 picks up $\qquad y = a\cos\omega t$

$$\therefore \qquad \langle I_{R_1}\rangle = \frac{1}{2}a^2$$

R_2 picks up $\qquad y = a\cos\omega t$

$$\therefore \qquad \langle I_{R_2}\rangle = a^2\langle\cos^2\omega t\rangle = \frac{a^2}{2}$$

Thus, R_1 and R_2 pick up the same signal.

(iii) If D is switched off.

R_1 picks up $y = a\cos\omega t$

$$\therefore \qquad \langle I_{R_1}\rangle = \frac{1}{2}a^2$$

R_2 picks up $\quad y = 3\,a\cos\omega t$

$$\therefore \quad \langle I_{R_2}\rangle = 9a^2 < \cos^2\omega t > = \frac{9a^2}{2}$$

Thus, R_2 picks up larger signal compared to R_1.

(iv) Thus, a signal at R_1 indicates B has been switched off and an enhanced signal at R_2 indicates D has been switched off.

Q.22 The optical properties of a medium are governed by the relative permittivity (ε_r) and relative permeability (μ_r). The refractive index is defined as $\sqrt{\mu_r \varepsilon_r} = n$. For ordinary material, $\varepsilon_r > 0$ and $\mu_r > 0$ and the positive sign is taken for the square root.

In 1964, a Russian scientist V. Veselago postulated the existence of material with $\varepsilon_r < 0$ and $\mu_r < 0$. Since then such metamaterials have been produced in the laboratories and their optical properties studied. For such materials $n = -\sqrt{\mu_r\,\varepsilon_r}$. As light enters a medium of such refractive index the phases travel away from the direction of propagation.

(i) According to the description above show that if rays of light enter such a medium from air (refractive index = 1) at an angle θ in 2nd quadrant, then the refracted beam is in the 3rd quadrant.

(ii) Prove that Snell's law holds for such a medium.

Ans. Let us assume that the given postulate is true, then two parallel rays would proceed as shown in the figure below.

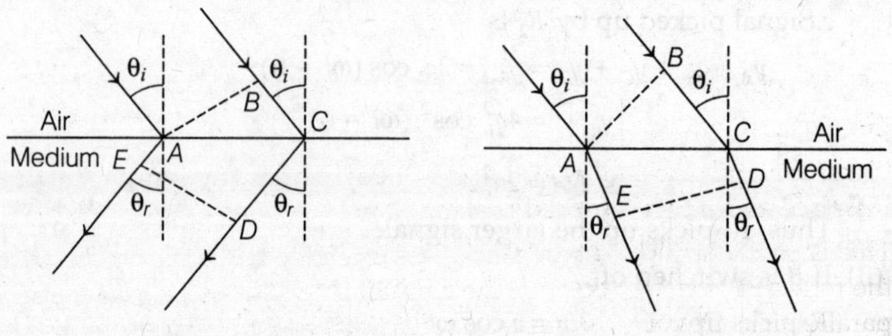

(i) $\qquad\qquad\qquad\qquad$ (ii)

(i) Let AB represent the incident wavefront and DE represent the refracted wavefront. All points on a wavefront must be in same phase and in turn, must have the same optical path length.

Thus $$-\sqrt{\varepsilon_r\mu_r}\,AE = BC - \sqrt{\varepsilon_r\mu_r}\,CD$$

or $$BC = \sqrt{\varepsilon_r\mu_r}\,(CD - AE)$$

$$BC > 0,\ CD > AE$$

This shows that the postulate is reasonable. If however, the light proceeded in the sense it does for ordinary material (*viz.* in the fourth quadrant, Fig. 2)

Then, $$-\sqrt{\varepsilon_r\mu_r}\,AE = BC - \sqrt{\varepsilon_r\mu_r}\,CD$$

or $$BC = \sqrt{\varepsilon_r\mu_r}\,(CD - AE)$$

As $AE > CD$, therefore $BC < 0$ which is not possible. Hence, we can say that the refracted rays lie in the third quadrant.

(ii) From Fig. (i) $BC = AC \sin\theta_i$

and $CD - AE = AC \sin\theta_r$

As $BC = \sqrt{\mu_r \varepsilon_r}$ $[CD - AE = BC]$

$$AC \sin\theta_i = \sqrt{\varepsilon_r \mu_r}\ AC \sin\theta_r$$

or $$\frac{\sin\theta_i}{\sin\theta_r} = \sqrt{\varepsilon_r \mu_r} = n$$

Which proves Snell's law.

***Q.23** To ensure almost 100% transmittivity, photographic lenses are often coated with a thin layer of dielectric material. The refractive index of this material is intermediated between that of air and glass (which makes the optical element of the lens). A typically used dielectric film is MgF_2 ($n = 1.38$). What should the thickness of the film so that at the centre of the visible spectrum (5500 Å) there is maximum transmission.

Ans. In this figure, we have shown a dielectric film of thickness d deposited on a glass lens.

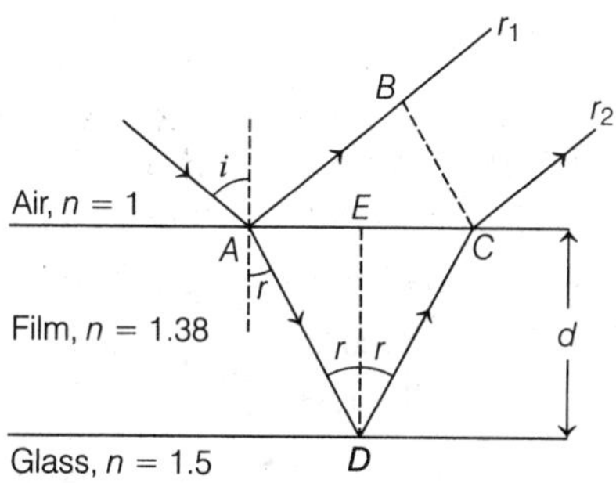

Refractive index of film = 1.38 and refractive index of glass = 1.5.

Given, $\lambda = 5500$ Å.

Consider a ray incident at an angle i. A part of this ray is reflected from the air-film interface and a part refracted inside.

This is partly reflected at the film-glass interface and a part transmitted. A part of the reflected ray is reflected at the film-air interface and a part transmitted as r_2 parallel to r_1. Of course successive reflections and transmissions will keep on decreasing the amplitude of the wave.

Hence, rays r_1 and r_2 shall dominate the behaviour. If incident light is to be transmitted through the lens, r_1 and r_2 should interfere destructively. Both the reflections at A and D are from lower to higher refractive index and hence, there is no phase change on reflection. The optical path difference between r_2 and r_1 is

$$n(AD + CD) - AB$$

If d is the thickness of the film, then

$$AD = CD = \frac{d}{\cos r}$$

$$AB = AC \sin i$$

$$\frac{AC}{2} = d \tan r$$

Note (✱) Topics related to these question have been removed from latest NCERT.

$\therefore \qquad AC = 2d \tan r$

Hence, $AB = 2d \tan r \sin i$.

Thus, the optical path difference $= \dfrac{2nd}{\cos r} - 2d \tan r \sin i$

$$= 2 . \frac{\sin i \, d}{\sin r \cos r} - 2d \frac{\sin r}{\cos r} \sin i$$

$$= 2d \sin i \left[\frac{1 - \sin^2 r}{\sin r \cos r} \right]$$

$$= 2nd \cos r$$

For these waves to interfere destructively path difference $= \dfrac{\lambda}{2}$.

$$\Rightarrow \qquad 2nd \cos r = \frac{\lambda}{2}$$

$$\Rightarrow \qquad nd \cos r = \frac{\lambda}{4} \qquad \ldots \text{(i)}$$

For photographic lenses, the sources are normally in vertical plane

$$\therefore \qquad i = r = 0°$$

From Eq. (i), $\qquad nd \cos 0° = \dfrac{\lambda}{4}$

$$\Rightarrow \qquad d = \frac{\lambda}{4n}$$

$$= \frac{5500 \text{ Å}}{4 \times 1.38} \approx 1000 \text{ Å}$$

Chapter 11

Dual Nature of Radiation and Matter

Multiple Choice Questions (MCQs)

Q.1 A particle is dropped from a height H. The de-Broglie wavelength of the particle as a function of height is proportional to

(a) H (b) $H^{1/2}$ (c) H^0 (d) $H^{-1/2}$

Thinking Process The de-Broglie wavelength λ is given by $\lambda = \frac{h}{mv}$.

Ans. *(d)* Velocity of a body falling from a height H is given by

$$v = \sqrt{2gH}$$

We know that de-broglie wavelength

$$\lambda = \frac{h}{mv} = \frac{h}{m\sqrt{2gH}} \Rightarrow = \frac{h}{m\sqrt{2g}\sqrt{H}}$$

Here, $\frac{h}{m\sqrt{2g}}$ is a constant say 'K'.

So, $$\lambda = K\frac{1}{\sqrt{H}} \Rightarrow \lambda \propto \frac{1}{\sqrt{H}}$$

$\Rightarrow$ $$\lambda \propto H^{-1/2}$$

Q.2 The wavelength of a photon needed to remove a proton from a nucleus which is bound to the nucleus with 1 MeV energy is nearly

(a) 1.2 nm (b) 1.2×10^{-3} nm (c) 1.2×10^{-6} nm (d) 1.2×10 nm

Thinking Process Energy of a photon is $E = \frac{hc}{\lambda}$, where λ is the minimum wavelength of the photon required to eject the proton from nucleus.

Ans. *(b)* Given in the question,

Energy of a photon, $E = 1\text{MeV} \Rightarrow = 10^6$ eV

Now, $$hc = 1240 \text{ eV nm}$$

Now, $$E = \frac{hc}{\lambda}$$

$\Rightarrow$ $$\lambda = \frac{hc}{E} = \frac{1240 \text{ eVnm}}{10^6 \text{ eV}}$$

$$= 1.24 \times 10^{-3} \text{ nm}$$

Q.3 Consider a beam of electrons (each electron with energy E_0) incident on a metal surface kept in an evacuated chamber. Then,

(a) no electrons will be emitted as only photons can emit electrons
(b) electrons can be emitted but all with an energy, E_0
(c) electrons can be emitted with any energy, with a maximum of $E_0 - \phi$ (ϕ is the work function)
(d) electrons can be emitted with any energy, with a maximum of E_0

Ans. *(d)* When a beam of electrons of energy E_0 is incident on a metal surface kept in an evacuated chamber, electrons can be emitted with maximum energy E_0 (due to elastic collision) and with any energy less than E_0, when part of incident energy of electron is used in liberating the electrons from the surface of metal.

Q.4 Consider figure given below. Suppose the voltage applied to A is increased. The diffracted beam will have the maximum at a value of θ that

(a) will be larger than the earlier value
(b) will be the same as the earlier value
(c) will be less than the earlier value
(d) will depend on the target

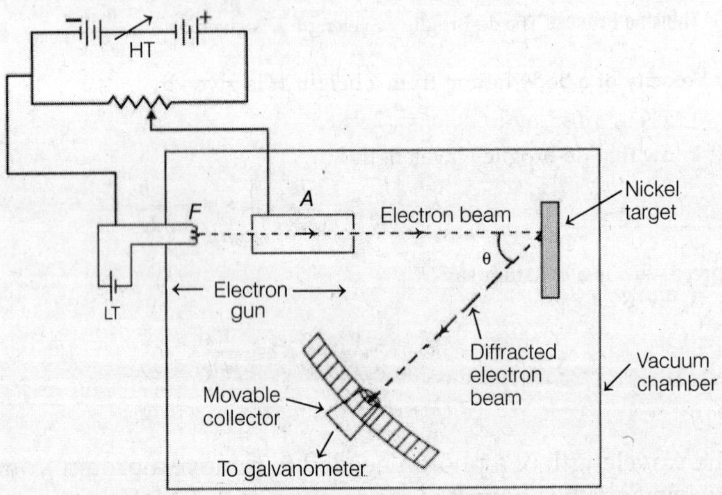

Thinking Process The figure given here shows the Davisson-Germer experiment which was held to verify the wave nature of electrons.

Ans. *(c)* In Davisson-Germer experiment, the de-Broglie wavelength associated with electron is

$$\lambda = \frac{12.27}{\sqrt{V}} \text{Å} \quad \text{...(i)}$$

where V is the applied voltage.

If there is a maxima of the diffracted electrons at an angle θ, then

$$2d\sin\theta = n\lambda \quad \text{...(ii)}$$

From Eq. (i), we note that if V is inversely proportional to the wavelength λ.

i.e., V will increase with the decrease in the λ.

From Eq. (ii), we note that wavelength λ is directly proportional to $\sin\theta$ and hence θ.

So, with the decrease in λ, θ will also decrease.

Thus, when the voltage applied to A is increased. The diffracted beam will have the maximum at a value of θ that will be less than the earlier value.

Q.5 A proton, a neutron, an electron and an α-particle have same energy. Then, their de-Broglie wavelengths compare as

(a) $\lambda_p = \lambda_n > \lambda_e > \lambda_\alpha$
(b) $\lambda_\alpha < \lambda_p = \lambda_n < \lambda_e$
(c) $\lambda_e < \lambda_p = \lambda_n > \lambda_\alpha$
(d) $\lambda_e = \lambda_p = \lambda_n = \lambda_\alpha$

Thinking Process The energy of any particle can be given by $k = \frac{1}{2}mv^2$

$$\Rightarrow \quad mv = \sqrt{2mk} \quad \text{...(i)}$$

Also, de-Broglie wavelength is given by

$$\lambda = \frac{h}{mv} = \frac{h}{\sqrt{2mk}} \quad \text{...(ii)}$$

Ans. ***(b)*** We know that the relation between λ and k is given by

$$\lambda = \frac{h}{\sqrt{2mk}}$$

Here, for the given value of energy k, $\frac{h}{\sqrt{2k}}$ is a constant.

Thus, $$\lambda \propto \frac{1}{\sqrt{m}}$$

$\therefore$ $$\lambda_p : \lambda_n : \lambda_e : \lambda_\alpha$$

$\Rightarrow$ $$= \frac{1}{\sqrt{m_p}} : \frac{1}{\sqrt{m_n}} : \frac{1}{\sqrt{m_e}} : \frac{1}{\sqrt{m_\alpha}}$$

Since, $m_p = m_n$, hence $\lambda_p = \lambda_n$

As, $m_\alpha > m_p$, therefore $\lambda_\alpha < \lambda_p$

As, $m_e < m_n$, therefore $\lambda_e > \lambda_n$

Hence, $\lambda_\alpha < \lambda_p = \lambda_n < \lambda_e$

Q.6 An electron is moving with an initial velocity $v = v_0\hat{i}$ and is in a magnetic field $\mathbf{B} = B_0\hat{\mathbf{j}}$. Then, it's de-Broglie wavelength

(a) remains constant
(b) increases with time
(c) decreases with time
(d) increases and decreases periodically

Ans. ***(a)*** Given, $\mathbf{v} = v_0\hat{\mathbf{i}}$ and $\mathbf{B} = B_0\hat{\mathbf{j}}$

Force on moving electron due to magnetic field is, $\mathbf{F} = -e(\mathbf{v} \times \mathbf{B})$

$$= -e[v_0\mathbf{i} \times B_0\mathbf{j}] \Rightarrow = -ev_0B_0\hat{\mathbf{k}}$$

As this force is perpendicular to $\mathbf{v}$ and $\mathbf{B}$, so the magnitude of $\mathbf{v}$ will not change, *i.e.*, momentum $(= mv)$ will remain constant in magnitude. Hence,

de-Broglie wavelength $\lambda = \frac{h}{mv}$ remains constant.

Q.7 An electron (mass m) with an initial velocity $\mathbf{v} = v_0\mathbf{i}(v_0 > 0)$ is in an electric field $\mathbf{E} = -E_0\hat{\mathbf{i}}$ (E_0 = constant > 0). It's de-Broglie wavelength at time t is given by

(a) $\dfrac{\lambda_0}{\left(1+\dfrac{eE_0}{m}\dfrac{t}{v_0}\right)}$ (b) $\lambda_0\left(1+\dfrac{eE_0 t}{mv_0}\right)$ (c) λ_0 (d) $\lambda_0 t$

Thinking Process De-Broglie wavelength is given by $\lambda = \dfrac{h}{mv}$

Ans. *(a)* Initial de-Broglie wavelength of electron,

$$\lambda_0 = \frac{h}{mv_0} \qquad ...(i)$$

Force on electron in electric field,

$$\mathbf{F} = -e\mathbf{E} = -e[-E_0\hat{\mathbf{i}}] = eE_0\hat{\mathbf{i}}$$

Acceleration of electron $\mathbf{a} = \dfrac{\mathbf{F}}{m} = -\dfrac{eE_0\hat{\mathbf{i}}}{m}$

Velocity of electron after time t,

$$\mathbf{v} = v_0\hat{\mathbf{i}} + \left(\frac{eE_0\hat{\mathbf{i}}}{m}\right)t = \left(v_0 + \frac{eE_0}{m}t\right)\hat{\mathbf{i}}$$

$$= v_0\left(1+\frac{eE_0}{mv_0}t\right)\hat{\mathbf{i}}$$

de - Broglie wavelength associated with electron at time t is

$$\lambda = \frac{h}{mv}$$

$$\Rightarrow \quad = \frac{h}{m\left[v_0\left(1+\dfrac{eE_0}{mv_0}t\right)\right]} = \frac{\lambda_0}{\left[1+\dfrac{eE_0}{mv_0}t\right]} \qquad \left[\because \lambda_0 = \frac{h}{mv_0}\right]$$

Q.8 An electron (mass m) with an initial velocity $\mathbf{v} = v_0\hat{\mathbf{i}}$ is in an electric field $\mathbf{E} = E_0\hat{\mathbf{j}}$. If $\lambda_0 = h/mv_0$, it's de-Broglie wavelength at time t is given by

(a) λ_0 (b) $\lambda_0\sqrt{1+\dfrac{e^2E_0^2t^2}{m^2v_0^2}}$ (c) $\dfrac{\lambda_0}{\sqrt{1+\dfrac{e^2E_0^2t^2}{m^2v_0^2}}}$ (d) $\dfrac{\lambda_0}{\left(1+\dfrac{e^2E_0^2t^2}{m^2v_0^2}\right)}$

Ans. *(c)* Initial de - Broglie wavelength of electron,

$$\lambda_0 = \frac{h}{mv_0}$$

Force on electron in electric field,

$$\mathbf{F} = -e\mathbf{E} = -eE_0\hat{\mathbf{j}}$$

Acceleration of electron, $\mathbf{a} = \dfrac{\mathbf{F}}{m} = -\dfrac{eE_0\hat{\mathbf{j}}}{m}$

It is acting along negative y-axis.

The initial velocity of electron along x-axis, $\mathbf{v}_{x_0} = v_0\hat{\mathbf{i}}$. Initial velocity of electron along y-axis, $\mathbf{v}_{y_0} = 0$.

Velocity of electron after time t along x-axis, $\mathbf{v}_x = v_0\hat{\mathbf{i}}$

($\because$ there is no acceleration along x-axis.)

Velocity of electron after time t along y-axis,

$$\mathbf{v}_y = 0 + \left(-\frac{eE_0}{m}\hat{\mathbf{j}}\right)t = -\frac{eE_0}{m}t\hat{\mathbf{j}}$$

Magnitude of velocity of electron after time t is

$$|\vec{v}| = \sqrt{v_x^2 + v_y^2} = \sqrt{v_0^2 + \left(\frac{-eE_0}{m}t\right)^2}$$

$\Rightarrow$ $$= v_0\sqrt{1 + \frac{e^2E_0^2t^2}{m^2v_0^2}}$$

de-Broglie wavelength, $$\lambda' = \frac{h}{mv}$$

$\Rightarrow$ $$= \frac{h}{mv_0\sqrt{1 + e^2E_0^2t^2/(m^2v_0^2)}}$$

$$= \frac{\lambda_0}{\sqrt{1 + e^2E_0^2t^2/m^2v_0^2}}$$

Multiple Choice Questions (More Than One Options)

Q.9 Relativistic corrections become necessary when the expression for the kinetic energy $\frac{1}{2}mv^2$, becomes comparable with mc^2, where m is the mass of the particle. At what de-Broglie wavelength, will relativistic corrections become important for an electron?

(a) $\lambda = 10\,\text{nm}$ (b) $\lambda = 10^{-1}\,\text{nm}$

(c) $\lambda = 10^{-4}\,\text{nm}$ (d) $\lambda = 10^{-6}\,\text{nm}$

Thinking Process If the speed corresponding to the de-Broglie wavelength is greater than the speed of light, then the relativistic corrections become important.

Ans. ***(c, d)*** de-Broglie wavelength

$$\lambda = \frac{h}{mv} \Rightarrow v = \frac{h}{m\lambda}$$

Here, $h = 6.6 \times 10^{-34}$ Js

and for electron, $m = 9 \times 10^{-31}$ kg

Now consider each option one by one

(a) $\lambda_1 = 10\,\text{nm} = 10 \times 10^{-9}\,\text{m} = 10^{-8}\,\text{m}$

$\Rightarrow$ $$v_1 = \frac{6.6 \times 10^{-34}}{(9 \times 10^{-31}) \times 10^{-8}}$$

$\Rightarrow$ $$= \frac{2.2}{3} \times 10^5 \approx 10^5\,\text{m/s}$$

(b) $\lambda_2 = 10^{-1}$ nm $= 10^{-1} \times 10^{-9}$ m $= 10^{-10}$ m

$$\Rightarrow \quad v_2 = \frac{6.6 \times 10^{-34}}{(9 \times 10^{-31}) \times 10^{-10}} \approx 10^7 \text{ m/s}$$

(c) $\lambda_3 = 10^{-4}$ nm $= 10^{-4} \times 10^{-9}$ m $= 10^{-13}$ m

$$\Rightarrow \quad v_3 = \frac{6.6 \times 10^{-34}}{(9 \times 10^{-31}) \times 10^{-13}} \approx 10^{10} \text{ m/s}$$

(d) $\lambda_4 = 10^{-6}$ nm $= 10^{-6} \times 10^{-9}$ m $= 10^{-15}$ m

$$\Rightarrow \quad v_4 = \frac{6.6 \times 10^{-34}}{9 \times 10^{-31} \times 10^{-15}} \approx 10^{12} \text{ m/s}$$

Thus, options (c) and (d) are correct as v_3 and v_4 is greater than 3×10^8 m/s.

Q.10 Two particles A_1 and A_2 of masses m_1, m_2 $(m_1 > m_2)$ have the same de-Broglie wavelength. Then,

(a) their momenta are the same
(b) their energies are the same
(c) energy of A_1 is less than the energy of A_2
(d) energy of A_1 is more than the energy of A_2

Ans. ***(a, c)*** de-Broglie wavelength $\lambda = \frac{h}{mv}$

where, $mv = p$ (momentum)

$$\Rightarrow \quad \lambda = \frac{h}{p} \Rightarrow p = \frac{h}{\lambda}$$

Here, h is a constant.

So, $$p \propto \frac{1}{\lambda} \Rightarrow \frac{p_1}{p_2} = \frac{\lambda_2}{\lambda_1}$$

But $$\lambda_1 = \lambda_2 = \lambda$$

Then, $$\frac{p_1}{p_2} = \frac{\lambda}{\lambda} = 1 \Rightarrow p_1 = p_2$$

Thus, their momenta are same.

Also, $$E = \frac{1}{2}mv^2 = \frac{1}{2}\frac{mv^2 \times m}{m} = \frac{1}{2}\frac{m^2v^2}{m} = \frac{1}{2}\frac{p^2}{m}$$

Here, p is constant $$E \propto \frac{1}{m}$$

$\therefore$ $$\frac{E_1}{E_2} = \frac{m_2}{m_1} < 1 \Rightarrow E_1 < E_2$$

Q.11 The de-Broglie wavelength of a photon is twice the de-Broglie wavelength of an electron. The speed of the electron is $v_e = \frac{c}{100}$. Then,

(a) $\frac{E_e}{E_p} = 10^{-4}$ (b) $\frac{E_e}{E_p} = 10^{-2}$

(c) $\frac{p_e}{m_e c} = 10^{-2}$ (d) $\frac{p_e}{m_e c} = 10^{-4}$

Ans. ***(b, c)*** Suppose, Mass of electron = m_e, Mass of photon = m_p,

Velocity of electron = v_e and Velocity of photon = v_p

Thus, for electron, de-Broglie wavelength

$$\lambda_e = \frac{h}{m_e v_e} = \frac{h}{m_e(c/100)} = \frac{100\,h}{m_e c} \text{ (given)} \quad \ldots\text{(i)}$$

Kinetic energy, $$E_e = \frac{1}{2} m_e v_e^2$$

$\Rightarrow$ $$m_e v_e = \sqrt{2E_e m_e}$$

so, $$\lambda_e = \frac{h}{m_e v_e} = \frac{h}{\sqrt{2m_e E_e}}$$

$\Rightarrow$ $$E_e = \frac{h^2}{2\lambda_e^2 m_e} \quad \ldots\text{(ii)}$$

For photon of wavelength λ_p, energy

$$E_p = \frac{hc}{\lambda_p} = \frac{hc}{2\lambda_e} \quad [\because \lambda_p = 2\lambda_e]$$

$\therefore$ $$\frac{E_p}{E_e} = \frac{hc}{2\lambda_e} \times \frac{2\lambda_e^2 m_e}{h^2} = \frac{\lambda_e m_e c}{h} = \frac{100h}{m_e c} \times \frac{m_e c}{h} = 100$$

So, $$\frac{E_e}{E_p} = \frac{1}{100} = 10^{-2}$$

For electron, $$p_e = m_e v_e = m_e \times c/100$$

So, $$\frac{p_e}{m_e c} = \frac{1}{100} = 10^{-2}$$

Q.12 Photons absorbed in matter are converted to heat. A source emitting n photon/sec of frequency ν is used to convert 1 kg of ice at 0°C to water at 0°C. Then, the time T taken for the conversion

(a) decreases with increasing n, with ν fixed

(b) decreases with n fixed, ν increasing

(c) remains constant with n and ν changing such that $n\nu$ = constant

(d) increases when the product $n\nu$ increases

Ans. ***(a, b, c)*** Energy spent to convert ice into water

$$= \text{mass} \times \text{latent heat}$$
$$= mL = (1000 \text{ g}) \times (80 \text{ cal/g}) = 80000 \text{ cal}$$

Energy of photons used = $nT \times E = nT \times h\nu$ $\quad [\because E = h\nu]$

So, $$nTh\nu = mL \Rightarrow T = \frac{mL}{nh\nu}$$

$\therefore$ $T \propto \frac{1}{n}$, when ν is constant.

$T \propto \frac{1}{\nu}$, when n is fixed.

$\Rightarrow$ $T \propto \frac{1}{n\nu}$.

Thus, T is constant, if $n\nu$ is constant.

Q.13 A particle moves in a closed orbit around the origin, due to a force which is directed towards the origin. The de-Broglie wavelength of the particle varies cyclically between two values λ_1, λ_2 with $\lambda_1 > \lambda_2$. Which of the following statement are true?

(a) The particle could be moving in a circular orbit with origin as centre
(b) The particle could be moving in an elliptic orbit with origin as its focus
(c) When the de-Broglie wavelength is λ_1, the particle is nearer the origin than when its value is λ_2
(d) When the de-Broglie wavelength is λ_2, the particle is nearer the origin than when its value is λ_1

Ans. ***(b, d)*** The de-Broglie wavelength of the particle can be varying cyclically between two values λ_1 and λ_2, if particle is moving in an elliptical orbit with origin as its one focus.

Consider the figure given below

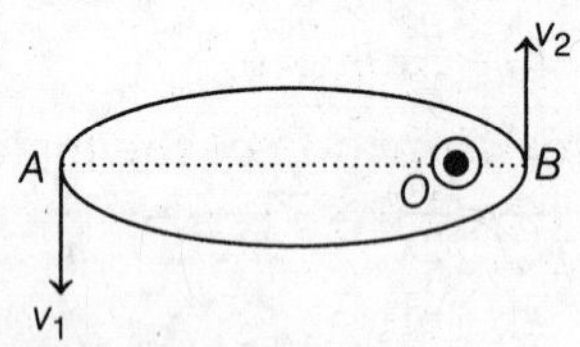

Let v_1, v_2 be the speed of particle at A and B respectively and origin is at focus O. If λ_1, λ_2 are the de-Broglie wavelengths associated with particle while moving at A and B respectively. Then,

$$\lambda_1 = \frac{h}{mv_1}$$

and $$\lambda_2 = \frac{h}{mv_2}$$

$\therefore$ $$\frac{\lambda_1}{\lambda_2} = \frac{v_2}{v_1}$$

since $$\lambda_1 > \lambda_2$$

$\therefore$ $$v_2 > v_1$$

By law of conservation of angular momentum, the particle moves faster when it is closer to focus.

Very Short Answer Type Questions

Q.14 A proton and an α-particle are accelerated, using the same potential difference. How are the de-Broglie wavelengths λ_p and λ_α related to each other?

Thinking Process The de-Broglie wavelength of a particle in terms of potential difference is given by $\lambda = \dfrac{h}{\sqrt{2mqv}}$

Ans. As,
$$\lambda = \frac{h}{\sqrt{2mqv}}$$
$$\therefore \quad \lambda \propto \frac{1}{\sqrt{mq}}$$
$$\frac{\lambda_p}{\lambda_\alpha} = \frac{\sqrt{m_\alpha q_\alpha}}{\sqrt{m_p q_p}} = \frac{\sqrt{4m_p \times 2e}}{\sqrt{m_p \times e}} = \sqrt{8}$$
$$\therefore \quad \lambda_p = \sqrt{8}\lambda_\alpha$$

i.e., wavelength of proton is $\sqrt{8}$ times wavelength of α-particle.

Q.15 (i) In the explanation of photoeletric effect, we assume one photon of frequency ν collides with an electron and transfers its energy. This leads to the equation for the maximum energy E_{max} of the emitted electron as

$$E_{max} = h\nu - \phi_0$$

where ϕ_0 is the work function of the metal. If an electron absorbs 2 photons (each of frequency ν), what will be the maximum energy for the emitted electron?

(ii) Why is this fact (two photon absorption) not taken into consideration in our discussion of the stopping potential?

Ans. (i) Here it is given that, an electron absorbs 2 photons each of frequency ν then $\nu' = 2\nu$ where, ν' is the frequency of emitted electron.

Given, $\quad E_{max} = h\nu - \phi_0$

Now, maximum energy for emitted electrons is

$$E'_{max} = h(2\nu) - \phi_0 = 2h\nu - \phi_0$$

(ii) The probability of absorbing 2 photons by the same electron is very low. Hence, such emissions will be negligible.

Q.16 There are materials which absorb photons of shorter wavelength and emit photons of longer wavelength. Can there be stable substances which absorb photons of larger wavelength and emit light of shorter wavelength.

Ans. Energy of photon of shorter wavelength will be high according to $E = \frac{hc}{\lambda}$ and energy of photon of longer wavelength will be low. So, when the materials which absorbs photons of shorter wavelength and emit photon of longer wavelength, the energy given out is less than the energy supplied.

But in second statement, the energy of the incident photon is low for the substances which has to absorb photons of larger wavelength and energy of emitted photon is high to emit light of shorter wavelength. This means in this statement material has to supply the energy for the emission of photons.

But this is not possible for a stable substances.

Q.17 Do all the electrons that absorb a photon come out as photoelectrons?

Ans. In photoelectric effect, we can observe that most electrons get scattered into the metal by absorbing a photon.

Thus, all the electrons that absorb a photon doesn't come out as photoelectron. Only a few come out of metal whose energy becomes greater than the work function of metal.

Q.18 There are two sources of light, each emitting with a power of 100 W. One emits X-rays of wavelength 1 nm and the other visible light at 500 nm. Find the ratio of number of photons of X-rays to the photons of visible light of the given wavelength?

Ans. Suppose wavelength of X-rays is λ_1 and the wavelength of visible light is λ_2.

Given, $P = 100\text{ W}$

$$\lambda_1 = 1 \text{ nm and } \lambda_2 = 500 \text{ nm}$$

Also, n_1 and n_2 represents number of photons of X-rays and visible light emitted from the two sources per sec.

So, $$P = n_1 \frac{hc}{\lambda_1} = n_2 \frac{hc}{\lambda_2} \Rightarrow \frac{n_1}{\lambda_1} = \frac{n_2}{\lambda_2}$$

$$\Rightarrow \frac{n_1}{n_2} = \frac{\lambda_1}{\lambda_2} = \frac{1}{500}$$

Short Answer Type Questions

Q.19 Consider figure for photoemission. How would you reconcile with momentum-conservation? Note light (photons) have momentum in a different direction than the emitted electrons.

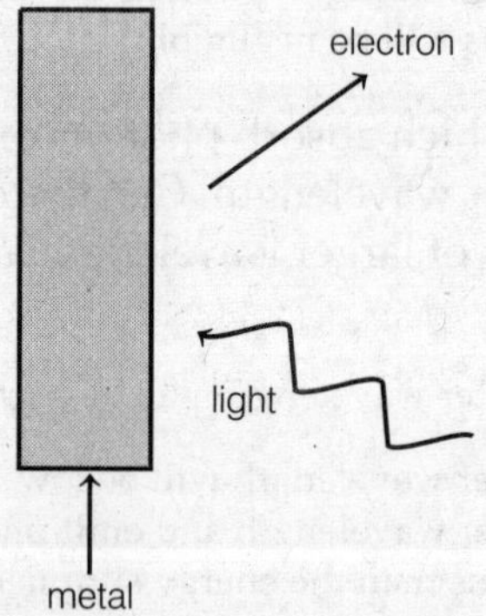

Ans. During photoelectric emission, the momentum of incident photon is transferred to the metal. At microscopic level, atoms of a metal absorb the photon and its momentum is transferred mainly to the nucleus and electrons.

The excited electron is emitted. Therefore, the conservation of momentum is to be considered as the momentum of incident photon transferred to the nucleus and electrons.

Q.20 Consider a metal exposed to light of wavelength 600 nm. The maximum energy of the electron doubles when light of wavelength 400 nm is used. Find the work function in eV.

Thinking Process Maximum energy = $h\nu - \phi$

Ans. Given,

For the first condition,

Wavelength of light $\lambda = 600\,\text{nm}$

and for the second condition,

Wavelength of light $\lambda' = 400\,\text{nm}$

Also, maximum kinetic energy for the second condition is equal to the twice of the kinetic energy in first condition.

i.e., $$K'_{max} = 2K_{max}$$

Here, $$K'_{max} = \frac{hc}{\lambda} - \phi$$

$$\Rightarrow \quad 2K_{max} = \frac{hc}{\lambda'} - \phi_0$$

$$\Rightarrow \quad 2\left(\frac{1240}{600} - \phi\right) = \left(\frac{1240}{400} - \phi\right) \quad [\because hc \simeq 1240\,\text{eVnm}]$$

$$\Rightarrow \quad \phi = 1240\left[\frac{2}{600} - \frac{1}{400}\right] = 1.03 eV$$

***Q.21** Assuming an electron is confined to a 1nm wide region, find the uncertainty in momentum using Heisenberg uncertainty principle $\left(\Delta x \times \Delta p \approx \frac{h}{2\pi}\right)$. You can assume the uncertainty in position Δx as 1 nm. Assuming $p \approx \Delta p$, find the energy of the electron in electronvolts.

Ans. Here, $\Delta x = 1\,\text{nm} = 10^{-9}$ m, $\Delta p = ?$

As $\Delta x\, \Delta p \approx \frac{h}{2\pi}$

$$\therefore \quad \Delta p = \frac{h}{2\pi \times \Delta x} = \frac{6.626 \times 10^{-34}}{2 \times 3.14 \times 10^{-9}}$$

$$\Delta p = 1.055 \times 10^{-25}\ \text{kgm/s}$$

We can treat Δp as p to find the energy of the electron.

$$\text{Energy} = \frac{p^2}{2m} = \frac{\Delta p^2}{2 \times m}$$

$$= \frac{(1.055 \times 10^{-25})^2}{2 \times 9.1 \times 10^{-31}} = 6.1 \times 10^{-21}\ \text{J}$$

Converting to eV by dividing by 1.6×10^{-19} J

$$E = \frac{6.1 \times 10^{-21}}{1.6 \times 10^{-19}}$$

$$= 3.8 \times 10^{-2}\ \text{eV}$$

Note (*) Topics related to these question have been removed from latest NCERT.

Q.22 Two monochromatic beams A and B of equal intensity I, hit a screen. The number of photons hitting the screen by beam A is twice that by beam B. Then, what inference can you make about their frequencies?

Ans. Suppose n_A is the number of photons falling per second of beam A and n_B is the number of photons falling per second of beam B.

Thus, $n_A = 2n_B$

Energy of falling photon of beam A, $E_A = h\nu_A$

Energy of falling photon of beam B, $E_B = h\nu_B$

Now, according to question,

$$\text{intensity of } A = \text{intensity of } B$$

$\therefore$ $$n_A h\nu_A = n_B h\nu_B$$

$\Rightarrow$ $$\frac{\nu_A}{\nu_B} = \frac{n_B}{n_A} = \frac{n_B}{2n_B}$$

$\Rightarrow$ $$\nu_B = 2\nu_A$$

Thus, from this relation we can infer that frequency of beam B is twice of beam A.

Q.23 Two particles A and B of de-Broglie wavelengths λ_1 and λ_2 combine to form a particle C. The process conserves momentum. Find the de-Broglie wavelength of the particle C. (The motion is one-dimensional)

Ans. Given from conservation of momentum,

$$|\mathbf{p}_C| = |\mathbf{p}_A| + |\mathbf{p}_B|$$

$\Rightarrow$ $$\frac{h}{\lambda_C} = \frac{h}{\lambda_A} + \frac{h}{\lambda_B} \qquad \left[\because \lambda = \frac{h}{mv} = \frac{h}{p} \Rightarrow p = \frac{h}{\lambda}\right]$$

$\Rightarrow$ $$\frac{h}{\lambda_C} = \frac{h\lambda_B + h\lambda_A}{\lambda_A\lambda_B}$$

$\Rightarrow$ $$\frac{\lambda_C}{h} = \frac{\lambda_A\lambda_B}{h\lambda_A + h\lambda_B} \Rightarrow \lambda_C = \frac{\lambda_A\lambda_B}{\lambda_A + \lambda_B}$$

Case I Suppose both p_A and p_B are positive,

then $$\lambda_C = \frac{\lambda_A\lambda_B}{\lambda_A + \lambda_B}$$

Case II When both p_A and p_B are negative,

then $$\lambda_C = \frac{\lambda_A\lambda_B}{\lambda_A + \lambda_B}$$

Case III When $p_A > 0$, $p_B < 0$ *i.e.*, p_A is positive and p_B is negative,

$$\frac{h}{\lambda_C} = \frac{h}{\lambda_A} - \frac{h}{\lambda_B} = \frac{(\lambda_B - \lambda_A)h}{\lambda_A\lambda_B} \Rightarrow \lambda_C = \frac{\lambda_A\lambda_B}{\lambda_B - \lambda_A}$$

Case IV $p_A < 0$, $p_B > 0$, *i.e.*, p_A is negative and p_B is positive,

$\therefore$ $$\frac{h}{\lambda_C} = \frac{-h}{\lambda_A} + \frac{h}{\lambda_B}$$

$\Rightarrow$ $$= \frac{(\lambda_A - \lambda_B)h}{\lambda_A\lambda_B} \Rightarrow \lambda_C = \frac{\lambda_A\lambda_B}{\lambda_A - \lambda_B}$$

Q.24 A neutron beam of energy E scatters from atoms on a surface with a spacing $d = 0.1$ nm. The first maximum of intensity in the reflected beam occurs at $\theta = 30°$. What is the kinetic energy E of the beam in eV?

Ans. Given, $d = 0.1\,\text{nm}$,

$$\theta = 30° \Rightarrow n = 1$$

Now, according to Bragg's law

$$2d\sin\theta = n\lambda \Rightarrow 2 \times 0.1 \times \sin 30° = 1\lambda$$

$\Rightarrow$ $$\lambda = 0.1\,\text{nm} = 10^{-10}\,\text{m}$$

Now, $$\lambda = \frac{h}{mv} = \frac{h}{p}$$

$\Rightarrow$ $$p = \frac{h}{\lambda} = \frac{6.62 \times 10^{-34}}{10^{-10}}$$

$\Rightarrow$ $$p = 6.62 \times 10^{-24}\ \text{kg-m/s}$$

Now, $$\text{KE} = \frac{1}{2}mv^2 = \frac{1}{2}\frac{m^2v^2}{m} = \frac{1}{2}\frac{p^2}{m}$$

$$= \frac{1}{2} \times \frac{(6.62 \times 10^{-24})^2}{1.67 \times 10^{-27}}\,\text{J} = 0.082\ \text{eV}$$

Long Answer Type Questions

Q.25 Consider a thin target (10^{-2} m square, 10^{-3} m thickness) of sodium, which produces a photocurrent of 100 μA when a light of intensity 100 W/m^2 ($\lambda = 660$ nm) falls on it. Find the probability that a photoelectron is produced when a photon strikes a sodium atom. [Take density of Na = 0.97 kg/m^3]

Thinking Process Absorption of two photons by an atom depends on the probability of photoemission by a single photon on a single atom.

Ans. Given, $$A = 10^{-2} \times 10^{-2}\ \text{m}^2$$

$\Rightarrow$ $$= 10^{-4}\ \text{m}^2$$

$$d = 10^{-3}\ \text{m}$$

$$i = 100 \times 10^{-6}\,\text{A} = 10^{-4}\,\text{A}$$

Intensity, $$I = 100\,\text{W/m}^2$$

$\Rightarrow$ $$\lambda = 660\ \text{nm} = 660 \times 10^{-9}\ \text{m}$$

$$\rho_{\text{Na}} = 0.97\,\text{kg/m}^3$$

Avogadro's number = 6×10^{26} kg atom

Volume of sodium target = $A \times d$

$$= 10^{-4} \times 10^{-3}$$

$\Rightarrow$ $$= 10^{-7}\ \text{m}^3$$

We know that 6×10^{26} atoms of Na weights = 23 kg

So, volume of 6×10^{6} Na atoms = $\frac{23}{0.97}\,\text{m}^3$.

Volume occupied by one Na atom $= \dfrac{23}{0.97 \times (6 \times 10^{26})} = 3.95 \times 10^{-26}\ \text{m}^3$

Number of Na atoms in target (n_{Na})

$$= \frac{10^{-7}}{3.95 \times 10^{-26}} = 2.53 \times 10^{18}$$

Let n be the number of photons falling per second on the target.

Energy of each photon $= hc / \lambda$

Total energy falling per second on target $= \dfrac{nhc}{\lambda} = IA$

$$\therefore \quad n = \frac{IA\lambda}{hc}$$

$$\Rightarrow \quad = \frac{100 \times 10^{-4} \times (660 \times 10^{-9})}{(6.62 \times 10^{-34}) \times (3 \times 10^{8})} = 3.3 \times 10^{16}$$

Let P be the probability of emission per atom per photon.

The number of photoelectrons emitted per second

$$N = P \times n \times (n_{\text{Na}})$$

$$= P \times (3.3 \times 10^{16}) \times (2.53 \times 10^{18})$$

Now, according to question,

$$i = 100\ \mu\text{A} = 100 \times 10^{-6} = 10^{-4}\ \text{A.}$$

Current, $\quad i = Ne$

$$\therefore \quad 10^{-4} = P \times (3.3 \times 10^{16}) \times (2.53 \times 10^{18}) \times (1.6 \times 10^{-19})$$

$$\Rightarrow \quad P = \frac{10^{-4}}{(3.3 \times 10^{16}) \times (2.53 \times 10^{18}) \times (1.6 \times 10^{-19})}$$

$$= 7.48 \times 10^{-21}$$

Thus, the probability of emission by a single photon on a single atom is very much less than 1. It is due to this reason, the absorption of two photons by an atom is negligible.

Mistake Alert ! *Ensure that the density and molar mass are used correctly to calculate the number of atoms in the target.*

Ensure that the density and molar mass are used correctly to calculate the number of atoms in the target

Q.26 Consider an electron in front of metallic surface at a distance d (treated as an infinite plane surface). Assume the force of attraction by the plate is given as $\dfrac{1}{4}\dfrac{q^2}{4\pi\varepsilon_0 d^2}$. Calculate work in taking the charge to an infinite distance from the plate. Taking $d = 0.1$ nm, find the work done in electron volts. [Such a force law is not valid for $d < 0.1$ nm]

Thinking Process Work done by an external agency $= +\dfrac{1}{4\pi\varepsilon_0} \cdot \dfrac{1}{4}\displaystyle\int_d^\infty \frac{q^2}{x^2}\, dx$

Ans. According to question, consider the figure as given below

From figure, $d = 0.1\,\text{nm} = 10^{-10}$ m,

$$F = \frac{q^2}{4 \times 4\pi\varepsilon_0 d^2}$$

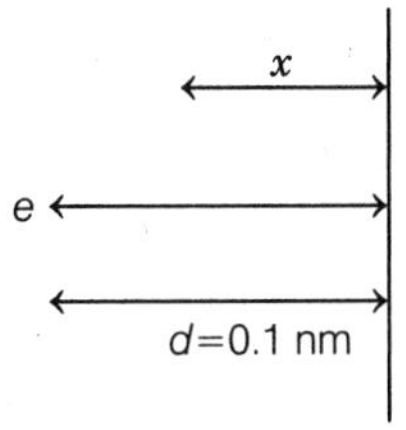

Let the electron be at distance x from metallic surface. Then, force of attraction on it is

$$F_x = \frac{q^2}{4 \times 4\pi\varepsilon_0 x^2}$$

Work done by external agency in taking the electron from distance d to infinity is

$$W = \int_d^{\infty} F_x\, dx = \int_d^{\infty} \frac{q^2 dx}{4 \times 4\pi\varepsilon_0} \frac{1}{x^2}$$

$$= \frac{q^2}{4 \times 4\pi\varepsilon_0}\left[\frac{1}{d}\right]$$

$$= \frac{(1.6 \times 10^{-19})^2 \times 9 \times 10^9}{4 \times 10^{-10}}\,\text{J}$$

$$= \frac{(1.6 \times 10^{-19})^2 \times (9 \times 10^9)}{(4 \times 10^{-10}) \times (1.6 \times 10^{-19})}\,\text{eV}$$

$$= 3.6\,\text{eV}$$

Q.27 A student performs an experiment on photoelectric effect, using two materials A and B. A plot of V_{stop} versus υ is given in figure.

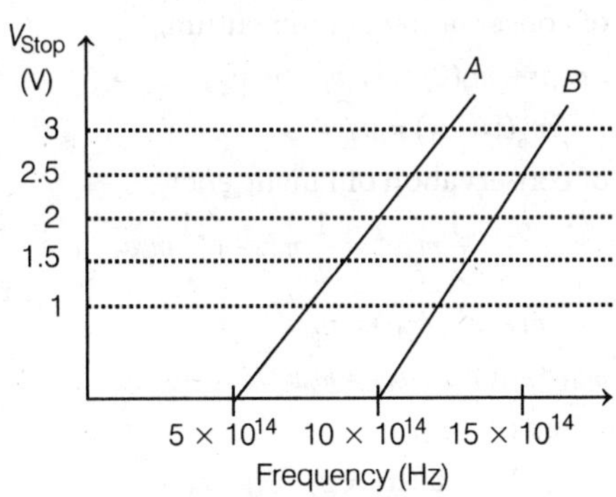

(i) Which material A or B has a higher work function?

(ii) Given the electric charge of an electron $= 1.6 \times 10^{-19}$ C, find the value of h obtained from the experiment for both A and B.

Comment on whether it is consistent with Einstein's theory.

Ans. (i) Given, thresholed frequency of A is given by $\nu_A = 5 \times 10^{14}$ Hz and

For B, $\nu_B = 10 \times 10^{14}$ Hz

We know that

Work function, $\phi = h\nu_0$ or $\phi_0 \propto \nu_0 \Rightarrow \phi_0 \propto \nu_0$

So, $$\frac{\phi_A}{\phi_B} = \frac{5 \times 10^{14}}{10 \times 10^{14}} < \frac{1}{2} < 1$$

$\Rightarrow$ $\phi_A < \phi_B$

Thus, work function of B is higher than A.

(ii) For metal A, slope $= \frac{h}{e} = \frac{2}{(10-5) \times 10^{14}}$

or $$h = \frac{2e}{5 \times 10^{14}} = \frac{2 \times 1.6 \times 10^{-19}}{5 \times 10^{14}}$$

$$= 6.4 \times 10^{-34} \text{ Js}$$

For metal B, slope $= \frac{h}{e} = \frac{2.5}{(15-10) \times 10^{14}}$

or $$h = \frac{2.5 \times e}{5 \times 10^{14}}$$

$$= \frac{2.5 \times 1.6 \times 10^{-19}}{5 \times 10^{14}} = 8 \times 10^{-34} \text{ Js}$$

Since, the value of h from experiment for metals A and B is different. Hence, experiment is not consistent with theory.

Q.28 A particle A with a mass m_A is moving with a velocity v and hits a particle B (mass m_B) at rest (one dimensional motion). Find the change in the de-Broglie wavelength of the particle A. Treat the collision as elastic.

Ans. As collision is elastic, hence laws of conservation of momentum and kinetic energy are obeyed.

According to law of conservation of momentum,

$$m_A v + m_B(0) = m_A v_1 + m_B v_2$$

$$\Rightarrow \quad m_A(v - v_1) = m_B v_2 \quad \text{...(i)}$$

According to law of conservation of kinetic energy,

$$\frac{1}{2} m_A v^2 = \frac{1}{2} m_A v_1^2 + \frac{1}{2} m_B v_2^2$$

$$\Rightarrow \quad m_A (v^2 - v_1^2) = m_B v_2^2$$

$$\Rightarrow \quad m_A(v - v_1)(v + v_1) = m_B {v_2}^2 \quad \text{...(ii)}$$

Dividing Eq. (ii) by Eq. (i),

we get, $$v + v_1 = v_2$$

or $$v = v_2 - v_1 \quad \text{...(iii)}$$

Solving Eqs. (i) and (iii), we get

$$v_1 = \left(\frac{m_A - m_B}{m_A + m_B}\right) v \text{ and } v_2 = \left(\frac{2m_A}{m_A + m_B}\right) v$$

$$\lambda_{\text{initial}} = \frac{h}{m_A v}$$

$$\lambda_{\text{final}} = \frac{h}{m_A v_1} = \frac{h(m_A + m_B)}{m_A(m_A - m_B)v}$$

$$\Delta\lambda = \lambda_{\text{final}} - \lambda_{\text{initial}} = \frac{h}{m_A v}\left[\frac{m_A + m_B}{m_A - m_B} - 1\right]$$

Mistake Alert! *Ensure you treat the collision as elastic, which means both momentum, and kinetic energy are conserved. Mistakely treating it as inelastic could lead to incorrect velocity and wavelength calculations.*

Q.29 Consider a 20 W bulb emitting light of wavelength 5000 Å and shining on a metal surface kept at a distance 2 m. Assume that the metal surface has work function of 2 eV and that each atom on the metal surface can be treated as a circular disk of radius 1.5 Å.

(i) Estimate number of photons emitted by the bulb per second. [Assume no other losses]

(ii) Will there be photoelectric emission?

(iii) How much time would be required by the atomic disk to receive energy equal to work function (2 eV)?

(iv) How many photons would atomic disk receive within time duration calculated in (iii) above?

(v) Can you explain how photoelectric effect was observed instantaneously?

Ans. Given, $P = 20$ W, $\lambda = 5000$ Å $= 5000 \times 10^{-10}$ m

$d = 2$ m, $\phi_0 = 2$ eV, $r = 1.5$ Å $= 1.5 \times 10^{-10}$ m

(i) Number of photon emitted by bulb per second is $n' = \dfrac{P}{hc/\lambda} = \dfrac{P\lambda}{hc}$

$$= \frac{20 \times (5000 \times 10^{-10})}{(6.62 \times 10^{-34}) \times (3 \times 10^8)}$$

$$\Rightarrow \quad = 5 \times 10^{19} \text{s}^{-1}$$

(ii) Energy of the incident photon $= \dfrac{hc}{\lambda} = \dfrac{(6.62 \times 10^{-34})(3 \times 10^8)}{5000 \times 10^{-10} \times 1.6 \times 10^{-19}}$

$$= 2.48 \text{ eV}$$

As this energy is greater than 2 eV (*i.e.*, work function of metal surface), hence photoelectric emission takes place.

(iii)

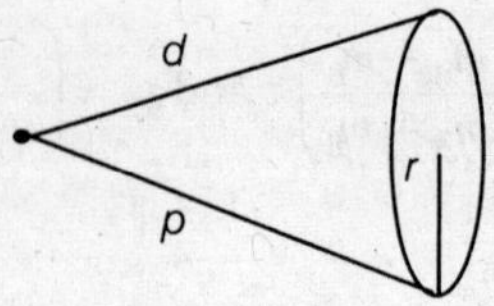

Let Δt be the time spent in getting the energy ϕ = (work function of metal).
Consider the figure,

$$\frac{P}{4\pi d^2} \times \pi r^2 \Delta t = \phi_0$$

$$\Rightarrow \quad \Delta t = \frac{4\phi_0 d^2}{Pr^2}$$

$$= \frac{4 \times (2 \times 1.6 \times 10^{-19}) \times 2^2}{20 \times (1.5 \times 10^{-10})^2} \approx 11.4 \text{ s}$$

(iv) Number of photons received by atomic disc in time Δt is

$$N = \frac{n' \times \pi r^2}{4\pi d^2} \times \Delta t$$

$$\Rightarrow \quad = \frac{n' r^2 \Delta t}{4d^2}$$

$$= \frac{(5 \times 10^{19}) \times (1.5 \times 10^{-10})^2 \times 11.4}{4 \times (2)^2} \approx 0.8 \approx 1$$

(v) In photoelectric emission, there is a collision between incident photon and free electron of the metal surface, which lasts for very very short interval of time ($\approx 10^{-9}$ s), hence we say photoelectric emission is instantaneous.

Chapter

12 Atoms

Multiple Choice Questions (MCQs)

Q.1 Taking the Bohr radius as $a_0 = 53$ pm, the radius of Li^{++} ion in its ground state, on the basis of Bohr's model, will be about

(a) 53 pm (b) 27 pm

(c) 18 pm (d) 13 pm

Thinking Process Since, the radii of the orbits increase inversely as atomic number Z *i.e.*,

$$r \propto \frac{1}{Z}.$$

Ans. *(c)* The atomic number of lithium is 3, therefore, the radius of Li^{++} ion in its ground state, on the basis of Bohr's model, will be about $\frac{1}{3}$ times to that of Bohr radius.

Therefore, the radius of lithium ion is $\frac{53}{3} \approx 18$ pm.

Q.2 The binding energy of a H-atom, considering an electron moving around a fixed nuclei (proton), is

$$B = -\frac{me^4}{8n^2\varepsilon_0^2h^2} \quad (m = \text{electron mass})$$

If one decides to work in a frame of reference where the electron is at rest, the proton would be moving around it. By similar arguments, the binding energy would be

$$B = -\frac{Me^4}{8n^2\varepsilon_0^2h^2} \quad (M = \text{proton mass})$$

This last expression is not correct, because

(a) n would not be integral

(b) Bohr-quantisation applies only to electron

(c) the frame in which the electron is at rest is not inertial

(d) the motion of the proton would not be in circular orbits, even approximately.

Thinking Process The electron revolves uniformly around nucleus have certain centripetal acceleration associated with it.

Ans. *(c)* When one decides to work in a frame of reference where the electron is at rest, the given expression is not true as it forms the non- inertial frame of reference.

Q.3 The simple Bohr model cannot be directly applied to calculate the energy levels of an atom with many electrons. This is because

(a) of the electrons not being subject to a central force
(b) of the electrons colliding with each other
(c) of screening effects
(d) the force between the nucleus and an electron will no longer be given by Coulomb's law

Thinking Process The electrostatic force of attraction between electron and nucleus is a central force which provide necessary centripetal force for circular motion of electron.

Ans. *(a)* The simple Bohr model cannot be directly applied to calculate the energy levels of an atom with many electrons. This is because of the electrons not being subject to a central force.

Q.4 For the ground state, the electron in the H-atom has an angular momentum $= h$, according to the simple Bohr model. Angular momentum is a vector and hence there will be infinitely many orbits with the vector pointing in all possible directions. In actuality, this is not true,

(a) because Bohr model gives incorrect values of angular momentum
(b) because only one of these would have a minimum energy
(c) angular momentum must be in the direction of spin of electron
(d) because electrons go around only in horizontal orbits

Thinking Process Bohr's second postulate defines these stable orbits. This postulate states that the electron revolves around the nucleus only in those orbits for which the angular momentum is integral multiple of $\frac{h}{2\pi}$, where h is the Planck's constant ($h = 6.6 \times 10^{-34}$ J-s).

Ans. *(a)* In the simple Bohr model, only the magnitude of angular momentum is kept equal to some integral multiple of $\frac{h}{2\pi}$, where, h is Planck's constant and thus, the Bohr model gives incorrect values of angular momentum.

Q.5 O_2 molecule consists of two oxygen atoms. In the molecule, nuclear force between the nuclei of the two atoms

(a) is not important because nuclear forces are short-ranged
(b) is as important as electrostatic force for binding the two atoms
(c) cancels the repulsive electrostatic force between the nuclei
(d) is not important because oxygen nucleus have equal number of neutrons and protons

Thinking Process The nuclear force is much stronger than the Coulomb force acting between charges or the gravitational forces between masses. The nuclear binding force has to dominate over the Coulomb repulsive force between protons inside the nucleus. This happens only because the nuclear force is much stronger than the Coulomb force. The nuclear force between two nucleons falls rapidly to zero as their distance is more than a few femtometres.

Ans. *(a)* In the molecules, nuclear force between the nuclei of the two atoms is not important because nuclear forces are short-ranged.

Q.6 Two H atoms in the ground state collide inelastically. The maximum amount by which their combined kinetic energy is reduced is

(a) 10.20 eV (b) 20.40 eV (c) 13.6 eV (d) 27.2 eV

Thinking Process The lowest state of the atom, called the ground state, is that of the lowest energy, with the electron revolving in the orbit of smallest radius, the Bohr radius, a_0. The energy of this state ($n = 1$), E_1 is -13.6 eV.

Ans. ***(a)*** The total energy associated with the two H-atoms in the ground state colliding elastically $= 2 \times (13.6 \text{ eV}) = 27.2$ eV.

The maximum amount by which their combined kinetic energy is reduced when any one of them goes into first excited state after the inelastic collision.

The total energy associated with the two H-atoms after the collision

$$= \left(\frac{13.6}{2^2}\right) + (13.6) = 17.0 \text{ eV}$$

Therefore, maximum loss of their combined kinetic energy

$$= 27.2 - 17.0 = 10.2 \text{ eV}$$

Q.7 A set of atoms in an excited state decays

(a) in general to any of the states with lower energy

(b) into a lower state only when excited by an external electric field

(c) all together simultaneously into a lower state

(d) to emit photons only when they collide

Thinking Process The electron of atoms in excited states can fall back to a state of lower energy, emitting a photon in the process.

Ans. ***(a)*** A set of atoms in an excited state decays in general to any of the states with lower energy.

Multiple Choice Questions (More Than One Options)

Q.8 An ionised H-molecule consists of an electron and two protons. The protons are separated by a small distance of the order of angstrom. In the ground state,

(a) the electron would not move in circular orbits

(b) the energy would be $(2)^4$ times that of a H-atom

(c) the electron's, orbit would go around the protons

(d) the molecule will soon decay in a proton and a H-atom

Thinking Process A hydrogen molecule contains two electrons and two protons whereas ionised H-molecule consists of an electron and two protons.

Ans. ***(a, c)*** The protons are separated by a small distance of the order of angstrom. In the ground state the electron would not move in circular orbits, the electron's, orbit would go around the protons.

Q.9 Consider aiming a beam of free electrons towards free protons. When they scatter, an electron and a proton cannot combine to produce a H-atom.

(a) Because of energy conservation
(b) Without simultaneously releasing energy in the form of radiation
(c) Because of momentum conservation
(d) Because of angular momentum conservation

Ans. ***(a, b)*** When beam of free electrons is aiming towards free protons, they scatter but an electron and a proton cannot combine to produce a H-atom because of energy conservation and without simultaneously releasing energy in the form of radiation.

Q.10 The Bohr model for the spectra of a H-atom

(a) will not be applicable to hydrogen in the molecular from
(b) will not be applicable as it is for a He-atom
(c) is valid only at room temperature
(d) predicts continuous as well as discrete spectral lines

Thinking Process Niel's Bohr proposed a model for hydrogenic (single electron) atoms in order to explain the line spectra emitted by atoms, as well as the stability of atoms.

Ans. ***(a, b)*** The Bohr model for the spectra of a H-atom will not be applicable to hydrogen in the molecular form. And also, it will not be applicable as it is for a He-atom.

Q.11 The Balmer series for the H-atom can be observed

(a) if we measure the frequencies of light emitted when an excited atom falls to the ground state
(b) if we measure the frequencies of light emitted due to transitions between excited states and the first excited state
(c) in any transition in a H-atom
(d) as a sequence of frequencies with the higher frequencies getting closely packed

Thinking Process The various lines in the atomic spectra are produced when electrons jump from higher energy state to a lower energy state and photons are emitted. These spectral lines are called emission lines.

Ans. ***(b, d)*** Balmer series for the H-atom can be observed if we measure the frequencies of light emitted due to transitions between higher excited states and the first excited state and as a sequence of frequencies with the higher frequencies getting closely packed.

Q.12 Let $E_n = \dfrac{-1\, me^4}{8\varepsilon_0^2 n^2 h^2}$ be the energy of the nth level of H-atom. If all the H-atoms are in the ground state and radiation of frequency $\dfrac{(E_2 - E_1)}{h}$ falls on it,

(a) it will not be absorbed at all
(b) some of atoms will move to the first excited state
(c) all atoms will be excited to the $n = 2$ state
(d) no atoms will make a transition to the $n = 3$ state

Thinking Process When an atom absorbs a photon that has precisely the same energy needed by the electron in a lower energy state to make transitions to a higher energy state, the process is called absorption.

Ans. ***(b, d)*** When all the H-atoms are in the ground state and radiation of frequency $\frac{(E_2 - E_1)}{h}$ falls on it, some of atoms will move to the first excited state and no atoms will make a transition to the $n = 3$ state.

Q.13 The simple Bohr model is not applicable to He^4 atom because

(a) He^4 is an inert gas
(b) He^4 has neutrons in the nucleus
(c) He^4 has one more electron
(d) electrons are not subject to central forces

Thinking Process Neil's Bohr proposed a model for hydrogenic (single electron) atoms in order to explain the line spectra emitted by atoms, as well as the stability of atoms.

Ans. ***(c, d)*** The simple Bohr model is not applicable to He^4 atom because He^4 has one more electron and electrons are not subject to central forces.

Very Short Answer Type Questions

Q.14 The mass of a H-atom is less than the sum of the masses of a proton and electron. Why is this?

Thinking Process Einstein showed that mass is another form of energy and one can convert mass-energy into other forms of energy, say kinetic energy and *vice-versa*. Einstein gave the famous mass-energy equivalence relation $E = mc^2$ where the energy equivalent of mass m is related by the above equation and c is the velocity of light.

Ans. Since, the difference in mass of a nucleus and its constituents, ΔM, is called the mass defect and is given by

$$\Delta M = [Zm_p + (A - Z)m_n] - M$$

Also, the binding energy is given by B= mass defect $(\Delta M) \times c^2$.

Thus, the mass of a H-atom is

$$m_p + m_e - \frac{B}{c^2}, \text{ where } B \approx 13.6 \text{ eV is the binding energy.}$$

Q.15 Imagine removing one electron from He^4 and He^3. Their energy levels, as worked out on the basis of Bohr model will be very close. Explain why?

Ans. On removing one electron from He^4 and He^3, the energy levels, as worked out on the basis of Bohr model will be very close as both the nuclei are very heavy as compared to electron mass. Also after removing one electron from He^4 and He^3 atoms, they contain one electron and are hydrogen like atoms.

Q.16 When an electron falls from a higher energy to a lower energy level, the difference in the energies appears in the form of electromagnetic radiation. Why cannot it be emitted as other forms of energy?

Thinking Process The accelerated electron produces electric as well as magnetic field hence electromagnetic energy.

Ans. The electrons are charged particles. When an electron falls from a higher energy to a lower energy level, it accelerates. We known accelerating charged particles radiate energy in the form of electromagnetic radiations.

Q.17 Would the Bohr formula for the H-atom remain unchanged if proton had a charge $(+4/3)e$ and electron a charge $(-3/4)e$, where $e = 1.6 \times 10^{-19}$ C. Give reasons for your answer.

Thinking Process The electrostatic force of attraction between positively charged nucleus and negatively charged electrons provides necessary centripetal force of revolution. Also, the magnitude of electrostatic force $F \propto q_1 q_2$.

Ans. If proton had a charge $(+4/3)\,e$ and electron a charge $(-3/4)\,e$, then the Bohr formula for the H-atom would remain same, since the Bohr formula involves only the product of the charges which remain constant for given values of charges.

Q.18 Consider two different hydrogen atoms. The electron in each atom is in an excited state. Is it possible for the electrons to have different energies but the same orbital angular momentum according to the Bohr model?

- **Concept Insight** Bohr's postulate states that the electron revolves around the nucleus only in those orbits for which the angular momentum is some integral multiple of $\frac{h}{2\pi}$, where h is Planck's constant ($h = 6.6 \times 10^{-34}$ J-s). Thus, the angular momentum (L) of the orbiting electron is quantised. *i.e.*, $L = \frac{nh}{2\pi}$

Ans. According to Bohr model electrons having different energies belong to different levels having different values of n. So, their angular momenta will be different, as

$$L = \frac{nh}{2\pi} \text{ or } L \propto n$$

Short Answer Type Questions

Q. 19 Positronium is just like a H-atom with the proton replaced by the positively charged anti-particle of the electron (called the positron which is as massive as the electron). What would be the ground state energy of positronium?

Thinking Process The reduced mass m of two particle system of masses m_1 and m_2 is given by $\frac{1}{m} = \frac{1}{m_1} + \frac{1}{m_2}$

Ans. The total energy of the electron in the stationary states of the hydrogen atom is given by

$$E_n = -\frac{me^4}{8n^2 \varepsilon_0^2 h^2}$$

where m is the reduced mass of electron and proton. Also, the total energy of the electron in the ground state of the hydrogen atom is -13.6 eV. For H-atom, reduced mass is m_e, whereas for positronium, the reduced mass is

$$m \approx \frac{m_e}{2}$$

Hence, the total energy of the electron in the ground state of the positronium atom is

$$\frac{-13.6}{2}\text{ eV} = -6.8\text{ eV}$$

Q.20 Assume that there is no repulsive force between the electrons in an atom but the force between positive and negative charges is given by Coulomb's law as usual. Under such circumstances, calculate the ground state energy of a He-atom.

Thinking Process The total energy of the electron in the n th stationary state of hydrogen like atom of atomic number Z is given by $E_n = Z^2 \frac{-13.6}{n^2}$ eV.

Ans. For a He -nucleus with charge $2e$ and electrons of charge $-e$, the energy level in ground state is

$$E_n = Z^2 \frac{-13.6}{n^2}\text{ eV} = 2^2 \frac{-13.6}{1^2}\text{ eV} = -54.4\text{eV}$$

Thus, the ground state will have two electrons each of energy E and the total ground state energy would be $-(4 \times 13.6)\text{eV} = -54.4\text{eV}$.

Q. 21 Using Bohr model, calculate the electric current created by the electron when the H-atom is in the ground state.

Thinking Process The electric current due to revolution of charge is given by $i = \frac{q}{T} = q\left(\frac{1}{T}\right) = q \times n$, where n is frequency.

Ans. The electron in Hydrogen atom in ground state revolves in a circular path whose radius is equal to the Bohr radius (a_n). Let the velocity of electron is v.

$\therefore$ Number of revolutions per unit time $= \frac{2\pi a_0}{v}$

The electric current is given by $i = \frac{q}{t}$, if q charge flows in time t. Here, $q = e$

The electric current is given by $i = \frac{2\pi a_0}{v} e$.

Q. 22 Show that the first few frequencies of light that is emitted when electrons fall to nth level from levels higher than n, are approximate harmonics (*i.e.*, in the ratio $1:2:3\ldots$) when $n >> 1$.

Thinking Process The problem is based on the explanation of spectrum of hydrogen atom.

Ans. The frequency of any line in a series in the spectrum of hydrogen like atoms corresponding to the transition of electrons from $(n+p)$ level to nth level can be expressed as a difference of two terms;

$$\nu_{mn} = cRZ^2\left[\frac{1}{(n+p)^2} - \frac{1}{n^2}\right]$$

where, $m = n + p, (p = 1, 2, 3, \ldots)$ and R is Rydberg constant.

For $p << n$

$$\nu_{mn} = cRZ^2\left[\frac{1}{n^2}\left(1+\frac{p}{n}\right)^{-2} - \frac{1}{n^2}\right]$$

$$\nu_{mn} = cRZ^2\left[\frac{1}{n^2} - \frac{2p}{n^3} - \frac{1}{n^2}\right]$$

[By binomial theorem, $(1+x)^n = 1 + nx$ if $|x| < 1$]

$$\nu_{mn} = cRZ^2\frac{2p}{n^3} \simeq \left(\frac{2cRZ^2}{n^3}\right)p$$

Thus, the first few frequencies of light that is emitted when electrons fall to the nth level from levels higher than n are approximate harmonic (*i.e.*, in the ratio 1 : 2 : 3 ...) when $n >> 1$.

Q.23 What is the minimum energy that must be given to a H-atom in ground state so that it can emit an H_γ line in Balmer series? If the angular momentum of the system is conserved, what would be the angular momentum of such H_γ photon?

Thinking Process The third line in Balmer series in the spectrum of hydrogen atom is H_γ.

Ans. H_γ in Balmer series corresponds to transition $n = 5$ to $n = 2$. So, the electron in ground state *i.e.*, from $n = 1$ must first be placed in state $n = 5$.

Energy required for the transition from $n = 1$ to $n = 5$ is given by

$$E = E_1 - E_5 = 13.6 - 0.54 = 13.06 \text{ eV}$$

Since, angular momentum is conserved,

angular momentum corresponding to H_γ photon = change in angular momentum of electron

$$= L_5 - L_2 = \frac{5h - 2h}{2\pi} = \frac{3h}{2\pi} = \frac{3 \times 6.63 \times 10^{-34}}{2 \times 3.14}$$

$$= 3.17 \times 10^{-34} \text{ kg-m}^2/\text{s}$$

Long Answer Type Questions

Q.24 The first four spectral lines in the Lyman series of a H-atom are $\lambda = 1218$Å, 1028Å, 974.3Å and 951.4Å. If instead of Hydrogen, we consider deuterium, calculate the shift in the wavelength of these lines.

Thinking Process The reduced mass m of two particle system of masses m_1 and m_2 is given by $\frac{1}{m} = \frac{1}{m_1} + \frac{1}{m_2}$.

Ans. The total energy of the electron in the stationary states of the hydrogen atom is given by

$$E_n = -\frac{me^4}{8n^2\varepsilon_0^2 h^2}$$

where m that occurs in the Bohr formula is the reduced mass of electron and proton in hydrogen atom.

By Bohr's model,

$$h\nu_{if} = E_{n_i} - E_{n_f}$$

On simplifying,

$$\nu_{if} = \frac{me^4}{8\varepsilon_0^2 h^3}\left(\frac{1}{n_f^2} - \frac{1}{n_i^2}\right)$$

Since, $$\lambda \propto \frac{1}{\mu}$$

Thus, $$\lambda_{if} \propto \frac{1}{\mu} \quad \text{...(i)}$$

where μ is the reduced mass. (here, μ is used in place of m)

Reduced mass for H, $$\mu_H = \frac{m_e}{1+\frac{m_e}{M}} = m_e\left(1-\frac{m_e}{M}\right)$$

Reduced mass for D, $$\mu_D = m_e\left(1-\frac{m_e}{2M}\right)$$

Now, the wavelength is $\frac{\lambda_H}{\lambda_D}$

$$\frac{\lambda_D}{\lambda_H} = \frac{\mu_H}{\mu_D} = \frac{m_e\left(1-\frac{m_e}{2M}\right)}{m_e\left(1-\frac{m_e}{M}\right)}$$

$$\Rightarrow \quad \frac{\mu_H}{\mu_D} = \left(1-\frac{m_e}{2M}\right)\left(1-\frac{m_e}{M}\right)^{-1}$$

$$\Rightarrow \quad \frac{\mu_H}{\mu_D} = \left(1-\frac{m_e}{2M}\right)\left(1+\frac{m_e}{M}\right)$$

Since $$\frac{m_e^2}{2M^2} \approx 0$$

$$\therefore \quad \frac{\mu_H}{\mu_D} = 1-\frac{m_e}{2M} = 1-\frac{1}{2\times 1840}$$

$$\lambda_D = \lambda_H \times (0.99973)$$

On substituting the values,

Thus, lines are 1217.7Å, 1027.7Å, 974.04Å, 951.143Å.

Thus, shift in wavelength $(\lambda_D - \lambda_H) = 0.3$Å

Q.25 Deutrium was discovered in 1932 by Harold Urey by measuring the small change in wavelength for a particular transition in ^1H and ^2H. This is because, the wavelength of transition depend to a certain extent on the nuclear mass. If nuclear motion is taken into account, then the electrons and nucleus revolve around their common centre of mass.

Such a system is equivalent to a single particle with a reduced mass μ, revolving around the nucleus at a distance equal to the electron-nucleus separation. Here $\mu = m_e M/(m_e + M)$, where M is the nuclear mass and m_e is the electronic mass. Estimate the percentage difference in wavelength for the 1st line of the Lyman series in ^1H and ^2H. (mass of ^1H nucleus is 1.6725×10^{-27} kg, mass of ^2H nucleus is 3.3374×10^{-27} kg, Mass of electron $= 9.109 \times 10^{-31}$ kg.)

- **Concept Insight** The percentage difference in wavelength is given by

$$100 \times \frac{\Delta\lambda}{\lambda_H} = \frac{\lambda_D - \lambda_H}{\lambda_H} \times 100, \quad \text{where signs are as usual.}$$

Ans. The total energy of the electron in the nth state of the hydrogen like atom of atomic number Z is given by

$$E_n = -\frac{\mu Z^2 e^4}{8\varepsilon_0^2 h^2}\left(\frac{1}{n^2}\right)$$

where signs are as usual and the μ that occurs in the Bohr formula is the reduced mass of electron and proton .

Let μ_H be the reduced mass of Hydrogen and μ_D that of Deutrium. Then, the frequency of the 1st Lyman line in hydrogen is $h\nu_H = \frac{\mu_H e^4}{8\varepsilon_0^2 h^2}\left(1 - \frac{1}{4}\right) = \frac{\mu_H e^4}{8\varepsilon_0^2 h^2} \times \frac{3}{4}$.

Thus, the wavelength of the transition is $\lambda_H = \frac{4}{3} \times \frac{8\varepsilon_0^2 h^3 c}{\mu_H e^4}$.

The wavelength of the transition for the same line in Deutrium is $\lambda_D = \frac{4}{3} \times \frac{8\varepsilon_0^2 h^3 c}{\mu_D e^4}$.

$$\therefore \quad \Delta\lambda = \lambda_D - \lambda_H$$

Hence, the percentage difference is

$$100 \times \frac{\Delta\lambda}{\lambda_H} = \frac{\lambda_D - \lambda_H}{\lambda_H} \times 100 = \frac{\frac{1}{\mu_D} - \frac{1}{\mu_H}}{\frac{1}{\mu_H}} \times 100 = \frac{\mu_H - \mu_D}{\mu_D}$$

$$= \frac{\frac{m_e M_H}{m_e + M_H} - \frac{m_e M_D}{m_e + M_D}}{\frac{m_e M_D}{m_e + M_D}} \times 100$$

$$= \left[\frac{m_e M_H (m_e + M_D)}{m_e M_D (m_e + M_H)} - 1\right] \times 100$$

Since, $m_e << M_H << M_D$

$$\frac{\Delta\lambda}{\lambda_H}\times 100 = \left[\frac{M_H}{M_D}\cdot\frac{M_D\left(1+\frac{m_e}{M_D}\right)}{M_H\left(1+\frac{m_e}{M_H}\right)} - 1\right]\times 100$$

$$= \left[\left(1+\frac{m_e}{M_D}\right)\left(1+\frac{m_e}{M_H}\right)^{-1} - 1\right]\times 100 = \left[1+\frac{m_e}{M_D}-\frac{m_e}{M_H}-1\right]\times 100$$

[By binomial theorem, $(1+x)^n = 1+nx$ is $|x|<1$]

$$\approx m_e\left[\frac{1}{M_D}-\frac{1}{M_H}\right]\times 100$$

$$= -9.1\times 10^{-31}\left[\frac{1}{1.6725\times 10^{-27}}-\frac{1}{3.3374\times 10^{-27}}\right]\times 100$$

$$= -9.1\times 10^{-4}[0.5979-0.2996]\times 100$$

$$= -2.714\times 10^{-2}\%$$

Q.26 If a proton had a radius R and the charge was uniformly distributed, calculate using Bohr theory, the ground state energy of a H-atom when (i) $R = 0.1\text{Å}$ and (ii) $R = 10\text{Å}$.

Thinking Process In this problem, expressions are to be derived in two cases namely for a point nucleus in H-atom and for a spherical nucleus of radius R.

Ans. (i) The electrostatic force of attraction between positively charged nucleus and negatively charged electrons (Coulomb force) provides necessary centripetal force of revolution.

$$\frac{mv^2}{r_B} = \frac{e^2}{r_B^2}\cdot\frac{1}{4\pi\varepsilon_0}$$

By Bohr's postulates in ground state, we have

$$mvr = \frac{h}{2\pi}$$

On solving,

$$\therefore \quad m\frac{h^2}{4\pi^2 m^2 r_B^2}\cdot\frac{1}{r_B} = +\left(\frac{e^2}{4\pi\varepsilon_0}\right)\frac{1}{r_B^2}$$

$$\therefore \quad \frac{h^2}{4\pi^2 m}\cdot\frac{4\pi\varepsilon_0}{e^2} = r_B = 0.51\ \text{Å}$$ [This is Bohr's radius]

The potential energy is given by

$$-\left(\frac{e^2}{4\pi r_0}\right)\cdot\frac{1}{r_B} = -27.2\text{eV};$$

$$\text{KE} = \frac{mv^2}{2} = \frac{1}{2}m\cdot\frac{h^2}{4\pi^2 m^2 r_B^2} = \frac{h}{8\pi^2 m r_B^2} = +13.6\text{ eV}$$

Total energy at ground state = KE + PE = 13.6 ev − 27.2 ev = −13.6 ev

Now, for a spherical nucleus of radius R,

If $R < r_B$, same result.

(ii) If $R >> r_B$ the electron moves inside the sphere with radius r'_B (r'_B = new Bohr radius).

Charge inside $r_B'^4 = e\left(\frac{r_B'^3}{R^3}\right)$

$$\therefore \quad r'_B = \frac{h^2}{4\pi^2 m}\left(\frac{4\pi\varepsilon_0}{e^2}\right)\frac{R^3}{r_B'^3}$$

$$r_B'^4 = (0.51\text{Å})\cdot R^3 \qquad [R = 10\text{ Å}]$$

$$= 510(\text{Å})^4$$

$$\therefore \quad r'_B \simeq (510)^{1/4}\text{ Å} < R$$

$$\text{KE} = \frac{1}{2}mv^2 = \frac{m}{2}\cdot\frac{h^2}{4\pi^2 m^2 r_B'^2} = \frac{h^2}{8\pi^2 m r_B'^2}$$

$$= \left(\frac{h^2}{8\pi^2 m r_B^2}\cdot\right)\left(\frac{r_B^2}{r_B'^2}\right) = (13.6\text{ eV})\frac{(0.51)^2}{(510)^{1/2}} = \frac{3.54}{22.6} = 0.16\text{ eV}$$

$$\text{PE} = +\left(\frac{e^2}{4\pi\varepsilon_0}\right)\cdot\left(\frac{r_B'^2 - 3R^2}{2R^3}\right)$$

$$= +\left(\frac{e^2}{4\pi\varepsilon_0}\cdot\frac{1}{r_B}\right)\cdot\left(\frac{r_B(r_B'^2 - 3R^2)}{R^3}\right) = +(27.2\text{eV})\left[\frac{0.51(\sqrt{510} - 300)}{1000}\right]$$

$$= +(27.2\text{eV})\cdot\frac{-141}{1000} = -3.83\text{ eV}$$

Total Energy at ground state = KE + PE = 0.16 ev − 3.83 ev = −3.67 ev

Q.27 In the Auger process an atom makes a transition to a lower state without emitting a photon. The excess energy is transferred to an outer electron which may be ejected by the atom (This is called an Auger, electron). Assuming the nucleus to be massive, calculate the kinetic energy of an $n = 4$ Auger electron emitted by Chromium by absorbing the energy from a $n = 2$ to $n = 1$ transition.

- **Concept Insight** As the nucleus is massive, recoil momentum of the atom may be neglected and the entire energy of the transition may be considered transferred to the Auger electron. As there is a single valence electron in Cr, the energy states may be thought of as given by the Bohr model.

Ans. The energy of the nth state $E_n = -Z^2 R\frac{1}{n^2}$

Where, R is the Rydberg constant and $Z = 24$.

The energy released in a transition from 2 to 1 is $\Delta E = Z^2 R\left(1 - \frac{1}{4}\right) = \frac{3}{4}Z^2 R$.

The energy required to eject a $n = 4$ electron is $E_4 = Z^2 R\frac{1}{16}$.

Thus, the kinetic energy of the Auger electron is

$$\text{KE} = Z^2 R\left(\frac{3}{4} - \frac{1}{16}\right) = \frac{1}{16}Z^2 R$$

$$= \frac{11}{16} \times 24 \times 24 \times 13.6\text{eV}$$

$$= 5385.6\text{eV}$$

Q.28 The inverse square law in electrostatic is $|\mathbf{F}| = \dfrac{e^2}{(4\pi\varepsilon_0)r^2}$ for the force between an electron and a proton. The $\left(\dfrac{1}{r}\right)$ dependence of $|\mathbf{F}|$ can be understood in quantum theory as being due to the fact that the particle of light (photon) is massless. If photons had a mass m_p, force would be modified to $|\mathbf{F}| = \dfrac{e^2}{(4\pi\varepsilon_0)r^2}\left[\dfrac{1}{r^2} + \dfrac{\lambda}{r}\right]\cdot \exp(-\lambda r)$ where $\lambda = \dfrac{m_p c}{\hbar}$ and $\hbar = \dfrac{h}{2\pi}$. Estimate the change in the ground state energy of a H-atom if m_p were 10^{-6} times the mass of an electron.

Ans. For $m_p = 10^{-6}$ times the mass of an electron, the energy associated with it is given by

$$m_pc^2 = 10^{-6} \times \text{electron mass} \times c^2$$
$$\approx 10^{-6} \times 0.5 \text{ MeV}$$
$$\approx 10^{-6} \times 0.5 \times 1.6 \times 10^{-13}$$
$$\approx 0.8 \times 10^{-19}\text{J}$$

The wavelength associated with is given by

$$\frac{\hbar}{m_pc} = \frac{\hbar c}{m_pc^2} = \frac{10^{-34} \times 3 \times 10^8}{0.8 \times 10^{-19}}$$
$$\approx 4 \times 10^{-7}\text{m} >> \text{Bohr radius}$$
$$|\mathbf{F}| = \frac{e^2}{4\pi\varepsilon_0}\left[\frac{1}{r^2} + \frac{\lambda}{r}\right]\exp(-\lambda r)$$

where, $$\lambda^{-1} = \frac{\hbar}{m_pc} \approx 4 \times 10^{-7}\, m >> r_B$$

$\therefore$ $$\lambda << \frac{1}{r_B} \text{ i.e., } \lambda r_B << 1$$

$$U(r) = -\frac{e^2}{4\pi\varepsilon_0}\cdot\frac{\exp(-\lambda r)}{r}$$

$$mvr = \hbar \quad \therefore \quad v = \frac{\hbar}{mr}$$

Also, $$\frac{mv^2}{r} = \left(\frac{e^2}{4\pi\varepsilon_0}\right)\left(\frac{1}{r^2} + \frac{\lambda}{r}\right)$$

$\therefore$ $$\frac{\hbar^2}{mr^3} = \left(\frac{e^2}{4\pi\varepsilon_0}\right)\left[\frac{1}{r^2} + \frac{\lambda}{r}\right]$$

$\therefore$ $$\frac{\hbar^2}{m} = \left(\frac{e^2}{4\pi\varepsilon_o}\right)[r + \lambda r^2]$$

If $\lambda = 0$ $$r = r_B = \frac{\hbar}{m}\cdot\frac{4\pi\varepsilon_0}{e^2}$$

$$\frac{\hbar^2}{m} = \frac{e^2}{4\pi\varepsilon_0}\cdot r_B$$

Since, $\lambda^{-1} >> r_B$, put $r = r_B + \delta$

$\therefore$ $r_B = r_B + \delta + \lambda(r_B^2 + \delta^2 + 2\delta r_B)$; neglect δ^2

or $0 = \lambda r_B^2 + \delta(1 + 2\lambda r_B)$

$$\delta = \frac{-\lambda r_B^2}{1 + 2\lambda r_B} \approx \lambda r_B^2(1 - 2\lambda r_B) = -\lambda r_B^2$$

Since, $\lambda r_B << 1$

$$\therefore \quad V(r) = -\frac{e^2}{4\pi\varepsilon_0} \cdot \frac{\exp(-\lambda\delta - \lambda r_B)}{r_B + \delta}$$

$$\therefore \quad V(r) = -\frac{e^2}{4\pi\varepsilon_0} \frac{1}{r_B}\left[\left(1 - \frac{\delta}{r_B}\right) \cdot (e^{-\lambda r})\right]$$

$$\cong (-27.2\text{eV}) \text{ remains unchanged}$$

$$\text{KE} = -\frac{1}{2}mv^2 = \frac{1}{2}m \cdot \frac{h^2}{m^2r^2} = \frac{h^2}{2m(r_B + \delta)^2} = \frac{h^2}{2mr_B^2}\left(1 - \frac{2\delta}{r_B}\right)$$

$$= (13.6\text{eV})[1 + 2\lambda r_B]$$

$$\text{Total energy} = -\frac{e^2}{4\pi\varepsilon_0 r_B} + \frac{h^2}{2mr_B^2}[1 + 2\lambda r_B]$$

$$= -27.2 + 13.6[1 + 2\lambda r_B] \text{ eV}$$

Change in energy $= 13.6 \times 2\lambda r_B \text{eV} = 27.2\lambda r_B \text{eV}$

Q.29 The Bohr model for the H-atom relies on the Coulomb's law of electrostatics. Coulomb's law has not directly been verified for very short distances of the order of angstroms. Supposing Coulomb's law between two opposite charge $+q_1, -q_2$ is modified to

$$|\mathbf{F}| = \frac{q_1q_2}{(4\pi\varepsilon_0)} \frac{1}{r^2}, r \geq R_0$$

$$= \frac{q_1q_2}{4\pi\varepsilon_0} \frac{1}{R_0^2}\left(\frac{R_0}{r}\right)^{\varepsilon}, r \leq R_0$$

Calculate in such a case, the ground state energy of a H-atom, if $E = 0.1$, $R_0 = 1$ Å.

Thinking Process The question offers hypothetical situation in dealing with the total energy of the electron of hydrogen atom.

Ans. Considering the case, when $r \leq R_0 = 1$ Å

Let $\varepsilon = 2 + \delta$

$$F = \frac{q_1q_2}{4\pi\varepsilon_0} \cdot \frac{R_0^{\delta}}{r^{2+\delta}}$$

where, $$\frac{q_1q_2}{4\pi\varepsilon_0} = (1.6 \times 10^{-19})^2 \times 9 \times 10^9$$

$$= 23.04 \times 10^{-29} \text{ N-m}^2 = \Lambda \text{ (let)}$$

The electrostatic force of attraction between positively charged nucleus and negatively charged electrons (Coulomb force) provides necessary centripetal force.

$$\frac{q_1 q_2}{4\pi\varepsilon_0}\cdot\frac{R_0^{\delta}}{r^{2+\delta}}=\frac{mv^2}{r} \quad \text{or} \quad v^2=\frac{\Lambda R_0^{\delta}}{mr^{1+\delta}} \qquad \ldots\text{(i)}$$

$$mvr = n\hbar \Rightarrow r=\frac{n\hbar}{mv}=\frac{n\hbar}{m}\left[\frac{m}{\Lambda R_0^{\delta}}\right]^{1/2} r^{1/2+\delta/2}$$

[Applying Bohr's second postulate]

Solving this for r, we get $r_n=\left[\frac{n^2\hbar^2}{m\,\Lambda\,R_0^{\delta}}\right]^{\frac{1}{1-\delta}}$

where, r_n is radius of nth orbit of electron.

For $n = 1$ and substituting the values of constant, we get

$$r_1=\left[\frac{\hbar^2}{m\,\Lambda\,R_0^{\delta}}\right]^{\frac{1}{1-\delta}}$$

$$r_1=\left[\frac{1.05^2\times10^{-68}}{9.1\times10^{-31}\times2.3\times10^{-28}\times10^{+19}}\right]^{\frac{1}{2.9}}$$

$$=8\times10^{-11}$$

$$=0.08\,\text{nm} \qquad (<0.1\,\text{nm})$$

This is the radius of orbit of electron in ground state of hydrogen atom.

$$v_n=\frac{n\hbar}{mr_n}=n\hbar\left(\frac{m\,\Lambda\,R_0^{\delta}}{n^2\hbar^2}\right)^{\frac{1}{1-\delta}}.$$

For $n = 1$, $v_1=\frac{\hbar}{mr_1}=1.44\times10^{6}$ m/s

[This is the speed of electron in ground state]

$$\text{KE}=\frac{1}{2}mv_1^2=9.43\times10^{-19}\ \text{J}=5.9\text{eV}$$

[This is the KE of electron in ground state]

PE till $R_0=-\frac{\Lambda}{R_0}$ [This is the PE of electron in ground state at $r = R_0$]

PE from R_0 to $r=+\Lambda R_0^{\delta}\int_{R_0}^{r}\frac{dr}{r^{2+\delta}}=+\frac{\Lambda R_0^{\delta}}{-1-\delta}\left[\frac{1}{r^{1+\delta}}\right]_{R_0}^{r}$

[This is the PE of electron in ground state at R_0 to r]

$$=-\frac{\Lambda R_0^{\delta}}{1+\delta}\left[\frac{1}{r^{1+\delta}}-\frac{1}{R_0^{1+\delta}}\right]=-\frac{\Lambda}{1+\delta}\left[\frac{R_0^{\delta}}{r^{1+\delta}}-\frac{1}{R_0}\right]$$

$$\text{PE}=-\frac{\Lambda}{1+\delta}\left[\frac{R_0^{\delta}}{r^{1+\delta}}-\frac{1}{R_0}+\frac{1+\delta}{R_0}\right]$$

$$\text{PE}=-\frac{\Lambda}{-0.9}\left[\frac{R_0^{-1.9}}{r^{-0.9}}-\frac{1.9}{R_0}\right]$$

$$=\frac{2.3}{0.9}\times10^{-18}[(0.8)^{0.9}-1.9]\,\text{J}=-17.3\ \text{eV}$$

Total energy is $(-17.3+5.9)=-11.4$ eV

This is the required TE of electron in ground state.

Chapter

13

Nuclei

Multiple Choice Questions (MCQs)

Q.1 Suppose we consider a large number of containers each containing initially 10000 atoms of a radioactive material with a half-life of 1 yr. After 1 yr,

(a) all the containers will have 5000 atoms of the material

(b) all the containers will contain the same number of atoms of the material but that number will only be approximately 5000

(c) the containers will in general have different numbers of the atoms of the material but their average will be close to 5000

(d) none of the containers can have more than 5000 atoms

Ans. *(c)* Radioactivity is a process due to which a radioactive material spontaneously decays. In half-life ($t = 1$ yr) of the material, on an average half the number of atoms will decay.

Therefore, the containers will in general have different number of atoms of the material, but their average will be approx 5000.

Q.2 The gravitational force between a H-atom and another particle of mass m will be given by Newton's law

$$F = G\frac{M.m}{r^2}, \text{ where } r \text{ is in km and}$$

(a) $M = m_{\text{proton}} + m_{\text{electron}}$

(b) $M = m_{\text{proton}} + m_{\text{electron}} - \frac{B}{c^2}$ $(B = 13.6 \text{ eV})$.

(c) M is not related to the mass of the hydrogen atom.

(d) $M = m_{\text{proton}} + m_{\text{electron}} - \frac{|V|}{c^2}$ ($|V|$ = magnitude of the potential energy of electron in the H-atom.)

Ans. *(b)* Given, $F = \frac{GMm}{r^2}$

M = effective mass of hydrogen atom

$= \text{mass of electron} + \text{mass of proton} - \frac{B^2}{C}$

where, B is BE of hydrogen atom = 13.6 eV.

Q.3 When a nucleus in an atom undergoes a radioactive decay, the electronic energy levels of the atom

(a) do not change for any type of radioactivity
(b) change for α and β-radioactivity but not for γ-radioactivity
(c) change for α-radioactivity but not for others
(d) change for β-radioactivity but not for others

Ans. ***(b)*** β particle carries one unit of negative charge and an α-particle carries 2 units of positive change and γ (particle) carries no charge, therefore electronic energy levels of the atom change for α and β decay, but not for γ-decay.

Q.4 M_x and M_y denote the atomic masses of the parent and the daughter nuclei respectively in radioactive decay. The Q-value for a β^- decay is Q_1 and that for a β^+ decay is Q_2. If m_e denotes the mass of an electron, then which of the following statements is correct?

(a) $Q_1 = (M_x - M_y)c^2$ and $Q_2 = [M_x - M_y - 2m_e]c^2$
(b) $Q_1 = (M_x - M_y)c^2$ and $Q_2 = (M_x - M_y)c^2$
(c) $Q_1 = (M_x - M_y - 2m_e)c^2$ and $Q_2 = (M_x - M_y + 2c_e)c^2$
(d) $Q_1 = (M_x - M_y + 2m_e)c^2$ and $Q_2 = (M_x - m_y + 2m_e)c^2$

Ans. ***(a)*** Let the nucleus is ${}_ZX^A$. β^+ decay is represented as

$$ {}_ZX^A \rightarrow {}_{Z-1}y^A + {}_{+1}e^0 + \nu + Q_2 $$

$$ \therefore \quad Q_2 = [m_n({}_ZX^A) - m_n({}_{Z-1}y^A) - m_e]c^2 $$
$$ = [m_n({}_ZX^A) + Zm_e - m_n({}_{Z-1}Y^A) - (Z-1)m_e - 2m_e]c^2 $$
$$ = [m({}_ZX^A) - m({}_{Z-1}Y^A) - 2m_e]c^2 $$
$$ = (M_x - M_y - 2m_e)c^2 $$

β^- decay is represented as

$$ {}_ZX^A \rightarrow {}_{Z+1}A^Y + {}_{-1}e^0 + \bar{\nu} + Q_1 $$
$$ Q_1 = [m_n({}_ZX^A) - m_n({}_{Z+1}Y^A) - m_e]c^2 $$
$$ = [m_n({}_ZX^A) + zm_e - m_n({}_{Z+1}Y^A) - (Z+1)m_e]c^2 $$
$$ = [m({}_ZX^A) - m({}_{Z-1}Y^A)]c^2 $$
$$ = (M_x - M_y)c^2 $$

Q.5 Tritium is an isotope of hydrogen whose nucleus triton contains 2 neutrons and 1 proton. Free neutrons decay into $p + \bar{e} + \bar{\nu}$. If one of the neutrons in Triton decays, it would transform into He^3 nucleus. This does not happen. This is because

(a) triton energy is than that of a He^3 nucleus
(b) the electron created in the beta decay process cannot remain in the nucleus
(c) both the neutons in triton have to decay simultaneously resulting in a nucleus with 3 protons, which is not a He^3 nucleus.
(d) free neutrons decay due to external perturbations which is absent in triton nucleus

Thinking Process Isotopes of an element have same atomic numbers and different mass numbers.

Ans. ***(a)*** Tritium $({}_1H^3)$ contains 1 proton and 2 neutrons. A neutron decays as $n \longrightarrow p + \bar{e} + \bar{\nu}$, the nucleus may have 2 protons and one neutron, *i.e.*, tritium will transform into ${}_2He^3$ (2 protons and 1 neutron).

Triton energy is less than that of ${}_2He^3$ nucleus, *i.e.*, transformation is not allowed energetically.

Q.6 Heavy stable nuclei have more neutrons than protons. This is because of the fact that

(a) neutrons are heavier than protons
(b) electrostatic force between protons are repulsive
(c) neutrons decay into protons through beta decay
(d) nuclear forces between neutrons are weaker than that between protons

Ans. ***(b)*** Stable heavy nuclei have more neutrons than protons. This is because electrostatic force between protons is repulsive , which may reduce stability.

Q.7 In a nuclear reactor, moderators slow down the neutrons which come out in a fission process. The moderator used have light nuclei. Heavy nuclei will not serve the purpose, because

(a) they will break up
(b) elastic collision of neutrons with heavy nuclei will not slow them down
(c) the net weight of the reactor would be unbearably high
(d) substances with heavy nuclei do not occur in liquid or gaseous state at room temperature

Thinking Process When there is an elastic collision between two bodies of same mass their velocities are exchanged.

Ans. ***(b)*** According to the question, the moderator used have light nuclei (like proton). When protons undergo perfectly elastic collision with the neutron emitted their velocities are exchanged, *i.e.*, neutrons come to rest and protons move with the velocity of neutrons.

Heavy nuclei will not serve the purpose because elastic collisions of neutrons with heavy nuclei will not slow them down.

Multiple Choice Questions (More Than One Options)

Q.8 Fusion processes, like combining two deuterons to form a He nucleus are impossible at ordinary temperatures and pressure.The reasons for this can be traced to the fact

(a) nuclear forces have short range
(b) nuclei are positively charged
(c) the original nuclei must be completely ionised before fusion can take place
(d) the original nuclei must first break up before combining with each other

Ans. ***(a, b)*** Two deuterons can combine to form a He atom when their nuclei come close enough so that nuclear fusion can occur. Since, the electrostatic repulsion between the two nuclei increases drastically at short distances, therefore to overcome this repulsion, very high temperature and pressure is required.

Q.9 Samples of two radioactive nuclides A and B are taken λ_A and λ_B are the disintegration constants of A and B respectively. In which of the following cases, the two samples can simultaneously have the same decay rate at any time?

(a) Initial rate of decay of A is twice the initial rate of decay of B and $\lambda_A = \lambda_B$
(b) Initial rate of decay of A is twice the initial rate of decay of B and $\lambda_A > \lambda_B$
(c) Initial rate of decay of B is twice the initial rate of decay of A and $\lambda_A > \lambda_B$
(d) Initial rate of decay of B is same as the rate of decay of A at $t = 2\text{h}$ and $\lambda_B < \lambda_A$

- **Concept Insight** According to rutherford and soddy law for radioactive decay, "At any instant, the rate of decay of radioactive atoms is proportional to the number of atoms present at that instant".

Ans. ***(b, d)*** The two samples of the two radioactive nuclides A and B can simultaneously have the same decay rate at any time if initial rate of decay of A is twice the initial rate of decay of B and $\lambda_A > \lambda_B$. Also, when initial rate of decay of B is same as rate of decay of A at $t = 2\text{h}$ and $\lambda_B < \lambda_A$.

Q.10 The variation of decay rate of two radioactive samples A and B with time is shown in figure.
Which of the following statements are true?

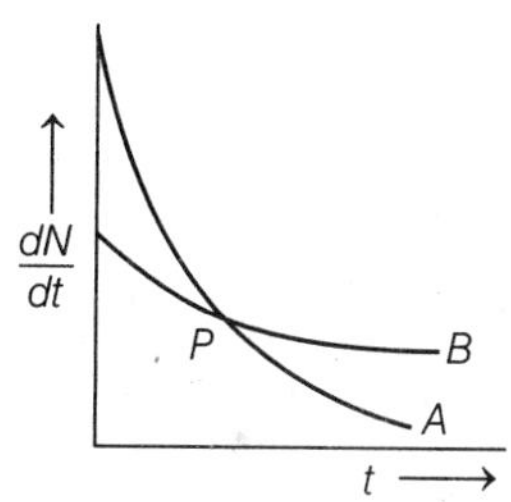

(a) Decay constant of A is greater than that of B, hence A always decays faster than B.
(b) Decay constant of B is greater than that of A but its decay rate is always smaller than that of A.
(c) Decay constant of A is greater than that of B but it does not always decay faster than B.
(d) Decay constant of B is smaller than that of A but still its decay rate becomes equal to that of A at a later instant.

Ans. ***(c, d)*** From the given figure, it is clear that slope of curve A is greater than that of curve B.

So rate of decay is faster for A than that of B.

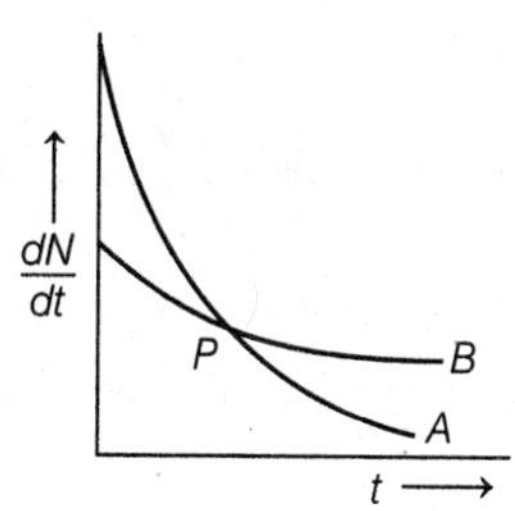

We know that $\left(\frac{dN}{dt}\right) \propto \lambda$, at any instant of time, hence we can say that $\lambda_A > \lambda_B$. At point P shown in the diagram the two curve intersect.

Hence at point P, rate of decay for both A and B is the same.

Very Short Answer Type Questions

Q.11 He_2^3 and He_1^3 nuclei have the same mass number. Do they have the same binding energy?

Ans. Nuclei He_2^3 and He_1^3 have the same mass number. He_2^3 has two proton and one neutron. He_1^3 has one proton and two neutron. The repulsive force between protons is missing in $_1He^3$ so the binding energy of $_1He^3$ is greater than that of $_2He^3$.

Q.12 Draw a graph showing the variation of decay rate with number of active nuclei.

Ans. We know that, rate of decay, $\frac{-dN}{dt} = \lambda N$

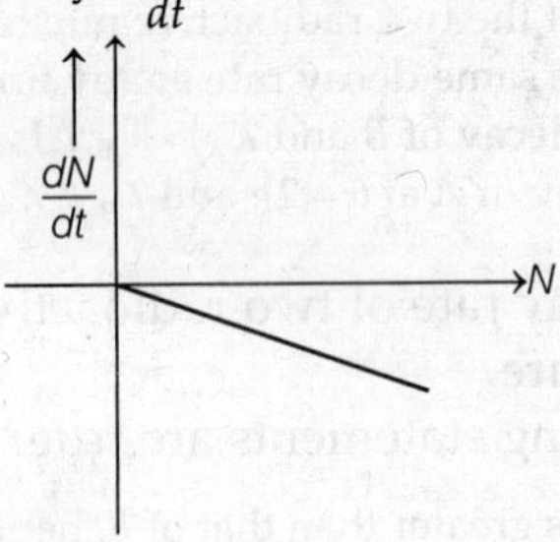

where decay constant (λ) is constant for a given radioactive material. Therefore, graph between N and $\frac{dN}{dt}$ is a straight line as shown in the diagram.

Q.13 Which sample A or B shown in figure has shorter mean-life?

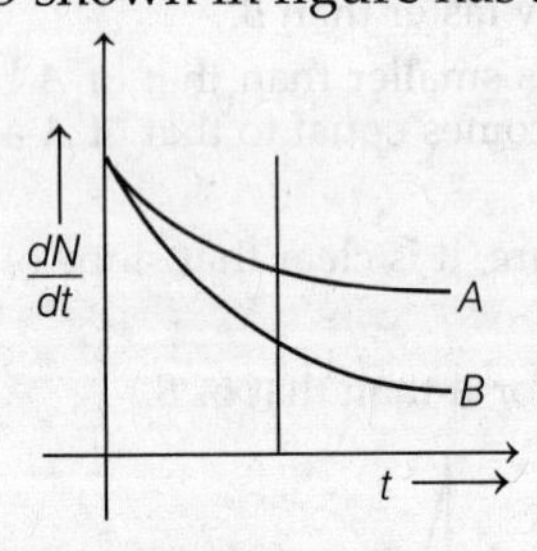

Ans. From the given figure, we can say that,

$$t = 0, \left(\frac{dN}{dt}\right)_A = \left(\frac{dN}{dt}\right)_B \Rightarrow (N_0)_A = (N_0)_B$$

Considering any instant t by drawing a line perpendicular to time axis, we find that $\left(\frac{dN}{dt}\right)_A > \left(\frac{dN}{dt}\right)_B$

$$\Rightarrow \quad \lambda_A N_A > \lambda_B N_B$$

$$\because \quad N_A > N_B \quad \text{(rate of decay of } B \text{ is slower)}$$

$$\therefore \quad \lambda_B > \lambda_A$$

$$\Rightarrow \quad \tau_A > \tau_B \quad \left[\because \text{Average life, } \tau = \frac{1}{\lambda}\right]$$

Thus, the mean-life of sample B is shorter than that of sample A.

Q.14 Which one of the following cannot emit γ radiation and why? Excited nucleus, excited electron.

Ans. Excited electron cannot emit γ radiation because energy of electronic energy levels is in the range of eV and not MeV (mega electron volt).
γ-radiations have energy of the order of MeV.

Q.15 In pair annihilation, an electron and a positron destroy each other to produce gamma radiations. How is the momentum conserved?

Ans. In pair annihilation, an electron and a positron destroy each other to produce 2γ photons which move in opposite directions to conserve linear momentum. The annihilation is shown below ${}_0e^{-1} + {}_0e^{+1} \rightarrow 2\gamma$ ray photons.

Short Answer Type Questions

Q.16 Why do stable nuclei never have more protons than neutrons?

Ans. Because protons are positively charged and repel one another electrically.

This repulsion becomes so great in nuclei with more than 10 protons that an excess of neutrons which produce only attractive forces, is required for stability.

Q.17 Consider a radioactive nucleus A which decays to a stable nucleus C through the following sequence

$$A \rightarrow B \rightarrow C$$

Here B is an intermediate nuclei which is also radioactive. Considering that there are N_0 atoms of A initially, plot the graph showing the variation of number of atoms of A and B *versus* time.

- **Concept Insight** In this problem we use the concept of decay law of unstable radioactive nuclei which states that the rate at which a radioactive substance decays is directly proportional to the number of undecayed nuclei present at any time.

Ans. Consider the situation shown in the graph.

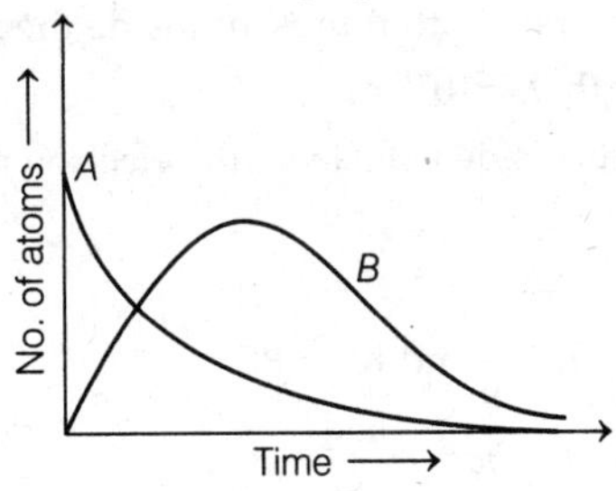

At $t = 0$, $N_A = N_0$ (maximum) while $N_B = 0$. As time increases, N_A decreases exponentially and the number of atoms of B increases. They becomes (N_B) maximum and finally drop to zero exponentially by radioactive decay law.

Q.18 A piece of wood from the ruins of an ancient building was found to have a ^{14}C activity of 12 disintegrations per minute per gram of its carbon content. The ^{14}C activity of the living wood is 16 disintegrations per minute per gram. How long ago did the tree, from which the wooden sample came, die? (Given, half-life of $^{14}C = 5760$ yr.)

Thinking Process Carbon dating is a technique that uses the decay of carbon – 14 (^{14}C) to estimate the age of organic materials, such as wood and leather.

Ans. Given, $R = 12$ dis/min per g, $R_0 = 16$ dis/min per g, $T_{1/2} = 5760$ yr

Let t be the span of the tree.

According to radioactive decay law,

$$R = R_0 e^{-\lambda t} \quad \text{or} \quad \frac{R}{R_0} = e^{-\lambda t} \quad \text{or} \quad e^{\lambda t} = \frac{R_0}{R}$$

Taking log on both the sides

$$\lambda t \log_e e = \log_e \frac{R_0}{R} \Rightarrow \lambda t = \left(\log_{10} \frac{16}{12}\right) \times 2.303$$

$$t = \frac{2.303(\log 4 - \log 3)}{\lambda}$$

$$= \frac{2.303(0.6020 - 0.4771) \times 5760}{0.6931} \qquad \left(\because \lambda = \frac{0.6931}{T_{1/2}}\right)$$

$$= 2390 \cdot 46 \text{ yr}$$

Q.19 Are the nucleons fundamental particles, or do they consist of still smaller parts? One way to find out is to probe a nucleon just as Rutherford probed an atom. What should be the kinetic energy of an electron for it to be able to probe a nucleon? Assume the diameter of a nucleon to be approximately 10^{-15} m.

Thinking Process We have to use de-Broglie formula ($\lambda = h/p$) to find momentum of the particle.

Ans. Each particle (neutron and proton) present inside the nucleus is called a nucleon.

Let λ be the wavelength, $\lambda = 10^{-15}$ m

To detect separate parts inside a nucleon, the electron must have wavelength less than 10^{-15} m.

We know that,

$$\lambda = \frac{h}{p} \text{ and KE} = \text{PE} \qquad \text{...(i)}$$

$$\text{Energy} = \frac{hc}{\lambda} \qquad \text{...(ii)}$$

From Eq.(i) and Eq. (ii),

$$\text{kinetic energy of electron} = \text{PE} = \frac{hc}{\lambda} = \frac{6.63 \times 10^{-34} \times 3 \times 10^8}{10^{-15} \times 1.6 \times 10^{-19}} \text{ eV}$$

$$\text{KE} = 10^9 \text{ eV}$$

Q.20 A nuclide 1 is said to be the mirror isobar of nuclide 2. If $Z_1 = N_2$ and $Z_2 = N_1$.(a) what nuclide is a mirror isobar of $^{23}_{11}$Na? (b) Which nuclide out of the two mirror isobars have greater binding energy and why?

- **Concept Insight** In this problem we use the concept of mirror isobar and binding energy concept. Mirror isobars are pairs of nuclei with the same mass number (A) but different atomic (Z). Such that one nucleus has Z protons and the other has $(A - Z)$ protons. Their proton and neutron numbers are interchanged.
  Binding energy is the energy required to disassemble a nucleus into its constituent protons and neutrons. It reflects the stability of a nucleus. The higher the binding energy the more stable the nucleus.

Ans. (a) According to question, a nuclide 1 is said to be mirror isobar of nuclide 2, if $Z_1 = N_2$ and $Z_2 = N_1$.

Now in $_{11}\text{Na}^{23}, Z_1 = 11, N_1 = 23 - 11 = 12$

$\therefore$ Mirror isobar of $_{11}\text{Na}^{23}$ is $_{12}\text{Mg}^{23}$, for which $Z_2 = 12 = N_1$ and $N_2 = 23 - 12 = 11 = Z_1$

(b) As $^{23}_{12}$Mg contains even number of protons (12) against $^{23}_{11}$Na which has odd number of protons (11), therefore $^{23}_{11}$Mg has greater binding energy than $_{11}\text{Na}^{23}$.

Long Answer Type Questions

Q.21 Sometimes a radioactive nucleus decays into a nucleus which itself is radioactive. An example is

$$^{38}\text{Sulphur} \xrightarrow[=2.48\text{h}]{\text{half-life}} {}^{38}\text{Cl} \xrightarrow[=0.62\text{ h}]{\text{half-life}} {}^{38}\text{Ar (stable)}$$

Assume that we start with 1000 ^{38}S nuclei at time $t = 0$. The number of ^{38}Cl is of count zero at $t = 0$ and will again be zero at $t = \infty$. At what value of t, would the number of counts be a maximum?

- **Concept Insight** To solve this problem concept of chain of two decays will be used. For the process, $A \rightarrow B \rightarrow C$, the law of decay is $\frac{dN_B}{dt} = \lambda_B N_B + \lambda_A N_A$.

Ans. Consider the chain of two decays

$$^{38}\text{S} \xrightarrow[2.48\text{h}]{} {}^{38}\text{Cl} \xrightarrow[0.62\text{h}]{} {}^{38}\text{Ar}$$

At time t, Let ^{38}S have $N_1(t)$ active nuclei and ^{38}Cl have $N_2(t)$ active nuclei.

$$\frac{dN_1}{dt} = -\lambda_1 N_1 = \text{rate of formation of Cl}^{38}.$$

Also, $$\frac{dN_2}{dt} = -\lambda_2 N_2 + \lambda_1 N_1$$

But $$N_1 = N_0 e^{-\lambda_1 t}$$

$$\frac{dN_2}{dt} = \lambda_1 N_0 e^{-\lambda_1 t} - \lambda_2 N_2$$

Multiplying by $e^{\lambda_2 t} dt$ and rearranging

$$e^{\lambda_2 t} dN_2 + \lambda_2 N_2 e^{\lambda_2 t} dt = \lambda_1 N_0 e^{(\lambda_2 - \lambda_1)t} dt \quad \text{...(i)}$$

Integrating both sides of eq. (i), we get

$$\int e^{\lambda_2 t} dN_2 + \lambda_2 N_2 \int e^{\lambda_2 t} dt = \lambda_1 N_0 \int e^{(\lambda_2 - \lambda_1)t} dt$$

$$(N_2 e^{\lambda_2 t} - N_2 \lambda_2 \int e^{\lambda_2 t} dt + \lambda_2 N_2 \int e^{\lambda_2 t} dt = \frac{\lambda_1 N_0}{(\lambda_2 - \lambda_1)} e^{(\lambda_2 - \lambda_1)} + C$$

Where, C is a constant of integration.

$$N_2 e^{\lambda_2 t} = \frac{N_0 \lambda_1}{\lambda_2 - \lambda_1} e^{(\lambda_2 - \lambda_1)t} + C$$

Since, at $t = 0$, $N_2 = 0$, $C = -\dfrac{N_0 \lambda_1}{(\lambda_2 - \lambda_1)}$

$$\therefore \quad N_2 e^{\lambda_2 t} = \frac{N_0 \lambda_1}{\lambda_2 - \lambda_1}[(e^{(\lambda_2 - \lambda_1)t} - 1)] \quad \text{...(ii)}$$

$$N_2 = \frac{N_0 \lambda_1}{\lambda_2 - \lambda_1}(e^{-\lambda_1 t} - e^{-\lambda_2 t})$$

For maximum count, $\dfrac{dN_2}{dt} = 0$

$$\lambda_1 N_0 e^{-\lambda_1 t} - \lambda_2 N_2 = 0$$

$$\Rightarrow \quad \frac{N_0}{N_2} = \frac{\lambda_2}{\lambda_1} e^{\lambda_1 t}$$

$$e^{\lambda_2 t} - \frac{\lambda_2}{\lambda_1} \cdot \frac{\lambda_1}{(\lambda_2 - \lambda_1)} e^{\lambda_1 t}[e^{(\lambda_2 - \lambda_1)t} - 1] = 0$$

or

$$e^{\lambda_2 t} - \frac{\lambda_2}{(\lambda_2 - \lambda_1)} e^{\lambda_2 t} + \frac{\lambda_2}{(\lambda_2 - \lambda_1)} e^{\lambda_1 t} = 0$$

$$1 - \frac{\lambda_2}{(\lambda_2 - \lambda_1)} + \frac{\lambda_2}{(\lambda_2 - \lambda_1)} e^{(\lambda_1 - \lambda_2)t} = 0$$

$$\frac{\lambda_2}{(\lambda_2 - \lambda_1)} e^{(\lambda_1 - \lambda_2)t} = \frac{\lambda_2}{(\lambda_2 - \lambda_1)} - 1$$

$$e^{(\lambda_1 - \lambda_2)t} = \frac{\lambda_1}{\lambda_2}$$

$$t = \left(\log_e \frac{\lambda_1}{\lambda_2}\right) \Big/ (\lambda_1 - \lambda_2)$$

$$= \frac{\log_e\left(\frac{2.48}{0.62}\right)}{2.48 - 0.62}$$

$$= \frac{\log_e 4}{1.86} = \frac{2.303 \times 2 \times 0.3010}{1.86} \qquad \left(\because \lambda = \frac{0.693}{T_{1/2}}\right)$$

$$= 0.745 \text{ s}$$

Mistake Alert ! *Do not apply directly the formula of radioactivity. Apply formulae related to chain decay.*

Q.22 Deuteron is a bound state of a neutron and a proton with a binding energy $B = 2.2$ MeV. A γ-ray of energy E is aimed at a deuteron nucleus to try to break it into a (neutron + proton) such that the n and p move in the direction of the incident γ-ray. If $E = B$, show that this cannot happen. Hence, calculate how much bigger than B must be E be for such a process to happen.

Thinking Process Apply conservation of energy as well as conservation of momentum.

Ans. Given, binding energy, $B = 2.2$ MeV

From the energy conservation law,

$$E - B = K_n + K_p = \frac{p_n^2}{2m} + \frac{p_p^2}{2m} \quad \text{...(i)}$$

From conservation of momentum,

$$p_n + p_p = \frac{E}{c} \quad \text{...(ii)}$$

As $E = B$, Eq. (i) $p_n^2 + p_p^2 = 0$

It can only happen if $p_n = p_p = 0$

So, the Eq. (ii) cannot be satisfied and the process cannot take place.

Let $E = B + X$, where $X << B$ for the process to take place.

Put value of p_n from Eq. (ii) in Eq. (i), we get

$$X = \frac{\left(\frac{E}{c} - p_p\right)}{2m} + \frac{p_p^2}{2m}$$

or $$2p_p^2 - \frac{2Ep_p}{c} + \frac{E^2}{c^2} - 2mX = 0$$

Solving using quadratic formula, we get

$$p_p = \frac{\frac{2E}{c} \pm \sqrt{\frac{4E^2}{c^2} - 8\left(\frac{E^2}{c^2} - 2mX\right)}}{4}$$

For the real and equal value p_p, the discriminant is positive

$$\frac{4E^2}{c^2} = 8\left(\frac{E^2}{c^2} - 2mX\right)$$

$$16mX = \frac{4E^2}{c^2}$$

$$X = \frac{E^2}{4mc^2} \approx \frac{B^2}{4mc^2} \quad [\because X << B \Rightarrow E \cong B]$$

Q.23 The deuteron is bound by nuclear forces just as H-atom is made up of p and e bound by electrostatic forces. If we consider the force between neutron and proton in deuteron as given in the form a coulomb potential but with an effective charge e'

$$F = \frac{1}{4\pi\varepsilon_0} \cdot \frac{e'^2}{r}$$

estimate the value of (e'/e) given that the binding energy of a deuteron is 2.2 MeV.

Ans. The binding energy is H-atom

$$E = \frac{me^4}{8\varepsilon_0^2 h^2} = 13.6 \text{ eV} \quad \text{...(i)}$$

If proton and neutron had charge e' each and were governed by the same electrostatic force, then in the above equation we would need to replace electronic mass m by the reduced mass m' of proton-neutron and the electronic charge e by e'.

$$m' = \frac{M \times M}{M + M} = \frac{M^2}{2M} = \frac{M}{2}$$

$$= \frac{1836}{2} \text{ m} = 918 \text{ m}$$

Here, M represents mass of a neutron/proton

$$\therefore \quad \text{Binding energy} = \frac{918m(e')^4}{8\varepsilon_0^2 h^2} = 2.2 \text{ MeV} \quad \ldots\text{(ii)}$$

Dividing Eqs. (ii) and (i), we get

$$918\left(\frac{e'}{e}\right)^4 = \frac{2.2 \text{ MeV}}{13.6 \text{ eV}} = \frac{2.2 \times 10^6}{13.6}$$

$$\left(\frac{e'}{e}\right)^4 = \frac{2.2 \times 10^6}{13.6 \times 918} = 176.21$$

$$\frac{e'}{e} = (176.21)^{1/4} = 3.64$$

Q.24 Before the neutrino hypothesis, the beta decay process was thought to be the transition.

$$n \to p + \bar{e}$$

If this was true, show that if the neutron was at rest, the proton and electron would emerge with fixed energies and calculate them. Experimentally, the electron energy was found to have a large range.

Ans. Before β-decay, neutron is at rest. Hence, $E_n = m_n c^2$, $p_n = 0$

$$\mathbf{p}_n = \mathbf{p}_p + \mathbf{p}_e$$

Or
$$\mathbf{p}_p + \mathbf{p}_e = 0 \Rightarrow |\mathbf{p}_p| = |\mathbf{p}_e| = \mathbf{p}$$

Also,
$$E_p = (m_p^2 c^4 + p_p^2 c^2)^{\frac{1}{2}}$$

$$E_e = (m_e^2 c^4 + p_e^2 c^2)^{\frac{1}{2}}$$

From conservation of energy,

$$(m_p^2 c^4 + p^2c^2)^{\frac{1}{2}} + (m_e^2 c^4 + p^2c^2)^{\frac{1}{2}} = m_n c^2$$

$$m_p c^2 \approx 936 \text{MeV}, \; m_n c^2 \approx 938 \text{MeV}, \; m_e c^2 = 0.51 \text{MeV}$$

Since, the energy difference between n and p is small, pc will be small, $pc \ll m_p c^2$, while pc may be greater than $m_e c^2$

$$\Rightarrow \quad m_p c^2 + \frac{p^2c^2}{2m_p^2 c^4} \simeq m_n c^2 - pc$$

To first order $\quad pc \simeq m_n c^2 - m_p c^2 = 938 \text{MeV} - 936 \text{MeV} = 2 \text{MeV}$

This gives the momentum of proton or neutron. Then,

$$E_p = (m_p^2 c^4 + p^2c^2)^{\frac{1}{2}} = \sqrt{936^2 + 2^2}$$
$$\simeq 936 \text{ MeV}$$
$$E_e = (m_e^2 c^4 + p^2c^2)^{\frac{1}{2}}$$
$$= \sqrt{(0.51)^2 + 2^2}$$
$$\simeq 2.06 \text{ MeV}$$

Mistake Alert ! *Incorrectly calculating the mass difference between the neutron and proton and not including the neutrino's contribution leading to wrong energy calculations.*

Q.25 The activity R of an unknown radioactive nuclide is measured at hourly intervals. The results found are tabulated as follows

t(h)	0	1	2	3	4
$R(MB_q)$	100	35.36	12.51	4.42	1.56

(i) Plot the graph of R *versus* t and calculate half-life from the graph.

(ii) Plot the graph of In $\left(\frac{R}{R_0}\right)$ *versus* t and obtain the value of half-life from the graph.

Thinking Process The problem is based on decay law and half-life.

Ans. (i) When we plot the graph of R versus t, we obtain an exponential curve as shown.

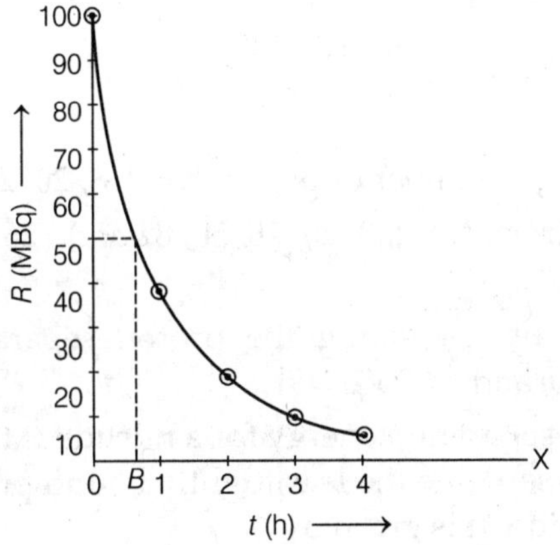

From the graph we can say that activity R reduces to 50% in $t = OB \approx 40$ min

So, $t_{1/2} \approx 40$ min.

(ii) In the table given below, we have listed values of $R(\text{MB}_q)$ and $\ln\left(\frac{R}{R_0}\right)$.

$t(h)$	0	1	2	3	4
$R(\text{MB}_q)$	100	35.36	12.51	4.42	1.56
$\frac{R}{R_0}$	—	−1.04	−2.08	−3.11	−4.16

The adjacent figure shows the graph of $\ln(R/R_0)$ *versus t*.

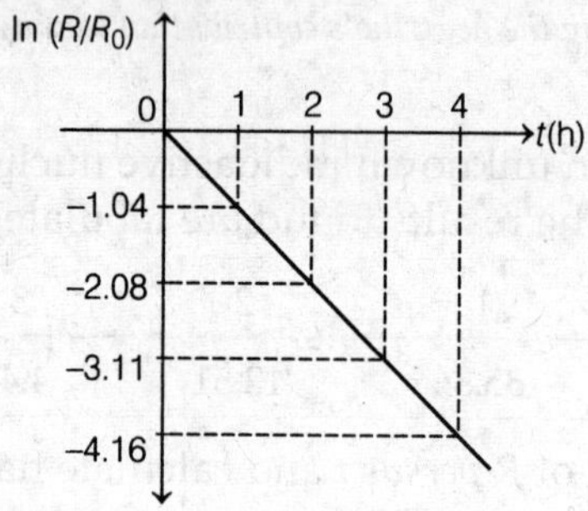

Slope of this graph $= -\lambda$

from the graph, $\quad \text{Slope} = -\left(\frac{-4.16-(-3.11)}{1}\right) = 1.05\text{h}^{-1}$

Half-life, $\quad T_{1/2} = \frac{0.693}{\lambda}$

$$= \frac{0.693}{1.05} = 0.66\text{ h}$$

$$= 39.6\text{ min}$$

$$\approx 40\text{ min}$$

Q.26 Nuclei with magic number of proton $Z = 2, 8, 20, 28, 50, 52$ and magic number of neutrons $N = 2, 8, 20, 28, 50, 82$ and 126 are found to be very stable.

(i) Verify this by caculating the proton separation energy S_p for $^{120}\text{Sn}(Z = 50)$ and $^{121}\text{Sb}(Z = 51)$.

The proton separation energy for a nuclide is the minimum energy required to separate the least tightly bound proton from a nucleus of that nuclide. It is given by

$$S_p = (M_{z-1,\ N} + M_{\text{H}} - M_{\text{Z, N}})c^2.$$

Given, $^{119}\text{In} = 118.9058\text{ u},$

$^{120}\text{Sn} = 199.902199\text{ u},$

$^{121}\text{Sb} = 120.903824\text{ u},$

$^{1}\text{H} = 1.0078252\text{ u}.$

(ii) What does the existence of magic number indicate?

Ans. (i) The proton separation energy is given by

$$S_{p\text{Sn}} = (M_{119.70} + M_H - M_{120,70})c^2$$
$$= (118.9058 + 1.0078252 - 119.902199)c^2$$
$$= 0.0114362c^2$$

Similarly

$$S_{p\text{Sp}} = (M_{120,70} + M_{\text{H}} - M_{121,70})c^2$$
$$= (119.902199 + 1.0078252 - 120.903822)c^2$$
$$= 0.0059912c^2$$

Since, $S_{p\text{Sn}} > S_{p\text{Sb}}$, Sn nucleus is more stable than Sb nucleus.

(ii) The existence of magic numbers indicates that the shell structure of nucleus is similar to the shell structure of an atom. This also explains the peaks in binding energy/nucleon curve.

Chapter 14

Semiconductor Electronics: Materials, Devices and Simple Circuits

Multiple Choice Questions (MCQs)

Q.1 The conductivity of a semiconductor increases with increase in temperature, because

(a) number density of free current carries increases
(b) relaxation time increases
(c) both number density of carries and relaxation time increase
(d) number density of carries increases, relaxation time decreases but effect of decrease in relaxation time is much less than increase in number density

Ans. ***(d)*** The conductivity of a semiconductor increases with increase in temperature, because the number density of current carries increases, relaxation time decreases but effect of decrease in relaxation is much less than increase in number density.

Q.2 In figure given below V_0 is the potential barrier across a *p-n* junction, when no battery is connected across the junction

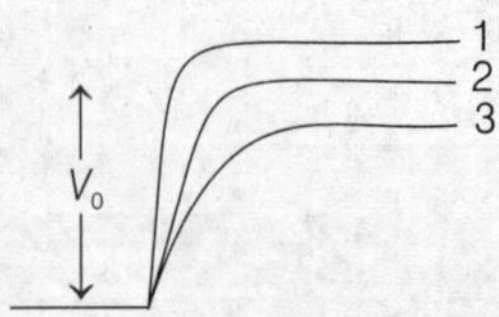

(a) 1 and 3 both correspond to forward bias of junction
(b) 3 corresponds to forward bias of junction and 1 corresponds to reverse bias of junction
(c) 1 corresponds to forward bias and 3 corresponds to reverse bias of junction
(d) 3 and 1 both correspond to reverse bias of junction

Thinking Process Go through the working of *p-n* junction.

Ans. ***(b)*** The height of the potential barrier is decreased when *p-n* junction is forward biased, it opposes the potential barrier junction. When *p-n* junction is reverse biased, it supports the potential barrier junction, resulting increase in potential barrier across the junction.

Thus, curve 3 corresponds to forward bias and curve 1 corresponds to reverse bias.

Q.3 In figure given below, assuming the diodes to be ideal

(a) D_1 is forward biased and D_2 is reverse biased and hence current flows from A to B.
(b) D_2 is forward biased and D_1 is reverse biased and hence no current flows from B to A and *vice-versa*.
(c) D_1 and D_2 are both forward biased and hence current flows from A to B.
(d) D_1 and D_2 are both reverse biased and hence no current flows from A to B and *vice-versa*.

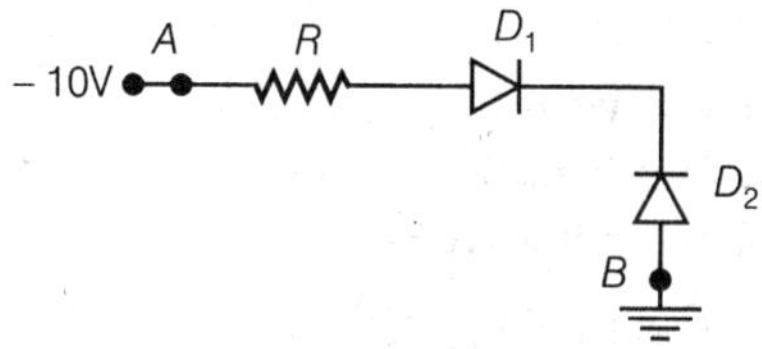

Thinking Process Check the polarity of the diodes.

Ans. ***(b)*** In the given circuit p-side of p-n function D_1 is connected to lower voltage and n-side of D_1 connected to higher voltage.

Thus D_1 is reverse biased.

The p -side of p-n junction D_2 is at higher potential and n-side of D_2 is at lower potential. Therefore D_2 is forward biased.

Hence, current flows through the junction B to A.

Q.4 A 220 V AC supply is connected between points A and B (figure). What will be the potential difference V across the capacitor?

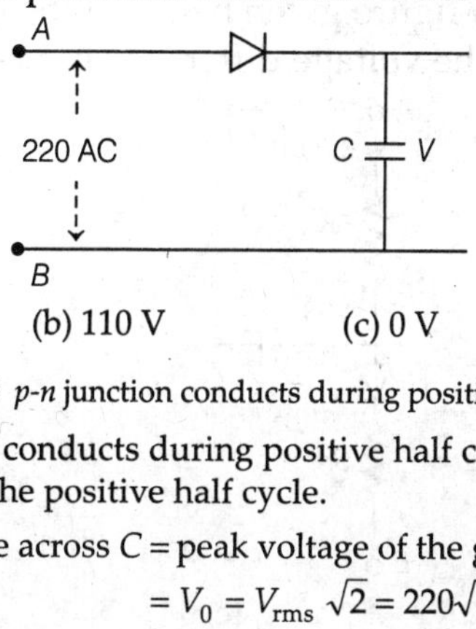

(a)220V (b) 110 V (c) 0 V (d) $220\sqrt{2}$V

Thinking Process p-n junction conducts during positive half cycle only.

Ans. ***(d)*** As p-n junction conducts during positive half cycle only, the diode connected here will work in the positive half cycle.

Potential difference across C = peak voltage of the given AC voltage

$$= V_0 = V_{rms}\sqrt{2} = 220\sqrt{2}\text{ V}.$$

Q.5 Hole is

(a) an anti-particle of electron
(b) a vacancy created when an electron leaves a covalent bond
(c) absence of free electrons
(d) an artificially created particle

Ans. ***(b)*** The concept of hole describes the lack of an electron at a position where one could exist in an atom or atomic lattice. If an electron is excited into a higher state, it leaves a hole in its old state.

Thus, hole can be defined as a vacancy created when an electron leaves a covalent bond.

Q.6 The output of the given circuit in figure given below,

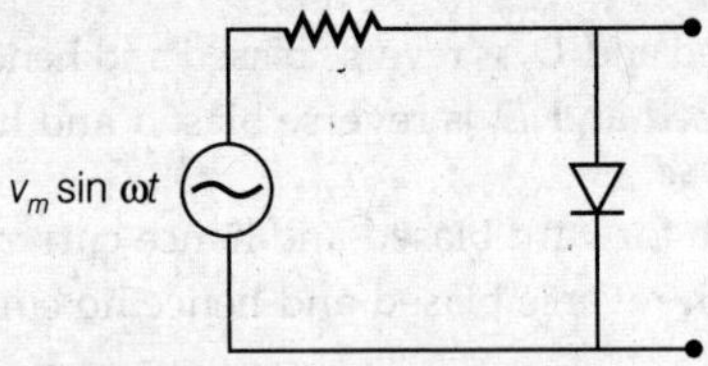

(a) would be zero at all times
(b) would be like a half wave rectifier with positive cycles in output
(c) would be like a half wave rectifier with negative cycles in output
(d) would be like that of a full wave rectifier

Thinking Process For positive half cycle of input AC voltage, the p-n junction is forward biased and for negative half cycle of input AC voltage the p-n junction is reversed biased.

Ans. ***(c)*** Due to forward biased during positive half cycle of input AC voltage, the resistance of *p-n* junction is low. The current in the circuit is maximum. In this situation, a maximum potential difference will appear across resistance connected in series of circuit. This result into zero output voltage across *p-n* junction.

Due to reverse biase during negative half cycle of AC voltage, the resistance of *p-n* junction becomes high which will be more than resistance in series. That is why, there will be voltage across *p-n* junction with negative cycle in output.

Q.7 In the circuit shown in figure given below, if the diode forward voltage drop is 0.3 V, the voltage difference between *A* and *B* is

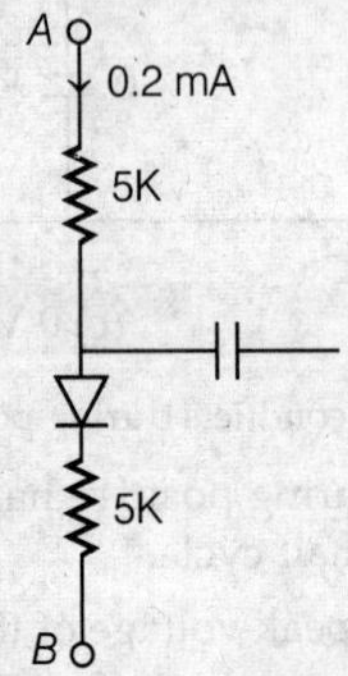

(a) 1.3 V (b) 2.3 V (c) 0 (d) 0.5 V

Ans. ***(b)*** Consider the given figure here, suppose the potential difference between *A* and *B* is *V*. $r_1 = 5\ \text{k}\Omega$ and $r_2 = 5\ \text{k}\Omega$ are resistance in series connection.

Then,
$$V - 0.3 = [(r_1 + r_2)\ 10^3] \times (0.2 \times 10^{-3})]$$
$$= [(5 + 5)\ 10^3] \times (0.2 \times 10^{-3})$$
$$= 10 \times 10^3 \times 0.2 \times 10^{-3} = 2$$
$$\Rightarrow \quad V = 2 + 0.3 = 2.3\ \text{V}$$

Multiple Choice Questions (More Than One Options)

***Q.8** Truth table for the given circuit is

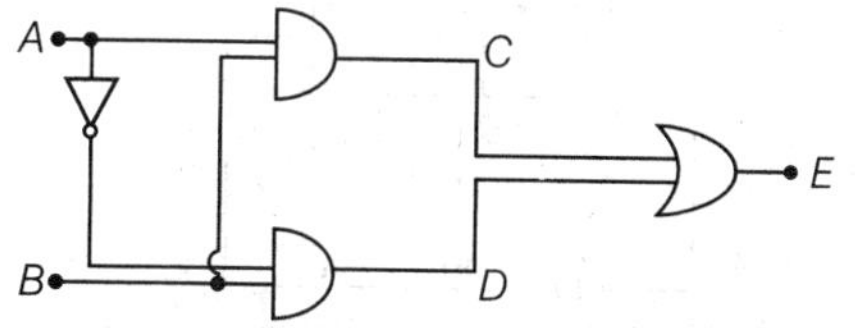

(a)

A	B	E
0	0	1
0	1	0
1	0	1
1	1	0

(b)

A	B	E
0	0	1
0	1	0
1	0	0
1	1	0

(c)

A	B	E
0	0	0
0	1	1
1	0	0
1	1	1

(d)

A	B	E
0	0	0
0	1	1
1	0	1
1	1	0

Ans. ***(c)*** Here, $C = A.B$ and $D = \overline{A}.B$

$$E = C + D = (A.B) + (\overline{A}.B)$$

The truth table of this arrangement of gates can be given by

A	B	$\overline{A}$	$C = A.B$	$d = \overline{A}.B$	$E = (C + D)$
0	0	1	0	0	0
0	1	1	0	1	1
1	0	0	0	0	0
1	1	0	1	0	1

Q.9 When an electric field is applied across a semiconductor

(a) electrons move from lower energy level to higher energy level in the conduction band

(b) electrons move from higher energy level to lower energy level in the conduction band

(c) holes in the valence band move from higher energy level to lower energy level

(d) holes in the valence band move from lower energy level to higher energy level

Thinking Process Electrons are negatively charged and its energy increases when electric fields is applied.

Ans. ***(a, c)*** When electric field is applied across a semiconductor, the electrons in the conduction band get accelerated and acquire energy. They move from lower energy level to higher energy level. While the holes in valence band move from higher energy level to lower energy level, where they will be having more energy.

Q.10 Consider an *n-p-n* transitor with its base-emitter junction forward biased and collector base junction reverse biased. Which of the following statements are true?

(a) Electrons crossover from emitter to collector

(b) Holes move from base to collector

(c) Electron's move from emitter to base

(d) Electrons from emitter move out of base without going to the collector.

Note (✱) Topics related to these question have been removed from latest NCERT.

Thinking Process Draw the figure as given in the question.

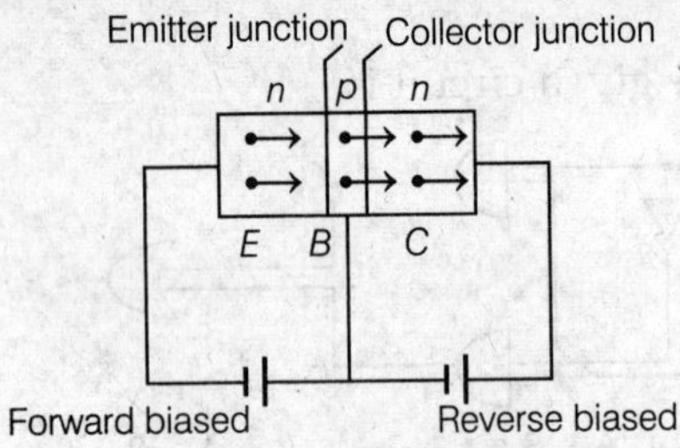

Ans. ***(a, c)*** Here emitter-base junction is forward biased *i.e.*, the positive pole of emitter base battery is connected to base and its negative pole to emitter. Also, the collector base junction is reverse biased, *i.e.*, the positive pole of the collector base battery is connected to collector and negative pole to base.

Thus, electron move from emmiter to base and crossover from emitter to collector.

****Q.11** Figure given below shows that transfer characteristics of a base biased *CE* transistor. Which of the following statements are true?

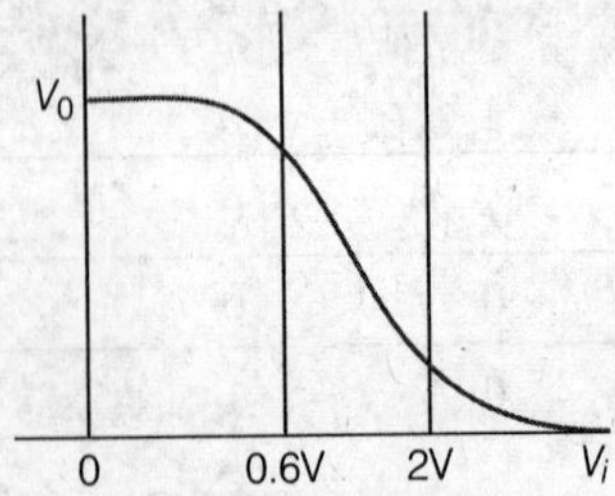

(a) At $V_i = 0.4$ V, transistor is in active state

(b) At $V_i = 1$ V, it can be used as an amplifier

(c) At $V_i = 0.5$ V, it can be used as a switch turned off

(d) At $V_i = 2.5$ V, can be used as a switch turned on

Ans. ***(b, c, d)*** From the given transfer characteristics of a base biased common emitter transistor, we note that

(i) when $V_i = 0.4$ V, there is no collection current. The transistor circuit is in activ state and is used as an amplifier.

(ii) when $V_i = 1$V (This is in between 0.6V to 2V), the transistor circuit is in activ state and is used as an amplifier.

(iii) when $V_i = 0.5$ V, there is no collector current. The transistor is in cut off stat The transistor circuit can be used as a switch turned off.

(iv) when $V_i = 2.5$ V, the collector current becomes maximum and transistor is i saturation state and can used as switch turned on state.

****Q.12*** In a *n-p-n* transistor circuit, the collector current is 10 mA. If 95 per cen of the electrons emitted reach the collector, which of the following statements are true?

(a) The emitter current will be 8 mA

(b) The emitter current will be 10.53 m

(c) The base current will be 0.53 mA

(d) The base current will be 2 mA

Note (✱) Topics related to these question have been removed from latest NCERT.

Thinking Process The collector current is the 95% of electrons reaching the collector after emission.

Ans. *(b, c)* Here, $I_c = 10 \text{ mA},$

Also, $I_c = \dfrac{95}{100} I_e$

$\Rightarrow$ $I_e = \dfrac{10 \times 100}{95} = 10.53 \text{ mA}$

Also, $I_b = I_e - I_c = 10.53 - 10 = 0.53 \text{ mA}$

Q.13 In the depletion region of a diode

(a) there are no mobile charges
(b) equal number of holes and elections exist, making the region neutral
(c) recombination of holes and electrons has taken place
(d) immobile charged ions exist

Ans. *(a, b, d)* The space-charge regions on both the sides of *p-n* junction which has immobile ions and entirely lacking of any charge carriers will form a region called depletion region of a diode. The number of ionized acceptors on the *p*-side equals the number of ionized donors on the *n*-side.

Q.14 What happens during regulation action of a Zener diode?

(a) The current and voltage across the Zener remains fixed
(b) The current through the series Resistance (R_s) changes
(c) The Zener resistance is constant
(d) The resistance offered by the Zener changes

Ans. *(b, d)* During regulation action of a Zener diode, the current through the R_s changes and resistance offered by the Zener changes. The current through the Zener changes but the voltage across the Zener remains constant.

Q.15 To reduce the ripples in rectifier circuit with capacitor filter

(a) R_L should be increased
(b) input frequency should be decreased
(c) input frequency should be increased
(d) capacitors with high capacitance should be used

Ans. *(a, c, d)* Ripple factor (r) is inversely proportional to R_L, C and ν.

Thus to reduce r, R_L should be increased, input frequency ν should be increased and capacitance C should be increased.

Q.16 The breakdown in a reverse biased *p-n* junction is more likely to occur due to

(a) large velocity of the minority charge carriers if the doping concentration is small
(b) large velocity of the minority charge carriers if the doping concentration is large
(c) strong electric field in a depletion region if the doping concentration is small
(d) strong electric field in the depletion region if the doping concentration is large

Ans. *(a, d)* In reverse biasing, the minority charge carriers will be accelerated due to reverse biasing, which on striking with atoms cause ionization resulting secondary electrons and thus more number of charge carriers. When doping concentration is large, there will be large number of ions in the depletion region, which will give rise to a strong electric field.

Very Short Answer Type Questions

Q.17 Why are elemental dopants for Silicon or Germanium usually chosen from group XIII or group XV?

Ans. The size of the dopant atom should be such that their presence in the pure semiconductor does not distort the semiconductor but easily contribute the charge carriers on forming covalent bonds with Si or Ge atoms, which are provided by group XIII or group XV elements.

Q.18 Sn, C, Si and Ge are all group XIV elements. Yet, Sn is a conductor, C is an insulator while Si and Ge are semiconductors. Why?

Thinking Process The property of conduction level of any element depends on the energy gap between its conduction band and valence band.

Ans. A material is a conductor if in its energy band diagram, there is no energy gap between conduction band and valence band. For insulator, the energy gap is large and for semiconductor the energy gap is moderate.

The energy gap for Sn is 0 eV, for C is 5.4 eV, for Si is 1.1 eV and for Ge is 0.7 eV, related to their atomic size. Therefore Sn is a conductor, C is an insulator and Ge and Si are semiconductors.

Q.19 Can the potential barrier across a *p-n* junction be measured by simply connecting a voltmeter across the junction?

Ans. We cannot measure the potential barrier across a *p-n* junction by a voltmeter because the resistance of voltmeter is very high as compared to the junction resistance.

Q.20 Draw the output waveform across the resistor in the given figure.

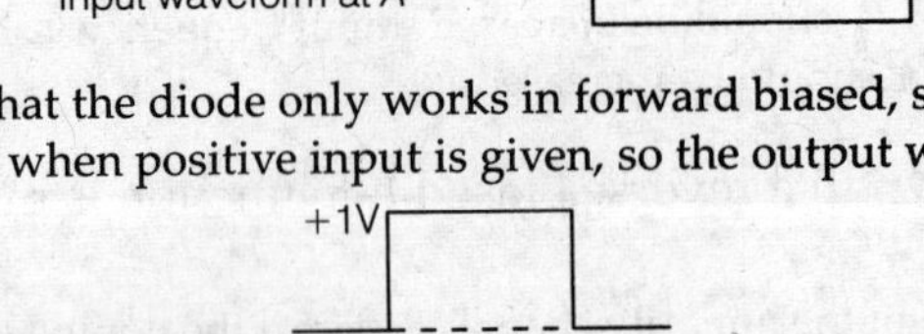

Input waveform at *A*

Ans. As we know that the diode only works in forward biased, so the output is obtained only when positive input is given, so the output waveform is

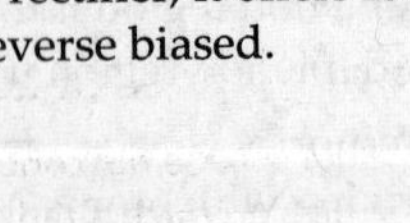

The diode acts as half wave rectifier, it offers low resistance when forward biased and high resistance when reverse biased.

Q.21 The amplifiers X, Y and Z are connected in series. If the voltage gains of X, Y and Z are 10, 20 and 30, respectively and the input signal is 1 mV peak value, then what is the output signal voltage (peak value)

(i) if DC supply voltage is 10 V?

(ii) if DC supply voltage is 5 V?

Thinking Process $\frac{\text{Output signal voltage}}{\text{Input signal voltage}} = \text{Total voltage amplification}$

Ans. Given, $Av_x = 10,$

$Av_y = 20,$

$Av_z = 30;$

$$\Delta V_i = 1\,\text{mV} = 10^{-3}\,\text{V}$$

Now, $$\frac{\text{Output Signal Voltage }(\Delta V_0)}{\text{Input Signal Voltage }(\Delta V_i)} = \text{Total voltage amplification}$$

$$= Av_x \times Av_y \times Av_z$$

$$\Rightarrow \quad \Delta V_0 = Av_x \times Av_y \times Av_z \times \Delta V_i$$

$$= 10 \times 20 \times 30 \times 10^{-3}$$

$$= 6\text{ V}$$

(i) If DC supply voltage is 10 V, then output is 6 V, since theoretical gain is equal to practical gain, *i.e.*, output can never be greater than 6 V.

(ii) If DC supply voltage is 5 V, *i.e.*, $V_{cc} = 5$ V. Then, output peak will not exceed 5 V.

Hence $V_0 = 5$ V.

Mistake Alert ! *Students sometimes uses the formula for total voltage amplification as* $Av_x + Av_y + Av_z$, *which is incorrect.*

The correct formula would be

$$Av_x + Ax_y + Ay_z.$$

***Q.22** In a CE transistor amplifier, there is a current and voltage gain associated with the circuit. In other words there is a power gain. Considering power a measure of energy, does the circuit violate conservation of energy?

Ans. In CE transistor amplifier, the power gain is very high. In this circuit, the extra power required for amplified output is obtained from DC source. Thus, the circuit used does not violet the law of conservation.

Note (*****) Topics related to these question have been removed from latest NCERT.

Short Answer Type Questions

Q.23 (i) Name the type of a diode whose characteristics are shown in figure. (a) and (b).

(ii) What does the point P in fig. (a) represent?

(iii) What does the points P and Q in fig. (b) represent?

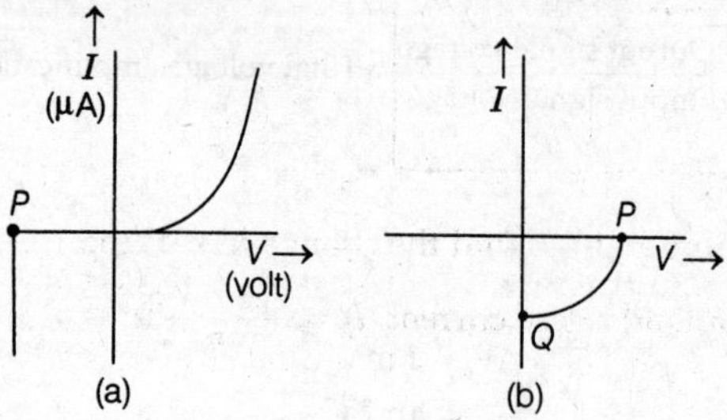

Ans. (i) The characteristic curve (a) is of Zener diode and curve (b) is of solar cell.

(ii) The point P in fig. (a) represents Zener break down voltage.

(iii) In fig. (b), the point Q represents zero voltage and negative current. It means light falling on solar cell with atleast minimum threshold frequency gives the current in opposite direction to that due to a battery connected to solar cell. But for the point Q, the battery is short circuited. Hence represents the short circuit current.

In fig. (b), the point P represents some positive voltage on solar cell with zero current through solar cell.

It means, there is a battery connected to a solar cell which gives rise to the equal and opposite current to that in solar cell by virtue of light falling on it.

As current is zero for point P, hence we say P represents open circuit voltage.

Q.24 Three photo diodes D_1, D_2 and D_3 are made of semiconductors having band gaps of 2.5eV, 2eV and 3eV, respectively. Which ones will be able to detect light of wavelength 6000 Å?

Ans. Given, wavelength of light $\lambda = 6000\,Å = 6000 \times 10^{-10}$ m

Energy of the light photon

$$E = \frac{hc}{\lambda} = \frac{6.6 \times 10^{-34} \times 3 \times 10^{8}}{6000 \times 10^{-10} \times 1.6 \times 10^{-19}} \text{ eV} = 2.07 \text{ eV}$$

The incident radiation which is detected by the photodiode having energy should be greater than the band-gap. So, it is only valid for diode D_2. Then, diode D_2 will detect this radiation.

Mistake Alert ! *Make sure to convert Å to meters correctly (6000 Å = 6000×10^{-10} m).*

Q.25 If the resistance R_1 is increased (see figure), how will the readings of the ammeter and voltmeter change?

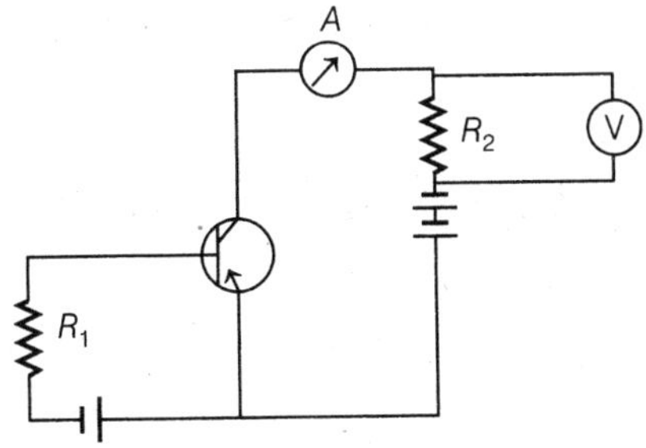

Ans. Consider the circuit in fig. (b) to find the change in reading.

As we know the formula for base current, $I_B = \dfrac{V_{BB} - V_{BE}}{R_1}$

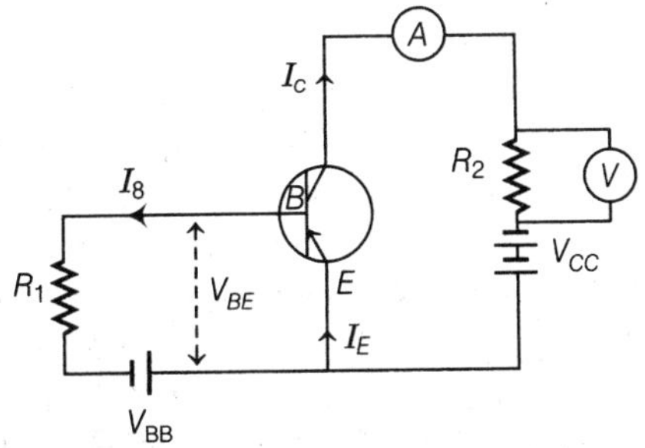

As R_1 is increased, I_B is decreased.

Now, the current in ammeter is collector current I_C.

$I_C = \beta I_B$ as I_B decreased I_C also decreased and the reading of voltmeter and ammeter also decreased.

***Q.26** Two car garages have a common gate which needs to open automatically when a car enters either of the garages or cars enter both. Devise a circuit that resembles this situation using diodes for this situation.

Ans. As car enters in the gate, any one or both are opened.

The device is shown.

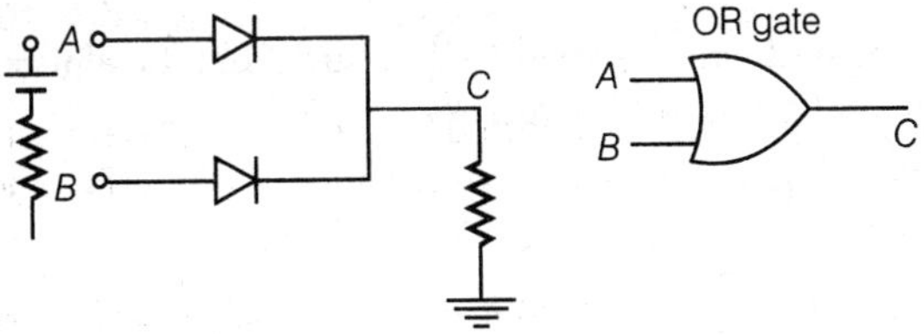

Note (✱) Topics related to these question have been removed from latest NCERT.

So, OR gate gives the desired output.

A	*B*	*C*
0	0	0
0	1	1
1	0	1
1	1	1

***Q.27** How would you set up a circuit to obtain NOT gate using a transistor?

Ans. The NOT gate is a device which has only one input and one output *i.e.*, $\overline{A} = Y$ means Y equals NOT *A*. This gate cannot be realised by using diodes. However it can be realised by making use of a transistor. *This can be seen in the figure given below*

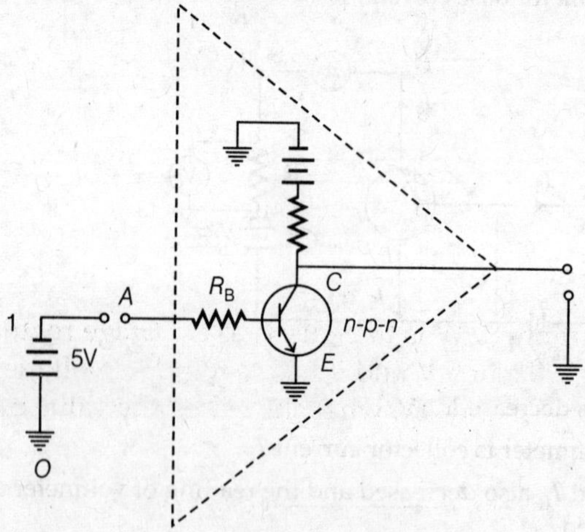

A	Y
0	1
1	0

Here, the base *B* of the transistor is connected to the input *A* through a resistance R_b and the emitter *E* is earthed. The collector is connected to 5 V battery. The output *Y* is the voltage at *C* w.r.t. earth. The resistor R_b and R_c are so chosen that if emitter-base junction is unbiased, the transistor is in cut off mode and if emitter-base junction is forward biased by 5V, the transistor is in saturation state.

Q.28 Explain why elemental semiconductor cannot be used to make visible LEDs.

Ans. In elemental semiconductor, the band gap is such that the emission are in infrared region and not in visible region.

$$\lambda = \frac{hc}{E_g} = \frac{1242}{E_g} \text{ eVnm}$$

For Si ; $E_g = 1.1$ eV, $\lambda = \frac{1242}{1.1} = 1129$ nm

For Ge ; $E_g = 0.72$ eV, $\lambda = \frac{1242}{0.72} = 1725$ nm

Note (✱) Topics related to these question have been removed from latest NCERT.

***Q.29** Write the truth table for the circuit shown in figure given below.

Name the gate that the circuit resembles.

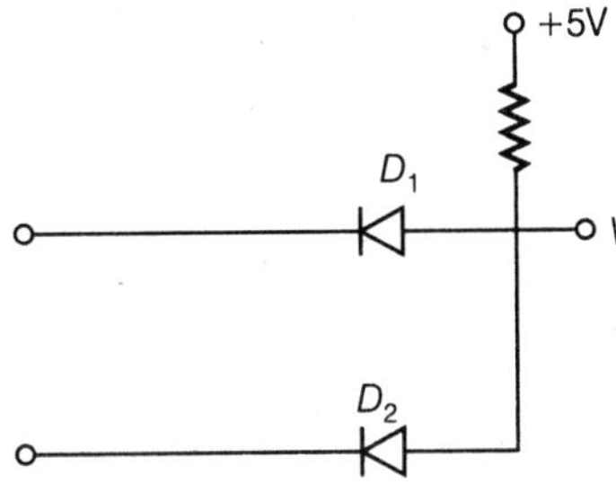

Ans. The circuit resemble AND gate. The boolean expression of this circuit is, $V_0 = A.B$ *i.e.*, V_0 equals A AND B. *The truth table of this gate is as given below*

A	B	$V_0 = A \cdot B$
0	0	0
0	1	0
1	0	0
1	1	1

***Q.30** A Zener of power rating 1 W is to be used as a voltage regulator. If Zener has a breakdown of 5 V and it has to regulate voltage which fluctuated between 3 V and 7 V, what should be the value of R_s for safe operation (see figure)?

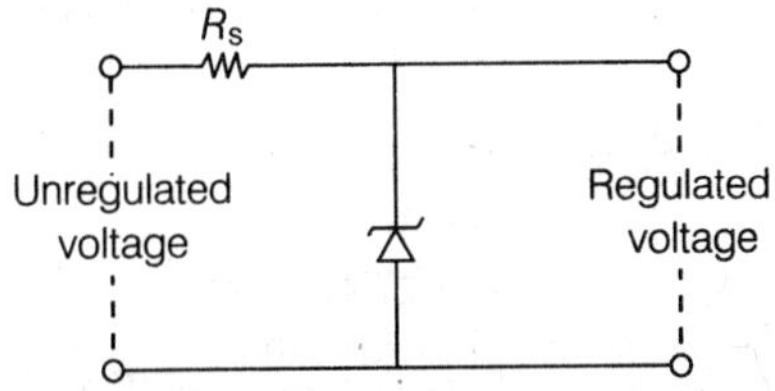

Ans. Given,

$$\text{power} = 1\,\text{W}$$
$$\text{Zener breakdown } V_z = 5\,\text{V}$$
$$\text{Minimum voltage } V_{min} = 3\,\text{V}$$
$$\text{Maximum voltage } V_{max} = 7\,\text{V}$$
$$\text{Current } I_{Z_{max}} = \frac{P}{V_Z} = \frac{1}{5} = 0.2\text{ A}$$

The value of R_s for safe operation $R_s = \dfrac{V_{max} - V_Z}{I_{Z_{max}}} = \dfrac{7-5}{0.2} = \dfrac{2}{0.2} = 10\,\Omega$

Note (✱) Topics related to these question have been removed from latest NCERT.

Long Answer Type Questions

Q.31 If each diode in figure has a forward bias resistance of 25 Ω and infinite resistance in reverse bias, what will be the values of the currents I_1, I_2, I_3 and I_4?

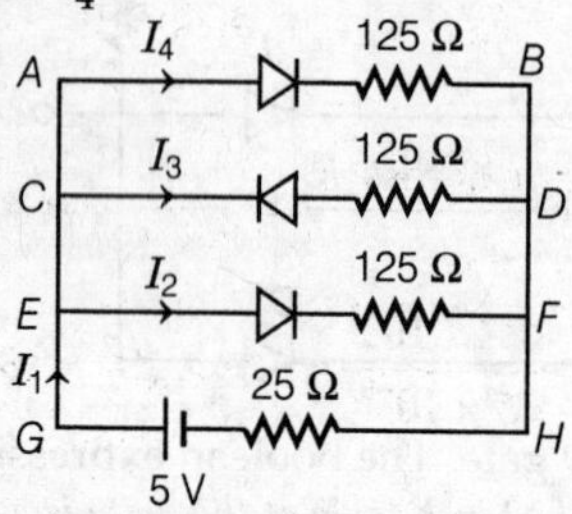

Ans. Given, Forward biased resistance = 25 Ω

Reverse biased resistance = ∞

As the diode in branch *CD* is in reverse biased which having resistance infinite, so

$$I_3 = 0$$

Resistance in branch $AB = 25 + 125 = 150\ \Omega$ say R_1

Resistance in branch $EF = 25 + 125 = 150\ \Omega$ say R_2

AB is parallel to *EF*.

So, Resultant resistance, $\frac{1}{R'} = \frac{1}{R_1} + \frac{1}{R_2} = \frac{1}{150} + \frac{1}{150} = \frac{2}{150}$

$\Rightarrow$ $R' = 75\ \Omega$

Total resistance, $R = R' + 25 = 75 + 25 = 100\ \Omega$

Current, $I_1 = \frac{V}{R} = \frac{5}{100} = 0.05$ A

$I_1 = I_2 + I_3 + I_4$ (Here $I_3 = 0$)

So, $I_1 = I_2 + I_4$

Here, the resistances R_1 and R_2 is same.

i.e., $I_4 = I_2$ $[\because I_2 = I_4]$

$\therefore$ $I_1 = 2I_2$

$\Rightarrow$ $I_2 = \frac{I_1}{2} = \frac{0.05}{2} = 0.025$ A and $I_4 = 0.025$ A

Thus, $I_1 = 0.05$ A, $I_2 = 0.025$ A, $I_3 = 0$ and $I_4 = 0.025$ A

***Q.32** In the circuit shown in figure, when the input voltage of the base resistance is 10 V, V_{BE} is zero and V_{CE} is also zero. Find the values of I_B, I_C and β.

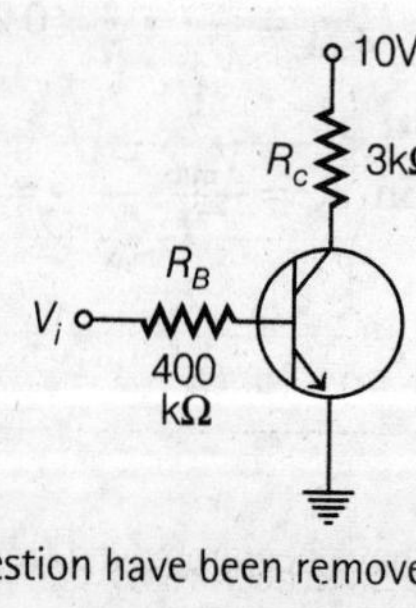

Note (✱) Topics related to these question have been removed from latest NCERT.

Ans. Given, Voltage across $R_B = 10\text{ V}$

Resistance $R_B = 400\text{ k}\Omega$

$$V_{BE} = 0,\ V_{CE} = 0\ \ R_C = 3\text{ k}\Omega$$

$$I_B = \frac{\text{Voltage across } R_B}{R_B} = \frac{10}{400 \times 10^3} = 25 \times 10^{-6}\text{ A} = 25\,\mu\text{A}$$

Voltage across $R_C = 10\text{ V}$

$$I_C = \frac{\text{Voltage across } R_C}{R_C} = \frac{10}{3 \times 10^3} = 3.33 \times 10^{-3}\text{ A} = 3.33\text{ mA}$$

$$\beta = \frac{I_C}{I_B} = \frac{3.33 \times 10^{-3}}{25 \times 10^{-6}} = 1.33 \times 10^2 = 133$$

***Q.33** Draw the output signals C_1 and C_2 in the given combination of gates.

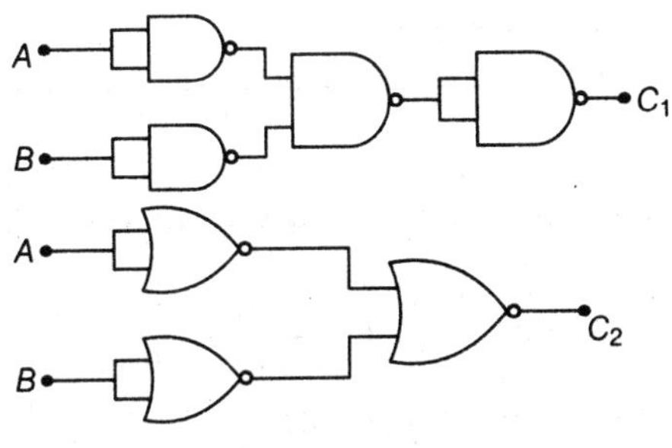

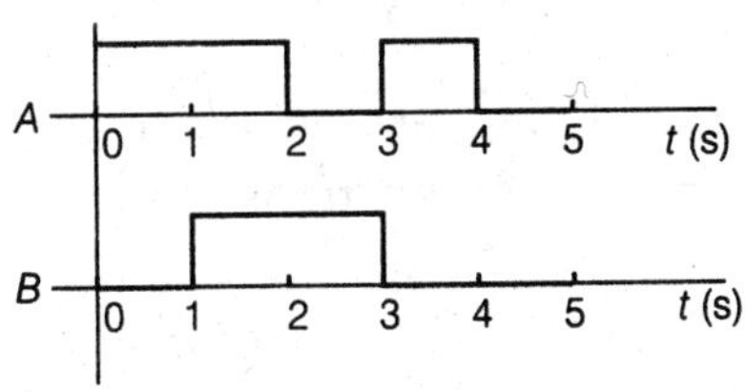

Ans. First draw the truth table of C_1 and C_2.

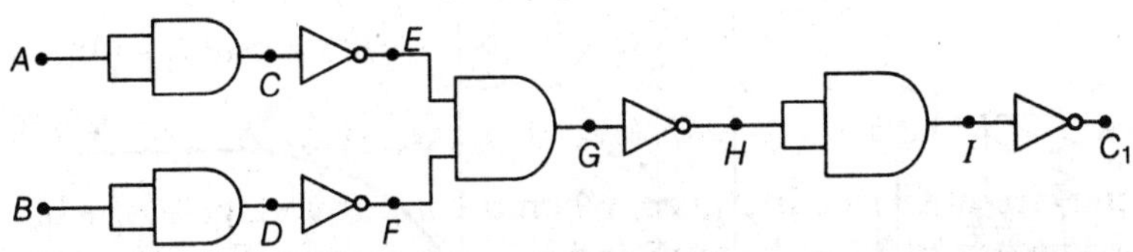

A	B	C	D	E	F	G	H	I	C_1
0	0	0	0	1	1	1	0	0	1
1	0	1	0	0	1	0	1	1	0
0	1	0	1	1	0	0	1	1	0
1	1	1	1	0	0	0	1	1	0

Note (*) Topics related to these question have been removed from latest NCERT.

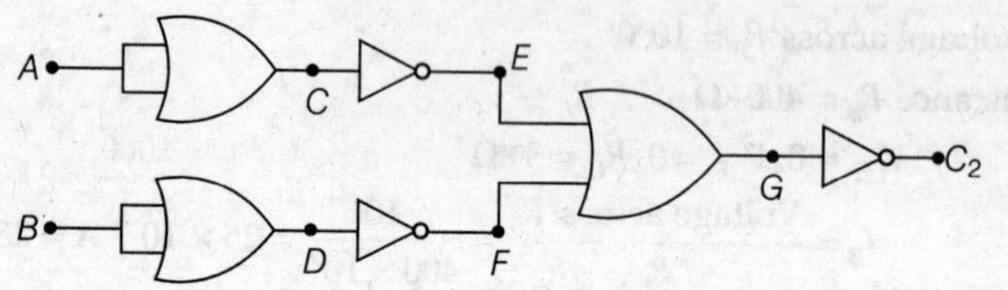

A	B	C	D	E	F	G	C_1
0	0	0	0	1	1	1	1
1	0	1	0	0	1	1	0
0	1	0	1	1	0	1	0
1	1	1	1	0	0	0	0

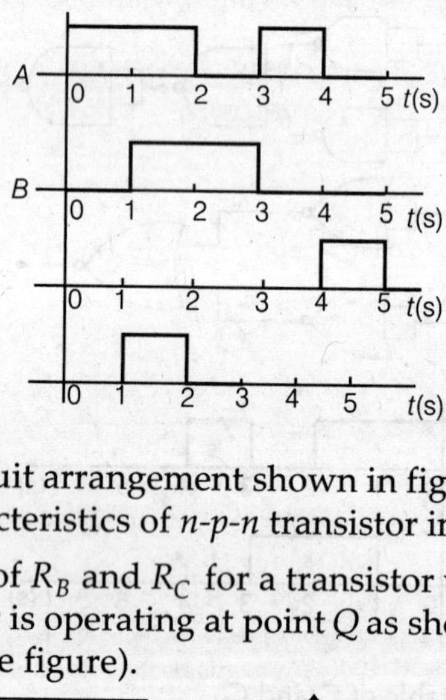

***Q.34** Consider the circuit arrangement shown in figure for studying input and output characteristics of *n-p-n* transistor in CE configuration.

Select the values of R_B and R_C for a transistor whose $V_{BE} = 0.7$ V, so that the transistor is operating at point Q as shown in the characteristics (see figure).

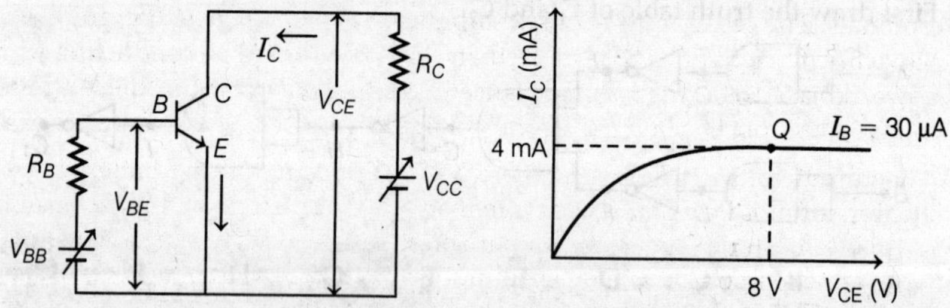

Given that the input impedance of the transistor is very small and $V_{CC} = V_{BB} = 16$ V, also find the voltage gain and power gain of circuit making appropriate assumptions.

Ans. Given,
$$V_{BE} = 0.7 \text{ V}, V_{CC} = V_{BB} = 16 \text{ V}$$
$$V_{CE} = 8 \text{ V} \quad \text{(from graph)}$$
$$I_C = 4 \text{ mA} = 4 \times 10^{-3} \text{ A}, I_B = 30 \, \mu\text{A} = 30 \times 10^{-6} \text{ A}$$

Note (✱) Topics related to these question have been removed from latest NCERT.

For the output characteristic at θ,

$$V_{CC} = I_C R_C + V_{CE}$$

$$R_C = \frac{V_{CC} - V_{CE}}{I_C} = \frac{16 - 8}{4 \times 10^{-3}} = \frac{8 \times 1000}{4} = 2\,\text{k}\Omega$$

Using the relation,

$$V_{BB} = I_B R_B + V_{BE}$$

$$R_B = \frac{V_{BB} - V_{BE}}{I_B} = \frac{16 - 0.7}{30 \times 10^{-6}} = 510 \times 10^3\ \Omega = 510\,\text{k}\Omega$$

$$\beta = \frac{I_C}{I_B} = \frac{4 \times 10^{-3}}{30 \times 10^{-6}} = 133$$

$$\text{Voltage gain} = \beta\,\frac{R_C}{R_B} = \frac{133 \times 2 \times 10^3}{510 \times 10^3} = 0.52$$

$$\text{Power gain} = \beta \times \text{Voltage gain} = 133 \times 0.52 = 69$$

Q.35 Assuming the ideal diode, draw the output waveform for the circuit given in fig., explain the waveform.

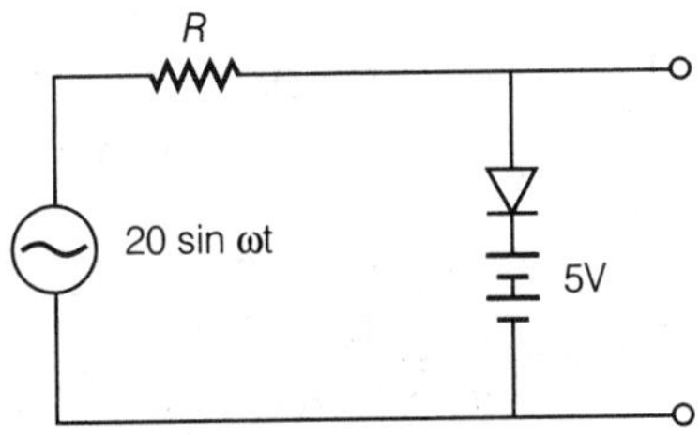

Thinking Process An ideal diode is a diode that acts like a perfect conductor when voltage is applied forward biased and like a perfect insulator when voltage is applied reverse biased.

Ans. When the input voltage is equal to or less than 5 V, diode will be reverse biased. It will offer high resistance in comparison to resistance (R) in series. Now, diode appears in open circuit. The input waveform is then passed to the output terminals. The result with sin wave input is to dip off all positive going portion above 5 V. If input voltage is more than + 5 V, diode will be conducting as if forward biased offering low resistance in comparison to R. But there will be no voltage in output beyond 5 V as the voltage beyond + 5 V will appear across R.

When input voltage is negative, there will be opposition to 5 V battery in p-n junction input voltage becomes more than – 5 V, the diode will be reverse biased. It will offer high resistance in comparison to resistance R in series. Now junction diode appears in open circuit. The input wave form is then passed on to the output terminals. The output waveform is shown here in the fig.

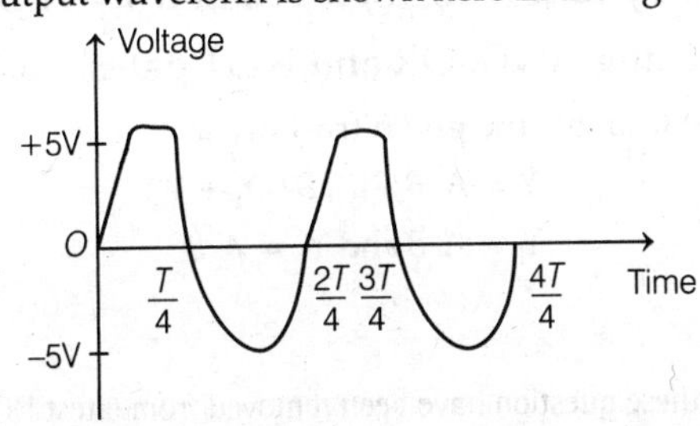

Q.36 Suppose a n-type wafer is created by doping Si crystal having 5×10^{28} atoms/m^3 with 1 ppm concentration of As. On the surface 200 ppm boron is added to create 'p' region in this wafer. Considering $n_i = 1.5 \times 10^{16}\ \text{m}^{-3}$, (i) Calculate the densities of the charge carriers in the n and p regions. (ii) Comment which charge carriers would contribute largely for the reverse saturation current when diode is reverse biased.

Ans. When As is implanted in Si crystal, n - type wafer is created. The number of majority carriers electrons due to doping of As is

$$n_e = N_D = \frac{1}{10^6} \times 5 \times 10^{28}$$

$$= 5 \times 10^{22} / \text{m}^3$$

Number of minority charge carriers (holes) in n-type wafer is

$$n_h = \frac{n_i^2}{n_e} = \frac{(1.5 \times 10^{16})^2}{5 \times 10^{22}}$$

$$= 0.45 \times 10^{10} / \text{m}^3$$

When B is implanted in Si crystal, p-type wafer is created with number of holes,

$$n_h = N_A = \frac{200}{10^6} \times (5 \times 10^{28}) = 1 \times 10^{25} / \text{m}^3$$

Minority carriers (electrons) created in p - type wafer is

$$n_e = \frac{n_i^2}{n_h} = \frac{(1.5 \times 10^{16})^2}{1 \times 10^{25}}$$

$$= 2.25 \times 10^7 / \text{m}^3$$

When p-n junction is reverse biased, the minority carrier holes of n-region wafer ($n_h = 0.45 \times 10^{10} / \text{m}^3$) would contribute more to the reverse saturation current than minority carrier electrons ($n_e = 2.25 \times 10^7 / \text{m}^3$) of p region wafer.

***Q.37** An X-OR gate has following truth table.

A	B	Y
0	0	0
0	1	1
1	0	1
1	1	0

It is represented by following logic relation $Y = \overline{A}.B + A.\overline{B}$

Build this gate using AND, OR and NOT gates.

Ans. Given, the logic relation for the given truth table is

$$Y = \overline{A}.B + A.\overline{B} = Y_1 + Y_2$$

when $\quad Y_1 = A.B$ and $Y_2 = A.\overline{B}$

Note (✱) Topics related to these question have been removed from latest NCERT.

Y_1 can be obtained as output of AND gate I for which one Input is of A through NOT gate and another input is of B. Y_2 can be obtained as output of AND gate II for which one input is of A and other input is of B through NOT gate.

Now, Y_2 can be obtained as output from OR gate, where, Y_1 and Y_2 are input of OR gate. *Thus, the given table can be obtained from the logic circuit given below.*

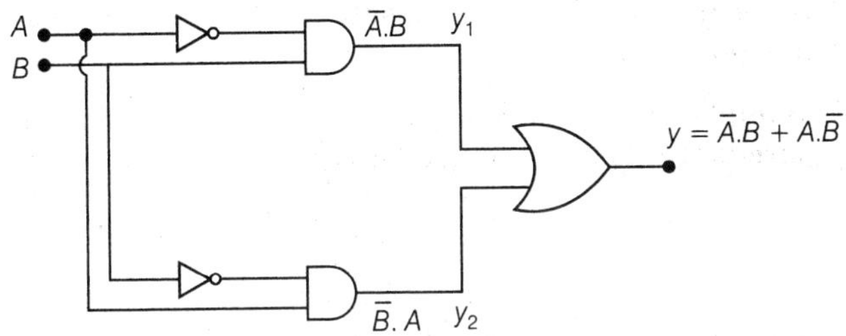

Q.38 Consider a box with three terminals on top of it as shown in figure (a).

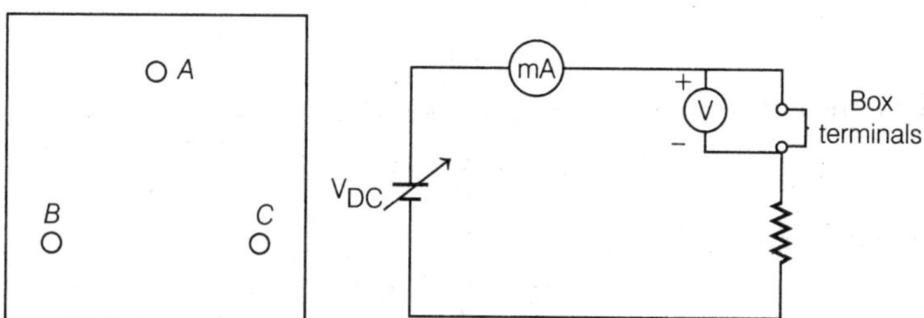

(a) (b)

Three components namely, two germanium diodes and one resistor are connected across these three terminals in some arrangement.

A student performs an experiment in which any two of these three terminals are connected in the circuit shown in figure (b).

The student obtains graphs of current-voltage characteristics for unknown combination of components between the two terminals connected in the circuit. The graphs are

(i) when A is positive and B is negative

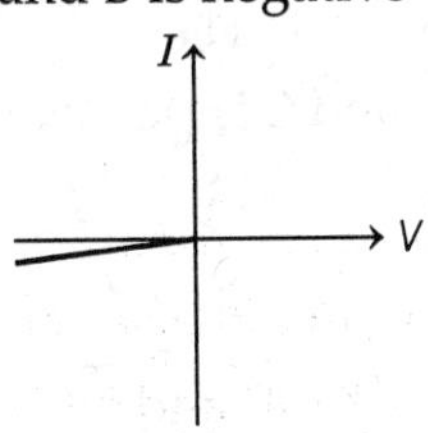

(c)

(ii) when A is negative and B is positive

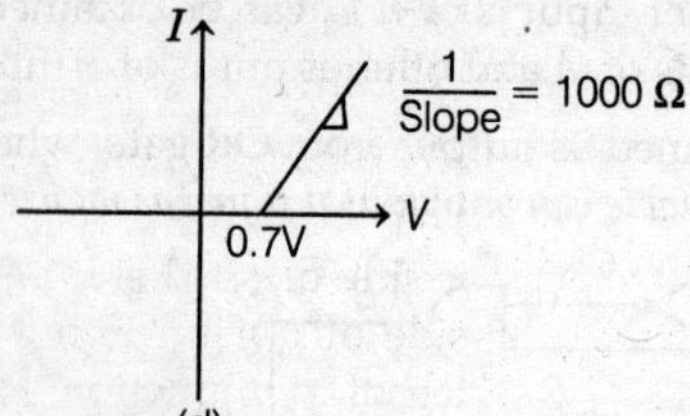

(d)

(iii) when B is negative and C is positive

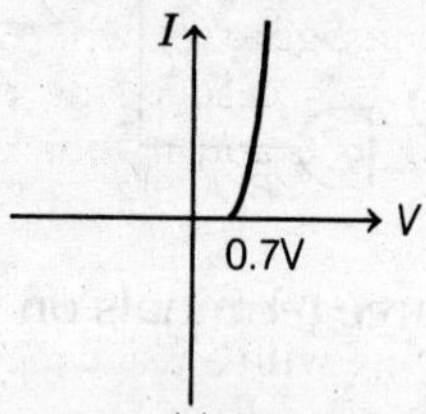

(e)

(iv) when B is positive and C is negative

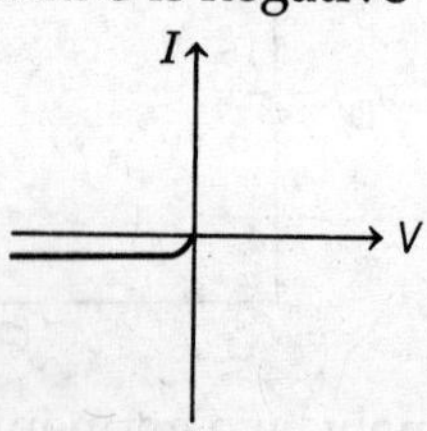

(f)

(v) when A is positive and C is negative

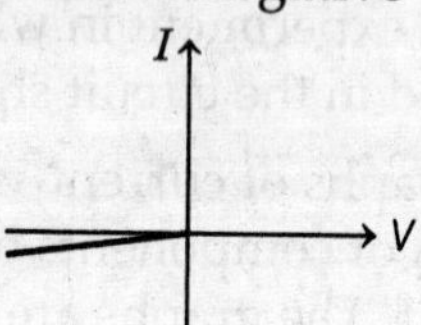

(g)

(vi) when A is negative and C is positive

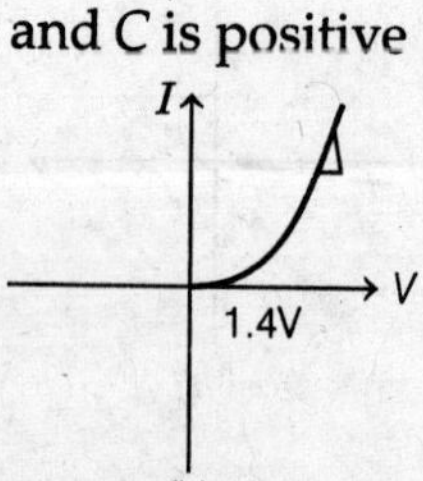

(h)

From these graphs of current - voltage characteristic shown in fig. (c) to (h) determine the arrangement of components between A, B, and C.

Note (✱) Topics related to these question have been removed from latest NCERT.

Ans. (a) In *V-I* graph of condition (i), a reverse characteristics is shown in fig. (c). Here A is connected to n- side of p-n junction I and B is connected to p-side of p-n junction I with a resistance in series.

(b) In *V-I* graph of condition (ii), a forward characteristics is shown in fig. (d), where 0.7 V is the knee voltage of p-n junction I 1/slope = (1/1000) Ω.

It means A is connected to n-side of p-n junction I and B is connected to p-side of p-n junction I and resistance R is in series of p-n junction I between A and B.

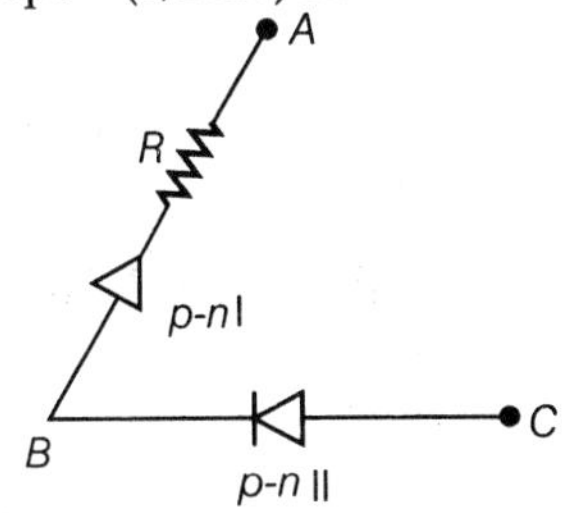

(c) In *V-I* graph of condition (iii), a forward characteristics is shown in figure (e), where 0.7 V is the knee voltage. In this case p-side of p-n junction II is connected to C and n-side of p-n junction II to B.

(d) In *V-I* graphs of conditions (iv), (v), (vi) also concludes the above connection of p-n junctions I and II along with a resistance R.

Thus, the arrangement of p-n I, p-n II and resistance R between A, B and C will be as shown in the figure.

***Q.39** For the transistor circuit shown in figure, evaluate V_E, R_B, R_E, given $I_C = 1$ mA, $V_{CE} = 3$ V, $V_{BE} = 0.5$ V and $V_{CC} = 12$ V, $\beta = 100$.

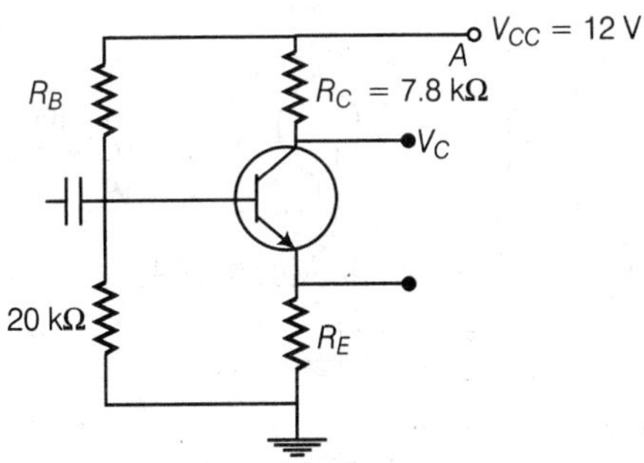

Ans. Consider the figure given below

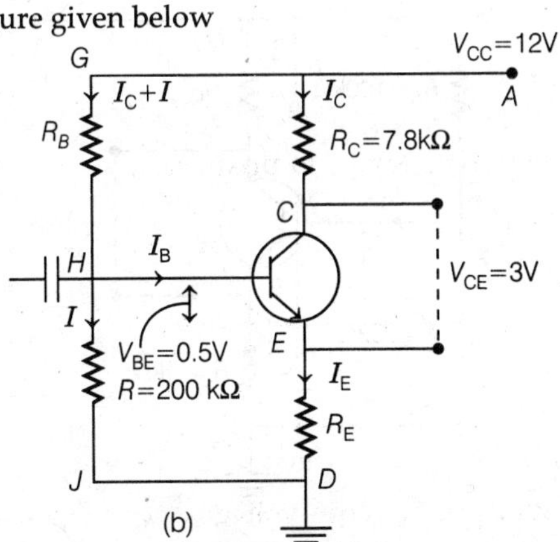

(b)

Note (✱) Topics related to these question have been removed from latest NCERT.

$$I_C \approx I_E \quad \text{[As base current is very small.]}$$

$$R_C = 7.8 \text{ k}\Omega$$

From the figure, $I_C(R_C + R_E) + V_{CE} = 12$

$$(R_E + R_C) \times 1 \times 10^{-3} + 3 = 12$$

$$R_E + R_C = 9 \times 10^3 = 9 \text{ k}\Omega$$

$$R_E = 9 - 7.8 = 1.2 \text{ k}\Omega$$

$$V_E = I_E \times R_E$$

$$= 1 \times 10^{-3} \times 1.2 \times 10^3 = 1.2 \text{ V}$$

Voltage $V_B = V_E + V_{BE} = 1.2 + 0.5 = 1.7 \text{ V}$

Current $I = \dfrac{V_B}{20 \times 10^3} = \dfrac{1.7}{20 \times 10^3} = 0.085 \text{ mA}$

Resistance $R_B = \dfrac{12 - 1.7}{\dfrac{I_C}{\beta} + 0.085} = \dfrac{10.3}{0.01 + 0.085}$ [Given, $\beta = 100$]

$$= 108 \text{ k}\Omega$$

***Q.40** In the circuit shown in figure, find the value of R_C.

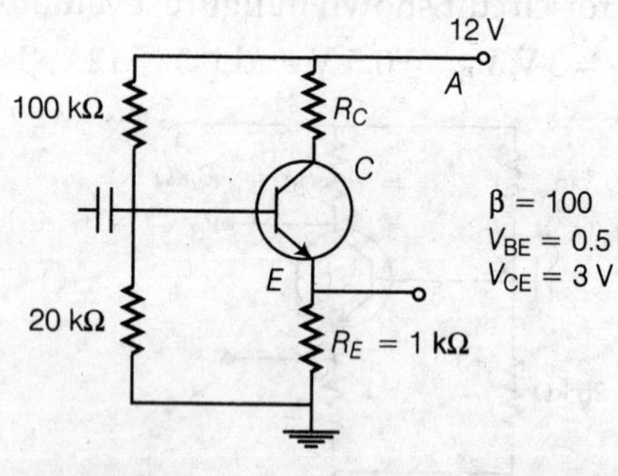

Ans. Consider the figure given below

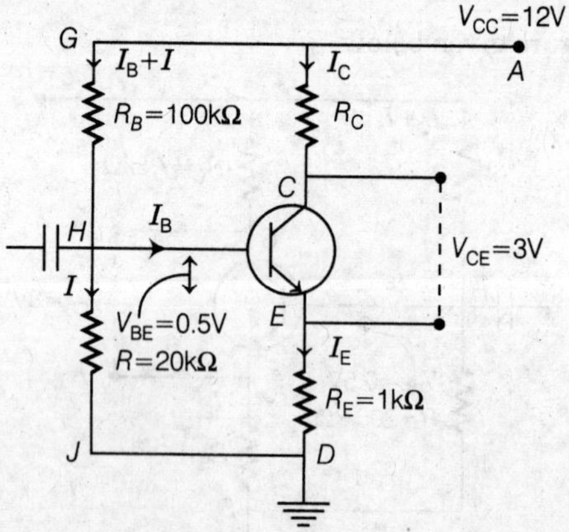

Note (*) Topics related to these question have been removed from latest NCERT.

$$I_E = I_C + I_B \text{ and } I_C = \beta I_B \quad \ldots\text{(i)}$$

$$I_C R_C + V_{CE} + I_E R_E = V_{CC} \quad \ldots\text{(ii)}$$

$$R I_B + V_{BE} + I_E R_E = V_{CC} \quad \ldots\text{(iii)}$$

$\because$
$$I_E \approx I_C = \beta I_B$$

From Eq. (iii),

$$(R_B + \beta R_E) I_B = V_{CC} - V_{BE}$$

$\Rightarrow$
$$I_B = \frac{V_{CC} - V_{BE}}{R_B + \beta \cdot R_E}$$

$$= \frac{12 - 0.5}{80 + 1.2 \times 100} = \frac{11.5}{200} \text{ mA}$$

From Eq. (ii),

$$(R_C + R_E) = \frac{V_{CE} - V_{BE}}{I_C} = \frac{V_{CC} - V_{CE}}{\beta I_B} \quad (\because I_C = \beta I_B)$$

$$(R_C + R_E) = \frac{2}{11.5}(12 - 3)\text{ k}\Omega = 1.56 \text{ k}\Omega$$

$$R_C + R_E = 1.56$$

$$R_C = 1.56 - 1 = 0.56 \text{ k}\Omega$$

Chapter 15

Communication Systems*

Multiple Choice Questions (MCQs)

Q.1 Three waves *A*, *B* and *C* of frequencies 1600 kHz, 5 MHz and 60 MHz, respectively are to be transmitted from one place to another. Which of the following is the most appropriate mode of communication?

(a) *A* is transmitted *via* space wave while *B* and *C* are transmitted *via* sky wave
(b) *A* is transmitted *via* ground wave, *B via* sky wave and *C via* space wave
(c) *B* and *C* are transmitted *via* ground wave while *A* is transmitted *via* sky wave
(d) *B* is transmitted *via* ground wave while *A* and *C* are transmitted *via* space wave

Thinking Process Mode of communication depend on the frequencies of a wave.

Ans. ***(b)*** Mode of communication frequency range

Ground wave propagation – 530 kHz to 1710 kHz
Sky wave propagation –1710 kHz to 40 MHz
Space wave propagation – 54MHz to 4.2GHz

Q.2 A 100m long antenna is mounted on a 500m tall building. The complex can become a transmission tower for waves with λ

(a) ~ 400 m (b) ~ 25 m (c) ~ 150 m (d) ~ 2400 m

Ans. ***(a)*** Given, length of the antenna (l) is given by

$$l = 100\,\text{m}$$

we know that, wavelength of the wave which can be transmitted by

$$\lambda \sim 4l = 4 \times 100 = 400\,\text{m}$$

Wavelength (λ) is nearly equal to 400 m.

Q.3 A 1 kW signal is transmitted using a communication channel which provides attenuation at the rate of – 2dB per km. If the communication channel has a total length of 5 km, the power of the signal received is

[gain in dB $= 10\log\left(\frac{P_0}{P_i}\right)$]

(a) 900 W (b) 100 W (c) 990 W (d) 1010 W

Note (✱) This chapter has been deleted from latest NCERT.

Ans. **(b)** Given, power of signal transmitted is given $P_i = 1\,\text{kW} = 1000\text{ W}$

Rate of attenuation of signal = – 2dB / km

Length of total path = 5 km

Thus, $$\text{gain in } dB = 5 \times (-2) = -10\text{ dB}$$

Also, $$\text{gain in } dB = 10 \log\left(\frac{P_0}{P_i}\right) \quad \ldots\text{(i)}$$

Here P_0 is the power of the received signal.

Putting the given values in Eq. (i),

$$-10 = 10 \log\left(\frac{P_0}{P_i}\right) = -10 \log\left(\frac{P_i}{P_0}\right)$$

$$\Rightarrow \quad \log\frac{P_i}{P_0} = 1 \Rightarrow \log\frac{P_i}{P_0} = \log 10$$

$$\Rightarrow \quad \frac{P_i}{P_0} = 10 \Rightarrow 1000\text{W} = 10\,P_0$$

$$\Rightarrow \quad P_o = 100\text{ W}$$

Q.4 A speech signal of 3 kHz is used to modulate a carrier signal of frequency 1 MHz, using amplitude modulation. The frequencies of the side bands will be

(a) 1.003 MHz and 0.997 MHz (b) 3001 kHz and 2997 kHz
(c) 1003 kHz and 1000 kHz (d) 1 MHz and 0.997 MHz

Thinking Process The amplitude modulated signal consists of the carrier wave of frequency ω_c with two additional sinusoidal waves, one of frequency $(\omega_c - \omega_m)$ and other of frequency $(\omega_c + \omega_m)$. These two waves are called side bands and their frequencies are called side band frequency.

Ans. **(a)** Given, frequency of carrier signal is $\omega_c = 1\,\text{MHz}$

and frequency of speech signal = 3 kHz

$$= 3 \times 10^{-3}\text{ MHz}$$
$$= 0.003\text{ MHz}$$

Now, we know that,

Frequencies of side bands $= (\omega_c \pm \omega_m)$

$$= (1 \pm 0.003)$$
$$= 1.003\text{ MHz and } 0.997\text{ MHz}$$

Q.5 A message signal of frequency ω_m is superposed on a carrier wave of frequency ω_c to get an Amplitude Modulated Wave (AM). The frequency of the AM wave will be

(a) ω_m (b) ω_c (c) $\frac{\omega_c + \omega_m}{2}$ (d) $\frac{\omega_c - \omega_m}{2}$

Thinking Process In amplitude modulation, the frequency of modulated wave is equal to the frequency of carrier wave.

Ans. **(b)** Here, according to the question, frequency of carrier wave is ω_c.

Thus the amplitude modulated wave also has frequency ω_c.

Q.6 I-V characteristics of four devices are shown in figure.

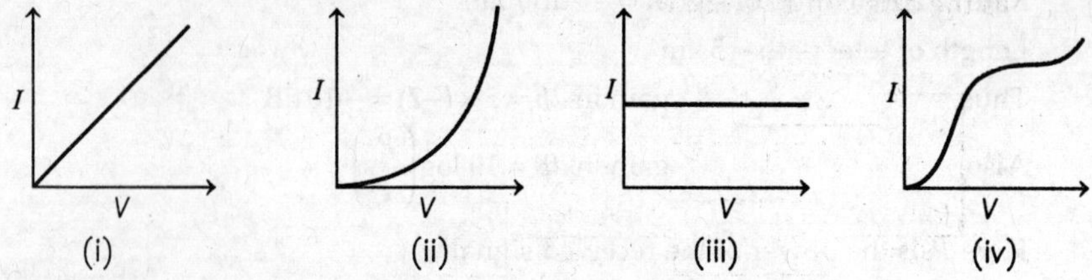

Identify devices that can be used for modulation

(a) (i) and (iii)
(b) only (iii)
(c) (ii) and some regions of (iv)
(d) All the devices can be used

- **Concept Insight** A square law device is something where either current or voltage depends on the square of the other.

Ans. ***(c)*** The device which follows square law is used for modulation purpose.
Characteristics shown by (i) and (iii) corresponds to linear devices.
Characteristics shown by (ii) corresponds to square law device. Some part of (i) also follow square law.
Hence, (ii) and (iv) can be used for modulation.

Q.7 A male voice after modulation-transmission sounds like that of a female to the receiver. The problem is due to

(a) poor selection of modulation index (selected $0 < m < 1$)
(b) poor bandwidth selection of amplifiers
(c) poor selection of carrier frequency
(d) loss of energy in transmission.

Thinking Process The frequency of male voice less than that of a female voice.

Ans. ***(b)*** Here, in this question, the frequency of modulated signal received becomes more, which is possible with the poor bandwidth selection of amplifiers.
This happens because bandwidth in amplitude modulation is equal to twice the frequency of modulating signal.
But, the frequency of male voice is less than that of a female.

Q. 8 A basic communication system consists of

A. transmitter.
B. information source.
C. user of information.
D. channel.
E. receiver.

Choose the correct sequence in which these are arranged in a basic communication system.

(a) ABCDE
(b) BADEC
(c) BDACE
(d) BEADC

Ans. ***(b)*** A communication system is the set-up used in the transmission and reception of information from one place to another.

The whole system consist of several elements in a sequence. It can be represented as the diagram given below

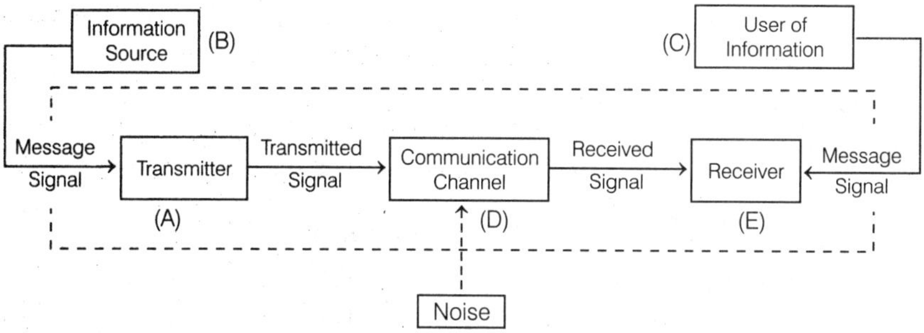

Q.9 Identify the mathematical expression for amplitude modulated wave

(a) $A_c \sin[\{\omega_c + k_1 V_m(t)\}t + \phi]$
(b) $A_c \sin\{\omega_c t + \phi + k_2 V_m(t)\}$
(c) $\{A_c + k_2 V_m(t)\}\sin(\omega_c t + \phi)$
(d) $A_c V_m(t)\sin(\omega_c t + \phi)$

Thinking Process An arbitrary change in phase angle of the modulating signal is given by ϕ.

Ans. *(c)* Consider a sinusoidal modulating signal represented by

$$m(t) = A_m \sin\omega_m t \quad \text{...(i)}$$

where, A_m = Amplitude of modulating signal ω_m = Angular frequency $= 2\pi V_m = \phi V_m$

Also consider a sinusoidal carrier wave represented by $C(t) = A_c \sin\omega_c t$ ...(ii)

Thus, modulated wave is given by

$$C_m(t) = (A_c + A_m \sin\omega_m t)\sin\omega_c t$$

$$= A_c[1 + \frac{A_m}{A_c} \sin\omega_m t)\sin\omega_c t$$

Here, $\frac{A_m}{A_c} = M$

$\Rightarrow$ $C_m(t) = (A_c + A_c \times \mu \sin\omega_m t)\sin\omega_c t$ ...(iii)

Now, we know that $A_c \times \mu = K$ [wave constant]

and $\sin\omega_m t = V_m$ [wave velocity]

Thus, Eq. (iii) becomes

$$C_m(t) = (A_c + K \times V_m)\sin\omega_c t$$

Now, consider a change in phase angle by ϕ then $\sin\omega_c t \to \sin(\omega_c t + \phi)$

Thus, $C_m(t) = (A_c + KV_m)(\sin\omega_c + \phi)$

Multiple Choice Questions (More Than One Options)

Q.10 An audio signal of 15 kHz frequency cannot be transmitted over long distances without modulation, because

(a) the size of the required antenna would be at least 5 km which is not convenient
(b) the audio signal can not be transmitted through sky waves
(c) the size of the required antenna would be at least 20 km, which is not convenient
(d) effective power transmitted would be very low, if the size of the antenna is less than 5 km

Thinking Process Transmission of a signal depends on three factors. These are size of antenna, medium of transmission and power of transmitted wave.

Ans. *(a, b, d)* Given, frequency of the wave to be transmitted is

$$\nu_m = 15 \text{ kHz} = 15 \times 10^3 \text{ Hz}$$

$$\text{Wavelength } \lambda_m = \frac{c}{\nu_m} = \frac{3 \times 10^8}{15 \times 10^3} = \frac{1}{5} \times 10^5 \text{ m}$$

$$\text{Size of the antenna required, } l = \frac{\lambda}{4} = \frac{1}{4} \times \left(\frac{1}{5} \times 10^5\right)$$

$$= 5 \times 10^3 \text{ m} = 5 \text{km}$$

The audio signals are of low frequency waves. Thus, they cannot be transmitted through sky waves as they are absorbed by atmosphere.

If the size of the antenna is less than 5 km, the effective power transmission would be very low because of deviation from resonance wavelength of wave and antenna length.

Q.11 Audio sine waves of 3 kHz frequency are used to amplitude modulate a carrier signal of 1.5 MHz. Which of the following statements are true?

(a) The side band frequencies are 1506 kHz and 1494 kHz
(b) The bandwidth required for amplitude modulation is 6kHz
(c) The bandwidth required for amplitude modulation is 3 MHz
(d) The side band frequencies are 1503 kHz and 1497 kHz

Thinking Process Here, in this question, options are giving the value of side band frequencies and band width of amplitude modulation. So, first of all find this quantities.

Ans. *(b, d)* Given, $\omega_m = 3 \text{ kHz}$

$$\omega_c = 1.5 \text{ MHz} = 1500 \text{ kHz}$$

Now, side band frequencies

$$\omega_c \pm \omega_m = (1500 \pm 3)$$

$$= 1503 \text{ kHz and } 1497 \text{ kHz}$$

Also, $\text{bandwidth} = 2\omega_m = 2 \times 3 = 6 \text{ kHz}$

Q.12 A TV transmission tower has a height of 240 m. Signals broadcast from this tower will be received by LOS communication at a distance of (assume the radius of earth to be $(6.4 \times 10^6$ m)

(a) 100 km (b) 24 km (c) 55 km (d) 50 km

Thinking Process Range $d_T = \sqrt{2Rh_T}$

Ans. ***(b,c,d)*** Given, height of tower $h = 240$ m

For LOS (line of sight) communication.

The maximum distance on earth from the transmitter upto which a signal can be received is given by

$$d = \sqrt{2Rh} \quad \text{...(i)}$$

Here R is the radius of the earth *i.e.*, $R = 6.4 \times 10^6$ m

Putting all these values in Eq. (i),

we get $$d = \sqrt{2Rh} = \sqrt{2 \times 6.4 \times 10^6 \times 240}$$

$$= 55.4 \times 10^3 \text{ m} = 55.4 \text{ km}$$

Thus, the range of 55.4 km covers the distance 24 km, 55 km and 50 km.

Q.13 The frequency response curve (figure) for the filter circuit used for production of AM wave should be

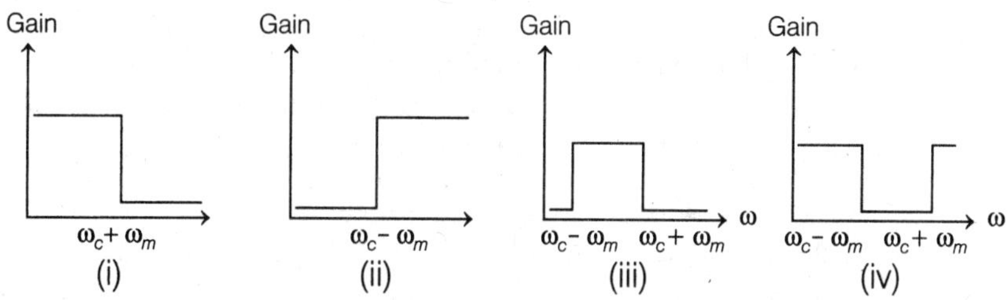

(a) (i) followed by (ii) (b) (ii) followed by (i)

(c) (iii) (d) (iv)

Ans. ***(a, b, c)*** Here, for the production of amplitude modulated wave, bandwidth is given by = frequency of upper side band – frequency of lower side band

$$= \omega_{USB} - \omega_{LSB} = (\omega_c + \omega_m) - (\omega_c - \omega_m)$$

Q.14 In amplitude modulation, the modulation index m, is kept less than or equal to 1 because

(a) $m > 1$, will result in interference between carrier frequency and message frequency, resulting into distortion

(b) $m > 1$, will result in overlapping of both side bands resulting into loss of information

(c) $m > 1$, will result in change in phase between carrier signal and message signal

(d) $m > 1$, indicates amplitude of message signal greater than amplitude of carrier signal resulting into distortion

Ans. ***(b, d)*** The modulation index (m) of amplitude modulated wave is

$$m = \frac{\text{amplitude of message signal } (A_m)}{\text{amplitude of carrier signal } (A_c)}$$

If $m > 1$, then $A_m > A_c$.

In this situation, there will be distortion of the resulting signal of amplitude modulated wave. Maximum modulation frequency (m_f) of A_m wave is

$$m_f = \frac{\Delta v_{max}}{v_m(\max)}$$

$$= \frac{\text{frequency deviation}}{\text{maximum frequency value of modulating wave}}$$

If $m_f > 1$, then $\Delta v_{max} > v_m$. It means, there will be overlapping of both side bands of modulated wave resulting into loss of information.

Very Short Answer Type Questions

Q.15 Which of the following would produce analog signals and which would produce digital signals?

(a) A vibrating tuning fork

(b) Musical sound due to a vibrating sitar string

(c) Light pulse

(d) Output of NAND gate

Ans. Analog and digital signals are used to transmit information, usually through electric signals. In both these technologies, the information such as any audio or video is transformed into electric signals.

The difference between analog and digital technologies is that in analog technology, information is translated into electric pulses of varying amplitude. In digital technology, translation of information is into binary formal (zero or one) where each bit is representative of two distinct amplitudes.

Thus, (a) and (b) would produce analog signal and (c) and (d) would produce digital signals.

Q.16 Would sky waves be suitable for transmission of TV signals of 60 MHz frequency?

Ans. A signal to be transmitted through sky waves must have a frequency range of 1710 kHz to 40 MHz.

But, here the frequency of TV signals are 60 MHz which is beyond the required range.

So, sky waves will not be suitable for transmission of TV signals of 60 MHz frequency.

Q.17 Two waves A and B of frequencies 2MHz and 3MHz, respectively are beamed in the same direction for communication *via* sky wave. Which one of these is likely to travel longer distance in the ionosphere before suffering total internal reflection?

Ans. As the frequency of wave B is more than wave A, it means the refractive index of wave B is more than refractive index of wave A (as refractive index increases with frequency increases).

For higher frequency wave (*i.e.,* higher refractive index) the angle of refraction is less *i.e.,* bending is less. So, wave B travel longer distance in the ionosphere before suffering total internal reflection.

Q.18 The maximum amplitude of an AM wave is found to be 15 V while its minimum amplitude is found to be 3 V. What is the modulation index?

Ans. Let A_c and A_m be the amplitudes of carrier wave and modulating wave respectively. So,

$$\text{Maximum amplitude} \longrightarrow A_{max} = A_c + A_m = 15\text{ V} \quad \text{...(i)}$$

$$\text{Minimum amplitude} \longrightarrow A_{min} = A_c - A_m = 3\text{ V} \quad \text{...(ii)}$$

Adding Eqs. (i) and (ii), we get

$$2A_c = 18$$

or $$A_c = 9\text{ V}$$

and $$A_m = 15 - 9 = 6\text{ V}$$

$$\text{Modulating index of wave } \mu = \frac{A_m}{A_c} = \frac{6}{9} = \frac{2}{3}$$

Q.19 Compute the LC product of a tuned amplifier circuit required to generate a carrier wave of 1 MHz for amplitude modulation.

Thinking Process For tuned amplifier $f = \frac{1}{2\pi\sqrt{LC}}$

Ans. Given, the frequency of carrier wave is 1 MHz.

Formula for the frequency of tuned amplifier,

$$\frac{1}{2\pi\sqrt{LC}} = 1\text{MHz}$$

$$\sqrt{LC} = \frac{1}{2\pi \times 10^6}$$

$$LC = \frac{1}{(2\pi \times 10^6)^2} = 2.54 \times 10^{-14}\text{ S}$$

Thus, the product of LC is 2.54×10^{-14} S.

Q.20 Why is a AM signal likely to be more noisy than a FM signal upon transmission through a channel?

Ans. In case of AM, the instantaneous voltage of carrier waves is varied by the modulating wave voltage. So, during the transmission, noise signals can also be added and receiver assumes noise a part of the modulating signal.

In case of FM, the frequency of carrier waves is changed as the change in the instantaneous voltage of modulating waves. This can be done by mixing and not while the signal is transmitting in channel. So, noise does not affect FM signal.

Short Answer Type Questions

Q.21 Figure shows a communication system. What is the output power when input signal is of 1.01 mW? [Gain in dB $= 10 \log_{10} (P_0 / P_i)$]

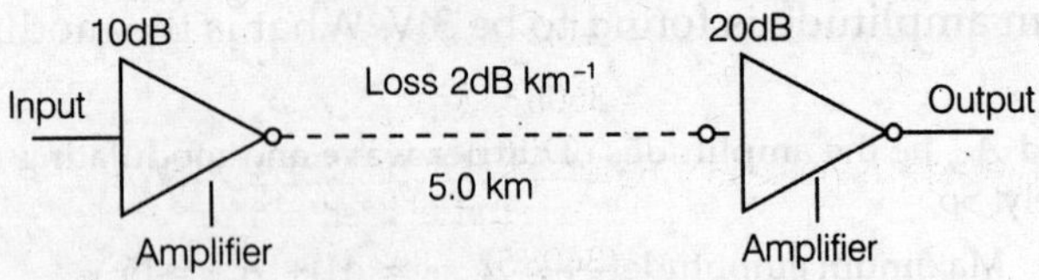

Ans. The distance travelled by the signal is 5 km

Loss suffered in path of transmission = 2 dB/km

So, total loss suffered in 5 km $= -2 \times 5 = -10$ dB

Total amplifier gain = 10 dB + 20 dB = 30 dB

Overall gain in signal = 30 − 10 = 20 dB

According to the question, gain in dB $= 10 \log_{10} \frac{P_0}{P_i}$

$$\therefore \quad 20 = 10 \log_{10} \frac{P_0}{P_i}$$

$$\text{or} \quad \log_{10} \frac{P_0}{P_i} = 2$$

Here, $P_i = 1.01$ mW and P_0 is the output power.

$$\therefore \quad \frac{P_0}{P_i} = 10^2 = 100$$

$$\Rightarrow \quad P_0 = P_i \times 100 = 1.01 \times 100$$

$$\text{or} \quad P_0 = 101 \text{ mW}$$

Thus, the output power is 101 mW.

Q.22 A TV transmission tower antenna is at a height of 20 m. How much service area can it cover if the receiving antenna is (i) at ground level, (ii) at a height of 25 m? Calculate the percentage increase in area covered in case (ii) relative to case (i).

Ans. Given, height of antenna $h = 20$ m

Radius of earth $= 6.4 \times 10^6$ m

At the ground level,

(i) Range $= \sqrt{2hR} = \sqrt{2 \times 20 \times 6.4 \times 10^6}$

$$= 16000 \text{ m} = 16 \text{ km}$$

$$\text{Area covered } A = \pi \, (\text{range})^2$$

$$= 3.14 \times 16 \times 16 = 803.84 \text{ km}^2$$

(ii) At a height of $H = 25$ m from ground level

$$\text{Range} = \sqrt{2hR} + \sqrt{2HR}$$

$$= \sqrt{2 \times 20 \times 6.4 \times 10^6} + \sqrt{2 \times 25 \times 6.4 \times 10^6}$$

$$= 16 \times 10^3 + 17.9 \times 10^3$$
$$= 33.9 \times 10^3 \text{ m}$$
$$= 33.9 \text{ km}$$

$$\text{Area covered} = \pi\,(\text{Range})^2$$
$$= 3.14 \times 33.9 \times 33.9$$
$$= 3608.52 \text{ km}^2$$

$$\text{Percentage increase in area} = \frac{\text{Difference in area}}{\text{Initial area}} \times 100$$
$$= \frac{(3608.52 - 803.84)}{803.84} \times 100$$
$$= 348.9\%$$

Thus, the percentage increase in area covered is 348.9%

Q.23 If the whole earth is to be connected by LOS communication using space waves (no restriction of antenna size or tower height), what is the minimum number of antennas required? Calculate the tower height of these antennas in terms of earth's radius.

Thinking Process Range $d_T = \sqrt{2Rh_t}$

Ans. Consider the figure given below to solve this question

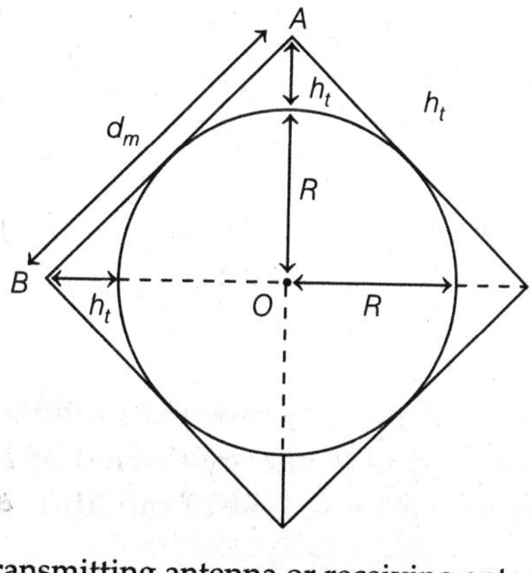

Suppose the height of transmitting antenna or receiving antenna in order to cover the entire surface of earth through communication is h_t and radius of earth is R

Then, maximum distance

$$d_m^2 = (R + h_t)^2 + (R + h_t)^2$$
$$= 2(R + h_t)^2 \qquad \text{...(i)}$$

As,
$$d_m = \sqrt{2h_t R} + \sqrt{2h_t R} = 2\sqrt{2h_t R}$$

From equation (i)

$\therefore$
$$8h_t R = 2(R + h_t)^2$$

$\Rightarrow$
$$4h_t R = R^2 + 2Rh_t + h_t^2$$

$\Rightarrow$
$$R^2 - 2h_t R + h_t^2 = 0$$

$\Rightarrow$
$$(R - h_t)^2 = 0$$

$\Rightarrow$
$$R = h_t$$

Since, space wave frequency is used so $\lambda << h_t$,hence only tower height is to be taken into consideration. In three dimensions of earth, 6 antenna towers of each of height $h_t = R$ would be used to cover the entire surface of earth with communication programme.

Q.24 The maximum frequency for reflection of sky waves from a certain layer of the ionosphere is found to be $f_{max} = 9(N_{max})^{1/2}$, where N_{max} is the maximum electron density at that layer of the ionosphere.

On a certain day it is observed that signals of frequencies higher than 5 MHz are not received by reflection from the F_1 layer of the ionosphere while signals of frequencies higher than 8 MHz are not received by reflection from the F_2 layer of the ionosphere. Estimate the maximum electron densities of the F_1 and F_2 layers on that day.

Ans. The maximum frequency for reflection of sky waves

$$f_{max} = 9(N_{max})^{1/2}$$

where, N_{max} is a maximum electron density.

For F_1 layer, $f_{max} = 5\,\text{MHz}$

So, $5 \times 10^6 = 9(N_{max})^{1/2}$

Maximum electron density

$$N_{max} = \left(\frac{5}{9} \times 10^6\right)^2 = 3.086 \times 10^{11}/\text{m}^3$$

For F_2 layer, $f_{max} = 8\,\text{MHz}$

So, $8 \times 10^6 = 9(N_{max})^{1/2}$

Maximum electron density

$$N_{max} = \left(\frac{8 \times 10^6}{9}\right)^2 = 7.9 \times 10^{11}/\text{m}^3$$

Q.25 On radiating (sending out) and AM modulated signal, the total radiated power is due to energy carried by $\omega_c, \omega_c - \omega_m$ and $\omega_c + \omega_m$. Suggest ways to minimise cost of radiation without compromising on information.

Ans. In amplitude modulated signal, only side band frequencies contain information. Thus only $(\omega_c + \omega_m)$ and $(\omega_c - \omega_m)$ contain information.

Now, according to question, the total radiated power is due to energy carried by

$$\omega_c, (\omega_c - \omega_m) \text{ and } (\omega_c + \omega_m).$$

Thus to minimise the cost of radiation without compromising on information ω_c can be left and transmitting. $(\omega_c + \omega_m)$, $(\omega_c - \omega_m)$ or both $(\omega_c + \omega_m)$ and $(\omega_c - \omega_m)$.

Long Answer Type Questions

Q.26 The intensity of a light pulse travelling along a communication channel decreases exponentially with distance x according to the relation $I = I_0 e^{-\alpha x}$, where I_0 is the intensity at $x = 0$ and α is the attenuation constant.

(a) Show that the intensity reduces by 75 % after a distance of $\left(\frac{\ln 4}{\alpha}\right)$.

(b) Attenuation of a signal can be expressed in decibel (dB) according to the relation $\text{dB} = 10 \log_{10}\left(\frac{I}{I_0}\right)$. What is the attenuation in dB/km for an optical fibre in which the intensity falls by 50 % over a distance of 50 km?

Ans. **(a)** Given, the intensity of a light pulse $I = I_0 e^{-\alpha x}$

where, I_0 is the intensity at $x = 0$ and α is constant.

According to the question, $I = 25\%$ of $I_0 = \frac{25}{100} \cdot I_0 = \frac{I_0}{4}$

Using the formula mentioned in the question,

$$I = I_0 e^{-\alpha x}$$

$$\frac{I_0}{4} = I_0 e^{-\alpha x} \text{ or } \frac{1}{4} = e^{-\alpha x}$$

Taking log on both sides, we get

$$\ln 1 - \ln 4 = -\alpha x \ln e \qquad (\because \ln e = 1)$$

$$-\ln 4 = -\alpha x$$

$$x = \frac{\ln 4}{\alpha}$$

Therefore, at distance $x = \frac{\ln 4}{\alpha}$, the intensity is reduced to 75% of initial intensity.

(b) Let α be the attenuation in dB/km. If x is the distance travelled by signal, then

$$10 \log_{10}\left(\frac{I}{I_0}\right) = -\alpha x \qquad \ldots\text{(i)}$$

where, I_0 is the intensity initially.

According to the question, $I = 50\%$ of $I_0 = \frac{I_0}{2}$ and $x = 50$ km

Putting the value of x in Eq. (i), we get

$$10\log_{10} \frac{I_0}{2I_0} = -\alpha \times 50$$

$$10\,[\log 1 - \log 2] = -50\,\alpha$$

$$\frac{10 \times 0.3010}{50} = \alpha$$

$\therefore$ The attenuation for an optical fibre

$$\alpha = 0.0602 \text{ dB/km}$$

Q.27 A 50 MHz sky wave takes 4.04 ms to reach a receiver *via* re-transmission from a satellite 600 km above Earth's surface. Assuming re-transmission time by satellite negligible, find the distance between source and receiver. If communication between the two was to be done by Line of Sight (LOS) method, what should size and placement of receiving and transmitting antenna be?

Ans. Let the receiver is at point A and source is at B.

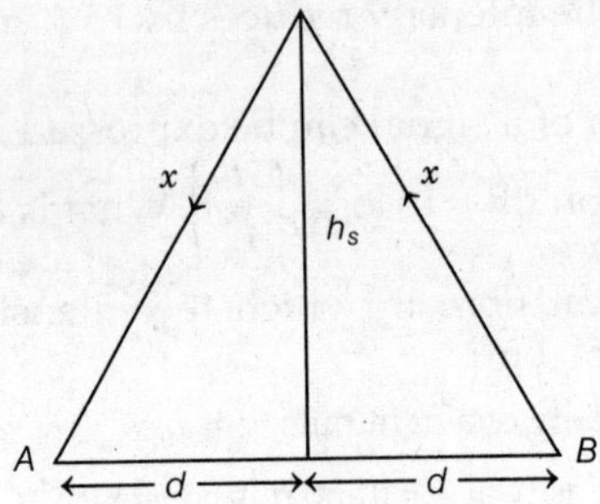

$$\text{Velocity of waves} = 3 \times 10^8 \text{ m/s}$$

$$\text{Time to reach a receiver} = 4.04 \text{ ms} = 4.04 \times 10^{-3} \text{ s}$$

Let the height of satellite is $h_s = 600$ km

$$\text{Radius of earth} = 6400 \text{ km}$$

Size of transmitting antenna $= h_T$

We know that, $\dfrac{\text{Distance travelled by wave}}{\text{Time}} = \text{Velocity of waves}$

$$\frac{2x}{4.04 \times 10^{-3}} = 3 \times 10^8$$

or
$$x = \frac{3 \times 10^8 \times 4.04 \times 10^{-3}}{2}$$
$$= 6.06 \times 10^5 = 606 \text{ km}$$

Using Phythagoras theorem,

$$d^2 = x^2 - h_s^2 = (606)^2 - (600)^2 = 7236$$

or
$$d = 85.06 \text{ km}$$

So, the distance between source and receiver $= 2d$

$$= 2 \times 85.06 = 170 \text{ km}$$

The maximum distance covered on ground from the transmitter by emitted EM waves

$$d = \sqrt{2Rh_T}$$

or
$$\frac{d^2}{2R} = h_T$$

or
$$\text{size of antenna } h_T = \frac{7236}{2 \times 6400}$$

$$= 0.565 \text{ km} = 565 \text{ m}$$

Q.28 An amplitude modulated wave is as shown in figure. Calculate

(i) the percentage modulation, (ii) peak carrier voltage and

(iii) peak value of information voltage

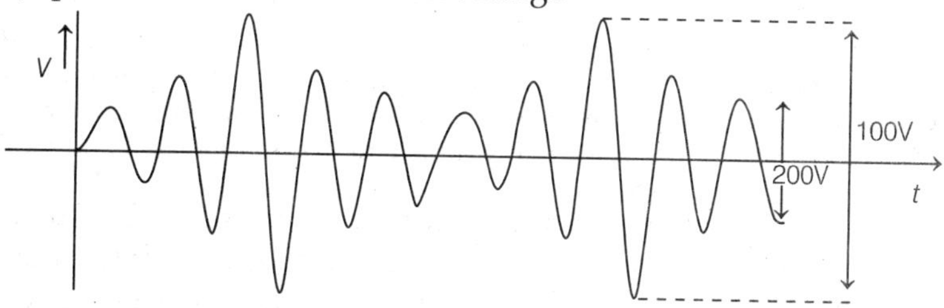

Ans. From the diagram,

$$\text{Maximum voltage } V_{max} = \frac{100}{2} = 50 \text{ V}$$

$$\text{Minimum voltage } V_{min} = \frac{20}{2} = 10 \text{ V}$$

(i) Percentage modulation, $\mu = \frac{V_{max} - V_{min}}{V_{max} + V_{min}} \times 100 = \frac{50 - 10}{50 + 10} \times 100$

$$= \frac{40}{60} \times 100 = 66.67\%$$

(ii) Peak carrier voltage, $V_c = \frac{V_{max} + V_{min}}{2} = \frac{50 + 10}{2} = 30 \text{ V}$

(iii) Peak value of information voltage,

$$V_m = \mu V_c = \frac{66.67}{100} \times 30 = 20 \text{ V}$$

Q.29 (i) Draw the plot of amplitude *versus* ω for an amplitude modulated were whose carrier wave (ω_c) is carrying two modulating signals, ω_1 and ω_2 ($\omega_2 > \omega_1$).

(ii) Is the plot symmetrical about ω_c? Comment especially about plot in region $\omega < \omega_c$.

(iii) Extrapolate and predict the problems one can expect if more waves are to be modulated.

(iv) Suggest solutions to the above problem. In the process can one understand another advantage of modulation in terms of bandwidth?

Ans. (i) The plot of amplitude versus ω can be shown in the figure below

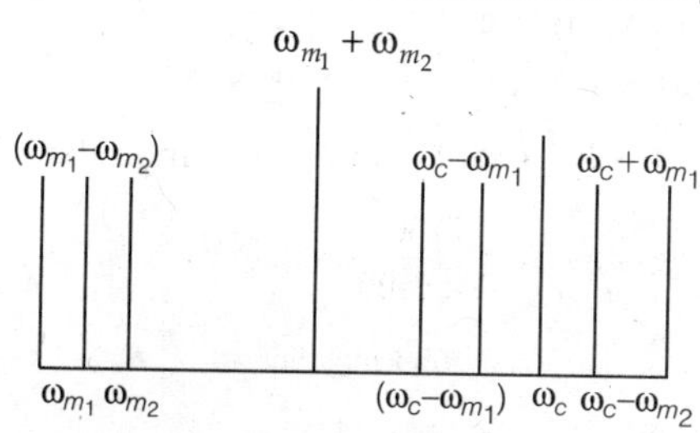

(ii) From figure, we note that frequency spectrum is not symmetrical about ω_c. Crowding of spectrum is present for $\omega < \omega_c$.

(iii) If more waves are to be modulated then there will be more crowding in the modulating signal in the region $\omega < \omega_c$. That will result more chances of mixing of signals.

(iv) To accommodate more signals, we should increase bandwidth and frequency carrier waves ω_c. This shows that large carrier frequency enables to carry more information (*i.e.*, more ω_m) and the same will in turn increase bandwidth.

Q.30 An audio signal is modulated by a carrier wave of 20 MHz such that the bandwidth required for modulation is 3kHz. Could this wave be demodulated by a diode detector which has the values of R and C as

(i) $R = 1\text{ k}\Omega, C = 0.01\,\mu\text{F}$.

(ii) $R = 10\text{ k}\Omega, C = 0.01\,\mu\text{F}$.

(iii) $R = 10\text{ k}\Omega, C = 0.1\,\mu\text{F}$.

Ans. Given, carrier wave frequency $f_c = 20$ MHz

$$= 20 \times 10^6 \text{ Hz}$$

Bandwidth required for modulation is

$$2 f_m = 3\text{kHz} = 3 \times 10^3 \text{ Hz}$$

$$\Rightarrow \quad f_m = \frac{3 \times 10^3}{2} = 1.5 \times 10^3 \text{ Hz}$$

Demodulation by a diode is possible if the condition $\frac{1}{f_c} << RC < \frac{1}{f_m}$ is satisfied

Thus, $$\frac{1}{f_c} = \frac{1}{20 \times 10^6} = 0.5 \times 10^{-7} \quad \text{..(i)}$$

and $$\frac{1}{f_m} = \frac{1}{1.5 \times 10^3}\text{ Hz} = 0.7 \times 10^{-3}\text{ s} \quad \text{....(ii)}$$

Now, gain through all the options of R and C one by one, we get

(i) $RC = 1\text{k}\,\Omega \times 0.01\,\mu\text{F} = 10^3\,\Omega \times (0.01 \times 10^{-6}\text{F}) = 10^{-5}\text{s}$

Here, condition $\frac{1}{f_c} << RC < \frac{1}{f_m}$ is satisfied.

Hence it can be demodulated.

(ii) $RC = 10\text{ k}\Omega \times 0.01\,\mu\text{F} = 10^4\,\Omega \times 10^{-8}\text{ F} = 10^{-4}\text{s}$

Here condition $\frac{1}{f_c} << RC < \frac{1}{f_m}$ is satisfied.

Hence, it can be demodulated.

(iii) $RC = 10\text{ k}\Omega \times 1\mu\mu F = 10^4\ \Omega \times 10^{-12}\text{ F} = 10^{-8}\text{s}$

Here, condition $\frac{1}{f_c} > RC$, so this cannot be demodulated.